Southern Local Color

Southern Local Color

Stories of Region, Race, and Gender

EDITED BY BARBARA C. EWELL

AND PAMELA GLENN MENKE

WITH NOTES BY ANDREA HUMPHREY

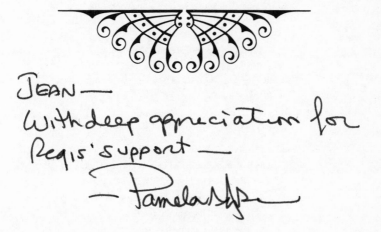

Jean —
With deep appreciation for
Regis' support —
— Pamela

The University of Georgia Press · *Athens and London*

© 2002 by the University of Georgia Press

Athens, Georgia 30602

All rights reserved

Designed by Betty Palmer McDaniel

Set in 11.5 on 13 Walbaum by G & S Typesetters, Inc.

Printed and bound by Maple-Vail

The paper in this book meets the guidelines for
permanence and durability of the Committee on
Production Guidelines for Book Longevity of the
Council on Library Resources.

Printed in the United States of America

06   05   04   03   02   C   5   4   3   2   1

06   05   04   03   02   P   5   4   3   2   1

Library of Congress Cataloging-in-Publication Data

Southern local color : stories of region, race, and gender /
edited by Barbara C. Ewell and Pamela Glenn Menke ;
with notes by Andrea Humphrey.

p.   cm.

Includes bibliographical references.

ISBN 0-8203-2316-0 (alk. paper) –

ISBN 0-8203-2317-9 (pbk. : alk. paper)

1. Southern States—Social life and customs—Fiction.

2. Short stories, American—Southern States.

3. Race relations—Fiction.   4. Sex role—Fiction.

I. Ewell, Barbara C.   II. Menke, Pamela Glenn, 1940–.

III. Humphrey, Andrea.

PS551 .S557   2001

813'.01083275—dc21   2001027722

British Library Cataloging-in-Publication Data available

Contents

Preface

THE SINGLE VOICE OF THIS VOLUME represents many pleasantly exhausting hours of shared research and lively conversation as we continually edited and expanded one another's insights. Enriching us personally and professionally, the collaborative process through which this anthology emerged has been one of its richest and most satisfying dimensions.

In ordering and selecting the stories, we have attempted to provide some sense of the development of local color as well as its geographic and thematic range. The authors thus appear in the order that they first published a short story with a southern setting, whether or not that particular story is included. When a writer is represented by more than one story, those are presented chronologically. The stories themselves have been reproduced in the form of their original publication, correcting only what appear to be minor mechanical errors.

Since issues of length and representativeness inevitably prevented the inclusion of many fine stories and several distinguished writers (most notably, Ruth McEnery Stuart and James Lane Allen), we have compiled a list of other interesting stories and short-fiction collections by each author as well as a selection of those by other writers whom we could not include. A general bibliography as well as primary and secondary sources for each represented author are also provided. Some sources for page citations in the introduction are in the author bibliographies.

Acknowledgments

WE EXPRESS OUR GRATITUDE to our editors at the University of Georgia Press, Barbara Ras and Jennifer Comeau, and to Daniel Simon; to the anonymous readers, whose criticism and praise improved this work; to former Regis student Melinda Riego DeDios, who provided early and important technical support for our project; to the Regis College security and secretarial staffs; to the Loyola University Institute for Ministry staff; and, most particularly, to our colleagues Sister Betty Cawley, CSJ, Suzanne Dietzl, Patricia Elliott, David Estes, Robert Frye, Anne Gowdy, Joan Wylie Hall, Sister Leila Hogan, CSJ, Julianne Maher, Jennifer Morrison, Ellen Munley, Marjorie Pryse, and Janna Saslaw.

We are also grateful to our student readers who helped to identify noteworthy portions of the stories: Kate Brown, Karen Joubert, Larry Rodrigue, and Rebecca Whitney of Loyola and the Regis student members of the spring 1999 Major American Writers course. Special thanks as well to the distinguished faculty mentors who shaped our passion for literature, especially in its nineteenth-century southern versions: Louis J. Rubin Jr., C. Carroll Hollis, C. Hugh Holman, Louise Cowan, and Walter R. Davis. Without the financial support of the Regis College Virginia Pyne Kaneb Faculty Scholar grant and Regis Faculty Development Fund, this project would have been impossible. The Grants and Leaves Committee of Loyola University and the Dean of City College, Marcel Dumestre, also provided support. We also thank our generous New Orleans friends Sister Denise Bourgeois, OP, and Sister Judene Lillie, OP. Our heartfelt thanks also goes to our colleague Andrea Humphrey, who not only developed much of the annotated material for this anthology but also generously provided many hours of technical and research support. Finally, our most profound gratitude and deep regard go to Jerry Speir and Sheila Clark Geha, whose good cheer and constant support made possible what would otherwise have been an insurmountable task.

The editors and publisher gratefully acknowledge permission to reprint the following copyrighted works:

Introduction

IN 1870 BRET HARTE signed a contract with the *Atlantic Monthly* for $10,000: literary gold had been discovered in the frontier mining camps of California. Harte's spirited tale, "The Luck of Roaring Camp" (1868), had swept its author into national prominence. The bawdy (but mostly good-hearted), rough-neck gamblers, drunks, and prostitutes of Harte's stories titillated a northeastern reading public curious about the West, hungry for entertainment, and eager to fashion a national identity from the regional fabrics that the Civil War had nearly rent. Other writers soon followed Harte's cue, and the tradition of "local color," a fashion that captivated the reading public in the 1880s and 1890s, was established.

A burgeoning new magazine market encouraged a stream of short fiction portraying unfamiliar customs and ordinary folk and affirming a renewed sense of unity in the nation's rich diversity. The country's distant reaches drew closer in the short stories, travelogues, and sketches of hundreds of writers, including Sarah Orne Jewett, Celia Thaxter, and Mary Wilkins Freeman of New England; Harte and Mark Twain, and later Sui Sin Far, Mary Austin, and Jack London of the West and desert Southwest; and Edward Eggleston, Octave Thanet, and Hamlin Garland of the Midwestern prairies. But it was the South — whose sectional differences were perceived most acutely — that, for the sake of national unity, most required the country's imaginative comprehension. Although stories with New England and Midwestern locales were popular, those with western and especially with southern settings dominated the market in the last two decades of the nineteenth century. *Scribner's Monthly* declared in 1881: "New England is no longer king. Her great literary school is dying out. . . . The South and the West are hereafter to be reckoned upon in making up the account of our literary wealth" (Hubbell 724).

This anthology offers a representative collection of these nineteenth-century stories set in the southern United States, known both in their own time and in literary history as "local color." Apart from their intrinsic interest as effective and varied fiction, the precipitous decline of these stories in the next century from extraordinary popularity to a "minor" place in literary history raises provocative questions about literary fashion, about shifting canons of taste and value, about definitions and persistence of genres, and about the cultural purposes literature can serve. As recent scholars have recognized, local color is a far more complex phenomenon than has generally been appreciated. Moreover, its southern expression is particularly relevant in comprehending the critical role of the South in the cultural development of the United States. To understand the re-formulation of the South and of the nation that southern local color both reflected and engendered is to apprehend more fully the inherently fluid, interdependent, and unsettling cultural identities that comprise American literary expressions and realities. The following discussion explores some of these questions as it positions southern local color within its contemporary socio-historical and literary contexts, outlines its principal characteristics and forms, and, finally, assesses its shifting significance in literary history.

The Precursors

The precursors of American local color and its southern forms appeared during the early nineteenth century as part of a general effort in the 1830s to find specifically "American" literary expressions. Among the relevant developments of that formative period were the early experiments of Washington Irving and later Nathaniel Hawthorne in writing short prose tales, and the shapely stories of Edgar Allan Poe, collected in 1840 as *Tales of the Grotesque and Arabesque.* John Pendleton Kennedy inaugurated the plantation literary tradition, while Caroline Hentz became the first to adopt the popular tropes of northern domestic fiction to southern settings. Within the same decade of the 1840s, Augustus Baldwin Longstreet won acclaim for his irreverently funny *Georgia Scenes,* and William Gilmore Simms published his romances of Georgia and South Carolina, replete with colorful outlaws, low-class mountaineers, and aristocratic heroes. A growing abolitionist movement encouraged the first published slave narratives, establishing influential formal models for black fiction. And, beginning about 1830, minstrel shows sprang up throughout the South, promulgating lively characters and an expressive language that drew heavily on African American oral traditions and proved a fertile resource for much later southern writing. The ingredients for southern local color were beginning to take shape.

Growing out of the eighteenth-century English sketch, the legends of Washington Irving's internationally successful *Sketch Book*, published in installments beginning in 1819, are generally acknowledged to have inaugurated the American short story. Irving transformed older European material, particularly German folk tales, into legends of the "fairy mountain" Catskills and the "drowsy, dreamy" Hudson Valley in "Rip Van Winkle" and "The Legend of Sleepy Hollow." Even though Irving's art is much indebted to his European sources, four of his thirty-two *Sketch Book* entries employed native settings. Irving's professed interest in the "familiar and faithful exhibition of senses in common life" and "the half-concealed vein of humor" influenced his contemporaries Kennedy and Longstreet, whose own southern stories echoed Irving's comedy and presented portraits of local customs and characters (1824 letter, Current-Garcia and Hitchcock 6).

Fellow New Englander Nathaniel Hawthorne also drew on Irving's work. Frustrated by publishers' rejections, Hawthorne burned his first collection, *Seven Tales of My Native Land*, but his fascination with his Puritan past resulted in such stories as "Young Goodman Brown," eventually collected in *Mosses from an Old Manse* (1846), and provided the backdrop for other tales and novels, including his classic *The Scarlet Letter* (1850). Expanding the dimensions of the short story, Hawthorne was more interested in inner motivations than in the realistic surfaces of character and place, and while his literary canvas is regionally specific, setting serves primarily as an allegorical and symbolic landscape for human struggles with self-truths and evil.

More than Irving or Hawthorne, Poe was interested in literary form and the production of tightly crafted, sensational effects, as in "Ligeia" (1838), "The Fall of the House of Usher" (1839), and "The Tell-Tale Heart" (1843). Reviewing Hawthorne's *Twice-Told Tales,* Poe also articulated the first theory of the short story, defining its essential elements as brevity, economy of writing, and a unified arrangement of character, setting, and situations to achieve an intense effect. Like Hawthorne, Poe found in the short story a perfect medium for what Hawthorne called in his preface to *The House of the Seven Gables* (1851) the "marvelous" rather than the "probable and ordinary."

Though both writers perceived the novelty of the form, Poe also understood its dependence on the emergence, in the 1840s, of a new literary market: the magazine. Beginning in 1830 with *Godey's Lady's Book*, these popular new monthlies were the successors of "annuals" or "gift-books," which had provided both Irving and Hawthorne with publishing venues for their short prose tales. The monthly magazines, often directed at female readers, generated a profitable market for short fiction and thereby established a symbiosis that would define the evolution of the genre in the United States. As Poe himself declared, the short story was the child of the American magazine.

AGRARIAN IDYLLS, DOMESTIC HEROINES, AND SOUTHWEST HUMOR

While southern writers adapted similar aesthetics of sensation and sentiment in their fiction, they drew on material quite different from Irving's or Hawthorne's. In *Swallow Barn; or a Sojourn in the Old Dominion* (1832), for example, John Pendleton Kennedy fashioned his "romance" from a detailed portrayal of the Tidewater countryside, a distinguished Virginian ancestry, and a white, planter hierarchy enfranchised by happily devoted slaves. *Swallow Barn*'s central character, Frank Meriwether, is "a thorough-bred Virginian" who "emphatically" considers Richmond "as the centre of civilization." Revered by his many slaves, who are "very happy under his dominion," Meriwether has little regard for merchants or for cities, whose inhabitants he believes are "hollow hearted and insincere, and altogether wanting in that substantial intelligence and honesty" of landed aristocracy. Anticipating a key strategy of later local colorists, Kennedy presented his narrator as a visiting New Yorker, possibly modeled on Irving, Kennedy's friend and a frequent visitor, but also emulating popular travel books about the South, including New York native James Kirke Paulding's *Letters from the South* (1817). The reports of *Swallow Barn* are sprinkled with the lively humor and realistic detail favored by readers, and Kennedy's portrait of the James River plantation and its denizens contained all the elements of the Old South myth later embraced by postbellum plantation apologists and many southern local colorists.

But Kennedy's plantation formula was most successfully adopted by the women writers who grafted its elements onto another popular form, the domestic novel. Introduced in 1822 by Catharine Sedgwick, the domestic or sentimental novel generated considerable fortunes for many northern women writers, including Fanny Fern, E. D. E. N. Southworth, Susan Warner, and Harriet Beecher Stowe. Incorporating elaborate descriptions of ordinary life, its plots focused on an ideally virtuous woman, whose tribulations revealed the possibilities for heroism in the domestic contexts to which most white women were confined. Southern writers like Caroline Hentz, Caroline Gilman, and Maria McIntosh, followed by a generation of younger writers, including Mary Virginia Terhune (Marion Harland) and Augusta Evans, recentered the plantation narrative on the aristocratic mistress instead of its master, creating, as Elizabeth Moss argues, a distinctively feminine fictional agenda (22). Thus while the southern domestic novelists, like their male contemporaries, incorporated gradually more explicit defenses of slavery, they did so in terms of the southern female aristocrat's responsibility for keeping the family structure intact—and thus saving the South.

The astonishing popularity of the southern domestic novel on both sides of the Mason-Dixon line (Evans claimed that her works sold nearly half a million copies [Moss 3]) attests to the power of its argument. But it was a northerner who ultimately marshaled its elements most effectively: Harriet Beecher Stowe, with her devastating attack on slavery, *Uncle Tom's Cabin; or, Life among the Lowly* (1852). Southern novelists, male and female, launched a barrage of fictional responses to Stowe, but only actual war settled the matter. Nonetheless, southern domestic fiction and its plantation kin firmly established the elements of planter life in the national imagination, both north and south. It also set its dominant tone: Augusta Evans's 1864 novel, *Macaria, or Altars of Sacrifice*, was already a panegyric to a lost cause (Moss 169), while Kennedy, who had revised and reissued *Swallow Barn* the year before, waxed nostalgic in his new introduction, recalling the "mellow, bland, and sunny luxuriance" of Virginia's "old-time society." Two decades after the war, this fantasy South would rise again from the pens of Page and other southern writers in another popular genre, local color.

Alongside plantation fiction and the literary innovations of Hawthorne and Poe, another mode also flourished in the South from the 1830s to the 1860s, frontier humor. It was labeled "Southwest" because the southern territories were largely "southwest" of the more settled eastern seaboard. When Bret Harte struck the literary gold fields of local color in the 1870s, the territory was not unfamiliar. Longstreet and his successors (including Mark Twain in tall tales like "The Notorious Jumping Frog of Calaveras County" [1865]), created high comedy out of the narrative distance between genteel narrators (and readers) and the raw, "natural" common folk, whose starkly different life and customs were being recounted. The

Southwest humorists exploited a wide variety of southern settings: Georgia (William Tappan Thompson, *Major Jones's Courtship,* 1843); Alabama (Johnson Jones Hooper, *Some Adventures of Captain Simon Suggs,* 1846); Louisiana (Thomas Bangs Thorpe, *The Big Bear of Arkansas,* 1841; Henry Clay Lewis, *Odd Leaves from the Life of a Louisiana "Swamp Doctor,"* 1858; and Tennessee (George Washington Harris, *Sut Lovingood Yarns,* 1867). The genre's characteristic misspellings, dialect, puns, and sayings were also taken up by northern writers like Maine-born Charles Farrar Browne, whose stage recreation of his semi-literate and provincial persona Artemus Ward would greatly influence Twain. While the antics of the uneducated, isolated backwoods and mountain folk were often exaggerated in the Southwest sketches, the excess and "oddities" of their communities and landscapes contributed significantly to the later development of southern local color.

WILLIAM GILMORE SIMMS: THE FATHER OF SOUTHERN LOCAL COLOR

The Southwest humorists won the praise of William Gilmore Simms, who, the year he died, even tried his hand at the tall tale in "How Sharp Snaffles Got His Capital and His Wife" (*Harper's Magazine,* October 1870). Read infrequently today, Simms was nationally renowned prior to the Civil War and, like many southern writers, financially dependent on northern presses and audiences. An ardent champion of southern writing, he also promoted an authentic American literature cut loose from its British and European antecedents. In 1842 he declared himself "an ultra-American" and a "born Southron." Plantation owner, slave holder, prolific author, and, above all, southern advocate, Simms anticipated in his historical romances and short fiction many of the tangled ideologies and features of much postwar southern local color, including competing national/regional allegiances, rigid class distinctions, an interest in common folk, and the skillful uses of detail, dialect, and exotic local landscapes.

Many of Simms's stories, particularly the "The Lazy Crow; A Story of the Cornfield" and "Caloya; Or, The Loves of the Driver," collected in *The Wigwam and the Cabin* (1845), drew on another important resource for later southern fiction: African and Native American folklore, along with titillating hints of interracial relationships. The unacknowledged fascination of white readers with the "other" cultures of America was already evident in the popularity of works as diverse as Longfellow's *Song of Hiawatha* (1855), the minstrel shows, with their adaptations of slave songs and customs, and the politically inspired slave narratives of Frederick

Douglass (1845), William Wells Brown (1847), Harriet Jacobs (1861), and many others. Capitalizing on these interests, Simms's tales augur many of the most popular tropes of postwar fiction, including plantation benevolence and hijinks, dialect, gender roles delimited by race and class, nonwhite customs, and allusions to voudou. In defending his portrayals of mixed-race relationships, Simms insisted that literature must resist polite hypocrisies and depict the natural passions shared by all, regardless of race. Simms recognized the subtle power of his "local" material and perceptively declared in his preface to the collection's 1856 edition that "[the subject] is local, sectional—and to be national in literature, one needs must be sectional" (4). The uneasy task of being "national in literature" by being "sectional" became the province of local color in the 1870s. Although Simms's version of a historically and culturally diverse South was marked by aristocratic heroism, class differentials, and nostalgic pastoralism, his vision influenced such ideologically dissimilar southern writers as the plantation apologist Page and the radical reformer Cable.

The Crucible of History

But if the various elements of southern local color can thus be identified well before mid-century, it was the Civil War and its tumultuous aftermath that furnished the historical crucible that molded those elements into a distinct genre, one that proved profoundly useful in the post-war reconstruction of national identity. Certainly, the end of the Civil War marked a traumatic moment in the identity both of the South as a region and of the nation as a whole. Although broadly defined differences between the southern and New England colonies had been present since the earliest seventeenth-century European settlements in North America, climate and geography as well as political, economic, and religious variations had served to sharpen those distinctions over the years. The issue of slavery, which had divided the constitutional conventions, eventually focused these conflicts into a catastrophic, four-year civil war. The military defeat of the South, marked by General Robert E. Lee's surrender of the Army of the Confederate States of America at Appomattox Court House on April 9, 1865, confirmed that the southern states would not be a separate nation, but it also solidified their status as a separate region. The war had consolidated southern white people with very different political and economic interests—upcountry small farmers from North Carolina and Tennessee as well as the owners of vast rice or cotton plantations from Georgia and Louisiana—into a single southern foe. Similarly, the costs of war and defeat had been spread across social classes and political allegiances. If the Civil War, as New England social critic Orestes Brownson observed, served to give the United States "a distinct consciousness of its own national existence," southerners' defeat clarified their awareness that they occupied a distinctly regional space within that nation (Foner 24).

THE PROMISES OF RECONSTRUCTION UNFULFILLED

The abolition of slavery made a profound difference in southern culture. Although the Emancipation Proclamation of 1863 initially affected only slaves in the Confederacy (exempting about a million slaves in border states and Union-occupied areas), by 1865 the status of nearly four million people had been radically changed from chattel to citizen. One of the freedmen's first responses to that new status was widespread migration. Formerly confined to plantations and forbidden to travel without passes, many ex-slaves took to the road for a variety of reasons: to seek out separated family members, to return to familiar places, to pursue better work opportunities, or just to test their new license. Most freedmen, however, traveled only a few miles, and many ended up in nearby southern towns and cities, where some felt "freedom was free-er" and where black populations often doubled after the war.

Emancipation dramatically reconfigured the labor force. The southern economy was based on agriculture and had been devastated by the war: crops, farm animals, and machinery had been destroyed, savings and capital were depleted, one-fifth of the white male population was dead, with many more wounded or maimed, and the black labor force now demanded wages and control over its toil. Freedmen and whites struggled to redefine their relationships within these new contexts. Former slaves demanded respect and proper compensation for their labor while former masters tried to reimpose their own notions of control and market value. Land owners, facing acute labor shortages, often courted freedmen with promises of good wages and land but then expressed outrage when the workers, unfairly treated or simply attracted by better offers, abandoned their places. In the cities, black workers similarly struggled for autonomy and opportunity as the concept of wage labor gradually took a tenuous hold in the region.

Critical to these redefinitions of labor relationships was the larger national project of the reconstruction of the South. Northern victory brought with it conflicting notions of how to reincorporate the rebellious states back into the Union, with the Radical Republicans urging retaliation upon whites and full civil rights for blacks. An intense political struggle ensued, which resulted in the impeachment of President Lincoln's successor, Andrew Johnson, whose southern sympathies ultimately offended the Republican majority. Congress soon settled on a relatively progressive path to reshape the relationships between southern blacks and whites. It readmitted the southern states, established the Freedmen's Bureaus to assist blacks in the transition from slavery, and passed civil rights legislation, including the Fourteenth and Fifteenth amendments, which gave black suffrage a Constitutional guarantee.

Reconstruction formally lasted from 1865 until 1877, when the contested election of Rutherford B. Hayes (in which a Republican victory was basically bartered for the return of white political control in the South) marked the virtual end of federal intervention in southern race relations. Almost as much as the war itself, Reconstruction helped to redefine southern life. In its earliest and briefly successful period, between 1868 and 1872, Republican policies encouraged a series of political and social reforms in the region, including the establishment of public school systems, hospitals, and asylums, protective labor laws, modernized tax codes and judicial systems, and remarkably biracial democratic governments in many states. White resistance to the loss of economic and political supremacy was fierce, however. Sporadic violence against blacks gave way to the formation of more organized terrorist groups, like the Ku Klux Klan, founded in Tennessee in 1865, and Louisiana's Knights of the White Camellia (1867); both groups attempted to control postwar elections by intimidating black and liberal white voters, who often responded with force. The passage of the national "Enforcement Acts" in 1870–71, which made violence against citizens a federal matter, helped to suppress these vigilante groups by 1872, although their tactics continued as a feature of southern life for many years. The effort to reshape southern social structures through national legislation was not without repercussions.

White resistance was not the only force that disabled the early promise of Reconstruction. There was also widespread political corruption (which, in the era of urban gangs like New York's notorious Tweed Ring, was hardly a southern phenomenon), a persistent lack of investment capital, and a major economic depression, the Panic of 1873, which shifted national attention away from the problems of the South and swept many Republicans from office. What had begun as an extension of abolitionist idealism—to end slavery and to integrate black people fully into the American political and economic order—was becoming a distracting liability. The real accomplishments of Reconstruction began to be viewed, even in the northern press, as failures. Influential reports on the South sponsored by liberal northern newspapers and journals, such as "The Prostrate State" (1874) written for the *New York Tribune* or "The Cotton States" (1875) for the *New York Herald*, reinforced the notion that the general disarray of the South was the result of incompetent "Negro government" and that prosperity could only return with white rule. That sentiment was enacted across the South in a series of violently contested elections by "Redeemers," conservative white Democrats who wrested control of state and local governments, beginning as early as 1870 in Virginia and North Carolina. When the Grant administration failed to intervene aggressively to protect the radical regime in Mississippi in the critical elections of 1875, "Reconstruction itself was doomed" and, with it, any notion that its aspirations marked a positive moment in U.S. history (Foner 563).

What was at stake in Reconstruction was ultimately the concept of white supremacy or, to put it differently, the disempowerment of blacks. Especially in the final decades before the war, as the contradictions of slavery in a presumably egalitarian nation became more untenable, slavery had been increasingly justified by arguments of racial inferiority, often buttressed by biblical and even anthropological evidence. When the "peculiar institution" was finally dismantled, white southerners clung to white supremacy as a final vestige of the economic and political power to which they were accustomed and believed they deserved. Reconstruction materially threatened that power, and even after its formal demise, white southerners fought strenuously to preserve the racial distinctions that would reinstate their prerogatives.

The new conservative state governments thus began to undo systematically the toehold of blacks in political and economic affairs. Ultimately, their aim was disenfranchisement: to make the Fourteenth and Fifteenth Amendments "dead letters on the statute-book." To that end, they drastically reduced state budgets and taxes (together with the social services they supported), passed antilabor laws, and revised the criminal codes and property laws in an undisguised effort to restore power to the old propertied castes and the new mercantile elite. Gradually recognizing that the federal government would not interfere, southern states began to impose restrictions designed to eliminate black male votes: poll taxes, property requirements, literacy and "understanding" tests, which required that prospective voters interpret a section of the Constitution to the local registrar's satisfaction, and even the infamous "grandfather clause," which exempted from any requirements all men and their descendants who could vote before 1867 — further disadvantaging the former slaves. Many of these restrictions were incorporated into constitutions rewritten in many southern states in the 1890s. The effect of such provisions was not only to eliminate most black voters but also many poor whites, thus ensuring that the white upper classes would retain much of their antebellum economic and political power.

SEGREGATION AND VIOLENCE: REDEFINING RACE AND GENDER

Racial segregation was a critical feature of black disempowerment during this period. Reconstruction had marked a somewhat fluid period of interaction as blacks and whites tentatively explored their new social and economic relationships. Some public schools in cities like New Orleans and even the University of South Carolina (from 1873 to 1877) were briefly integrated, while most public transportation and even theaters and taverns were in some areas nominally open to blacks and whites alike. However, when in 1883 the Supreme Court invalidated the 1875 Civil Rights Act, the states began to enact a series of laws requiring "separate but equal" accommodations. Upheld by the courts in 1890 and then affirmed in 1896 by the famous Louisiana test case, *Plessy v. Ferguson,* these laws became collectively known as Jim Crow. Jim Crow legislation, named for an antebellum minstrel performer, ratified the needs of whites to justify and consolidate their power through caste distinctions, which were then marked by physical and social distance. Racial difference became identified with racial inferiority; for despite the rhetoric of "separate but equal" (which some black leaders like Booker T. Washington tentatively endorsed), the reality was always separate and decidedly unequal, from railroads to restaurants, from "colored" water fountains to "whites only" hospitals, from schools and bawdy houses to prisons and cemeteries. By restricting any contact between blacks and whites as equals or peers, segregation enforced an ideology of profound difference; by maintaining that difference as asymmetric, it magnified the desired perception of white superiority. As Edward Ayers observes, the actual implementation of racial segregation was an uneven process across the region and was driven by a variety of forces; however, by the turn of the century when the word "segregation" actually entered the language, it was firmly in place throughout the South. It remained entrenched until after World War II and the emergence of the Civil Rights movement of the 1950s and 1960s (Ayers 145).

Violence, essential in maintaining slavery, was a necessary corollary to segregation's blatant injustices; blacks did not always submit peacefully to the revocation of their freedoms. Black resistance was evident in lawsuits, boycotts, and riots, among them the 1898 Wilmington, North Carolina, race riots on which Charles Chesnutt based his 1901 novel, *The Marrow of Tradition*. Federal protections for freedmen were gradually withdrawn, first in the presence of the military, then in the courts, and, by the 1890s, even in the sympathies of the northern public. As a result, whites became increasingly able to suppress black resistance through violent means. Lynchings proliferated in the 1880s: between 1882 and 1900, over eleven hundred black men (and at least a score of black women) were executed by white mobs in the South, often after cruel torture (Tolnay and Beck 271). The most common targets were "uppity" blacks, those who had presumed to challenge white rule or had perhaps achieved a modicum of financial success. The most widely held justification for lynching was the crime of raping a white woman, the most scandalous instance of unwanted physical contact across the barriers of race.

The insistence that rape was the reason for lynching revealed a critical nexus in the South between race and gender. Indeed, as Ayers points out, the more intimate the space, the more stringent the rules of segregation. Memphis journalist Ida B. Wells, who began a courageous anti-lynching campaign in the 1890s, was the first to document the fact that only about one-third of lynchings even involved an actual charge of rape (207). Nonetheless, as in Paul Laurence Dunbar's story "The Lynching of Jube Benson" (1902), the protection of white womanhood from the vicious sexual attacks of black men remained the mantra of lynch law. As one proponent succinctly put it, lynching was "the white woman's guarantee against rape by niggers" (Wilson 175). In fact, the status of the white woman was closely tied to the status of blacks in general and to black men in particular. The traditional superiority of southern white men depended on the subservience of both white women and blacks. Transferred onto black men, the threat of male sexual violence helped to contain white women, while the defense of female honor justified the brutal punishment of black men. Black women, as the embodiment of a female sexuality impermissible to white women, remained equally vulnerable to rape and to retribution.

Central to these interrelationships was the figure of the white southern belle: the beautiful, charming, genteel, and submissive mistress of the patriarchal southern household. A familiar ideal in antebellum literature and society, the aristocratic white woman anchored southern conceptions of domestic and social order. For, as LeeAnn Whites and others have demonstrated, gender roles in the South were not, as in the North, shaped by the notion of "separate spheres," in which men governed the public realms of money and politics while women occupied and controlled the private domestic spaces. Instead, southern conceptions of gender depended on "economically autonomous" households in which men provided material support in return for female dependence and submission (Whites 10). The willing—and thus "natural"—subservience of the southern woman mirrored and contained the unwilling, if equally ordained, compliance of the black slaves, who were also part of the exemplary southern household. As Marjorie Spruill Wheeler points out, "the war and Reconstruction initiated a series of social and economic changes that gradually altered Southern gender relations," but those changes strengthened rather than severed the connections between race and gender that those relations implied (*New Women* 9).

Although the Civil War reshaped gender in both the North and the South, military defeat and the wholesale loss of property and slaves gave many returning Confederate soldiers an especially acute sense of their failure as men (Edwards 113). The only remaining component of the patriarchal household, which had defined southern male identity, was its loyal women. In contrast, for white women, the war and its difficult aftermath had provided a new sense of empowerment, as they managed struggling businesses and failing plantations (as did author Kate Chopin) and assumed greater public roles in the war effort. Both men and women struggled after the war to regain some semblance of their prewar gender identity, and both found it in the magnification of the role of women. For white men, particularly in the upper classes, female loyalty and submission were the sole remnants of their maleness as defined by their "head of household" status. For white women, more complexly, that same loyal support was the principal means by which they could reconstruct their devastated men as providers (if they had returned at all) and, in so doing, could also maintain some sense of their wartime empowerment "as the 'makers' of their men" (Whites 13).

Of course, for black men and women, as for many lower-class whites, the reshaping of gender roles unfolded differently. Freedom enabled blacks to construct their roles along the model of the patriarchal family, an op-

portunity expressly denied them during slavery. For black men, the war
and military service allowed them to claim a manhood that slavery had
denied. After the war, the control of their own labor, as well as their
wives', enabled them to act as providers. Their vehement resistance to
gang labor, with its overtones of slavery, became a point of critical contention in the Reconstruction labor market. Emancipation enabled black
women to insist on their own domestic importance and to return their allegiance, as well as their labor, to their husbands and families. During the
years of Reconstruction, in particular, their adamant refusal to work in
the fields under the authority of other men became a central symbol of
their new status as women. Later, as sharecropping replaced wage labor
among freedmen, women's fieldwork was seen as properly contributing to
the family rather than as demeaning (J. Jones 58–59).

Another important aspect of shifting gender roles was the national
movement for female suffrage. Before the war, the links between abolitionism and woman suffrage had discouraged much public support for wom-
en's rights in the South. However, after a number of black men moved into
public office and exercised their electoral privileges during Reconstruction, many white women began to find the subject more compelling. As
Wheeler notes, the "Negro problem" (understood as the enfranchisement
of several million people considered by many southern whites as "un-
fit for political participation") did not cause white women to want the
vote so much as it gave them "a reason to suspect that they could win it"
("Woman Suffrage" 38, 39). The formation of new constitutional conventions throughout the South provided an early venue for the enlargement
of women's political rights. Arkansas, North Carolina, and Texas considered including woman suffrage in their 1868 conventions, and the matter
came up again when the conservative white "redeemers" rewrote constitutions in the 1870s (Green 6–7).

Following these debates, equal suffrage organizations began to develop
sporadically in most southern states, along with women's clubs, which
were a principal source of female self-education throughout the nation.
These groups, which included many upper-class white women (such as author and activist Sarah Barnwell Elliot), began to lobby state legislatures
on a variety of issues and achieved some modest success, including admis-
sion to colleges and professional schools, service on government commis-
sions and boards, and reforms of inheritance and custody laws. However,
as southern women faced repeated defeats on such important issues as
child labor, many began to recognize the limits of their traditional femi-

nine role as "moral suasor." Despite the self-proclaimed chivalry of southern politicians in assuming the burden of politics, many southern white
women became less convinced that their protection and that of children
weighed very heavily at all against the financial interests of the cotton
mill owners and railroad barons (Wheeler, "Woman Suffrage" 34–35).
Finally in the 1890s, partly in response to the newly reorganized National
Women's Suffrage Association, which appreciated the potential and need
for southern support, the South saw its first organized effort for woman
suffrage.

But just as the "Negro problem" had precipitated many white southern
women into the struggle for suffrage, the "race issue" circumscribed their
efforts. White women, no less than white men, recognized in white supremacy and black disenfranchisement the underpinnings of their own
political and economic dominance and security. As Elna Green writes of
southern anti-suffragists, they "saw the world as an integrated whole:
class, gender and race relations were set in a permanent configuration,
each mutually enforcing the others. . . . A blow to any part of the edifice
endangered the integrity of the entire structure" (90–91). One consequence of this perception were the racialist strategies that southern white
women, together with their complicitous northern sisters, employed on behalf of suffrage. In the 1880s and 1890s, for example, southern suffragists
argued that extending the vote to women would help dilute black electoral strength, especially since white women outnumbered black women.
At the same time, many white leaders, like Kate Gordon of Louisiana, insisted on seeking suffrage from the states; they feared that a federal mandate would weaken the ability of states to maintain local "control" over its
black citizens. However, when Mississippi's Jim Crow laws were upheld
by the Supreme Court in *Williams v. Mississippi* (1898), it became clear
that the federal government would not resist the erosion of black civil
rights nor the steady drift toward legalized segregation. As a result,
woman suffrage lost any serious support in white legislatures. Instead, the
links between white women's empowerment and black advancement became all the more apparent. Ironically, as white women had seen in black
suffrage an opportunity to secure their own enfranchisement, the southern hierarchy now perceived in female autonomy an alarming threat to
the postwar redefinitions of southern (white) manhood, especially in regard to women.

If southern female suffrage was thus crippled by such mixed allegiances, white women became a vital (and often willing) tool in the con-

solidation of white supremacy. Women's loyal submission to white men thus served as a central prop to the renewed southern patriarchy. Protecting her status became a paramount expression of manliness. The principal menace to this regime was of course the black man—whose existence directly challenged the racial exclusiveness of the new southern manhood. Political and economic disenfranchisement steadily eroded black men's claims to "manhood" as providers and autonomous heads of households. At the same time, legal segregation, supported by lynch law, demonstrated white men's absolute right to protect their own women from any contact with such "beasts." Stripped of the "natural" authority and dignity of true (white) manhood, black men became imaginatively reduced to mere physicality—mindless strength and unharnessed desire. White women, dependent and vulnerable, were divested of any real agency, while black women bore the brunt of both sexual vulnerability and a racialized physicality.

Such at least were the ideological models of postwar white supremacy. In fact, as the violence of lynching and the eventual success of woman suffrage indicate, these redefinitions of race and gender were hardly seamless. Even their uneven implementation required a series of ritualizations, the most important of which was a redefined meaning of the Civil War itself.

TURNING THE "LOST CAUSE" INTO THE NEW SOUTH

Many scholars have attempted to explain how the South managed to redefine itself after the war, reshaping a slave society into an apartheid state, drawing out of the ruins of the old plantation South a new and more industrialized region, and ultimately transforming a decided military defeat into a great moral victory. As C. Vann Woodward, the most influential commentator on this era, concluded, the South after the war was schizophrenic. Its "divided mind" at once looked backward to what it had lost and forward to what it hoped to become: "The deeper the involvements in commitments to the New Order, the louder the protests of loyalty to the Old" (155).

One unlikely component of these transformations, as Gaines Foster explains, was the glorification of the Confederate veteran. Memorial rituals and monuments took shape gradually after the war, at first simply to give meaning to the tremendous loss and suffering southerners had experienced, but eventually to celebrate the courage and valor expended on behalf of a "Lost Cause." Throughout the 1880s and 1890s, organizations like the United Confederate Veterans (formed in New Orleans in 1889) and the United Daughters of the Confederacy (founded in 1895) established and maintained a virtual cult of the glorious southern soldier (Foster 103, 108).

By the 1880s, the North was signaling its own willingness to join in this uncritical celebration of southern heroism, particularly in the popular press. Between 1884 and 1887, for example, the prestigious *Century* published a long series of articles entitled "Battles and Leaders of the Civil War," noting that the time had been reached when "motives will be weighed without malice, and valor praised without distinction of uniform" (Foster 69). The series included Mark Twain's bitterly humorous account of his own short-lived Confederate service, "The Private History of a Campaign that Failed" (1885). The increased focus on honorable military service and glory erased the "lost cause" and the serious issues (such as race relations and states' rights) that the war had never really settled. Instead, the celebration of the Confederacy in literature and in social ritual became a ready (if relatively neutral and extremely popular) tool in the service of various contemporary purposes, from the support of white supremacy to the furtherance of political campaigns, from national reconciliation to the founding of the New South.

The struggle of the southern states to redefine white authority in the decades of the eighties and nineties took place in the context of tremendous economic, technological, and social changes, not just in the South but in the nation as a whole. While southern industrialization had begun before 1880, manufacturing more than doubled in the majority of southern states during the eighties, and workers in the new textile and steel mills tripled (Foster 80). Wage labor and new marketing practices reshaped agriculture, emphasizing the role of small towns and encouraging the growth of inland market centers like Atlanta and Birmingham. The doubling of railroad mileage, initiated by the radical Republican governments during Reconstruction, not only helped to spread lumbering and cash crops like cotton into areas with fresh access to markets but also spurred a general population movement toward towns and cities. As urban areas grew, so did the professional classes of merchants, lawyers, doctors, and other businessmen. Their prosperity and proximity also encouraged the adoption of new urban amenities: electric lighting, telephones, modern sewer systems, and indoor plumbing.

Newspaper editors and city boosters began in the early 1880s to proclaim a New South, one ready to leave behind the old "backward" ways of resistance to such changes as wage labor and modern industry and eager to welcome collaboration with the North in the exploitation of its rich resources. The most famous of these spokesmen was young Henry Grady, who with Joel Chandler Harris coedited the *Atlanta Constitution.* His landmark 1886 speech to the New England Club in New York projected a powerful image of the South as a vigorous land "having nothing for which to apologize" and standing "upright, full-statured and equal among the people of the earth" (33). For her northern victors, Grady offered an explicitly feminized place, "misguided, perhaps, but beautiful in her suffering, and honest, brave and generous always" (23). He called on the country to engage in the noble duty of "uplifting and upbuilding" the region and assured his audience that in the New South "perfect harmony" reigns in every "household," that the devastated Confederate soldier is "a hero in gray with a heart of gold," and that "close and cordial relations" exist among the "free Negro" and his white comrades. In the South, intoned Grady, "we have sowed towns and cities in the place of theories, and put business above politics" (23, 30, 32, 33).

While calming northern investors and satisfying southern loyalists, this highly idealized image of the New South hardly quelled the widespread misgivings about the coming of a new industrialized regime and its effects on people's lives. One major manifestation of such unrest was the rise of populism. The movement reflected the displeasure of small farmers, often veterans, who had struggled through general depression, collapsing crop prices, land devaluation, and a plethora of policies that favored large planters and businesses. Even before "redemption," several radical organizations took shape in the South, the most influential of which was the Farmers' Alliance, whose first president was the much-admired former Confederate General Leonidas Polk. A remarkably integrated cooperative movement that proclaimed the benefits of North-South cooperation, the Alliance brought together thousands of small farmers, laborers, and other reformers intent on reshaping political power to serve their interests. Its successor and ally, the Populist or People's Party, proposed an egalitarian revision of the capitalist principles that shaped the Gilded Age. Although the movement had significant effects on southern elections in 1892, it succumbed to the forces of compromise in the next national elections (Ayers 250). The erosion of Populism's political base occurred, in part, from the differing views on racial reform among its northern and southern supporters. As Nina Silber points out, "Reunion sentiments could not mask the fact that southern Populists were committed to a brand of racial politics that was often antithetical to some of the northern farmer's reform-minded traditions" (101).

What Populists regarded as rapacious capitalism required a massive, underpaid work force supplied by waves of immigrants from Ireland, England, Asia, and southern and eastern Europe. Settling primarily in the urban north but also in many southern coastal cities, these immigrants, much like blacks throughout the South, represented a threat to traditional notions of power and mastery, already weakened by the cultural and economic shifts that had transformed rural, independent farmers and merchants into wage laborers under the control of distant managers and inexplicable economic forces. Grady struck a chord of nationalist pride in his New South speech when he invited native workers southward, declaring that "One Northern immigrant is worth fifty foreigners" (32). Increasingly, as Silber points out, northerners themselves began to see in southern conservatism an admirable ability to retain social control over inferior classes. The negative reaction to immigrants also fueled the decline of northern sympathy for the freedmen and allowed northerners to acquiesce quietly to the South's insistence in the 1890s that it knew best how to handle the Negro.

REDEFINING THE WAR: THE MARRIAGE OF NORTH AND SOUTH

Though the North's willingness to join southerners in redefining the meaning of the Civil War intensified in the 1890s, its foundations had been manifest almost as soon as the battle dust had cleared. The most conspicuous motivation was the bounty to be reaped by northern investors from the South's plentiful natural resources. However, as later southern novels demonstrate—even with such different ideological foundations as George W. Cable's *John March, Southerner* (1894) and Thomas Nelson Page's *Red Rock* (1898)—the most fertile resource the South contributed to a turbulent nation was not its mineral and agrarian riches but a highly idealized, hierarchical heritage based on an aristocratic class structure, courtly male behavior, and proper womanliness.

The reshaping of northerners' view of the South and of reunion reflected many of the same gender anxieties that afflicted white southerners in the decades after the war. Immigrants were adapting their unfamiliar social customs and languages to crowded urban districts. Increasing numbers of young women were entering northern mills and factories, and many powerful female voices were pressing for greater political and economic influence. As a result, northerners expressed increasing concern about the breakdown of gender spheres and a decline of sexual mores (Silber 9). Turning South, the industrialized and disempowered northern male began to view the southern belle nostalgically, as an epitome of womanhood, recognizing in her a pleasing figure over whom he could exert control. As early as the 1860s, the conflation of the South with the innocent belle "provided for the northern male a sweet, double victory; he was once again victorious, not only over the South, but also over womankind" (Silber 10). In political rhetoric as well as in fiction, essays, illustrations, and historical accounts, North-South reconciliation, depoliticized as a "marriage," became a pervasive trope. It also provided an immensely popular plot device in authors ranging from northerners like John DeForest to southerners like Cable, Harris, and Page. Even Chopin framed her first novel, *At Fault* (1890), with the salvific marriage of a northern entrepreneur and a widowed plantation mistress. The image of North-South bliss disguised or suppressed such uncomfortable moral issues as the reasons for the war in the first place and the unpleasant persistence of white poverty and black oppression.

The postwar shift in focus and sympathy—from perceiving the South as rebellious foe to a wayward, though noble, comrade and/or marital "partner"—was dramatic. While the practical effects of that metamorphosis unfolded with predictable unevenness, that it could occur at all was a direct consequence of certain profound changes in national publishing. While the magazine had been an important feature of American culture since the 1830s, the postbellum era brought a new surge in its growth. The establishment of the International Copyright Association in 1868 gave writers new incentives to publish, and the "magazine trade burgeoned outside eastern publishing centers" (Price and Smith 13). Even so, throughout the 1870s and 1880s the most influential journals remained the major monthlies of the Northeast: Boston's *Atlantic Monthly* and *Harper's Magazine* and New York's *Scribner's Monthly*, which became the *Century Magazine* in 1881. Presided over by discriminating editors such as William Dean Howells, Thomas Bailey Aldrich, Richard Watson Gilder, and Henry Mills Alden, and appealing to a relatively elite audience, these journals helped shape national literary taste and intellectual opinion. Though staunchly abolitionist and pro-Republican prior to the Civil War, by the 1870s they increasingly reflected northern weariness with Reconstruction and the desire for reconciliation, glossing over the deeply unresolved issues of race.

These prestigious journals were the most visible constituent of a wide range of periodicals that sprang up following the Civil War; in the concluding decades of the nineteenth century, the magazine was the primary vehicle for literary reading and entertainment. Ellery Sedgwick notes that 3,300 magazines were published in 1885; 5,500 in 1900. This explosion of the periodical market can be explained by a number of factors, including new printing technologies and extensive railroad-based distribution systems; however, an essential stimulus was an increasingly far-flung audience with a voracious appetite for education and entertainment, especially about some of the "other" places that constituted a rapidly expanding nation. The short story, primarily because of its brevity, became the staple feature of this escalating market, and southern local color was its dominant form. Opportunities for southern local-color literature blossomed. As the periodicals eagerly sought fiction and essays to fill their pages, authorship became a more lucrative and acceptable profession, particularly for those, like educated women, who had not always had ready access to publication or supplemental income.

As the century drew to a close, many concerns that after the war had seemed sharply divisive had been reconfigured into familiar if not altogether comfortable compromises. Issues that the war had magnified had faded from national view, though not entirely from consciousness. Segregation and de facto disenfranchisement had been allowed to resolve "the Negro problem" in the South, consigning black people to narrow definitions of citizenship and placating the poverty of many whites with the sop of racial superiority. Reconciliation had effectively erased the moral implications of the war and opened the resources of the South to full exploitation by northern capitalists in exchange for the return of political power to the hands of the southern planter classes. What had not yet been fully settled was the "woman question," but even the new outlines of gender relations were becoming clear.

THE WAR THAT ENDED THE WAR: 1898

The advent of another war precipitated many lingering issues. By the standards of the Civil War or even the Great War of the next century, the War of 1898 (often called the Spanish-American War) was not cataclysmic. It lasted for a short time (if one does not count, as the nation did not, the many years of guerrilla resistance in the Philippines), and U.S. casualties were limited. However, the war was a crucial event in U.S. history. It catapulted Theodore Roosevelt into the presidency in 1901 and, at the very end of Western Europe's most extensive period of empire-building, defined the United States as an imperial power. When it was over, the United States had annexed Hawaii and had gained Puerto Rico, Guam, and the Philippine Islands from Spain. The war also consolidated the delineation of American manhood. As Kristin Hoganson argues, that redefinition, especially among southerners, helped to confirm that the South as a region was finally "man enough" to rejoin and represent a nation whose own white manliness so transparently underwrote its imperial ambitions and status.

The fading of the Civil War into history and memory encouraged many to fear that the "manly character" essential to democratic government in the rough and tumble economy of the Gilded Age was fading with it. Practically speaking, many veterans had parlayed their wartime experience (whether Confederate or Union) into very successful political careers. Economic depression, the closing of the frontier, the unchecked rise of big business, and widespread corruption in both business and politics fostered the belief, however, that the country was becoming weak and effeminate, a concern that was hardly assuaged by women's insistence on political equity and greater economic opportunity (Hoganson 10–12). The outbreak of war generated a welcome opportunity to reassert the manliness of the nation, and much of the political rhetoric urging war was in terms of defending the nation's "honor." Many white southerners, immersed in the cult of the Confederacy and its Lost Cause, flocked to enlist, and even many black men, eager to use the war as a demonstration of the manhood denied by the impositions of white supremacy, signed up. As Hoganson demonstrates, however, the war and its idealization of "military manliness" actually narrowed rather than expanded the prerequisites of citizenship. Blacks could not be white, no matter how valiant, and women could be neither soldiers nor men.

By the end of the war, the nature of American identity that the Civil War had so profoundly unsettled had begun to precipitate into the shapes it would bear for most of the next hundred years. However, even in the first decade of this new century, tensions underlying that identity abided. While whiteness, maleness, and the preservation of union were reaffirmed, their preeminence was no longer uncontested: slavery was abolished, women would soon secure the enfranchisement they sought, and laborers and immigrants would shortly assert their own prerogatives and contributions to the American ideal. In the early 1900s, the consequences of these shifts in identity were writ large in social conflict and active dissent.

Led by men like W. E. B. Du Bois, a native of Massachusetts and the first black man to receive a degree from Harvard, and women like Alice Dunbar-Nelson and Ida B. Wells, African Americans began to organize themselves against the indignities and violence of Jim Crow. The National Association of Colored Women was founded in 1903 to resist lynching and peonage, followed seven years later by the influential National Association for the Advancement of Colored People. Exchanging the blunt oppressions of the South for better opportunities in the North during the Great Migrations surrounding World War I, blacks developed vibrant ethnic communities that fostered original forms of music, like the blues and jazz, and created the spirited atmosphere that would later give birth to the urban movement collectively known as the "New Negro" movement or, more popularly, the "Harlem Renaissance."

Both black and white women intensified their commitment to suffrage, a goal they finally achieved in 1919. As women pursued the vote, however, they also began to recognize the narrowness of that aim, a point that Elizabeth Cady Stanton had tried to make years before. The changes in women's lives—from a greater and growing presence in the workplace to the birth-control education advocated by Margaret Sanger—exacerbated the distance between traditional notions of femininity and the social reforms necessary to support women's new roles. Many women joined progressive movements, demanding reforms as various as the regulation of meat and food inspection, the control of rail and oil monopolies, and the abolition of child labor—an abuse particularly rampant in southern textile mills.

The explosive growth of the Progressive movement in the early twentieth century was largely a response to the unbridled exploitation of human and natural resources launched in the decades following the Civil War. The Robber Barons of the Gilded Age, who had created both the demand for new workers and their dismal conditions, faced a myriad of strikes, boycotts, and other organized resistance in the decades before and after 1900. Though the unions themselves were often exclusive, rejecting both women and black men, an exception was the Industrial Workers of the World formed in Chicago in 1905. Determined to create "One Big Union" not separated by gender or race or skills, the "Wobblies" represented one of the most powerful versions of the inclusive identity that mirrors the deliberate diversity of U.S. culture. A dramatic and popular force for social change, the IWW was gradually discredited by conservative forces that slowly suppressed such reforms after 1914, and the Wobblies' inclusive ideology tainted the very idea of socialism as anti-democratic for a whole century (Zinn 31–76). In many ways, the radical activism of the early twentieth century was a ripening of the profound social reorganization prompted by the Civil War and its unsettling aftermath. By the first decade of the new century, the South as an issue, and the local-color fiction that had served to articulate the conflicts of a nation redefining itself, had lost the public's interest. However, in the cauldron of the four earlier decades, and particularly in its popular literature, American identity had been profoundly redefined. No literary type was more integral or significant to the enterprise than southern local-color fiction.

MARKETING THE EXOTIC:
THE POSTBELLUM RISE OF SOUTHERN LOCAL COLOR

With the destruction of the regional economy and southerners struggling to reconstruct a coherent society, southern fiction had, in fact, lain dormant for almost a decade after the Civil War. The means for its resurgence—like so many other aspects of the South's recovery—eventually came from the North. In the 1870s, as magazines multiplied throughout the publishing centers of the Northeast, the most prestigious and widely circulated of them began to seek out southern material: among them, *Scribner's Monthly* (later *Century Magazine*), *Lippincott's*, *Harper's Magazine*, and, eventually, the *Atlantic Monthly*. Coupled with popular family periodicals like *Youth's Companion* and *Wide Awake* and a multitude of local newspapers, they created a fertile and lucrative venue for southern materials and for many new writers, who drew, in part, on the readership Simms, the Southwest humorists, and the domestic novelists had cultivated before the war.

One stimulus to this reinvigorated interest in the South was tourism. The prosperous extension of northern middle and upper classes and the expansion of the railroads made southern tourism an entertaining and instructional means of asserting social status. The postwar South, with its ruined mansions redolent of lost glory and the patent otherness of its rural inhabitants, both black and white, furnished a superb experience of the exotic for both physical and mental travelers. Northern journals encouraged touristic attitudes through numerous southern travelogues. In one of the most aggressive efforts to reacquaint readers with the South—and to identify promising southern writers—*Scribner's Monthly* sent Edward King and an illustrator on an excursion through the former Confederacy in 1872. Commencing the next year as *Scribner's* installments and published in three volumes in 1875, King's prodigious report celebrated "the current of travel pouring over the great roadways from New York to

New Orleans and from the West and St. Louis to the Atlantic coast" (722). His project encompassed more than 880,000 square miles of "fifteen ex-slave states" and the "Indian territories" and provided a compendium of rising southern commerce, social commentary, history, travel sketches, statistics, and, of course, illustrations. The extensive series proved an in-fluential tool in moderating attitudes toward the defeated South—and for promoting southern writers. During his sojourn in New Orleans, for example, King "discovered" New Orleans cotton warehouse clerk George Washington Cable. King encouraged *Scribner's* to publish Cable's first story in 1873, and southern local color was launched. *Harper's* also ran a series of southern articles in 1873–74 and, under the leadership of editor Henry Mills Alden, eventually published a number of southern writers, notably Grace King and James Lane Allen.

Century Magazine editor L. Frank Tooker explained that the readiness to publish southern authors was based on the "courtesy and tact of the South," with its willingness to remove the "old hostility," and on the value of the literature which "blazed a new path in America—a path marked by the most pronounced local color, irradiated by humor and ten-der romanticism" (Hubbell 728). While the *Atlantic* resisted the popular tide of southern materials until the 1880s, its influential editor William Dean Howells did publish former Confederate veteran (and Indiana native) George Cary Eggleston's "A Rebel's Recollections" and Twain's "True Story" in 1874, as well as Murfree's Tennessee mountain stories in the later 1870s.

The popularity of southern characters and settings even prompted a number of northern writers to try their hands at the genre, among them New England regionalists Sarah Orne Jewett and Mary Wilkins Freeman; none, however, enjoyed the earlier success of New Hampshire-born Con-stance Fenimore Woolson, whose first southern story, "Miss Elisabetha," appeared in *Appleton's Journal* in 1874.

The necessity for filling millions of pages (an estimated three million by 1890) opened national publishing opportunities for many new writers across the country. In effect, the proliferation of magazines and the short fiction they encouraged became a critical attendant to the nation's efforts to redefine its regional relationships and national identity. Southern local-color fiction, which promptly dominated the periodical market, was cru-cial in that redefinition.

While the local-color short story inherited both the model of Haw-thorne's and Poe's tales as well as the magazine markets that supported them, there were important distinctions. Postwar fiction, like the culture that produced it, was affected by a sharper skepticism and a stronger reliance on empirical measures of truth than antebellum literature. What Hawthorne and Simms as well as the plantation and domestic novelists variously understood as "romance" was replaced by a "new realism," championed by influential editors and novelists like Howells and Twain. As a distinct narrative aesthetic, realism's roots were continental, applied first to the accurate, unidealized descriptions of the novels of Gustave Flaubert. The term *la couleur locale* also developed in France in the 1850s, where Flaubert and Guy de Maupassant considered it "the essence of realism." In the United States, however, realism was promptly claimed as offering the most authentic version of American experience, and local color was regarded as one of its leading embodiments. As late as 1927, literary critic Vernon Parrington singled out southern writers Cable and Murfree to demonstrate that local color was an indigenous American form a "native growth, sprung from the soil, unconcerned with European technique" (3:238). But whether import or native, the hallmarks of local color were manifestly realistic: an accurate attention to detail, an emphasis on landscape, carefully created characters, provincial customs, and the peculiarities of local speech (dialect). But what also characterized local color was its interest in difference: not simply "realistic" portraits but portraits of some "other" places and experience, a role that the South—with its lively frontier humor traditions, racialized family structures, slaveholding rebel past, and renewed attractiveness both to tourists and investors—played like a natural.

THE ELEMENTS OF LOCAL COLOR:
EXOTIC SETTINGS, CHARACTERS, AND DIALECT

Since readers were usually assumed to share the perspectives—physical and social—of publishers in the urban northeast, much of the United States, particularly its rural reaches and inhabitants, was deemed "exotic." As a region whose dissimilarities had been profound enough to warrant civil war, the "Great South" was an especially "different" place. Its varied landscapes and isolated cultural pockets offered appealing sources of unfamiliarity for writers to deploy: the misty Tennessee mountains of Murfree and Elliott; the Florida marshes of Woolson; the southeastern plantations of Harris, Bonner, and Page; the Alabama and Texas of Davis; the North Carolina settlements of Chesnutt; and the Creole and Acadian

Louisiana of Cable, Hearn, Stuart, King, Chopin, and Dunbar-Nelson. Writers like Harris, Stuart, Octave Thanet, Ambrose Gonzales, and James Lane Allen placed other southern states, such as Georgia, Arkansas, South Carolina, and Kentucky into this fictional topography. Typically authors were associated by reputation with a particular place, though some, including Page, Davis, Harris, Bonner, and Twain, turned occasionally to other settings; others, like Paul Laurence Dunbar, adopted a variety of locales, including the generically southern, such as his unspecified "Happy Hollow," which Dunbar identified as whatever city or village blacks occupied as their own. The richness and strangeness of setting were so central to the genre that the local-color "sketch," in contrast to the more fully realized "story," often evoked just the flavor of an interesting place, as in Dunbar-Nelson's "Praline Woman" or any number of Hearn's reflective pieces.

The singularity of these "other" places was further confirmed by the "characters" who populated them. For the presumably urban (and implicitly urbane) reader, even the ordinary—"real"—lives of these folk were eccentric, quaint, charming, or surprisingly different. Writers quickly learned to exploit and even exaggerate such disparities. Perhaps the most distinctive feature of these "different" people—and the most difficult to convey on the printed page—was their speech. Careful phonetic transcriptions (which were often as much an obstacle for contemporary readers as for modern ones) became a signal element of local color's realism. Writers such as Twain, Harris, Bonner, Cable, Murfree, Hearn, Chesnutt, and Stuart took great pains to enunciate the varieties of southern dialect. Harris and Cable, among others, consciously pursued the essentially ethnographical task of accurately recording the differing speech patterns and customs of the souths they knew.

Nineteenth-century interest in dialect was part of a general concern about language, especially the provenance of English and Anglo-Saxon culture, and related anxieties about national identity. One popular view maintained that the country's various speech communities would eventually amalgamate into a national vernacular, brought about—as John Fiske speculated in 1891—by the "continuous business communication among large bodies of men" (660). The process of achieving a standard American speech, of course, would require melding the various local accents into a single national tongue. Seeking, among other ends, ways to advance commerce, reformists like Fiske argued that in "speech, as in other aspects of social life, the progress of mankind is from fragmentariness to solidarity" (664). Implicitly and often quite consciously, the representation of various speech patterns in local color insinuated a resistance to this "progressive" leveling process.

But as Gavin Jones demonstrates, dialect served any number of often contradictory functions during the Gilded Age, including the subordination of "other" spoken identities to a dominant cultural standard (46). Brodhead, North, and others have emphasized this demeaning function, especially in white representations of black speech, which marked African Americans' language (together with their persons) as inferior. In this sense, southern black dialect, as Walter Benn Michaels argues, augmented the work of Jim Crow by isolating race as an autonomous human characteristic (739). Becoming more than simply a marker of realism and locale, dialect helped to identify "blackness" or race as independent of region, ultimately transcending both place and skin tone ("not white" covered an infinite array of pigmentations), representable in the abstractions of speech as firmly as in the abstract laws of segregation. However, as Jones insists, in the hands of Dunbar or Chesnutt or Cable, dialect could also subvert those same hegemonies, by revealing either the inadequacy of representing another's speech or the interpenetration of standard and nonstandard speech, the indistinguishable creolization of black and white language and culture (46, 133).

Like dialect, the narrative perspective of much local-color fiction emphasized the marginality of its material. Self-consciously more "national," educated, and sophisticated than their characters, the writer and the story's narrator mediated between the reader and those various "others" who could not themselves claim any such shared identity and authority—a point duly emphasized by their phonetically marked speech. The local-color narrator was often an outsider, someone external to the action, who was yet able to observe and comment perceptively and, the reader assumed, accurately. Like dialect, that distance could nonetheless serve disparate intentions and often reflected a complex negotiation of those audiences. For example, southern writers King and Chesnutt, who were keenly aware—albeit from very different perspectives—of the biases and even ignorance of northern publishers and readers, were both self-conscious interpreters of their region's differences. More typical were Stuart and Murfree, who sought to differentiate themselves (and thus the social strata they occupied) from the folly or coarseness of those "other" black or mountain southerners they were presenting.

Southern communities and families, with their complex webs of class, racial, and gender relationships, provided a particularly fertile source of narrative tropes. As in antebellum domestic fiction, the formation of family often functioned as a figure of national reconciliation: North-South infatuations (usually leading to marriage) structured numerous tales, including Harris's "A Story of the War," Murfree's "The Star in the Valley," and Page's "Meh Lady." Merrill Skaggs has demonstrated the prominence of communal gatherings in southern stories, such as the Christmas visit in Page's "Unc' Edinburgh's Drowndin' " or the festivities in Davis's "A Bamboula." Black servants' identification with their white "family" provided another narrative mainstay: the faithfully loving black "Aunts," "Uncles," and "Gran'mammys" in the fiction of Page, Harris, and Bonner. But writers also exposed the ironies of such assumed loyalties, as in Twain's "A True Story," Dunbar's "Nelse Hatton's Vengeance," and many of Chesnutt's narratives, including his 1912 story "The Doll," "The Passing of Grandison," and all the Uncle Julius tales.

Just as a racialized dialect could expose character, a hidden racial heritage served as the pivot of many plots. Such stories depended on individuals of biracial or uncertain ancestry who "passed," sometimes unknowingly, as "pure" white, usually with disastrous consequences. Chopin's "Désirée's Baby" is the most famous instance of this story line, but Harris's "Where's Duncan?", Elliott's "The Heart of It," King's "The Little Convent Girl," and Dunbar-Nelson's "Sister Josepha" and "The Stones of the Village" all utilize the device. A complementary variant also emerged involving cross-race lovers and their same-race rivals, typically resulting in death for the black character. Cable's excerpt from *The Grandissimes* and Davis's "A Bamboula" both employ this pattern, while Chopin's unpublished story "The Storm" features a cross-class relationship. While such plots traded on the dangerous sensuality of mixed-heritage women, others tentatively explored the limited autonomy of white women, as in King's "La Grande Demoiselle," or even her abusive subjugation, as in Dunbar-Nelson's "Tony's Wife" or Chopin's "In Sabine." Still others mirrored the prevailing ideology that white women were venerated by white and black men alike. Many of Page's stories rest on this notion, as does Davis's "A Bamboula" and, in a quite different fashion, Dunbar's "The Lynching of Jube Benson," which unmasks the racial bigotry and violence such veneration conceals.

As Edward King began his "Great South" series for *Scribner's*, he carefully condemned the South's "unjust civilization of the past," but he also found its cultural riches not only "picturesque" but starkly different from "the prosaic and leveling civilization of the present" (2). That shift—seeing the inequities of southern society as simply a "picturesque" counter to the "prosaic" equality of a modern democracy—marked a profound turn in the relationship between the antithetical social and economic visions that had provoked the Civil War. This turn would only sharpen in the next two decades. King had predicted that the "Paradise Lost" of the South in twenty years "may just be Paradise Regained." His remark proved prophetic.

The Practice of Southern Local Color

THE FIRST SOUTHERN LOCAL-COLOR STORIES

The complex tensions in southern local color are evident in the fiction of its earliest practitioner, Louisianian and former Confederate officer George W. Cable. His outrage against racial injustice is evident in his first story "Bibi," which King admired. Its account of a rebellious slave tortured by his owner was too inflammatory, however, for either the *Atlantic Monthly* or *Scribner's*, both of which rejected it as distressing and violent. King did persuade *Scribner's* to publish the less troubling "'Sieur George" in 1873. The social criticism that typified Cable's early work is more contained and palatable in this story, which warns against the mental and social erosion of an effete Creole past. *Scribner's* then urged Cable to "work as religiously as if you had already Bret Harte's reputation—and perhaps you may have one as lasting" (Biklé 48). The magazine's conviction about the salability of Cable's work was confirmed by the rapid publication of six more stories (1873–76) that later formed the core of Cable's 1879 collection *Old Creole Days*. Immediately popular, Cable's fiction featured a dark strain of violence, social unrest, economic tension, and the racial complexities that King had encountered on his southern tour. But much of this darkness is suppressed or palliated by Cable's luxurious southern settings and romantic resolutions. Like King, Cable saw in the decadent charm of the old Creole world a reassuring contrast to the spirited brashness, even rudeness, of the emerging "Americain" society. Although Cable would eventually reject the plantation tradition and deplore its legacies, these early stories reveal his fascination with its voluptuous decadence— a fascination the reading public eagerly shared. *Jadis,* the title he originally proposed for his first collection, poignantly invoked these seductions. "Jadis," explained Cable, "signified, as near as I can give it in English, once, in the fairy-tale sense; 'once upon a time,' or 'in old times'" (Biklé 58). Such yearnings, together with the charming eccentricities of Creole and French Acadian life, established an enthusiastic audience for Louisiana fiction, which was satisfied by a host of talented writers, including Hearn in the 1880s and (Grace) King, Chopin, Stuart, and Dunbar-Nelson in the 1890s.

With his careful reproduction of Creole accents, Cable confirmed the integral role of dialect in southern local color. But it was black dialect that became its most familiar marker. Mark Twain, with obvious debts to his western yarns and Southwestern humor, first experimented with black dialect in two stories, both published in November 1874. In "Sociable Jimmy" the narrator, a public lecturer and visitor to an Illinois village, chats with a garrulous, ten-year-old black serving boy. Like that tale, Twain's first *Atlantic Monthly* publication, "A True Story: Repeated Word for Word as I Heard It," was based on an actual conversation. Both stories are framed by an uninformed but sophisticated listener. "A True Story," however, involves explicitly southern material, and its narrator emerges as foolishly unknowing, even culpable, while its informant, Aunt Rachel, grows in stature recounting the desperation of blacks' prewar bondage and the joy of northern-won freedom. In presenting her poignant account of injustice and resistance, Twain exposes both the horrors of slavery as well as his own (and the reader's) ignorant assumptions about the happy conditions of black folk. Such resistant perspectives appear early in southern local color, though they tended to remain, as in Twain and Cable, as undercurrents rather than main streams.

Twain's venerable black woman who cooks for white people is fictional kin to the slave "mammy" Sherwood Bonner is generally credited with creating in her dialect "Gran'mammy tales," first published in July 1875 and later collected in *Suwanee River Tales* (1884). Bonner's Gran'mammy, who generated a crucial type in southern local color, also laid bare the underlying foundation of racial interdependence. In the collected version of the story, Gran'mammy, who controls her plantation kitchen, pointedly ejects her own "tar-baby" grandchildren and, at the same time, adores the privileged white master's children, whom she raises; she loves God with "childlike simplicity" and exhibits an unfailing love for her white plantation family. Like Twain's spirited Aunt Rachel, Gran'mammy is a survivor, but she remains indissolubly linked to the white family she serves, emphasizing a significant strand in the tangle of southern kinship and heralding the many stereotypes, especially of blacks, that filled the repertoire of southern local color.

Although Bonner's stories were based on her Mississippi childhood, Gran'mammy shares much with Harris's Uncle Remus, the Georgian ex-slave who first appeared in a newspaper sketch in 1876. Newspapers were, like magazines, an important vehicle for local-color fiction, and both "Uncle Remus As a Rebel" (1877) and "The Story of Mr. Rabbit and Mr. Fox" (1879) were published in the *Atlanta Constitution,* which was rapidly becoming the voice of the reconstituted New South. The benign figure of Uncle Remus, willingly instructing whites about black culture, was, like Gran'mammy, a reassuring image of blacks' continued fidelity to the conventional southern models of society. The immense success of Harris's 1880 collection, *Uncle Remus: His Songs and Sayings* (the first printing sold ten thousand copies) confirmed the power of this folk figure, who captured the American imagination for decades. In collecting his early stories, however, Harris significantly revised the titles, improved the stories' dialect and ethnographical verisimilitude (Harris became revered as a folklore collector), and enhanced their incipient note of plantation nostalgia—all changes that reflected the shifting emphases of southern local color itself. For example, "Uncle Remus As a Rebel" was originally framed by a northern woman's report of Remus's account of events; in the collected version, Harris renamed it "A Story of the War" and shifted the focus from the fiercely protective rebel Remus, who shoots a Union soldier while safeguarding young Mistress Sally, to the postwar marriage of the Confederate Miss Sally with Marse John, a wounded Union officer. Prefacing the new volume with "Uncle Remus Initiates the Little Boy," Harris made the initiation of northern readers into the folkways and values of the South explicit. John and Sally's six-year-old son, figuratively the hope of a newly reunited nation, sits in the flickering firelight of Uncle Remus's cabin and begs for stories, often asking questions as Uncle Remus beguiles him with tale after tale of a dancing, singing, smoking, tobacco-chewing trickster rabbit, a thinly veiled portrait of the black freedmen, who were indeed still dancing ambivalently to the tunes of white society.

Although plantation life and black interpreters remained standard in southern local color, another important locale was the Appalachian mountain range of Virginia, Tennessee, Georgia, and Kentucky—a region first explored in the Sut Lovingood yarns of eastern Tennessee, composed primarily in the 1850s and 1860s by George Washington Harris, who was regarded as "the most original and gifted of the antebellum humorists" (Rubin 155). *Lippincott's Magazine,* established in 1868, was especially hospitable to southern writers, and in the early 1870s it printed two works by one Mary Noailles Murfree. But it was in the *Atlantic Monthly* that Murfree found her real niche, with the publication of "The Dancin' Party at Harrison's Cove" under her pen name, "Charles Egbert Craddock." This story of a quaint settlement of hill people nestled in "the wild spur of the Alleghenies" opened a literary passage for virtual wagon-loads of popular Appalachian mountain stories by a host of authors, including Bonner, Harris, Page, and Woolson. The mountain settings dramatized the independent, egalitarian spirit of its white inhabitants, who had occupied their land for generations. Here, declared Murfree in her collection *In the Tennessee Mountains,* was "pride, so intense that it recognizes no superior, so inordinate that one is tempted to cry out, 'Here are the true republicans!'" (186).

In contrast to the Civil War, where the struggle was over such far-reaching issues as legal servitude and political secession, the fictional rivalries in the hills stemmed from long-standing family discord or jealous courtships. Moreover, the disputes were settled by an acceptable man-play of untutored farmers and moonshiners, dedicated to maintaining codes of loyalty to one another and, more importantly, to the nation. For example, expressing his stalwart belief in the United States and the idiocy of a war to abolish slavery, one of Harris's hillbillies simply dismisses the issue altogether: "I hain't got none [slaves], and I hain't a-wantin' none"; "Them dad-blasted Restercrats a-secedin' out'n the Nunited States. . . . The Nunited States is big enough for me" (49–50). The mountaineers' isolation and their eccentric ways also provided broad opportunities for humor; however, the sophisticated visitors, who so often framed these stories, were also assured of a traditional folk wisdom that valued individuality over any foolish efforts at social reform or the intrusions of progress. With the exception of their illegal whiskey distilleries, the mountain men were vigorously anti-commercial, and, though often portrayed as shiftless, dense, and backward, they were also tenacious and spirited. "Men's men," they dominated rude households made livable by their compliant wives.

This formidably conservative male power, however, was frequently undercut by the "mountain pink" woman (to borrow Bonner's term for the sensuous type she introduced in her story "Jack and the Mountain Pink" [1883]). Curiosity, willfulness, and sensual desire propel these mountain women, almost unconsciously, into more fluid cultural spaces than the fixed heritage they are obliged to protect. Seeking romance with sophisticated outlanders, they often pay for their transgressive ventures into (typically) unrequited love with injury or death (as in Harris's "Trouble on Lost Mountain" [1886]). The mountain stories thus significantly modified the standard North-South marriage of much southern local color: the mountains typically kept the girl.

In this "unraced" mountain configuration of the South, racial heritage was pointedly invisible. The isolated (implicitly white) mountain man, not the (implicitly northern) visitor, represented the steadfast independence of the republic. Making just this point in an 1896 story, Kentucky writer John Fox Jr. established an unqualified English, egalitarian lineage for his mountaineer: "This last, silent figure, traced through Virginia, was closely linked by blood and speech with the common people of England. . . . Strikingly unchanged . . . [he is] the most distinctively national remnant in the American soil" and symbolizes "the development of the continent" (Skaggs 144). In the mountains, southern local-color fiction was particularly free to affirm its national allegiances, even as it confirmed the Anglo-Saxon complexion of that loyalty.

Although national reconciliation remained a prominent thematic feature in southern local color, some early writers did acknowledge the formidable obstacles to any easy reunion. The often disregarded stories of Woolson, who began publishing southern material in *Harper's* as early as 1875, were remarkable instances of that recognition. A northerner (born in New Hampshire and raised in Ohio), Woolson became familiar with Georgia, the Carolinas, Virginia, and Florida through periods of residency and travel—a fact that underscores the increasing popularity of the South as a vacation destination and the readiness with which many northerners took up southern material. Woolson's varied and realistic portraits reflected much of the anger, fluidity, and racial complexities of the Reconstruction South. Stories like "King David" and "Rodman the Keeper," for example, presented ruined, often bitter and unreconstructed white southerners and defiant, sometimes patriotic and sometimes recalcitrant blacks. In "Felipa" (1876), however, Woolson moved beyond those entrenched hostilities and stereotypes of the plantation South to Florida, the "wild . . . old-new land, with its deserted plantations, its skies of Paradise," and painted a liminal landscape of borderlands and border beings. Like other Woolson characters, the sensitive northerner of "Felipa," Catherine, is frustrated by her efforts to bring enlightenment and culture to a beleaguered region. But in deftly chronicling such northern intrusions, Woolson gave voice to just those forces that would reshape and silence a culturally rich, diverse, and often resistant South.

THE MYTH OF THE OLD SOUTH IN LOCAL COLOR

However, it was not Woolson's stories of a diverse South or even Murfree's mountain chronicles that created the lasting blueprint for what Paul H. Buck has called this "Dixie of the storybooks . . . the Arcady of American tradition" (244). That ambiguous honor was assumed by the plantation fiction of Virginian Thomas Nelson Page. The most popular southern writer of the 1880s and 1890s, Page offered an ideological solution for many of the troubling issues of the era: the erosion of white primacy, failed agrarianism, women's insistence on equality, and racial unrest. After publishing "Marse Chan" in the prestigious *Century* in 1884, Page became an immediate sensation. New England author Sarah Orne Jewett, Harriet Beecher Stowe's brother and distinguished orator Henry Ward Beecher, and once-ardent abolitionist Thomas Wentworth Higginson were all moved by the story (Hubbell 801). Harris declared it better than "everything else that has appeared since the War—or before the War, for that matter." Page's 1887 collection, *In Ole Virginia or Marse Chan and Other Stories,* established him as the high priest of Southern apologists. In her 1932 autobiography, Grace King, whose popular *Balcony Stories* appeared in 1893, recalls Page's significance for southern writers: "It is hard to explain in simple terms what Thomas Nelson Page meant to us in the South at that time. . . . His stories, short and simple . . . showed us with ineffable grace that although we were sore bereft, politically, we had now a chance in literature at last" (ix). King spoke for many white southerners who saw in southern local color a welcome opportunity to express to a predominantly northern readership their frustration with the radical changes that the demise of slavery had imposed on southern society.

Page created an idealized antebellum world in which that society could be positively experienced and publicly exonerated. In it, cheerfully loyal slaves were part of an extended family in which aristocratic cavaliers lived by a code of honor. In contrast to the disturbing turmoil of the 1880s and 1890s, his Old South rested upon a fixed social system that subordinated women and nonwhites. Both "Marse Chan" and "Unc' Edinburg's Drowndin'" illustrate Page's successful formula. A visiting white narrator encounters a black man, who was once the beloved slave of a noble, young aristocrat. The freedman now defines his life through that of his master;

"jes' like he shadow," says Edinburg of his master George. Old South memories of fox-hunting, dueling, dancing, loving, and happy "darkies" fill the stories. Sam declares in "Marse Chan," "Dem wuz good ole times, master—de bes' Sam ever see! . . . Niggers didn' had nothin't all to do— jus' hed to ten' to de feedin' an' cleanin' de hosses, an' doin' what de mars- ter tell 'em to do." The former young masters are invariably charming, handsome, kind, college-educated, and courageous. They defend their slaves, intervening in cruel sales and rescuing servants from fires and floods. These noble southerners fight bravely for the Confederacy, even though some, like Channing, argue against secession. They always love a spirited, wondrously attractive lady, at first unattainable because of family conflicts, but eventually won. The final union of master and mis- tress is then echoed in the marriage or relationships of their respective black servants.

Despite such happy resolutions, however, Page ultimately cannot erase the cruelties of slavery and the rigid hierarchies of plantation life that seep into his fictional society. Slaves are property to be bought and sold. Edin- burg is viciously whipped, and Channing's father, however generous, still patronizes and lashes his retainers. Sam and Edinburg remain as subordi- nate in the free present as in the idealized past. The stories' young white mistresses, Anne and Charlotte, are bound by family honor and are fully dependent upon male protection. Even the privileged white masters are inextricably obligated to their dependent women and slaves.

In this transparent "fantasy of white, male power" as Caroline Geb- hard terms it, the planter master is the embodiment of gentility, generos- ity, and white dominion ("Reconstructing" 136). That such a past was a fictional creation was unimportant to the reading public. They were con- tentedly breathing the stuff of romance or, as Ellen Glasgow, a later Vir- ginia author, phrased it in 1943, "the fragrance of dried-rose leaves" (140). Certainly, that fragrance was a refreshing change from the stench of mod- ern industrialism. Even more importantly, the patriarchal power implicit in this noblesse oblige fantasy fit well with a growing national imperial- ism, unqualified racism, and the concomitant resurgence of male virility. As Silber has insisted, this "new and invigorated image of southern white manhood" was well suited to the patriotic and imperialist impulses defin- ing the decade of the War of 1898 (12).

Page influenced a number of writers, among them Kentucky author James Lane Allen, who published his first story, "Two Gentlemen of the Old School," in 1888. Retitled "Two Gentlemen of Kentucky," the story appeared in his collection *Flute and Violin and Other Kentucky Tales and Romances* (1891). By excising Page's conventional love interest and introducing an omniscient author, Allen brought into focus the loving interrelationship between male master and former slave. Though preserving racial and class distinctions, the two become distorted mirror images of one another, enduring a disillusioning series of financial, religious, and social disappointments, and eventually lying buried, one beside the other. As Gebhard observes, Allen's sentimental reminiscences extended the male interdependence of master and body-servant to its implicit homoerotic conclusion ("Reconstructing" 133).

THE GOLDEN AGE OF LOCAL COLOR

Writers of the 1890s found a South already mostly imagined. Distracted by the predations of the robber barons and the labor struggles of the Gilded Age, the nation had largely abandoned the "Negro problem" to southern whites, who had worked rapidly to reinstate racism, segregation, and economic oppression in the place of chattel slavery. Even so, the popularity of southern local color did not wane, and many of the genre's finest writers produced some of their best work in this decade. The quality of their stories testifies both to the flexibility of local color in adapting to changing audiences and to its continuing usefulness as a tool in confirming the redefinitions of American identity.

One of the richest veins of local color, opened by Cable in the 1870s, continued to be mined with great effect by several talented Louisiana writers. Lafcadio Hearn, a close friend of Cable, virtually perfected the local-color sketch in the newspapers of Cincinnati and New Orleans in the 1880s. His brief anecdotes and reflections, in carefully crafted, impressionistic prose, provided rich evocations of the exotic places and characters of the urban South. Though he published several collections of these sketches and reviews, his best-known work was *Chita, a Memory of Last Island*, which Arlin Turner described in 1969 as "a small masterpiece . . . a small jewel, rapturously conceived and meticulously wrought, which has been duplicated not at all and surpassed rarely in the special category to which it belongs" (ix, xxiv). Hearn's subtle uses of language reflected both the seriousness with which he and others treated local-color materials as well as the modernist shifts that the short story had begun to anticipate.

Another fine stylist and New Orleans native, Grace King sympathized with Page's ideological reclamation of the Old South and was quite explicit in her efforts to counter what she viewed as Cable's distorted and unfair portrait of white Creole culture. Beginning with "Monsieur Motte" (1888), her stories were championed by *Century*'s influential editor, Richard Watson Gilder. Later a close friend of the Clemenses, King employed a nuanced prose to defend southern racial hierarchies, as in "The Little Convent Girl" (1893), where the discovery of a racial "taint" leads the story's namesake to suicide. However, King's searching fidelity to psychological realism, together with her commitment to the subversive value of feminine perspectives (charmingly suggested in "The Balcony Stories," her 1893 collection's preface), often unsettles the conservative surfaces of her fiction and gives it modernist undercurrents of uncertainty. At the same time, King's personal sense of the injustice of the war's aftermath, a perspective which many white southerners shared and which southern fiction helped to reinforce among northerners, is poignantly expressed in sketches like "La Grande Demoiselle" (1893).

A contemporary of both Hearn and King, Ruth McEnery Stuart shared King's sensitivity to the plight of women after the war and, like her, used local color to explore explicitly female perspectives, particularly in her Arkansas tales. Like Hearn, however, Stuart was also concerned with the accuracies of dialect and realistic description. Her extremely popular black dialect fiction, which first appeared in *Harper's* (1887), recapitulated a plantation mythology similar to Page's, though Stuart accented the deliberate humor of the Southwest traditions and the peculiarities of the southern delta. Stuart's urban fiction also introduces other ethnicities, including vivid (if occasionally unflattering) portraits of the New Orleans Italian community. Like Harris, Stuart provided northerners with a sense that white southerners "knew" and indeed could interpret African American culture, certainly better than they and even better than blacks themselves.

When she moved to New Orleans from Texas as a young wife in 1879, Mollie Moore Davis was already a widely published and well-known poet. Her turn to local-color fiction in the early 1880s attests to its enormous popularity and the seductive financial opportunities it offered. Davis wrote several novels and novellas as well as short stories. "A Bamboula" is a provocative rendering of much that made the genre popular. Set on a Louisiana plantation, the tale incorporates a range of exotic African American customs and beliefs, recalling William Gilmore Simms's early defense of southern "legends" as an important element of local material. Davis both echoes and revises Page and Allen, structuring her tale around the sexual and familial rivalries between black and white women, who are presumably sisters. Together with its internal racial stratifications, these elements suggest the genre's increasingly complicated portraits of black-white relations, a far cry from the unquestioning loyalty of Bonner's mammy.

The local-color writer with perhaps the most enduring reputation is, like the much-admired Cable, associated with Louisiana. While Kate Chopin is best known for her brilliant novel of female selfhood, *The Awakening* (1899), her contemporary reputation was based on her many stories and sketches depicting the lives of Louisiana's rural Acadians, French-speaking émigrés who settled the region in the 1770s. Although Chopin's deft rendering of women's lives gave her local-color tales depth and continuing relevance, she was also a subtle recorder of folkways and was particularly skillful at using fragments of French and minimal phonetic changes to convey her characters' lilting speech. Chopin rarely employed antebellum settings, but in both "Désirée's Baby" (1894) and "La Belle Zoraïde" (1894) she explores with surprising sensitivity the plight of mixed-race women in a racist culture. Elsewhere, Chopin demonstrated the potential of local color for examining complex contemporary issues, particularly the changes in women's lives. With an adroit blend of seriousness and humor, she explored wife abuse in "In Sabine" (1894) and female sensuality in her remarkable story "The Storm," which remained unpublished in her lifetime.

Prolific and popular, Sarah Barnwell Elliott was a social activist and Tennessee resident; like Chopin, Davis, King, and Dunbar-Nelson, she scrutinized the difficult alternatives faced by the mixed-race woman in her spirited tale of passing, "The Heart of It" (unpublished before her death in 1928). Increasingly common in southern local color in the eighties and nineties, the "tragic mulatta" (whose "white blood" permitted a somewhat greater identification and sympathy than did black heroines among white readers) epitomized the intricacy of contemporary perceptions of race, even as the character's narrow range of options reflected the nation's emergent, uneasy consensus about black inferiority.

BLACK WRITERS, WHITE READERS: DIVERSITY AND COMPLICITY

The complexity with which race is figured in southern local color appears most dramatically in the work of several important black writers who successfully asserted their own perspective within the genre's ambiguous parameters. Charles W. Chesnutt was the first to break the local-color "line" that restricted the genre to white authors. However, when his story "The

Goophered Grapevine" appeared in the *Atlantic* (1888), neither his editors nor his readers knew, since Chesnutt "wished his work to be considered on its own merit." Eventually, on September 8, 1891, he wrote his publisher Houghton Mifflin, describing himself as "an American of acknowledged African descent." Houghton Mifflin withheld this information until the appearance of his first short-story collection, *The Conjure Woman* (1899), however, partly out of concern for Chesnutt's privacy, but also for the weightier possibility that his work might be viewed less favorably (Render 10). In fact, a number of autobiographies and novels by blacks had appeared after the war with some success, including Frances E. W. Harper's *Sketches of Southern Life* (1872) and *Iola Leroy or Shadows Uplifted* (1892), her rendering of the tragic mulatta. But Chesnutt's stories drew on the established popularity of plantation literature, particularly on Harris's Uncle Remus. Chesnutt subtly transformed Harris's faithful, if elusive, ex-slave into the consummate freedman, Uncle Julius. A skillful trickster, Julius employs the black power of "conjuring" (or "goophering") in his tales to secure some form of personal or economic advantage. To assure the sympathies of the northern reader, Julius's tales are typically framed by the nondialect narration of a white Ohioan. Such structures permitted Chesnutt to expose with extraordinary power the profound suffering of slavery in a story like "Dave's Neckliss," in which the undeserved punishments for the alleged poaching of a ham result in madness and death. Chesnutt also adapted conservative tropes to subversive purposes. In "The Passing of Grandison" (1899), for example, the notion of unquestioned black fidelity to white interests enables slaves to escape to freedom in plain sight of their unsuspecting masters' (and readers') eyes—indeed with their masters' help. In later stories, especially those published in *The Crisis* (1912), a magazine with a primarily black audience, Chesnutt moved away from the plantation frames to explore the plight of the black professional classes in their struggle to rise above the continuing indignities of racism.

Another writer who used southern local color to criticize racist images was Paul Laurence Dunbar. Usually remembered not for his fiction but for his dialect poetry (for which Booker T. Washington lauded him as "the poet laureate of the Negro race"), Dunbar wrote four novels and four collections of short stories. Like Chesnutt, Dunbar worked to revise the prevailing imagery of African Americans as hopelessly unsophisticated, childish, wily, and shiftless. Both men understood how significantly such portrayals, in fiction as well as in the press, contributed to the intensify-

ing violence against black men and to the economic and social marginalization of all African Americans. Dunbar's stories, like Chesnutt's, disclose
the masking in which blacks must engage to maintain their dignity and
autonomy. "Nelse Hatton's Vengeance" (1898) examines the bonds between master and slave without the legal constraints of the "peculiar institution." The dignity and careful calculations of the black characters notably revised the fawning loyalty that Page and Allen had made standard
in the genre. "The Lynching of Jube Benson" (1904), on the other hand,
provides a much sharper indictment of contemporary race relations and
the racist fears undergirding lynching. Dunbar's penetrating analysis of
white guilt and regret for betrayal of the interracial family marked a momentous new note in southern local color.

Like her first husband Paul Laurence Dunbar, New Orleans native
Alice Dunbar-Nelson began her career as a poet, and her contemporary
literary reputation was based on her poetry. *The Goodness of St. Rocque*
(1899), the first collection of short stories by a black woman, is characterized by a poet's impressionistic use of language; its stories also reflect the
range and fluidity that southern local color had acquired by the turn of the
century. The dialect sketch, first ventured by Twain two decades earlier,
has become in "The Praline Woman" (1899) a subtle evocation of character and relationships in a compact monologue. The "tragic mulatta" trope
is adapted in "Sister Josepha" (1899) to a delicate appraisal of female selfhood and sexuality, while "Tony's Wife" (1899) probes female victimhood
through Italian and German ethnicities. Often racially coded, Dunbar-
Nelson's stories of Creole life rarely confront these potent issues directly,
though her remarkable collection depicts domestic violence, working-class
conflict, male duplicity, female economic oppression, and racial strife—
all pressing issues of the era. But if, as Elizabeth Ammons argues, these
stories are packaged to "pass" as local color and thus to be freed from "racial prescriptions" (60), they nonetheless consistently engage race (no less
than gender and class) in their own margins: the uncertain identity and
sexual dangers for a young woman on the perimeters of whiteness, or the
vulnerability of immigrant or "brown" women outside the slim legal protections of marriage or economic security

That Dunbar-Nelson's reticence, particularly about race, was amply
justified is manifest in the fate of her unpublished story, "The Stones of
the Village," which editors rejected in 1900 as unsuitable for audiences no
longer interested in "race stories." Certainly, to the story's central character, the costs of passing, even to achieve social standing (or literary fame),

are extremely high, as Dunbar-Nelson herself soon recognized. After the rejection of "Stones," she turned increasingly to activism and journalism as more effective ways to resist the hardening racism of the early twentieth century. Partly for that reason, Dunbar-Nelson's contributions to local color, like those of Chesnutt and Dunbar, have been largely overlooked. But as Violet Harrington Bryan astutely observes, taking them into account forces a profound reconsideration of the work of their white contemporaries, as well as a serious reevaluation of the meaning of "color" in local-color literature (77).

As the tradition and the century drew to a close, Dunbar-Nelson's guarded local-color fiction seemed to reflect all too accurately a world in which intimacy was absent and human contact was undermined by the deceptions that it required. "Who am I? What am I?" cries her "tropical beauty" Camille, whose only refuge from such uncertainties is the convent's "white veil." Almost three decades earlier in "Felipa," Woolson's young androgynous heroine attempts suicide by eating the poisonous sketching crayons of the visiting teacher-artist she so hopelessly loves. Like Camille's white habit and Felipa's assimilative desire, southern local color was ultimately a literature of colonization; its subjects were exotic hybrids that had to be codified and "civilized" in order to be manageable, if not altogether visible. The distinct regional differences that defined and partly stabilized its surfaces were also traversed by such deeply destabilizing factors as race, gender, and class. These implicit and explicit tensions permeate even the most traditional narratives, like those by Page and Harris, which sanction a return to an idealized hierarchy. Indeed, even Dunbar-Nelson's indeterminate characters, Page's Unc' Edinburg, and Harris's Uncle Remus are firmly framed by a patriarchal white world. In the last decades of the century, that world was severely threatened by the dark fluidity undermining the makeshift boundaries of the homogeneous nation the Civil War had been intended to restore. Southern local-color fiction offered a way to circumscribe some of that threat, at least until the nation had a chance to reassess itself and, partly through the imaginative work of that fiction, to reassert a more familiar version of its continuing cultural identity.

As Dunbar-Nelson's Tante Marie in "The Praline Woman" (1899) offers her wares with sweet words appropriate to each buyer, she fears a break in the Mississippi river levee, not unlike the dangerous break with established lives and customs that so many of the late stories of southern local color imply. The stark historical realities that infused the genre might be as sugar-coated as Tante Marie's words, but, as in Dunbar-Nelson's "The Goodness of St. Rocque" (1899), the "native black waters," representing the fluid perspectives that moved through southern local color, were held at bay at the end of the century only by white prescriptions of dominance.

Rereading Local Color: Twentieth-Century Perspectives

Applied to a wide range of writers, geographical regions, and literary impulses—including traditions of romance, sentiment, and humor— local color remains an elusive and contested genre. Though relegated by twentieth-century literary history to minor status, it has in recent years attracted new critical interest. Initially, that interest came from feminist critics, who observed parallels between the prominent place women and their concerns occupied in local color and its later devaluation; more recently, those issues have been further linked to functions of regionalism and nationalism. As literary theorists like Deleuze and Guattari suggest, however, a "minor literature," such as local color, is intrinsically politicized, embodying issues of power and group struggle that are critical to a given culture or period. That insight underlies much of the contention surrounding local color in literary history, even as it helps to illuminate the importance of southern local color in particular.

THE CULTURAL WORK OF LOCAL COLOR

Perhaps no issue was more critical to the late nineteenth century than the terms by which the reunited states would define themselves as a nation. Several recent scholars have drawn important attention to the central role that local color played in representing if not reconciling the era's conflicting anxieties about national identity. As Kate McCullough observes, the "struggle to create a unified national identity" was particularly urgent in these decades, given the nation's imperialist ambitions for expanding its global markets and territories and the "racial, regional, ethnic, and sexual divisions" produced in the wake of the Civil War. Literature, and local-color fiction in particular, became a "crucially important site for the production of this national fantasy" (2–3).

In the first place, the sheer variety of American culture—its different regions, ethnicities, accents—could be acknowledged and portrayed in local-color fiction. The intentional realism of that portraiture (the predominance of dialect, the careful description of geography and social customs, the focus on "common folk") made explicitly local characters and cultures available to and part of a broader "nation," one confronting willy nilly its own internally and externally expanding borders. Local color helped to mediate the distances between those different "others" (as defined by region or gender or race) and a wider national audience, who implicitly shared an "American" identity. One important aspect of that shared identity, as Amy Kaplan points out, was precisely the distance of that predominantly urban audience from its own recently rural roots, which were often nostalgically idealized in local-color fiction (251). The individuality, independence, and traditional wisdom of the rural "folk" that seemed so lost to the citizens of a modern industrialized nation could thus be preserved and affirmed without sacrificing the tacit superiority of its new urbanity and progressive "American" goals.

But while local color acknowledged the values of the past and, as Richard Brodhead argues, made marginality itself into a literary asset, it also used those "differences" as a way of containing that very diversity (117). The "explosive social conflicts of class, race, and gender" that were so distressingly present in urban life were, as Kaplan explains, conveniently "effaced" by rendering them in terms of region (251). The realism of the genre at once made these disturbing others visible, even as their real power to disturb was diffused by relegating them to an idealized folk past or places made remote by exaggerated difference: *other* people's funny ways of talking, the unusual places *they* lived, *their* old-fashioned ways. In these "other," exotic places of the country, the diversity of North American life could thus be both reported and kept at bay: the "old ways" could be maintained at the margins while the new realities of Darwinism and laissez-faire capitalism continued to establish themselves at the urban, industrialized, self-defined "centers" of the Northeast (Ewell 162).

One way that southern local-color fiction proved especially useful in defining a national identity was in fostering the re-imagination of a region whose differences had almost undone the Union. Through its fictional prisms, the prewar South and its contemporary heirs—an entire territory of cultural and social "rebels"—could be conveniently "reconstructed" from being dangerous enemies of the republic to a more acceptable role as custodians of traditional hierarchy. In the nation's imagination, then, the South was nostalgically recreated as the locus of values whose loss seemed intolerable to a society gripped by change. Despite dissenting portraits by Chesnutt, Dunbar, Dunbar-Nelson, and others, the image of the South as a poignantly Lost Cause became definitive. The national appeal of this particular icon was bitterly observed in 1888 by Albion Tourgée, whose own novels had resisted such idealization. "Our literature," he wrote, "has become not only Southern in type, but distinctly Confederate in sympathy" (8). Nearly a half-century later, W. J. Cash paid tribute to the enduring fantasy of the South as the "Happy-Happy Land . . . perpetually suspended in the great haze of memory . . . poised, somewhere between earth and sky, colossal, shining, and incomparably lovely—a Cloud-Cuckoo land" (127, 130).

The hierarchies whose maintenance most required this nostalgic image of the South were those of race and gender. Representing African Americans and white women in places where their roles were clearly defined helped to assuage the vague threat insinuated by emancipation and suffrage. African American men, for example, often the target of lynchings and figures of great fear, were sanctioned in local color by their quaint (and deliberately amusing) distance from the "reality" of economic and political inequality and by their fixed place at the bottom of the social ladder. Marked by dialect and isolated in rural backwaters, black Americans were seen to occupy a position that was clearly separate from and only presumptively equal to white Americans or even to the new immigrants flooding northern cities. This fictional containment was convincingly reiterated in the political sphere by the "separate but equal" 1896 findings of the Supreme Court, which legalized the erosion of rights supposedly won during the Civil War and hardened racial boundaries by legitimizing Jim Crow. By externalizing "color," local-color fiction, like the color line that it helped to establish, created a separate place, a "different" locality, in which to preserve and celebrate values and ways of being that were no longer tenable in a society whose very premises were in question.

The subordination of women, however, was less successfully sustained by local color. For white women, at least, the privileges of race and class gave them better control of the spaces of redefinition that the genre offered. By the 1890s, white women authors dominated local color, just as they had dominated domestic romance earlier in the century. Attracted, like other marginalized groups, by the increased access local color provided to publishing, women also found in the genre a valorization of the places to which they had largely been confined, the home and local community. Women writers could take up issues already familiar in domestic romance: family relationships, the loss of security in traditional roles, the limits of female agency, and now the absence of dependable men in the wake of a costly war. Deliberately distant from the urban "centers" where increased educational and economic opportunities were making dramatic changes in women's lives, local color offered an "ideal" place to explore unsettled contemporary debates about female status. Women writers also found in the genre both a satisfying professional status and a purposeful aesthetic. Writers like Chopin, King, Bonner, Elliot, Woolson, and Dunbar-Nelson consciously adapted the narrative strategies of local color to address sophisticated problems of morality, emotion, aesthetics, and sexuality. Committed to their craft as writers, they used the genre not only for some of their most serious fiction but also to attract a national audience for their work.

But while local color created rich regional landscapes and congenial fictional places for both women writers and other marginal groups, its limitations eventually confined them there. Shaped by discourses of race, gender, and region, local color—especially southern local color—was ultimately compromised by the purposes of nationalism and hierarchy that those discourses served. The South, which local color had helped to transform into a racialized and gendered space in which the nation (understood as the industrialized Northeast) might safely examine the vexing contradictions of its pluralist identity, now became the scapegoat of those discourses. As the United States more confidently grasped its own imperialist and masculinist authority, the challenges represented by a feminized South (as well as by "socially marginal" writers like white women or African Americans) had to be reinscribed as minor features of American identity. As McCullough explains, the literary South became the exotic and eroticized "other" of America (i.e., the North), even as southern letters was being "written out of 'real men's' literature, aligned with the losers and the women" (190). Indeed, as Gebhard suggests, not only their contributions to the strategies and techniques of realism but "a whole century of writing by women" had to be devalued in the face of this new version of the genuinely "American" ("Spinster" 80). Local color soon occupied its own ironically insulated place in literary history—to use Judith Fetterley's chilling image—as "the literary equivalent of apartheid or purdah" (*Provisions* 23).

THE SHAPE OF THE GENRE: ROMANCE, REALISM, AND REVISIONISM

One of the most telling aspects of the critical debate about local color has been precisely its relationship to realism and the extent to which local color constitutes a contribution to that dominant mode or a deviation from it. A parallel issue is the relationship of local color to regionalism. In both instances, what is at stake is the status of local color: whether it has contributed significantly to the mainstream of U.S. literary history or merely represents an interesting backwater.

Local color has always had strong affinities with nineteenth-century realism. Even when its overall effects were maudlin or artificial—usually the consequence of sentimental plots or ineptitude—the technical intentions of local color were directed toward truthful, and even anthropologically accurate, portraits of human experience. Local color was, in fact, closely related to nineteenth-century materialist philosophies (such as Darwinism) and notions of truth associated more with the physical, "scientific" surfaces of reality than its psychological depths. By the end of the century, however, such versions of realism increasingly began to seem superficial, particularly in the view of many early modernists, whose conceptions of "reality" gave greater weight to the psychological and the symbolic.

Certainly, for many early and influential critics like Vernon Parrington, realism remained the most pronounced feature of local color. Howells, an ardent nineteenth-century champion of realism and an influential author and editor, also praised the particularities of local color as evidence of its quality and its American-ness. Noting the "distinguished performance" of Harris, he described Cable as having "written one of the few American fictions which may be called great" (57). For Howells, the uniqueness and particularity of America's diverse places confirmed an individuality that only realism could represent. The contested site for serious fiction was for critics like Howells not between local color and realism but between a realism grounded in detail (like local color) and fiction mired in artifice and mechanical construction, like contemporary historical romances, which Howells considered useless "tarradiddles" (26).

By the 1890s, however, the term "local color" was falling out of vogue among "serious" authors. In an 1894 review of Hamlin Garland's *Crumbling Idols,* Chopin, herself an accomplished local-color writer who greatly admired both Grace King and Ruth Stuart as well as New Englanders Sarah Orne Jewett and Mary Wilkins Freeman, denounced the "provincialism" and "sentimentality" of "local colorists" such as Indiana poet James Whitcomb Riley (691). Responding to Garland's rejection of European traditions as corrupt and his praise for "veritism" (that is, strains of local color using "authentic" western and Midwestern settings),

Chopin (herself deeply influenced by Maupassant) called for immutable "human existence" as the theme most worthy of an author (691). A truly American literature had to deploy its uniquely colorful places in the service of ideas that transcended merely local concerns; and a serious American writer (as Chopin well understood) could not be identified as a "mere local colorist."

But if literary history thus began to represent the abandonment of local color in favor of more realistic or modernist modes, the regional impulse of local color persisted. For example, not long after Garland declared the West a promising subject, Jack London and Frank Norris were both reshaping the regional details and realist strategies of local-color fiction into their deterministic dramas of brute instinct. For these authors, Howell's carefully photographed, very real "grasshopper" and his "smiling aspects of life" became the human animal caught in a chain of predetermined circumstances (36, 74). But naturalism's darker assessment of the human condition relied on specific detail and careful description to achieve its effects no less than local color. Subject matter and moral stance rather than technique distinguished these presumably discrete genres of the 1890s. Not surprisingly, Norris, who believed that culture is a mere disguise for animal instincts, dismissed local color as "the drama of broken teacups" (Campbell 4). However, his repudiation of such "feminine" subjects only fortifies the claim by Campbell and others that naturalism itself arose, in part, as "a gender-based counter tradition not only to realism but to female-dominated local color writing" (5).

The emergence of modernism was itself a factor in the devaluation of local color. The technical requirements of the sketch and short story had encouraged the development of many of the impressionistic methods associated with modernist fiction. Chopin, King, Hearn, Dunbar-Nelson, and other local colorists anticipated modernism's preferences for brevity and fluidity and its emphasis on the alienated individual, shaped by and standing outside of an outworn culture. But like naturalism, American modernism was underwritten, as Gebhard argues, by the same nationalist, masculinist ideologies that required the devaluation of local color and the feminization of the South ("Spinster" 80). Rather than the diversity celebrated by local color, modernism demanded a more unified, more dominant consciousness. Only such a seemingly "universal" perspective would permit any control—artistic or social—over the dangerously fragmenting world that was whirling into view in the early decades of the century. Much of its cultural work accomplished—primarily the containment of a threatening pluralism—local color thus seemed particularly unsuited to literary modernism and its darker modes of realism. With the general masculinization of American letters, the consequences for local color were most sharply manifest in the development of the southern literary canon.

SOUTHERN REVISIONISM:
THE FUGITIVE-AGRARIANS AND THE SOUTHERN CANON

Between 1895 and 1915, as American literature began to establish its canons, a number of anthologies of southern literature were produced that reflected very different principles of selection. Susan Irons explains that, building on the work of earlier mid-century editors, the Preservationists proposed an inclusive southern heritage, including many women and popular writers of local color. The Revisionists, many of whom were associated with Vanderbilt University, had another agenda, one based on the New South principles of a progressive "readiness" for Northern interests. Applying what they termed critical standards, they pursued a more exclusive lineage, one whose white, male biases aligned it with the powerful literary culture of the North.

That the latter view prevailed had a great deal to do with the emergence at Vanderbilt after World War I of the century's most influential group of writers and critics, known as the Fugitive-Agrarians. Ambitious young white intellectuals—including poets and essayists like John Crowe Ransom, Allen Tate, Donald Davidson, Cleanth Brooks, and Robert Penn Warren—they were eager to assert the masculine seriousness of their own work in a region marked as feminine. Rejecting the writing of the previous generation for its "sentimentality," "romantic diction," and "local color," the Fugitive-Agrarians took great pains to distance themselves from it, either by leaping over it to claim the masculinity of the Southwest humorists as their true forbears or by marking the writing as unacceptably female: "the Charming Lady" whose time had clearly passed and with whom these new "men of letters" could have "no productive intercourse" (Donaldson 40). Preferring their self-proclaimed more objective, more homogeneous view of region, they effectively defined southern local color—indeed all local color—as an aberration in literary history, a literature of insignificant particularities and perspectives, superseded by a modernist version of realism that was more universal and thus more true.

Their estimation of the value and place of southern local color in American literary history soon became the standard judgment of the genre. Southern local-color fiction was represented in twentieth-century anthologies and literary history as an anomaly. Jay B. Hubbell's authoritative 1954 study, *The South in American Literature,* does not even index the term and pronounces the common judgement that "The literature of local color now seems . . . like an eddy rather than a part of the national literary tradition. [It] seems too local, too romantic, and too sentimental" (741).

RECLAIMING THE GENRE AND REEVALUATING SOUTHERN LOCAL COLOR

This erasure of local color as the dominant late-nineteenth-century literary mode was challenged in the last decades of the twentieth-century by feminist critics. Throughout the 1970s and 1980s, scholars sought diligently to reassert and redefine the value of many "lost" women writers whose concerns for women's identity and role seemed, on the one hand, the principal reason for their treatment as "minor" figures, and, on the other, a powerful motive for their reevaluation. Like domestic fiction, which had suffered a similar depreciation, the status of local color as a "minor literature" began to be reassessed as encoding fundamental issues of gender.

One of the first critics to value local color as a genre of particular importance to women was Ann Douglas (Wood). While she appreciated the fictional possibilities the genre offered women, Wood tended to concede the limitations of local color as art. She found local colorists "impoverished," at least in contrast with the buoyant optimism of their sentimental predecessors. Later scholars found in local color more subversive potential. Josephine Donovan, whose groundbreaking book on New England local color appeared in 1983, argues that the alternative knowledge offered by local-color fiction represents a "feminist subtext" that in turn provides a defense of women's "own life-world against the encroachments of modern normalizing disciplines that would relegate it to the status of deviant" ("Breaking" 231). A radical rereading of local color was proposed by Judith Fetterley and Marjorie Pryse, whose anthology, *American Women Regionalists* (1992), has been highly influential. Affirming the deliberate marginalization of women local colorists, they maintained that "regionalism" was a more appropriate term for representing the specific generic features that they sought to redeem. For them, "local color" denotes an irreducible complicity with a colonizing, hierarchical perspective, reflected in patronizing narrators who "hold up regional characters to potential ridicule by eastern readers" (xii). In contrast, regionalist women writers present "regional experience from within, so as to engage the reader's sympathy and identification" (xii). Emphasizing gendered perspectives and readerly empathy, Fetterley and Pryse highlighted the neglected critical contributions of women local colorists. Since their approach did not account for male practitioners, however, the terminology they introduced subtly distorts the genre by excluding some of its most troubling (and often most southern) material.

While Fetterley, Pryse, and other feminist critics have, in fact, found any effort to rehabilitate the term "futile" (Gebhard, "Spinster" 88), others, like Donovan, maintain that "local color," in defining a "minority literature," has greater "insurrectionary" force than "the tamer, more acceptable *regionalist*" ("Breaking" 233). Recent anthologists Elizabeth Ammons and Valerie Rohy likewise defend the term, both for its historical accuracy and because it does express the particularity and difference that are intrinsic to the genre. Contending that local color enacts an early version of contemporary multiculturalism, they conclude that "local color remains a paradoxical genre, an example of both the marginal and the central, deviance and social discipline, diversity and the imperative to nationalistic unity" (xxviii).

If the complexity of local color, including its crucial cultural work, has reaffirmed its importance in U.S. literary history, southern local color has been interestingly resistant to that reevaluation. And yet southern local color was both its most popular contemporary version as well as the site where gender, race, and region were most fully deployed in the creation of a devalued minority literature. In many ways, that resistance underlines the continuing importance of the issues that the South in general and southern local color in particular embody for American culture and literature; namely, how to reconcile its diversities (especially those of race and gender) with a unified national identity. Regionalism offered one late-nineteenth-century solution: by spatializing its internal differences, the nation created the illusion of resolving them. As the victorious North (more truly, the Northeast) reinforced its image as the center of American culture, the heritage and concerns of New England defined the true national legacy and the source of a reaffirmed national identity. The defeated South became the Other, as marginal to an imperial, masculinist

U.S. identity as women were in a patriarchal culture, a point underscored by the South's increasingly feminized image and its parallel economic decline. Issues peculiar to southern fiction, such as racial conflict and rigid class hierarchies, could be confined there: the South, not the nation, had problems with race, and thus race was not a national problem. Such a perceptual shift was possible in large measure because of the violent success of political segregation, which did in fact contain much racial dissension until the 1960s. Black writers like Chesnutt, Dunbar, and Dunbar-Nelson, who had found in the popularity of local color a means of articulating dissenting views of race to a national readership, witnessed the segregation of their work in racial rather than regional categories. Later black southerners, like Richard Wright or Zora Neale Hurston, were not even considered part of the southern regional renaissance of the twentieth century.

But if "race" writers were excluded from regionalism as the region itself was "raced," the gendering of the South was also linked to the erasure of local color. The Fugitive-Agrarians, who galvanized modern southern regionalism in the 1920s and '30s, successfully resisted their own marginalization as writers of the "feminine" South precisely by rejecting the literary movement that had defined their regional distinctiveness. Recapitulating the nationalist gestures of the late 1890s, they imposed on the South their own "unified" identity, one that conceded race as a problem (though primarily one of history) and traced its literary lineage as exclusively masculine (claiming the older Southwest humorists) and untainted by popular appeal (thus disavowing the local colorists). The conflation of popularity with the peripheral, which was also a function of modernism's own elitism, allowed the new regionalists to discount both the contributions and the challenges of local color to their modern, seamless South. By identifying the genre with its most popular (and often most complicit) male writers, like Page and Allen and Harris, they could, for example, credibly demonstrate the cultural inconsequence of that work. At the same time, writers like Cable, who had disputed white racial privilege, or Chopin, who had questioned traditional notions of female sexuality, could be dismissed as "marginal" to the "serious" traditions of southern writing; even those who wrote about the non-racialized areas of Appalachia or Florida could be tacitly ignored as "outside" its mainstream.

Even more disturbingly, the discrediting of local color truncated access to a supportive tradition of writing for at least the next half-century of southern women writers. To remain southern, women writers of the next generation had to disavow any identification with "feminine" values: to embrace them was to be considered "inferior"; to resist the traditional hierarchies they enforced was to be regarded as irrelevantly non-southern, truly "placeless." Talented white writers like Ellen Glasgow, Julia Peterkin, Flannery O'Connor, Eudora Welty, Caroline Gordon, Katherine Anne Porter, Lillian Hellman, and far too many others can thus be seen visibly struggling against a masculinized southern literary heritage that forced them either to deny or subvert their own identity as women writers.

Reclaiming southern local color—as this anthology seeks to do—thus implies a redefinition of both the meaning and the shape of the southern literary tradition as well as that of American letters. The 1890s were a pivotal moment in the history and literary culture of the United States. The sheer variety of local-color fiction, the heterogeneity of its many national versions, and the literary access it offered to a whole range of marginal voices suggests the openness of that discursive moment. Local-color fiction drew to itself a myriad of literary techniques and traditions: fostering the development of realism, adapting the tropes of domestic fiction, incorporating the discourses of slave narratives and those of plantation romance. Southern local color proved particularly capable of rendering the era's pressing issues of race, gender, and nation and, ultimately, of creating the terms by which those issues could (at least superficially) be resolved. Part of that resolution was the dismissal both of the genre and of the very openness that local color had permitted; the new regionalism was located solely in the South and was no longer "colored."

As the stories in this anthology suggest, nineteenth-century southern local color was a complex and fascinating genre, encompassing some of the era's most entertaining and well-crafted fiction. In its open spaces, writers of different genders, races, classes, and locales found opportunities to articulate a wide range of perspectives. Men like Cable, Chesnutt, and Dunbar, who sought to change the status of black Americans, found the genre as malleable as women like Chopin, Dunbar-Nelson, and Elliott, who challenged traditional notions of gender. Southern local color served both the implicit racism of Page and the unsettling complicity of the white Harris's Uncle Remus or Bonner's Gran'mammy—what Nobel laureate Toni Morrison has called the "sycophancy of white dependency" (9). But in stories by authors as varied as Cable, Twain, Chesnutt, Dunbar, Woolson, and Dunbar-Nelson, it also unmasked the severity of such interdependencies, including those of gender. And while it remained predominantly the province of white authors, it nonetheless gave black writers unique access to publication. Southern local color thus exposes the conflicting elements of a major transformation in U.S. culture, elements that both fostered a unified national identity even as they unsettled and subverted it. To study this fiction is to explore our national and regional identities in the making.

Southern Local Color

George Washington Cable

(1844–1925)

BORN IN NEW ORLEANS ON OCTOBER 12, 1844, George Washington Cable
was named for his energetic Virginian father, a descendant of German
immigrant Jakob Kobell. Although his father's German heritage would
be shared by some of Cable's protagonists, the austere Calvinism and New
England ancestry of his determined and deeply religious mother, Rebecca
Boardman, would shape Cable's life. Cable's fastidiousness would frustrate
his later friends like the earthy Mark Twain, just as his outspoken condemnation of racial inequities would eventually separate him from his beloved
Louisiana.

The Cables initially prospered in New Orleans, but by 1859 Cable's
father, who had suffered a series of financial reversals, was dead. At fourteen, Cable left school to support his mother and his two surviving sib-
lings. Confederate sympathizers, he and his family fled when Union soldiers occupied New Orleans in 1862. Cable (barely one hundred pounds)
served in the Mississippi Cavalry until the war concluded. He then secured
a position in a cotton warehouse, leaving to join a crew of river surveyors.
Having contracted malaria, he returned to accounting and began writing
his successful *Daily Picayune* columns. In 1869 he married delicate, pi-
ous Louise Bartlett, a New Orleanian with a similar New England background; their first of seven children was born the next year.

Stirred by Charles Gayarré's *Romance of the History of Louisiana*
(1848), Cable began researching colonial Louisiana history. His research
led him to the *Code Noir* (the "Black Code" that specified the treatment
of slaves and persons of color in the early 1800s) and to the legend of
Squire, a fugitive slave and insurrectionist leader of the 1850s, who was
known as Bras-Coupé and who, when captured, was disfigured in compliance with the Code. From this material emerged Cable's first story, "Bibi,"
presented in 1872 to *Scribner's* correspondent Edward King, who was
scouring the South for just such local color. Although the story was never

published and is now lost, its material became the centerpiece for Cable's *The Grandissimes* (1880). *Scribner's* cool reception of "Bibi" and the *Atlantic's* comment that it was "unmitigatedly distressful" affected the shape of Cable's subsequent fiction. Although he believed in the power of his "nightmare" tale, he was to learn again and again that the horrors of slavery, miscegenation, class conflict, and white cruelty had to be carefully rendered, even suppressed, if his fiction were to be successful.

In 1873 *Scribner's* did accept Cable's "'Sieur George," carefully edited to make it sufficiently clear and tasteful. With this artful account of moral decadence in New Orleans, Cable holds the distinction of quietly and unknowingly launching southern local color. During the next six years, Cable held three jobs to maintain financial solvency, struggled with ill health, and lost his son to a yellow fever epidemic; however, he also published six long stories and began an outline for a novel. His first collection, *Old Creole Days* (1879), garnered critical accolades; one reviewer declared Cable "a genius," linking him with the immensely popular Bret Harte.

Serialized in *Scribner's,* his first novel, *The Grandissimes* (1880), which secured his literary reputation, embodied his complex vision and artistic compromises with its exposé of racial conflict made palatable by luxurious southern settings and manipulated romantic resolutions. William Dean Howells, who continually expressed his regard for Cable, declared: "If some finer and nobler novel than *The Grandissimes* has been written in this land, any time, I have not read it." Though generally unread today, *The Grandissimes* is now recognized by critics as the precursor of twentieth-century southern fiction.

Cable followed this success with *Madame Delphine* (1881), a novella about the plight of the quadroon and the injustice of miscegenation. Fascinated like his friend Lafcadio Hearn with African and Creole materials, Cable published folk-culture songs, dances, and practices as well as the historical *Creoles of Louisiana* (1884). Both Joel Chandler Harris and Twain admired Cable and visited him in New Orleans in 1882. Cable, a small, dapper man with an excellent singing voice, soon toured with Twain to great acclaim (1884–85). In the late 1880s, Cable's stories based on Acadian culture, collected in *Bonaventure: A Prose Pastoral of Acadian Louisiana* (1888), created the first fictional market for Cajun materials—a market Kate Chopin would also find profitable.

Cable's fiction also focused on such contemporary causes as prison reform in *Dr. Sevier* (1882) and economic revitalization in his New South novel *John March, Southerner* (1895)—sometimes considered his masterpiece. However, Cable's social crusades increasingly alienated the South. He gained the ardent disapproval of fellow New Orleanians Gayarré and Grace King, not only for his occasionally unflattering portraits of Creoles but also for his insistence on "Negro" education and civil rights and his vigorous condemnation of Jim Crow laws. Unchastened and outspoken, Cable argued for freedmen's rights in speeches and essays, including a call for radical reform in *The Silent South* (1885), written the same year he moved to Northampton, Massachusetts, where he lived for the last half of his life.

Though Cable was a courageous social crusader whose vision of southern economic reform and race relations would prove prophetic, his voice was virtually lost in the closing decade of the century. Eventually, he turned away from public causes and problem-centered fiction. Although he remained an international celebrity, he was often in financial difficulty, a predicament eased through the ongoing assistance of industrial magnate Andrew Carnegie. Cable wrote several other books and five more novels, most of them historical romances like his most popular work *The Cavalier* (1901), which sold over one hundred thousand copies and became a successful Broadway play.

Soon after the death of his first wife in 1904, Cable entered a fulfilling marriage with Eva Colgate Stevenson. After her death in 1923, he married Hanna Cowing, a Northampton neighbor and friend of thirty-five years. Two years later, on January 31, 1925, he died while wintering in St. Petersburg, Florida. At Cable's memorial service, long-time friend and editor Robert Underwood Johnson avowed that Cable was "with the possible exception of Hawthorne and Poe . . . the greatest figure in American fiction" and that *The Grandissimes* "is not only the greatest novel to date but that it stands in the front rank of fiction of the world."

The following selection from *The Grandissimes* is based, presumably, on Cable's lost story "Bibi," since it presents the legend of the rebellious, enslaved African Bras-Coupé. Told by Raoul, a member of the distinguished Creole Grandissime family, the story's listener is *The Grandissimes'* protagonist, Joseph Frowenfeld, an outsider of German descent who has established a pharmacy in New Orleans. Joseph's steadfast good sense and courage have earned him the respect of the stubborn Old Louisiana defender and Grandissime patriarch Agricola, while his fierce commitment to racial justice has gained him the friendship of the younger and enlightened Grandissime, the mixed-blood Creole Honoré. Joseph is "learning" the cultural climate of New Orleans, and Raoul's two-part narrative is an essential lesson even as it serves Cable's passion for racial reform. The seduction of white privilege leads the powerful, voluptuous conjure woman Palmyre Philosophe to an unrequited love for the white Honoré instead of for the two men of African descent who adore her: Bras-Coupé and the white Honoré's half-African/half-white brother (also named Honoré), who at the novel's end commits suicide. The maiming effects of slavery are also reflected in the brutal death of Palymre's disciple, Clemence (briefly mentioned in the excerpt), who conspires to kill Agricola. The Bras-Coupé story itself indicts both slavery and the bigotry rampant in New Orleans and throughout the white South. The doomed unions and deaths of "Bras-Coupé" are reversed in the novel's romantic main plot, which concludes as Joseph and Honoré marry an impoverished but elegant and aristocratic widow and her daughter. This union, implies Cable, holds the beginning of a "new world" with honorable and humane solutions.

Works by George W. Cable

SHORT FICTION

Old Creole Days, 1879

Madame Delphine, 1881

Bonaventure, 1888

Strange True Stories of Louisiana, 1889

"Posson Jone" and Père Raphaël, 1909

NOVELS

The Grandissimes, 1880, rev. 1883, ed. Newton Arvin, 1957, ed. Michael Kreyling, 1988

Dr. Sevier, 1884

John March, Southerner, 1894

Strong Hearts, 1899

The Cavalier, 1901

Bylow Hill, 1902

Kinkaid's Battery, 1908

Gideon's Band, 1914

The Flower of the Chapdelaines, 1918

ESSAYS AND SOCIAL HISTORY

The Creoles of Louisiana, 1884

The Silent South, 1885

The Negro Question, 1890, ed. Arlin Turner, 1958

Further Readings

Benfey, Christopher E. G. *Degas in New Orleans: Encounters in the Creole World of Kate Chopin and George Washington Cable.* New York: Knopf, 1997.

Biklé, Lucy Leffingwell Cable. *George W. Cable: His Life and Letters.* New York: Russell & Russell, 1928.

Butcher, Philip. *George W. Cable.* New York: Twayne, 1962.

———. *George W. Cable: The Northampton Years.* New York: Columbia University Press, 1959.

Cardwell, Guy A. *Twins of Genius.* East Lansing: Michigan State College Press, 1953.

Cleman, John. *George Washington Cable Revisited.* New York: Twayne, 1996.

Ekstrom, Kjell. *George Washington Cable: A Study of His Early Life and Work.* Cambridge: Harvard University Press, 1950.

Ladd, Barbara. *Nationalism and the Color Line in George W. Cable, Mark Twain, and William Faulkner.* Baton Rouge: Louisiana State University Press, 1996.

Petry, Alice Hall. *A Genius in His Way: The Art of Cable's Old Creole Days.* Rutherford, N.J.: Fairleigh Dickinson University Press, 1988.

Richardson, Thomas J., ed. *The Grandissimes: Centennial Essays.* Jackson: University Press of Mississippi, 1981.

Roberson, William H. *George Washington Cable: An Annotated Bibliography.* Metuchen, N.J.: Scarecrow Press, 1982.

Rubin, Louis D., Jr. *George W. Cable: The Life and Times of a Southern Heretic.* New York: Pegasus, 1969.

Turner, Arlin. *George W. Cable: A Biography.* Durham, N.C.: Duke University Press, 1956.

———. *Mark Twain and G. W. Cable: The Record of a Literary Friendship.* East Lansing: Michigan State University Press, 1960.

———, ed. *Critical Essays on George W. Cable.* Boston: G. K. Hall, 1980.

The Story of Bras-Coupé

"A very little more than eight years ago," began Honoré—but not only Honoré, but Raoul also; and not only they, but another, earlier on the same day,—Honoré, the f. m. c.[1] But we shall not exactly follow the words of any one of these.

Bras-Coupé, they said, had been, in Africa and under another name, a prince among his people. In a certain war of conquest, to which he had been driven by *ennui,* he was captured, stripped of his royalty, marched down upon the beach of the Atlantic, and, attired as a true son of Adam, with two goodly arms intact, became a commodity. Passing out of first hands in barter for a looking-glass, he was shipped in good order and condition on board the schooner *Egalité,*[2] whereof Blank was master, to be delivered without delay at the port of Nouvelle Orleans (the dangers of fire and navigation excepted), unto Blank Blank. In witness whereof, He that made men's skins of different colors, but all blood of one, hath entered the same upon His book, and sealed it to the day of judgment.

Of the voyage little is recorded—here below; the less the better. Part of the living merchandise failed to keep; the weather was rough, the cargo large, the vessel small. However, the captain discovered there was room over the side, and there—all flesh is grass—from time to time during the voyage he jettisoned the unmerchantable.

Yet, when the reopened hatches let in the sweet smell of the land, Bras-Coupé had come to the upper—the favored—the buttered side of the world; the anchor slid with a rumble of relief down through the muddy fathoms of the Mississippi, and the prince could hear through the schooner's side the savage current of the river, leaping and licking about the bows, and whimpering low welcomes home. A splendid picture to the eyes of the royal captive, as his head came up out of the hatchway, was the little Franco-Spanish-American city that lay on the low, brimming bank. There were little forts that showed their whitewashed teeth; there was a green parade-ground, and yellow barracks, and cabildo,[3] and hospital, and cavalry stables, and customhouse, and a most inviting jail, convenient to the cathedral—all of dazzling white and yellow, with a black stripe marking the track of the conflagration of 1794,[4] and here and there among the low roofs a lofty one with round-topped dormer windows and a breezy belvedere[5] looking out upon the plantations of coffee and indigo beyond the town.

1. Free man of color.
2. "Equality" (Fr.).
3. Town hall.
4. The second of two city-wide fires in New Orleans, which resulted in rebuilding with brick.
5. A small house-top structure affording distant views.

When Bras-Coupé staggered ashore, he stood but a moment among a drove of "likely boys," before Agricola Fusilier, managing the business adventures of the Grandissime estate, as well as the residents thereon, and struck with admiration for the physical beauties of the chieftain (a man may even fancy a negro—as a negro), bought the lot, and loth to resell him with the rest to some unappreciative 'Cadian,[6] induced Don José Martinez overseer to become his purchaser.

Down in the rich parish of St. Bernard (whose boundary line now touches that of the distended city) lay the plantation, known before Bras-Coupé passed away, as La Renaissance. Here it was that he entered at once upon a chapter of agreeable surprises. He was humanely met, presented with a clean garment, lifted into a cart drawn by oxen, taken to a white-washed cabin of logs, finer than his palace at home, and made to comprehend that it was a free gift. He was also given some clean food, whereupon he fell sick. At home it would have been the part of piety for the magnate next the throne to launch him heavenward at once; but now, healing doses were administered, and to his amazement he recovered. It reminded him that he was no longer king.

His name, he replied to an inquiry touching that subject, was —————————, something in the Jaloff[7] tongue, which he by and by condescended to render into Congo: Mioko-Koanga, in French Bras-Coupé, the Arm Cut Off. Truly it would have been easy to admit, had this been his meaning, that his tribe, in losing him, had lost its strong right arm close off at the shoulder; not so easy for his high-paying purchaser to allow, if this other was his intent; that the arm which might no longer shake the spear or swing the wooden sword, was no better than a useless stump never to be lifted for aught else. But whether easy to allow or not, that was his meaning. He made himself a type of all Slavery, turning into flesh and blood the truth that all Slavery is maiming.

He beheld more luxury in a week than all his subjects had seen in a century. Here Congo girls were dressed in cottons and flannels worth, where he came from, an elephant's tusk apiece. Everybody wore clothes— children and lads alone excepted. Not a lion had invaded the settlement since his immigration. The serpents were as nothing; an occasional one coming up through the floor—that was all. True, there was more emaciation than unassisted conjecture could explain—a profusion of enlarged

6. Also Cajun, originally Acadian, descendants of French colonists expelled from Nova Scotia in 1755 by Britain after the French and Indian War, often disdained by earlier colonial families.

7. Or Wolof, a tribe of Senegal often considered fiercer than the others.

joints and diminished muscles, which, thank God, was even then confined to a narrow section and disappeared with Spanish rule.[8] He had no experimental knowledge of it; nay, regular meals, on the contrary, gave him anxious concern, yet had the effect—spite of his apprehension that he was being fattened for a purpose—of restoring the herculean puissance which formerly in Africa had made him the terror of the battle.

When one day he had come to be quite himself, he was invited out into the sunshine, and escorted by the driver (a sort of foreman to the overseer),[9] went forth dimly wondering. They reached a field where some men and women were hoeing. He had seen men and women—subjects of his—labor—a little—in Africa. The driver handed him a hoe; he examined it with silent interest—until by signs he was requested to join the pastime.

"What?"

He spoke, not with his lips, but with the recoil of his splendid frame and the ferocious expansion of his eyes. This invitation was a cataract of lightning leaping down an ink-black sky. In one instant of all-pervading clearness he read his sentence—WORK.

Bras-Coupé was six feet five. With a sweep as quick as instinct the back of the hoe smote the driver full in the head. Next, the prince lifted the nearest Congo crosswise, brought thirty-two teeth together in his wildly kicking leg and cast him away as a bad morsel; then, throwing another into the branches of a willow, and a woman over his head into a draining-ditch, he made one bound for freedom, and fell to his knees, rocking from side to side under the effect of a pistol-ball from the overseer. It had struck him in the forehead, and running around the skull in search of a penetrable spot, tradition—which sometimes jests—says came out despairingly, exactly where it had entered.

It so happened that, except the overseer, the whole company were black. Why should the trivial scandal be blabbed? A plaster or two made everything even in a short time, except in the driver's case—for the driver died. The woman whom Bras-Coupé had thrown over his head lived to sell *calas*[10] to Joseph Frowenfeld.

Don José, young and austere, knew nothing about agriculture and cared as much about human nature. The overseer often thought this, but never said it; he would not trust even himself with the dangerous criti-

---

8. Begun in 1769, fulfilling a secret 1762 treaty and much opposed by the French Colonists.

9. Plantation manager of work crews, usually white.

10. Fried rice cakes covered with powdered sugar.

cism. When he ventured to reveal the foregoing incidents to the señor he laid all the blame possible upon the man whom death had removed beyond the reach of correction, and brought his account to a climax by hazarding the assertion that Bras-Coupé was an animal that could not be whipped.

"Caramba!" [11] exclaimed the master, with gentle emphasis, "how so?"

"Perhaps señor had better ride down to the quarters," replied the overseer.

It was a great sacrifice of dignity, but the master made it.

"Bring him out."

They brought him out—chains on his feet, chains on his wrists, an iron yoke on his neck. The Spanish-Creole master had often seen the bull, with his long, keen horns and blazing eye, standing in the arena; but this was as though he had come face to face with a rhinoceros.

"This man is not a Congo," he said.

"He is a Jaloff," replied the encouraged overseer. "See his fine, straight nose; moreover, he is a *candio*—a prince. If I whip him he will die."

The dauntless captive and fearless master stood looking into each other's eyes until each recognized in the other his peer in physical courage, and each was struck with an admiration for the other which no after difference was sufficient entirely to destroy. Had Bras-Coupé's eye quailed but once—just for one little instant—he would have got the lash; but, as it was—

"Get an interpreter," said Don José; then, more privately, "and come to an understanding. I shall require it of you."

Where might one find an interpreter—one not merely able to render a Jaloff's meaning into Creole French, or Spanish, but with such a turn for diplomatic correspondence as would bring about an "understanding" with this African buffalo? The overseer was left standing and thinking, and Clemence, who had not forgotten who threw her into the draining-ditch, cunningly passed by.

"Ah, Clemence—"

"*Mo pas capabe! Mo pas capabe!* (I cannot, I cannot!) *Ya, ya, ya! 'oir Miché Agricol' Fusilier! ouala yune bon monture, oui!*" [12]—which was to signify that Agricola could interpret the very Papa Lébat.

"Agricola Fusilier! The last man on earth to make peace."

---

11. "Good gracious" (Sp.).

12. "Aye yi yi! Go see Monsieur ('Miche') Agricola Fusilier, there's a clever trickster, yes!" (Creole Fr.). Papa Lébat (or Legba) is a rather cranky voudou *loa*, or spirit, who guards crossroads.

But there seemed to be no choice, and to Agricola the overseer went. It was but a little ride to the Grandissime place.

"I, Agricola Fusilier, stand as an interpreter to a negro? H-sir!"

"But I thought you might know of some person," said the weakening applicant, rubbing his ear with his hand.

"Ah!" replied Agricola, addressing the surrounding scenery, "if I did not—who would? You may take Palmyre."

The overseer softly smote his hands together at the happy thought.

"Yes," said Agricola, "take Palmyre; she has picked up as many negro dialects as I know European languages."

And she went to the don's plantation as interpretess, followed by Agricola's prayer to Fate that she might in some way be overtaken by disaster. The two hated each other with all the strength they had. He knew not only her pride, but her passion for the absent Honoré. He hated her, also, for her intelligence, for the high favor in which she stood with her mistress, and for her invincible spirit, which was more offensively patent to him than to others, since he was himself the chief object of her silent detestation.

It was Palmyre's habit to do nothing without painstaking. "When Mademoiselle comes to be Señora," thought she—she knew that her mistress and the don were affianced—"it will be well to have Señor's esteem. I shall endeavor to succeed." It was from this motive, then, that with the aid of her mistress she attired herself in a resplendence of scarlet and beads and feathers that could not fail the double purpose of connecting her with the people of Ethiopia and commanding the captive's instant admiration.

Alas for those who succeed too well! No sooner did the African turn his tiger glance upon her than the fire of his eyes died out; and when she spoke to him in the dear accents of his native tongue, the matter of strife vanished from his mind. He loved.

He sat down tamely in his irons and listened to Palmyre's argument as a wrecked mariner would listen to ghostly church-bells. He would give a short assent, feast his eyes, again assent, and feast his ears; but when at length she made bold to approach the actual issue, and finally uttered the loathed word, *Work*, he rose up, six feet five, a statue of indignation in black marble.

And then Palmyre, too, rose up, glorying in him, and went to explain to master and overseer. Bras-Coupé understood, she said, that he was a slave—it was the fortune of war, and he was a warrior; but, according to a generally recognized principle in African international law, he could not reasonably be expected to work.

"As señor will remember I told him," remarked the overseer; "how can a man expect to plow with a zebra?"

Here he recalled a fact in his early experience. An African of this stripe had been found to answer admirably as a "driver" to make others work. A second and third parley, extending through two or three days, were held with the prince, looking to his appointment to the vacant office of driver; yet what was the master's amazement to learn at length that his Highness declined the proffered honor.

"Stop!" spoke the overseer again, detecting a look of alarm in Palmyre's face as she turned away, "he doesn't do any such thing. If Señor will let me take the man to Agricola——"

"No!" cried Palmyre, with an agonized look, "I will tell. He will take the place and fill it if you will give me to him for his own—but oh, messieurs, for the love of God—I do not want to be his wife!"

The overseer looked at the Señor, ready to approve whatever he should decide. Bras-Coupé's intrepid audacity took the Spaniard's heart by irresistible assault.

"I leave it entirely with Señor Fusilier," he said.

"But he is not my master; he has no right——"

"Silence!"

And she was silent; and so, sometimes, is fire in the wall.

Agricola's consent was given with malicious promptness, and as Bras-Coupé's fetters fell off it was decreed that, should he fill his office efficiently, there should be a wedding on the rear veranda of the Grandissime mansion simultaneously with the one already appointed to take place in the grand hall of the same house six months from that present day. In the meanwhile Palmyre should remain with Mademoiselle, who had promptly but quietly made up her mind that Palmyre should not be wed unless she wished to be. Bras-Coupé made no objection, was royally worthless for a time, but learned fast, mastered the "gumbo"[13] dialect in a few weeks, and in six months was the most valuable man ever bought for gourd dollars.[14] Nevertheless, there were but three persons within as many square miles who were not most vividly afraid of him.

13. Bantu for "okra," the vegetable used in Louisiana gumbo, a tasty, thickened soup. Applied here to English-French patois spoken among local slaves.

14. Haitian paper money, worth one-fifth of a U.S. dollar.

The first was Palmyre. His bearing in her presence was ever one of solemn, exalted respect, which, whether from pure magnanimity in himself, or by reason of her magnetic eye, was something worth being there to see. "It was royal!" said the overseer.

The second was not that official. When Bras-Coupé said—as, at stated intervals, he did say—"*Mo courri c'ez Agricole Fusilier 'pou oir' n'amourouse* (I go to Agricola Fusilier to see my betrothed)," the overseer would sooner have intercepted a score of painted Chickasaws than that one lover. He would look after him and shake a prophetic head. "Trouble coming; better not deceive that fellow"; yet that was the very thing Palmyre dared do. Her admiration for Bras-Coupé was almost boundless. She rejoiced in his stature; she revelled in the contemplation of his untamable spirit; he seemed to her the gigantic embodiment of her own dark, fierce will, the expanded realization of her lifetime longing for terrible strength. But the single deficiency in all this impassioned regard was—what so many fairer loves have found impossible to explain to so many gentler lovers— an entire absence of preference; her heart she could not give him—she did not have it. Yet after her first prayer to the Spaniard and his overseer for deliverance, to the secret surprise and chagrin of her young mistress, she simulated content. It was—artifice; she knew Agricola's power, and to seem to consent was her one chance with him. He might thus be beguiled into withdrawing his own consent. That failing, she had Mademoiselle's promise to come to the rescue, which she could use at the last moment; and that failing, there was a dirk [15] in her bosom, for which a certain hard breast was not too hard. Another element of safety, of which she knew nothing, was a letter from the Cannes Brulées. [16] The word had reached there that love had conquered—that, despite all hard words, and rancor, and positive injury, the Grandissime hand—the fairest of Grandissime hands—was about to be laid into that of one who without much stretch might be called a De Grapion; that there was, moreover, positive effort being made to induce a restitution of old gaming-table spoils. Honoré and Mademoiselle, his sister, one on each side of the Atlantic, were striving for this end. Don José sent this intelligence to his kinsman as glad tidings (a lover never imagines there are two sides to that which makes him happy), and, to add a touch of humor, told how Palmyre, also, was given to the chieftain. The letter that came back to the young Spaniard did not blame

15. Small dagger.

16. The De Grapion plantation; literally, "burned cane." Sugar cane leaves were burned before harvesting the succulent stalks.

him so much: *he* was ignorant of all the facts; but a very formal one to Agricola begged to notify him that if Palmyre's union with Bras-Coupé should be completed, as sure as there was a God in heaven, the writer would have the life of the man who knowingly had thus endeavored to dishonor one who *shared the blood of all De Grapions.* Thereupon Agricola, contrary to his general character, began to drop hints to Don José that the engagement of Bras-Coupé and Palmyre need not be considered irreversible; but the don was not desirous of disappointing his terrible pet. Palmyre, unluckily, played her game a little too deeply. She thought the moment had come for herself to insist on the match, and thus provoke Agricola to forbid it. To her incalculable dismay she saw him a second time reconsider and become silent.

The second person who did not fear Bras-Coupé was Mademoiselle. On one of the giant's early visits to see Palmyre he obeyed the summons which she brought him, to appear before the lady. A more artificial man might have objected on the score of dress, his attire being a single gaudy garment tightly enveloping the waist and thighs. As his eyes fell upon the beautiful white lady he prostrated himself upon the ground, his arms outstretched before him. He would not move till she was gone. Then he arose like a hermit who has seen a vision. "*Bras-Coupé 'n pas oulé oir zombis* (Bras-Coupé dares not look upon a spirit)." From that hour he worshipped. He saw her often; every time, after one glance at her countenance, he would prostrate his gigantic length with his face in the dust.

The third person who did not fear him was—Agricola? Nay, it was the Spaniard—a man whose capability to fear anything in nature or beyond had never been discovered.

Long before the end of his probation Bras-Coupé would have slipped the entanglements of bondage, though as yet he felt them only as one feels a spider's web across the face, had not the master, according to a little affectation of the times, promoted him to be his game-keeper. Many a day did these two living magazines of wrath spend together in the dismal swamps and on the meagre intersecting ridges, making war upon deer and bear and wildcat; or on the Mississippi after wild goose and pelican; when even a word misplaced would have made either the slayer of the other. Yet the months ran smoothly round and the wedding night drew nigh.[17] A goodly

---

17. An over-zealous Franciscan once complained bitterly to the bishop of Havana that people were being married in Louisiana in their own houses after dark and thinking nothing of it. It is not certain that he had reference to the Grandissime mansion; at any rate he was tittered down by the whole community (author's note).

company had assembled. All things were ready. The bride was dressed, the bridegroom had come. On the great back piazza, which had been inclosed with sail-cloth and lighted with lanterns, was Palmyre, full of a new and deep design and playing her deceit to the last, robed in costly garments to whose beauty was added the charm of their having been worn once, and once only, by her beloved Mademoiselle.

But where was Bras-Coupé?

The question was asked of Palmyre by Agricola with a gaze that meant in English, "No tricks, girl!"

Among the servants who huddled at the windows and door to see the inner magnificence a frightened whisper was already going round.

"We have made a sad discovery, Miché Fusilier," said the overseer. "Bras-Coupé is here; we have him in a room just yonder. But—the truth is, sir. Bras-Coupé is a voudou." [18]

"Well, and suppose he is; what of it? Only hush; do not let his master know it. It is nothing; all the blacks are voudous, more or less."

"But he declines to dress himself—has painted himself all rings and stripes, antelope fashion."

"Tell him Agricola Fusilier says, 'dress immediately!'"

"Oh, Miché, we have said that five times already, and his answer—you will pardon me—his answer is—spitting on the ground—that you are a contemptible *dotchian* (white trash)."

There is nothing to do but privily to call the very bride—the lady herself. She comes forth in all her glory, small, but oh, so beautiful! Slam! Bras-Coupé is upon his face, his finger-tips touching the tips of her snowy slippers. She gently bids him go and dress, and at once he goes.

Ah! now the question may be answered without whispering. There is Bras-Coupé, towering above all heads, in ridiculous red and blue regimentals; but with a look of savage dignity upon him that keeps every one from laughing. The murmur of admiration that passed along the thronged gallery leaped up into a shout in the bosom of Palmyre. Oh, Bras-Coupé—heroic soul! She would not falter. She would let the silly priest say his say—then her cunning should help her *not to be* his wife, yet to show his mighty arm how and when to strike.

"He is looking for Palmyre," said some, and at that moment he saw her.

"Ho-o-o-o-o!"

Agricola's best roar was a penny trumpet to Bras-Coupé's note of joy.

18. Adherent of African or Caribbean syncretic religion, often suppressed and feared by whites.

The whole masculine half of the in-door company flocked out to see what the matter was. Bras-Coupé was taking her hand in one of his and laying his other upon her head; and as some one made an unnecessary gesture for silence, he sang, beating slow and solemn time with his naked foot and with the hand that dropped hers to smite his breast:

> "'En haut la montagne, zami,
> Mo pé coupé canne, zami,
> Pou' fé i'a'zen' zami,
> Pou' mo baille Palmyre.
> Ah! Palmyre, Palmyre mo c'ere,
> Mo l'aimé'ou'—mo l'aimé ou'.'" [19]

"*Montagne?*" asked one slave of another, "*qui ce çà, montagne? gnia pas quiç' ose comme çà dans la Louisiana?* (What's a mountain? We haven't such things in Louisiana.)"

"*Mein ye gagnein plein montagnes dans l'Afrique,* listen!"

> "'Ah! Palmyre, Palmyre, mo' piti zozo,
> Mo l'aimé'ou'—mo l'aimé, l'aimé'ou.'" [20]

"Bravissimo!—" but just then a counter-attraction drew the white company back into the house. An old French priest with sandalled feet and a dirty face had arrived. There was a moment of hand-shaking with the good father, then a moment of palpitation and holding of the breath, and then—you would have known it by the turning away of two or three feminine heads in tears—the lily hand became the don's, to have and to hold, by authority of the Church and the Spanish king. And all was merry, save that outside there was coming up as villainous a night as ever cast black looks in through snug windows.

It was just as the newly wed Spaniard, with Agricola and all the guests,

19. "On the top of the mountain, my friends,
   I cut the cane, my friends,
   To make the offering, my friends,
   For my beautiful Palmyre.
   Ah! Palmyre, Palmyre, my dear,
   I love you, I love you." (Fr. Creole)
20. "I had plenty of mountains in Africa, listen!"
   "Ai! Palmyre, Palmyre, my little fool,
   I love you—I love you, I love you." (Fr. Creole)

were concluding the by-play of marrying the darker couple, that the hurricane struck the dwelling. The holy and jovial father had made faint pretence of kissing this second bride; the ladies, colonels, dons, etc.,—though the joke struck them as a trifle coarse—were beginning to laugh and clap hands again and the gowned jester to bow to right and left, when Bras-Coupé, tardily realizing the consummation of his hopes, stepped forward to embrace his wife.

"Bras-Coupé!"

The voice was that of Palmyre's mistress. She had not been able to comprehend her maid's behavior, but now Palmyre had darted upon her an appealing look.

The warrior stopped as if a javelin had flashed over his head and stuck in the wall.

"Bras-Coupé must wait till I give him his wife."

He sank, with hidden face, slowly to the floor.

"Bras-Coupé hears the voice of zombis; the voice is sweet, but the words are very strong; from the same sugar-cane comes *sirop* and *tafia;*[21] Bras-Coupé says to zombis, 'Bras-Coupé will wait; but if the *dotchians* deceive Bras-Coupé —' " he rose to his feet with his eyes closed and his great black fist lifted over his head—"Bras-Coupé will call Voudou-Magnan!"[22]

The crowd retreated and the storm fell like a burst of infernal applause. A whiff like fifty witches floated up the canvas curtain of the gallery and a fierce black cloud, drawing the moon under its cloak, belched forth a stream of fire that seemed to flood the ground; a peal of thunder followed as if the sky had fallen in, the house quivered, the great oaks groaned, and every lesser thing bowed down before the awful blast. Every lip held its breath for a minute—or an hour, no one knew—there was a sudden lull of the wind, and the floods came down. Have you heard it thunder and rain in those Louisiana lowlands? Every clap seems to crack the world. It has rained a moment; you peer through the black pane—your house is an island, all the land is sea.

However, the supper was spread in the hall and in due time the guests were filled. Then a supper was spread in the big hall in the basement, below stairs, the sons and daughters of Ham[23] came down like the fowls of

21. "Syrup" (Fr.). Tafia is Haitian rum made of low-grade cane sugar.

22. Among West Indians, the python god is worshiped in voudou ceremonies and believed to animate corpses.

23. Noah's youngest son was cursed for observing his father drunk and naked. Noah condemned Ham's sons, Cush, Egypt, Lybia, and Canaan, to slavery (Gen. 10:6).

the air upon a rice-field, and Bras-Coupé, throwing his heels about with the joyous carelessness of a smutted Mercury,[24] for the first time in his life tasted the blood of the grape. A second, a fifth, a tenth time he tasted it, drinking more deeply each time, and would have taken it ten times more had not his bride cunningly concealed it. It was like stealing a tiger's kittens.

The moment quickly came when he wanted his eleventh bumper. As he presented his request a silent shiver of consternation ran through the dark company; and when, in what the prince meant as a remonstrative tone, he repeated the petition—splitting the table with his fist by way of punctuation—there ensued a hustling up staircases and a cramming into dim corners that left him alone at the banquet.

Leaving the table, he strode upstairs and into the chirruping and dancing of the grand salon. There was a halt in the cotillion and a hush of amazement like the shutting off of steam. Bras-Coupé strode straight to his master, laid his paw upon his fellow-bridegroom's shoulder and in a thunder-tone demanded:

"More!"

The master swore a Spanish oath, lifted his hand and—fell, beneath the terrific fist of his slave, with a bang that jingled the candelabras. Dolorous stroke!—for the dealer of it. Given, apparently to him—poor, tipsy savage—in self-defence, punishable, in a white offender, by a small fine or a few days' imprisonment, it assured Bras-Coupé the death of a felon; such was the old *Code Noir*. (We have a *Code Noir* now, but the new one is a mental reservation, not an enactment.)[25]

The guests stood for an instant as if frozen, smitten stiff with the instant expectation of insurrection, conflagration and rapine (just as we do to-day whenever some poor swaggering Pompey[26] rolls up his fist and gets a ball through his body), while, single-handed and naked-fisted in a room full of swords, the giant stood over his master, making strange signs and passes and rolling out in wrathful words of his mother tongue

---

24. Wingfooted messenger of the Roman gods; as the Greek Hermes, he also guides the dead into the underworld.

25. The *Code Noir*, or Black Code, was issued in 1724 by the French monarchy to govern racial interactions in Louisiana. Maintained under Spanish rule, it later influenced nineteenth-century state law and racial attitudes.

26. A foolish Shakespearean braggart; in the nineteenth century, often applied to African American males.

what it needed no interpreter to tell his swarming enemies was a voudou malediction.

"*Nous sommes grigis!*" screamed two or three ladies, "we are bewitched!"

"Look to your wives and daughters!" shouted a Brahmin-Mandarin.

"Shoot the black devils without mercy!" cried a Mandarin-Fusilier,[27] unconsciously putting into a single outflash of words the whole Creole treatment of race troubles.

With a single bound Bras-Coupé reached the drawing-room door; his gaudy regimentals made a red and blue streak down the hall; there was a rush of frilled and powdered gentlemen to the rear veranda, an avalanche of lightning with Bras-Coupé in the midst making for the swamp, and then all without was blackness of darkness and all within was a wild commingled chatter of Creole, French, and Spanish tongues,—in the midst of which the reluctant Agricola returned his dress-sword to its scabbard.

While the wet lanterns swung on crazily in the trees along the way by which the bridegroom was to have borne his bride; while Madame Grandissime prepared an impromptu bridal chamber; while the Spaniard bathed his eye and the blue gash on his cheek-bone; while Palmyre paced her room in a fever and wild tremor of conflicting emotions throughout the night and the guests splashed home after the storm as best they could, Bras-Coupé was practically declaring his independence on a slight rise of ground hardly sixty feet in circumference and lifted scarce above the water in the inmost depths of the swamp.

And what surroundings! Endless colonnades of cypresses; long, motionless drapings of gray moss; broad sheets of noisome waters, pitchy black, resting on bottomless ooze; cypress knees[28] studding the surface; patches of floating green, gleaming brilliantly here and there; yonder where the sunbeams wedge themselves in, constellations of water-lilies, the many-hued iris, and a multitude of flowers that no man had named; here, too, serpents great and small, of wonderful colorings, and the dull and loathsome moccasin sliding warily off the dead tree; in dimmer recesses the cow alligator, with her nest hard by; turtles a century old; owls and bats, raccoons, opossums, rats, centipedes and creatures of like vileness; great

27. Brahmins were the highest or priestly class of India, while mandarins were Chinese officials; thus "double high-class." A *fusilier* (Fr.) is also a rifleman.

28. Cypress tree roots rise in the surrounding water like knees.

vines of beautiful leaf and scarlet fruit in deadly clusters; maddening mosquitoes, parasitic insects, gorgeous dragon-flies and pretty water-lizards: the blue heron, the snowy crane, the red-bird, the moss-bird, the night-hawk and the chuckwill's widow; a solemn stillness and stifled air only now and then disturbed by the call or whir of the summer duck, the dismal ventriloquous note of the rain-crow, or the splash of a dead branch falling into the clear but lifeless bayou.[29]

The pack of Cuban hounds that howl from Don José's kennels cannot snuff the trail of the stolen canoe that glides through the sombre blue vapors of the African's fastnesses.[30] His arrows send no tell-tale reverberations to the distant clearing. Many a wretch in his native wilderness has Bras-Coupé himself, in palmier days, driven to just such an existence, to escape the chains and horrors of the barracoons;[31] therefore not a whit broods he over man's inhumanity, but, taking the affair as a matter of course, casts about him for a future.

Bras-Coupé let the autumn pass, and wintered in his den.

Don José, in a majestic way, endeavored to be happy. He took his señora to his hall, and under her rule it took on for a while a look and feeling which turned it from a hunting-lodge into a home. Wherever the lady's steps turned—or it is as correct to say wherever the proud tread of Palmyre turned—the features of bachelor's hall disappeared; guns, dogs, oars, saddles, nets, went their way into proper banishment, and the broad halls and lofty chambers—the floors now muffled with mats of palmetto-leaf—no longer re-echoed the tread of a lonely master, but breathed a redolence of flowers and a rippling murmur of well-contented song.

But the song was not from the throat of Bras-Coupé's *"piti zozo."* Silent and severe by day, she moaned away whole nights heaping reproaches upon herself for the impulse—now to her, because it had failed, inexplicable in its folly—which had permitted her hand to lie in Bras-Coupé's and the priest to bind them together.

For in the audacity of her pride, or, as Agricola would have said, in the immensity of her impudence, she had held herself consecrate to a hopeless love. But now she was a black man's wife; and even he unable to sit at

29. From the Choctaw *bayuk*, a narrow, slow-moving, marshy outlet of a lake or river.

30. Secure place or stronghold.

31. Barracks or temporary housing for slaves or convicts.

her feet and learn the lesson she had hoped to teach him. She had heard of San Domingo,[32] and for months the fierce heart within her silent bosom had been leaping and shouting and seeing visions of fire and blood, and when she brooded over the nearness of Agricola and the remoteness of Honoré these visions got from her a sort of mad consent. The lesson she would have taught the giant was Insurrection. But it was too late. Letting her dagger sleep in her bosom, and with an undefined belief in imaginary resources, she had consented to join hands with her giant hero before the priest; and when the wedding had come and gone, like a white sail, she was seized with a lasting, fierce despair. A wild aggressiveness that had formerly characterized her glance in moments of anger—moments which had grown more and more infrequent under the softening influence of her Mademoiselle's nature—now came back intensified and blazed in her eye perpetually. Whatever her secret love may have been in kind, its sinking beyond hope below the horizon had left her fifty times the mutineer she had been before—the mutineer who has nothing to lose.

"She loves her *candio*,"[33] said the negroes.

"Simple creatures!" said the overseer, who prided himself on his discernment, "she loves nothing; she hates Agricola; it's a case of hate at first sight—the strongest kind."

Both were partly right; her feelings were wonderfully knit to the African; and she now dedicated herself to Agricola's ruin.

The señor, it has been said, endeavored to be happy; but now his heart conceived and brought forth its first-born fear, sired by superstition—the fear that he was bewitched. The negroes said that Bras-Coupé had cursed the land. Morning after morning the master looked out with apprehension toward his fields, until one night the worm came upon the indigo[34] and between sunset and sunrise every green leaf had been eaten up, and there was nothing left for either insect or apprehension, to feed upon.

And then he said—and the echo came back from the Cannes Brulées—that the very bottom culpability of this thing rested on the Grandissimes, and specifically on their fugleman Agricola, through his putting the hellish African upon him. Moreover, fever and death, to a degree unknown before, fell upon his slaves. Those to whom life was spared—but to whom strength did not return—wandered about the place like scare-

32. Site of several slave revolts from 1780 to 1800 spearheaded by Toussaint L'Ouverture.
33. "Prince."
34. Source of a deep-blue dye and a staple crop until the introduction of sugar cane in the 1780s.

crows, looking for shelter, and made the very air dismal with the reitera-tion, *"No' ouanga* (we are bewitched), *Bras-Coupé fe moi des grigis* (the voudou's spells are on me)." The ripple of song was hushed and the flow-ers fell upon the floor.

"I have heard an English maxim," wrote Colonel De Grapion to his kinsman, "which I would recommend you to put into practice—'Fight the devil with fire.'"

No, he would not recognize devils as belligerents.

But if Rome commissioned exorcists, could not he employ one?

No, he would not! If his hounds could not catch Bras-Coupé, why, let him go. The overseer tried the hounds once more and came home with the best one across his saddlebow, an arrow run half through its side.

Once the blacks attempted by certain familiar rum-pourings and noc-turnal charm-singing to lift the curse; but the moment the master heard the wild monotone of their infernal worship, he stopped it with a word.

Early in February came the spring, and with it some resurrection of hope and courage. It may have been—it certainly was, in part—because young Honoré Grandissime had returned. He was like the sun's warmth wherever he went; and the other Honoré was like his shadow. The fairer one quickly saw the meaning of these things, hastened to cheer the young don with hopes of a better future, and to effect, if he could, the restoration of Bras-Coupé to his master's favor. But this latter effort was an idle one. He had long sittings with his uncle Agricola to the same end, but they al-ways ended fruitless and often angrily.

His dark half-brother had seen Palmyre and loved her. Honoré would gladly have solved one or two riddles by effecting their honorable union in marriage. The previous ceremony on the Grandissime back piazza need be no impediment: all slave-owners understood those things. Following Honoré's advice, the f. m. c., who had come into possession of his paternal portion, sent to Cannes Brulées a written offer to buy Palmyre at any price that her master might name, stating his intent to free her and make her his wife. Colonel De Grapion could hardly hope to settle Palmyre's fate more satisfactorily, yet he could not forego an opportunity to indulge his pride by following up the threat he had hung over Agricola to kill whoso-ever should give Palmyre to a black man. He referred the subject and the would-be purchaser to him. It would open up to the old braggart a line of retreat, thought the planter of the Cannes Brulées.

But the idea of retreat had left Citizen Fusilier.

"She is already married," said he to M. Honoré Grandissime, f. m c.

"She is the lawful wife of Bras-Coupé; and what God has joined together let no man put asunder. You know it, sirrah. You did this for impudence, to make a show of your wealth. You intended it as an insinuation of equality. I overlook the impertinence for the sake of the man whose white blood you carry; but h-mark you, if you ever bring your Parisian airs and self-sufficient face on a level with mine again, h-I will slap it."

The quadroon,[35] three nights after, was so indiscreet as to give him the opportunity, and he did it—at that quadroon ball to which Dr. Keene alluded in talking to Frowenfeld.

But Don José, we say, plucked up new spirit.

"Last year's disasters were but fortune's freaks," he said. "See, others' crops have failed all about us."

The overseer shook his head.

"*C'est ce maudit cocodri' là bas* (It is that accursed alligator Bras-Coupé down yonder in the swamp)."

And by and by the master was again smitten with the same belief. He and his neighbors put in their crops afresh. The spring waned, summer passed, the fevers returned, the year wore round, but no harvest smiled. "Alas!" cried the planters, "we are all poor men!" The worst among the worst were the fields of Bras-Coupé's master—parched and shrivelled. "He does not understand planting," said his neighbors; "neither does his overseer. Maybe, too, it is true as he says, that he is voudoued."

One day at high noon the master was taken sick with fever.

The third noon after—the sad wife sitting by the bedside—suddenly, right in the centre of the room, with the open door behind him, stood the magnificent, half-nude form of Bras-Coupé. He did not fall down as the mistress's eyes met his, though all his flesh quivered. The master was lying with his eyes closed. The fever had done a fearful three days' work.

"*Mioko-koanga oulé so' femme* (Bras-Coupé wants his wife)."

The master started wildly and stared upon his slave.

"*Bras-Coupé oulé so' femme!*" repeated the black.

"Seize him!" cried the sick man, trying to rise.

But, though several servants had ventured in with frightened faces, none dared molest the giant. The master turned his entreating eyes upon his wife, but she seemed stunned, and only covered her face with her hands and sat as if paralyzed by a foreknowledge of what was coming.

Bras-Coupé lifted his great, black palm and commenced:

35. An individual born of one white parent and one parent who is half white and half black; here Honoré, f. m. c.

"*Mo cé voudrai que la maison ci là et tout ça qui pas femme' ici s'raient encore maudits!* (May this house and all in it who are not women be accursed)."

The master fell back upon his pillow with a groan of helpless wrath.

The African pointed his finger through the open window.

"May its fields not know the plough nor nourish the cattle that overrun it."

The domestics, who had thus far stood their ground, suddenly rushed from the room like stampeded cattle, and at that moment appeared Palmyre.

"Speak to him," faintly cried the panting invalid.

She went firmly up to her husband and lifted her hand. With an easy motion, but quick as lightning, as a lion sets foot on a dog, he caught her by the arm.

"*Bras-Coupé oulé so' femme,*" he said, and just then Palmyre would have gone with him to the equator.

"You shall not have her!" gasped the master.

The African seemed to rise in height, and still holding his wife at arm's length, resumed his malediction:

"May weeds cover the ground until the air is full of their odor and the wild beasts of the forest come and lie down under their cover."

With a frantic effort the master lifted himself upon his elbow and extended his clenched fist in speechless defiance; but his brain reeled, his sight went out, and when again he saw, Palmyre and her mistress were bending over him, the overseer stood awkwardly by, and Bras-Coupé was gone.

The plantation became an invalid camp. The words of the voudou found fulfilment on every side. The plough went not out; the herds wandered through broken hedges from field to field and came up with staring bones and shrunken sides; a frenzied mob of weeds and thorns wrestled and throttled each other in a struggle for standing-room—rag-weed, smart-weed, sneeze-weed, bind-weed, iron-weed—until the burning skies of mid-summer checked their growth and crowned their unshorn tops with rank and dingy flowers.

"Why in the name of—St. Francis," asked the priest of the overseer, "didn't the señora use her power over the black scoundrel when he stood and cursed, that day?"

"Why, to tell you the truth, father," said the overseer, in a discreet whisper, "I can only suppose she thought Bras-Coupé had half a right to do it."

"Ah, ah, I see; like her brother Honoré —looks at both sides of a question—a miserable practice; but why couldn't Palmyre use *her* eyes? They would have stopped him."

"Palmyre? Why Palmyre has become the best *mon ture* (Plutonian medium)[36] in the parish. Agricola Fusilier himself is afraid of her. Sir, I think sometimes Bras-Coupé is dead and his spirit has gone into Palmyre. She would rather add to his curse than take from it."

"Ah!" said the jovial divine, with a fat smile, "castigation would help her case; the whip is a great sanctifier. I fancy it would even make a Christian of the inexpugnable Bras-Coupé."

But Bras-Coupé kept beyond the reach alike of the lash and of the Latin Bible.

By and by came a man with a rumor, whom the overseer brought to the master's sick-room, to tell that an enterprising Frenchman was attempting to produce a new staple in Louisiana, one that worms would not annihilate. It was that year of history when the despairing planters saw ruin hovering so close over them that they cried to heaven for succor. Providence raised up Etienne de Boré.[37] "And if Etienne is successful," cried the newsbearer, "and gets the juice of the sugar-cane to crystallize, so shall all of us, after him, and shall yet save our lands and homes. Oh, Señor, it will make you strong again to see these fields all cane and the long rows of negroes and negresses cutting it, while they sing their song of those droll African numerals, counting the canes they cut," and the bearer of good tidings sang them for very joy:

An-o-qué,　An-o-bia,　Bia-tail-la,　Que-re-que,　Nal-le-oua,

Au-mon-dé, Au-tap-o-té, Au-pa-to-té, Au-qué-ré-qué,　Bo.[38]

"And Honoré Grandissime is going to introduce it on his lands," said Don José.

36. An agent of Pluto, Roman god of the underworld, someone who channels spirits of the dead.

37. In 1796, Boré developed a granulation process, making sugar cane profitable.

38. Uncertain language, but probably counting to ten.

"That is true," said Agricola Fusilier, coming in. Honoré, the indefatigable peace-maker, had brought his uncle and his brother-in-law for the moment not only to speaking but to friendly terms.

The señor smiled.

"I have some good tidings, too," he said; "My beloved lady has borne me a son."

"Another scion of the house of Grand—I mean Martinez!" exclaimed Agricola. "And now, Don José, let me say that *I* have an item of rare intelligence!"

The don lifted his feeble head and opened his inquiring eyes with a sudden, savage light in them.

"No," said Agricola, "he is not exactly taken yet, but they are on his track."

"Who?"

"The police. We may say he is virtually in our grasp."

It was on a Sabbath afternoon that a band of Choctaws [39] having just played a game of racquette [40] behind the city and a similar game being about to end between the white champions of two rival faubourgs,[41] the beating of tom-toms, rattling of mules' jawbones and sounding of wooden horns drew the populace across the fields to a spot whose present name of Congo Square still preserves a reminder of its old barbaric pastimes. On a grassy plain under the ramparts, the performers of these hideous discords sat upon the ground facing each other, and in their midst the dancers danced. They gyrated in couples, a few at a time, throwing their bodies into the most startling attitudes and the wildest contortions, while the whole company of black lookers-on, incited by the tones of the weird music and the violent posturing of the dancers, swayed and writhed in passionate sympathy, beating their breasts, palms and thighs in time with the bones and drums, and at frequent intervals lifting, in that wild African unison no more to be described than forgotten, the unutterable songs of the Babouille and Counjaille dances, with their ejaculatory burdens of "*Aie! Aie! Voudou Magnan!*" and "*Aie Calinda! Dancé Calinda!*" [42] The volume of sound rose and fell with the augmentation or diminution of the danc-

39. Lower Mississippi Valley tribe of the Muskogean Nation.

40. A version of lacrosse.

41. Suburbs outside the original city walls (Fr.).

42. Invocations to voudou spirits; the calinda was also a popular dance with African and Caribbean sources.

ers' extravagances. Now a fresh man, young and supple, bounding into the ring, revived the flagging rattlers, drummers and trumpeters; now a wearied dancer, finding his strength going, gathered all his force at the cry of "*Dancé zisqu'a mort!*" [43] rallied to grand finale and with one magnificent antic, fell, foaming at the mouth.

The amusement had reached its height. Many participants had been lugged out by the neck to avoid their being danced on, and the enthusiasm had risen to a frenzy, when there bounded into the ring the blackest of black men, an athlete of superb figure, in breeches of "Indienne" [44]— the stuff used for slave women's best dresses—jingling with bells, his feet in moccasins, his tight, crisp hair decked out with feathers, a necklace of alligator's teeth rattling on his breast and a living serpent twined about his neck.

It chanced that but one couple was dancing. Whether they had been sent there by advice of Agricola is not certain. Snatching a tambourine from a bystander as he entered, the stranger thrust the male dancer aside, faced the woman and began a series of saturnalian [45] antics, compared with which all that had gone before was tame and sluggish; and as he finally leaped, with tinkling heels, clean over his bewildered partner's head, the multitude howled with rapture.

Ill-starred Bras-Coupé. He was in that extra-hazardous and irresponsible condition of mind and body known in the undignified present as "drunk again."

By the strangest fortune, if not, as we have just hinted, by some design, the man whom he had once deposited in the willow bushes, and the woman Clemence, were the very two dancers, and no other, whom he had interrupted. The man first stupidly regarded, next admiringly gazed upon, and then distinctly recognized, his whilom driver. Five minutes later the Spanish police were putting their heads together to devise a quick and permanent capture; and in the midst of the sixth minute, as the wonderful fellow was rising in a yet more astounding leap than his last, a lasso fell about his neck and brought him, crashing like a burnt tree, face upward upon the turf.

"The runaway slave," said the old French code, continued in force by the Spaniards, "the runaway slave who shall continue to be so for one

43. "Dance until you die" (Fr. Creole).

44. Printed muslin imitating fabrics made in India.

45. Behaviors typical of the feast of Saturn: feasting and unrestrained merry-making.

month from the day of his being denounced to the officers of justice, shall have his ears cut off and shall be branded with the flower de luce[46] on the shoulder; and on a second offence of the same nature, persisted in during one month of his being denounced, he shall be hamstrung,[47] and be marked with the flower de luce on the other shoulder. On the third offence he shall die." Bras-Coupé had run away only twice. "But," said Agricola, "these 'bossals'[48] must be taught their place. Besides, there is Article 27 of the same code: 'The slave who, having struck his master, shall have produced a bruise, shall suffer capital punishment'—a very necessary law!" He concluded with a scowl upon Palmyre, who shot back a glance which he never forgot.

The Spaniard showed himself very merciful—for a Spaniard; he spared the captive's life. He might have been more merciful still; but Honoré Grandissime said some indignant things in the African's favor, and as much to teach the Grandissimes a lesson as to punish the runaway, he would have repented his clemency, as he repented the momentary truce with Agricola, but for the tearful pleading of the señora and the hot, dry eyes of her maid. Because of these he overlooked the offence against his person and estate, and delivered Bras-Coupé to the law to suffer only the penalties of the crime he had committed against society by attempting to be a free man.

We repeat it for the credit of Palmyre, that she pleaded for Bras-Coupé. But what it cost her to make that intercession, knowing that his death would leave her free, and that if he lived she must be his wife, let us not attempt to say.

In the midst of the ancient town, in a part which is now crumbling away, stood the Calaboza,[49] with its humid vaults, grated cells, iron cages and its whips; and there, soon enough, they strapped Bras-Coupé face downward and laid on the lash. And yet not a sound came from the mutilated but unconquered African to annoy the ear of the sleeping city.

("And you suffered this thing to take place?" asked Joseph Frowenfeld of Honoré Grandissime.

"My-de'-seh!" exclaimed the Creole, "they lied to me—said they would not harm him!")

---

46. *Fleur de lis,* official symbol of France and New Orleans.

47. Cutting the tendons or "hamstrings" behind the knees, thus permanently crippling.

48. "Vassals" or slaves.

49. "Calabozo" (Sp.), prison.

He was brought at sunrise to the plantation. The air was sweet with the smell of the weed-grown fields. The long-horned oxen that drew him and the naked boy that drove the team stopped before his cabin.

"You cannot put that creature in there," said the thoughtful overseer. "He would suffocate under a roof—he has been too long out-of-doors for that. Put him on my cottage porch." There, at last, Palmyre burst into tears and sank down, while before her on a soft bed of dry grass, rested the helpless form of the captive giant, a cloth thrown over his galled back, his ears shorn from his head, and the tendons behind his knees severed. His eyes were dry, but there was in them that unspeakable despair that fills the eye of the charger when, fallen in battle, he gazes with sidewise-bended neck upon the ruin wrought upon him. His eye turned sometimes slowly to his wife. He need not demand her now—she was always by him.

There was much talk over him—much idle talk; no power or circumstance has ever been found that will keep a Creole from talking. He merely lay still under it with a fixed frown; but once some incautious tongue dropped the name of Agricola. The black man's eyes came so quickly round to Palmyre that she thought he would speak; but no; his words were all in his eyes. She answered their gleam with a fierce affirmative glance, whereupon he slowly bent his head and spat upon the floor.

There was yet one more trial of his wild nature. The mandate came from his master's sick-bed that he must lift the curse.

Bras-Coupé merely smiled. God keep thy enemy from such a smile!

The overseer, with a policy less Spanish than his master's, endeavored to use persuasion. But the fallen prince would not so much as turn one glance from his parted hamstrings. Palmyre was then besought to intercede. She made one poor attempt; but her husband was nearer doing her an unkindness than ever he had been before; he made a slow sign for silence—with his fist; and every mouth was stopped.

At midnight following, there came, on the breeze that blew from the mansion, a sound of running here and there, of wailing and sobbing—another Bridegroom was coming, and the Spaniard, with much such a lamp in hand as most of us shall be found with, neither burning brightly nor wholly gone out, went forth to meet Him.

"Bras-Coupé," said Palmyre, next evening, speaking low in his mangled ear, "the master is dead; he is just buried. As he was dying, Bras-Coupé, he asked that you would forgive him."

The maimed man looked steadfastly at his wife. He had not spoken since the lash struck him, and he spoke not now; but in those large, clear eyes, where his remaining strength seemed to have taken refuge as in a citadel, the old fierceness flared up for a moment, and then, like an expiring beacon, went out.

"Is your mistress well enough by this time to venture here?" whispered the overseer to Palmyre. "Let her come. Tell her not to fear, but to bring the babe—in her own arms, tell her—quickly!"

The lady came, her infant boy in her arms, knelt down beside the bed of sweet grass and set the child within the hollow of the African's arm. Bras-Coupé turned his gaze upon it; it smiled, its mother's smile, and put its hand upon the runaway's face, and the first tears of Bras-Coupé's life, the dying testimony of his humanity, gushed from his eyes and rolled down his cheek upon the infant's hand. He laid his own tenderly upon the babe's forehead, then removing it, waved it abroad, inaudibly moved his lips, dropped his arm, and closed his eyes. The curse was lifted.

"*Le pauv' dgiab'!*" [50] said the overseer, wiping his eyes and looking fieldward. "Palmyre, you must get the priest."

The priest came, in the identical gown in which he had appeared the night of the two weddings. To the good father's many tender questions Bras-Coupé turned a failing eye that gave no answers; until, at length:

"Do you know where you are going?" asked the holy man.

"Yes," answered his eyes, brightening.

"Where?"

He did not reply; he was lost in contemplation, and seemed looking far away.

So the question was repeated.

"Do you know where you are going?"

And again the answer of the eyes. He knew.

"Where?"

The overseer at the edge of the porch, the widow with her babe, and Palmyre and the priest bending over the dying bed, turned an eager ear to catch the answer.

"To—" the voice failed a moment; the departing hero essayed again; again it failed; he tried once more, lifted his hand, and with an ecstatic, upward smile, whispered. "To—Africa"—and was gone.

50. *Le pauvre diable* (Creole Fr.), "the poor devil."

Samuel L. Clemens (Mark Twain)

(1835–1910)

SAMUEL CLEMENS (the fifth of six children) was born on November 30, 1835, in a tiny village on a Mississippi tributary. When young Sam was four, financial setbacks prompted the family's move to the bustling river town of Hannibal, which Clemens would memorialize as the fictional St. Petersburg. Although Clemens's well-born Kentucky father, John Marshall Clemens, was a poor businessman, his spirited and aristocratic Virginian mother, Jane Lampton, provided the children with a solidly moral education. It was Hannibal's rich river life, however, that informed Clemens's imagination. Though somewhat sickly, he eventually became a village prankster with his scruffy comrade, Tom Blankenship, the prototype for Huckleberry Finn. The family's genteel poverty worsened with his father's death when Clemens was eleven, and he soon left school to become a printer's apprentice, publishing his first sketch in 1851 while working for his brother Orion.

In his early twenties, Clemens used his journalistic skills to fund his wanderlust. In 1857, bound for the Amazon, he set out on a steamship heading for New Orleans but became fascinated with the Mississippi. Signing on as an apprentice pilot, for four years (1857–61) he proudly navigated the river and produced the accounts that first appeared in *Atlantic* articles and were expanded to become *Life on the Mississippi* (1883). With the perils of river travel heightened by the war, Clemens returned to Hannibal where he and some boisterous buddies formed a secret Confederate unit, a misadventure Twain fictionalized in 1885. Uneasy about active war involvement and struggling with his pro-Union/pro-slavery beliefs, Clemens was pleased to head out to Nevada, where Orion had been appointed territory secretary. Twain later transformed that journey into the rollicking adventures of *Roughing It* (1872).

The West and its promises of instant riches suited Clemens, who would chase golden dreams throughout his life. Accepting a position on the prominent *Virginia City Enterprise* in 1862, he became a popular satirist, legislative recorder, and outrageous humorist. He also adopted his enduring pseudonym, "Mark Twain," which he first signed to a witty letter in February 1863. That same year he met the flamboyant performer and writer Artemus Ward. Fired in 1864 from the *Enterprise* for debt and an illegal duel, Clemens headed to San Francisco where he worked briefly as a reporter, renewed his association with Ward, and met Bret Harte, who, six years later, would become the nation's most famous western writer. Though Clemens spent a few months prospecting in the Calaveras County hills, his real riches came from the miners' yarns. (One of his most famous re-tellings, "The Notorious Jumping Frog of Calaveras County," was initially crafted as a letter to an amused and appreciative Ward.) Though Twain later described it as a "villainous backwoods sketch," this superb tall tale opened the doorway to numerous publishing and travel opportunities.

In 1867 Twain traveled to New York, where he cleaned up his writings for a genteel collection, which sold poorly. Eager for a more profitable venture and armed with a publishing contract, Twain sailed abroad. On his return, fellow passenger Charles Langdon introduced Twain to his sister, the wealthy socialite Olivia (Livy), whom Twain married in 1870. Seeking to prove himself worthy of the affluent Langdons, Twain diligently revised and expanded his popular European travel letters into *Innocents Abroad* (1869). Though his father-in-law helped him buy an interest in a Buffalo, New York, newspaper, Twain was eager to be part of the prosperous and elite eastern publishing industry. Depressed by the unexpected death of his first son and still doubtful about his talents, Twain resettled his family in Hartford, Connecticut, near the intellectual Nook Farm community. Quarry Farm, the Langdons' summer retreat near Elmira, New York, nonetheless remained for him a healing and productive retreat.

After the birth of his first daughter, Twain sailed to London where he was an instant success, initiating a habit of European travel that eventually accumulated into eleven years abroad. Not long after his return, Twain collaborated with Nook Farm resident and editor Charles Dudley Warner to produce *The Gilded Age* (1873), an indictment of Reconstruction excesses. Only a modest success, the book was adapted as a play, which yielded substantial profits.

Back at Quarry Farm in the spring of 1874 for the birth of his third child, Twain experimented with black dialect in two stories published the following November: "Sociable Jimmy" set in Illinois and "A True Story, Repeated Word for Word As I Heard It." While the creative epithets of the talkative black Jimmy anticipated the inventive language of Huck Finn, the piece that attracted serious attention was Twain's deft rendering of a black woman's voice in "A True Story."

Challenged by his abolitionist sister-in-law to hear the story of former slave Mary Ann Cord, the Quarry Farm cook, Clemens turned the experience into a tour-de-force. "A True Story" overturns the condescending certainty of the listening "Misto C——" and validates the dignified strength of Aunt Rachel (Mary Ann). Clemens also establishes the Union debt to black soldiers, the brutality of slavery, and the white complicity of such pro-slavery advocates as he himself once had been. Aunt Rachel's double-voiced conclusion underscores the complex interaction of mistakenly superior white beliefs and "true" black humanity. This "rugged truth," as Twain's friend and admirer William Dean Howells described it, would later become a shaping force in Twain's sympathetic portrayal of *Huckleberry Finn*'s Jim, an achievement that in 1970 prompted Ralph Ellison to identify Twain as his "co-creator" of the "African [literary] voice." To Twain's delight, "A True Story" was published by the prestigious *Atlantic*, and Twain achieved literary respectability.

Although its publication was delayed until 1876, Twain also wrote a large portion of *The Adventures of Tom Sawyer* that summer and began *Adventures of Huckleberry Finn* (1885), which he worked on periodically for the next seven years. Although Clemens privately ridiculed Thomas Nelson Page's fawning freedmen and was much admired by prominent black authors like Charles Chesnutt, the ambivalent relationship between Huck Finn and Jim suggests the paradoxical Clemens, who could neither fully shed his deeply embedded racial attitudes nor fail to repudiate the disastrous effects of slavery. During this period, Clemens co-authored a play with Bret Harte and returned to the lecture circuit, this time with George W. Cable, whose small, elegant stature and lilting Creole songs and stories provided a brilliant pairing with shaggy Clemens's drawling down-home humor. Although he continued publishing in the 1880s, Clemens devoted much of his energy to various business schemes, all of which failed.

The final decade of the century was a tragic one. Beset with serious financial problems, the Clemenses settled in Europe. Clemens penned several potboilers, including *Tom Sawyer Abroad* (1894). Although by 1898 his lectures and publications reversed his finances, his personal losses were immense. One daughter died of meningitis; another was diagnosed as an epileptic; and his beloved Livy became an invalid. At the same time, Clemens was achieving the adulation and literary respectability for which he had yearned. Nonetheless, his personal despair and his dismal view of "the damned human race" were expressed in increasingly bitter satires and in an angry protest against U.S. imperialism.

Livy died in Florence in 1904, and another daughter in 1909. Four months later, a tired and grief-stricken Clemens, awaiting Haley's comet, which had flamed through the sky on his birth, died on April 21, 1910, one day after its return. His champion Howells provided a literary epitaph Clemens would have relished: "I knew them all and all the rest of our sages, poets, seers, critics, humorists; they were like one another and like other literary men, but Clemens was sole, incomparable, the Lincoln of our literature."

Works by Samuel L. Clemens (Mark Twain)

The Innocents Abroad, 1869

Roughing It, 1872

The Adventures of Tom Sawyer, 1876

A Tramp Abroad, 1880

The Prince and the Pauper, 1882

Life on the Mississippi, 1883

Adventures of Huckleberry Finn, 1885

A Connecticut Yankee in King Arthur's Court, 1889

The Tragedy of Pudd'nhead Wilson and the Comedy
of Those Extraordinary Twins, 1894

Personal Recollections of Joan of Arc, 1896

Following the Equator, 1897

Autobiography, 1924, ed. Charles Neider, 1959

Mark Twain's Mysterious Stranger Manuscripts, ed. William M. Gibson, 1969

What Is Man? and Other Philosophical Writings, ed. Paul Baender, 1973

Mark Twain: Collected Tales, Sketches, Speeches, and Essays, ed. Louis Budd, 1992

The Oxford Mark Twain, gen. ed. Shelley Fisher Fishkin, 1996

Further Readings

Cardwell, Guy A. *Twins of Genius*. East Lansing: Michigan State College Press, 1953.

Cox, James M. *Mark Twain: The Fate of Humor*. Princeton: Princeton University Press, 1966.

Duckett, Margaret. *Mark Twain and Bret Harte.* Norman: University of Oklahoma Press, 1964.

Fishkin, Shelley Fisher. *Lighting out for the Territory: Reflections on Mark Twain and American Culture.* New York: Oxford University Press, 1996.

———. *Was Huck Black? Mark Twain and African-American Voices.* New York: Oxford University Press, 1993.

Fulton, Joe B. *Mark Twain's Ethical Realism: The Aesthetics of Race, Class, and Gender.* Columbia: University of Missouri Press, 1997.

Griffith, Clark. *Achilles and the Tortoise: Mark Twain's Fictions.* Tuscaloosa: University of Alabama Press, 1998.

Hoffman, Andrew Jay. *Inventing Mark Twain: The Lives of Samuel Langhorne Clemens.* New York: William Morrow, 1997.

Howells, William Dean. *My Mark Twain: Reminiscences and Criticisms.* New York: Harper & Bros., 1910.

Kaplan, Justin. *Mr. Clemens and Mark Twain.* New York: Simon and Schuster, 1966.

Lauber, John. *The Inventions of Mark Twain.* New York: Hill and Wang, 1990.

LeMaster, J. R., and James D. Wilson, eds. *The Mark Twain Encyclopedia.* New York: Garland, 1993.

Lynn, Kenneth S. *Mark Twain and Southwestern Humor.* Boston: Little, Brown, 1959.

Quirk, Tom. *Mark Twain: A Study of the Short Fiction.* New York: Twayne, 1997.

Robinson, Forrest G., ed. *The Cambridge Companion to Mark Twain.* New York: Cambridge University Press, 1995.

———. *In Bad Faith: The Dynamics of Deception in Mark Twain's America.* Cambridge: Harvard University Press, 1986.

Skandera-Trombley, Laura E. *Mark Twain in the Company of Women.* Philadelphia: University of Pennsylvania Press, 1994.

Smith, Henry Nash. *Mark Twain: The Development of a Writer.* Cambridge, Mass.: Belknap Press, 1962.

Stoneley, Peter. *Mark Twain and the Feminine Aesthetic.* New York: Cambridge University Press, 1992.

Wecter, Dixon. *Sam Clemens of Hannibal.* Boston: Houghton Mifflin, 1952.

Wonham, Henry B. *Mark Twain and the Art of the Tall Tale.* New York: Oxford University Press, 1993.

A True Story, Repeated Word for Word As I Heard It

It was summer time, and twilight. We were sitting on the porch of the farm-house, on the summit of the hill, and "Aunt Rachel" was sitting respectfully below our level, on the steps—for she was our servant, and colored. She was of mighty frame and stature; she was sixty years old, but her eye was undimmed and her strength unabated. She was a cheerful, hearty soul, and it was no more trouble for her to laugh than it is for a bird to sing. She was under fire, now, as usual when the day was done. That is to say, she was being chaffed without mercy, and was enjoying it. She would let off peal after peal of laughter, and then sit with her face in her hands and shake with throes of enjoyment which she could no longer get breath enough to express. At such a moment as this a thought occurred to me, and I said:—

"Aunt Rachel, how is it that you've lived sixty years and never had any trouble?"

She stopped quaking. She paused, and there was a moment of silence. She turned her face over her shoulder toward me, and said, without even a smile in her voice:—

"Misto C——, is you in 'arnest?"

It surprised me a good deal; and it sobered my manner and my speech, too. I said:—

"Why, I thought—that is, I meant—why, you *can't* have had any trouble. I've never heard you sigh, and never seen your eye when there wasn't a laugh in it."

She faced fairly around, now, and was full of earnestness.

"Has I had any trouble? Misto C——, I's gwyne to tell you, den I leave it to you. I was bawn down 'mongst de slaves; I knows all 'bout slavery, 'case I ben one of 'em my own se'f. Well, sah, my ole man—dat's my husban'—he was lovin' an' kind to me, jist as kind as you is to yo' own wife. An' we had chil'en—seven chil'en—an' we loved dem chil'en jist de same as you loves yo' chil'en. Dey was black, but de Lord can't make no chil'en so black but what dey mother loves 'em an' wouldn't give 'em up, no, not for anything dat's in dis whole world.

"Well, sah, I was raised in ole Fo'ginny,[1] but my mother she was raised in Maryland; an' my *souls!* she was turrible when she'd git started! My *lan'!* but she'd make de fur fly! When she'd git into dem tantrums, she always had one word dat she said. She'd straighten herse'f up an' put her fists in her hips an' say, 'I want you to understan' dat I wa'nt bawn in de mash to be fool' by trash! I's one o' de ole Blue Hen's Chickens, *I* is!' 'Ca'se, you see, dat's what folks dat's bawn in Maryland calls deyselves, an' dey's proud of

1. Virginia.

it. Well, dat was her word. I don't ever forgit it, beca'se she said it so much, an' be ca'se she said it one day when my little Henry tore his wris' awful, an' most busted his head, right up at de top of his forehead, an' de niggers didn't fly aroun' fas' enough to 'tend to him. An' when dey talk' back at her, she up an' she says, 'Look-a-heah!' she says, 'I want you niggers to understan' dat I wa'nt bawn in de mash to be fool' by trash! I's one o' de ole Blue Hen's Chickens, *I* is!' an' den she clar' dat kitchen an' bandage' up de chile herse'f. So I says dat word, too, when I's riled.

"Well, bymeby my ole mistis say she's broke, an' she got to sell all de niggers on de place. An' when I heah dat dey gwyne to sell us all off at oction in Richmon',[2] oh, de good gracious! I know what dat mean!"

Aunt Rachel had gradually risen, while she warmed to her subject, and now she towered above us, black against the stars.

"Dey put chains on us an' put us on a stan' as high as dis po'ch—twenty foot high—an' all de people stood aroun', crowds an' crowds. An' dey'd come up dah an' look at us all roun', an' squeeze our arm, an' make us git up an' walk, an' den say, 'Dis one too ole,' or 'Dis one lame,' or 'Dis one don't 'mount to much.' An' dey sole my ole man, an' took him away, an' dey begin to sell my chil'en' an' take *dem* away, an' I begin to cry; an' de man say, 'Shet up yo' dam blubberin',' an' hit me on de mouf wid his han'. An' when de las' one was gone but my little Henry, I grab' *him* clost up to my breas' so, an' I ris up an' says, 'You shan't take him away,' I says; 'I'll kill de man dat tetches him!' I says. But my little Henry whisper an' say, 'I gwyne to run away, an' den I work an' buy yo' freedom.' Oh, bless de chile, he always so good! But dey got him—dey got him, de men did; but I took and tear de clo'es mos' off of 'em, an' beat 'em over de head wid my chain; an' *dey* give it to *me*, too, but I didn't mine dat.

"Well, dah was my ole man gone, an' all my chil'en, all my seven chil'en—an' six of 'em I hain't set eyes on ag'in to dis day, an' dat's twenty-two year ago las' Easter. De man dat bought me b'long' in Newbern,[3] an' he took me dah. Well, bymeby de years roll on an' de waw come. My marster he was a Confedrit colonel, an' I was his family's cook. So when de Unions took dat town, dey all run away an' lef' me all by myse'f wid de other niggers in dat mons'us big house. So de big Union officers move in dah, an' dey ask me would I cook for *dem*. 'Lord bless you,' says I, 'dat's what I's *for*.'

2. Richmond, the capital of Virginia.

3. A town in western Virginia.

"Dey wa'n't no small-fry officers, mine you, dey was de biggest dey *is;* an' de way dey made dem sojers mosey roun'! De Gen'l he tole me to boss dat kitchen; an' he say, 'If anybody come meddlin' wid you, you jist make 'em walk chalk;[4] don't you be afeard,' he say; 'you's 'mong frens, now.'

"Well, I thinks to myse'f, if my little Henry ever got a chance to run away, he'd make to de Norf, o' course. So one day I comes in dah whah de big officers was, in de parlor, an' I drops a kurtchy, so, an' I up an' tole 'em 'bout my Henry, dey a-listenin' to my troubles jist de same as if I was white folks; an' I says, 'What I come for is beca'se if he got away and got up Norf whah you gemmen comes from, you might 'a' seen him, maybe, an' could tell me so as I could fine him ag'in; he was very little, an' he had a sk-yar on his lef' wris', an' at de top of his forehead.' Den dey look mournful, an' de Gen'l say, 'How long sence you los' him?' an' I say, 'Thirteen year.' Den de Gen'l say, 'He wouldn't be little no mo' now—he's a man!'

"I never thought o' dat befo'! He was only dat little feller to *me,* yit. I never thought 'bout him growin' up an' bein' big. But I see it den. None o' de gemmen had run acrost him, so dey couldn't do nothin' for me. But all dat time, do' *I* didn't know it, my Henry *was* run off to de Norf, years an' years, an' he was a barber, too, an' worked for hisse'f. An' bymeby, when de waw come, he ups an' he says, 'I's done barberin',' he says; 'I's gwyne to fine my ole mammy, less'n she's dead.' So he sole out an' went to whah dey was recruitin', an' hired hisse'f out to de colonel for his servant; an' den he went all froo de battles everywhah, huntin' for his ole mammy; yes indeedy, he'd hire to fust one officer an' den another, tell he'd ransacked de whole Souf; but you see *I* didn't know nuffin 'bout *dis.* How was *I* gwyne to know it?

"Well, one night we had a big sojer ball; de sojers dah at Newbern was always havin' balls an' carryin' on. Dey had 'em in my kitchen, heaps o' times, 'ca'se it was so big. Mine you, I was *down* on sich doin's; beca'se my place was wid de officers, an' it rasp' me to have dem common sojers cavortin' roun' my kitchen like dat. But I alway' stood aroun' an' kep' things straight, I did; an' sometimes dey'd git my dander up, an' den I'd make 'em clar dat kitchen, mine I *tell* you!

"Well, one night—it was a Friday night—dey comes a whole platoon f'm a *nigger* ridgment dat was on guard at de house—de house was headquarters, you know—an' den I was jist a-*bilin'!* Mad? I was just a-*boomin'!* I swelled aroun', an' swelled aroun'; I jist was a-itchin' for 'em to do

4. Toe the (chalk) line; follow the rules strictly.

somefin for to start me. *An'* dey was a-waltzin' an' a-dancin'! *my!* but dey was havin' a time! an' I jist a-swellin' an' a-swellin' up! Pooty soon, 'long comes *sich* a spruce young nigger a-sailin' down de room wid a yaller wench roun' de wais'; an' roun' an' roun' an' roun' dey went, enough to make a body drunk to look at 'em; an' when dey got abreas' o' me, dey went to kin' o' balancin' aroun', fust on one leg an' den on t'other, an' smilin' at my big red turban, an' makin' fun, an' I ups an' says, '*Git* along wid you!—rubbage!' De young man's face kin' o' changed, all of a sudden, for 'bout a second, but den he went to smilin' ag'in, same as he was befo'. Well, 'bout dis time, in comes some niggers dat played music an' b'long' to de ban', an' dey *never* could git along widout puttin' on airs. An' de very fust air dey put on dat night, I lit into 'em! Dey laughed, an' dat made me wuss. De res' o' de niggers got to laughin', an' den my soul *alive* but I was hot! My eye was jist a-blazin'! I jist straightened myself up so—jist as I is now, plum to de ceilin', mos'—an' I digs my fists into my hips, an' I says, 'Look-a-heah!' I says, 'I want you niggers to understan' dat I wa'n't bawn in de mash to be fool' by trash! I's one o' de ole Blue Hen's Chickens, *I* is!' an' den I see dat young man stan' a-starin' an' stiff, lookin' kin' o' up at de ceilin' like he fo'got somefin, an' couldn't 'member it no mo'. Well, I jist march' on dem niggers—so, lookin' like a gen'l—an' dey jist cave' away befo' me an' out at de do'. An' as dis young man was a-goin' out, I heah him say to another nigger, 'Jim,' he says, 'you go 'long an' tell de cap'n I be on han' 'bout eight o'clock in de mawnin'; dey's somefin on my mine,' he says; 'I don't sleep no mo' dis night. You go 'long,' he says, 'an' leave me by my own se'f.'

"Dis was 'bout one o'clock in de mawnin'. Well, 'bout seven, I was up an' on han', gittin' de officers' breakfast. I was a-stoopin' down by de stove—jist so, same as if yo' foot was de stove—an' I'd opened de stove do' wid my right han'—so, pushin' it back, jist as I pushes yo' foot—an' I'd jist got de pan o' hot biscuits in my han' an' was 'bout to raise up, when I see a black face come aroun' under mine, an' de eyes a-lookin' up into mine, jist as I's a-lookin' up clost under yo' face now; an' I jist stopped *right dah*, an' never budged! jist gazed, an' gazed, so; an' de pan begin to tremble, an' all of a sudden I *knowed!* De pan drop' on de flo' an' I grab his lef' han' an' shove back his sleeve—jist so, as I's doin' to you—an' den I goes for his forehead an' push de hair back, so, an' 'Boy!' I says, 'if you an't my Henry, what is you doin' wid dis welt on yo' wris' an' dat sk-yar on yo' forehead? De Lord God ob heaven be praise', I got my own ag'in!'

"Oh, no, Misto C——, *I* hain't had no trouble. An' no *joy!*"

Constance Fenimore Woolson

(1840–1894)

CONSTANCE FENIMORE WOOLSON'S life was one of literary triumph and personal tragedy. Her birth in Claremont, New Hampshire, on March 5, 1840, was shortly followed by the deaths of her three sisters from scarlet fever. Another sister died soon after in Cleveland, Ohio, where her grieving family had relocated; two older sisters died not long after their marriages when Woolson was in her early teens, and, as she neared thirty, her vibrant father, highly successful stove manufacturer Charles Jarvis Woolson, passed away. Finally, her deeply troubled brother died mysteriously in California in 1883.

Nonetheless, Woolson's early years were marked by accomplishment and adventure. She accompanied her keenly observant father, a journalist before his marriage, on his trips throughout the Great Lakes region, and she spent delightful summers on Mackinac Island, Michigan. The island served as the setting for two early sketches and for her first novel, *Anne* (1882), which became the most popular serialization in *Harper's* publishing history. Woolson's middle name "Fenimore," briefly her pen name, reflected the literary heritage of her mother; Hannah Cooper Pomeroy was the niece of James Fenimore Cooper, whose "Leather-stocking Tales" (1820–41) about frontier scout Natty Bumppo had gained him international renown. Woolson was a special favorite of Cooper's unmarried sisters, one of whom was herself an author. During her frequent visits to Cooperstown, New York, Woolson, who never lost her love for nature, imaginatively relived Natty's exploits, hiking deep into the woods and rowing along the lake shore for hours.

She was an equally spirited student. The thriving city of Cleveland offered unusually fine educational opportunities for young women. First in Miss Hayden's School and then in the Cleveland Female Seminary, Woolson became an avid reader, a gifted writer, and an admired and popular student. Following her mother's educational tradition, she next attended

Madame Chegaray's, a fashionable New York boarding school that catered primarily to distinguished southern families. An outstanding student, she graduated at the top of her class. More importantly, as one of only three northerners, she became schooled in the nuances of affluent southern culture. The Civil War years, which soon followed, profoundly influenced Woolson, who later described them as affecting "the heart and spirit of my life." According to her sister, the war also engendered an infatuation with a childhood friend serving as a Union officer; however, the romance was short-lived, and Woolson remained single throughout her life.

Five years after the war's end, her father's death left Woolson the primary provider for her invalid mother. She closed their Cleveland home, moved to New York, and, with the assistance of her sister Clara's journalist father-in-law, began publishing short pieces in leading magazines. Soon after the move, Clara's husband was killed in a railroad accident. Recognizing her mother's need for a warmer climate, Woolson relocated with her mother, Clara, and Clara's daughter to St. Augustine, Florida. Enjoying the solitude and the exotic landscape, Woolson spent long, delighted hours rowing in the moss-shaded, snake-infested river swamps.

Her childhood memories and her travels became the substance of her increasingly popular fiction. Although she had published a number of stories in several leading magazines and had received a prize for *The Old Stone House*, a children's book written in 1872, she considered the short-story collection *Castle Nowhere: Lake-Country Sketches* (1875) her real literary debut. Its success encouraged Woolson to consider other publishing venues, and she became one of the first and certainly among the most empathetic northern authors to recognize the fictional value of the defeated South. From 1875 to 1879 she published twelve such stories, ten of which were collected in *Rodman the Keeper* (1880). These polished tales explore the war's aftermath with a finely edged realism. In "Felipa" (first published in *Lippincott's* in 1876), the volume's most poetic and intriguing tale, Woolson evokes the sensuous marginality of a Florida sea island and an indigenous child for whom the story is named. Felipa's androgynous paganism challenges the cultivated sense of race, class, and gender enjoyed by the island's sophisticated women visitors. The result is a remarkable commentary on the contaminating seduction of civilization and its artistic projects. Woolson's interest in the vulnerability of creative spirits like Felipa was repeated a few years later in what is currently her best-known story, the semi-autobiographical "Miss Grief" (1880). In that tale, sometimes read as a mirror of Woolson's relationship with Henry James, the eager, unpublished author Aaronna Moncrief travels to Europe to gain the assistance of an established and self-important male critic to whom she naively entrusts her artistic "body." After her mother's death in 1879, Woolson had moved permanently to Europe, living in England, Switzerland, and Italy. It was there that she initiated her long friendship with James. Woolson, who had favorably reviewed James's novels, met him in Florence. James, who usually had little use for literary women, admired her enthusiasm and intelligence and lavishly praised her artistry. Both American expatriates, Woolson and James maintained a lively friendship, sustained by correspondence through several long separations, for the remainder of Woolson's life.

Poet, essayist, novelist, writer of popular travel sketches and more than fifty short stories, Woolson exploited a variety of settings in her work, including the Midwest and Europe. But the South continued to draw her interest, particularly North Carolina and Florida, which provided settings for three of her five novels: *For the Major* (1883), *East Angels* (1886), and *Horace Chase* (1894). Though not widely read today, Woolson was an adept artist, a pioneer local colorist, and the first postwar northerner to capture the exotic sensuality and poignancy of the South. Her fiction was deeply esteemed, and critics even speculated she might become the American novelist laureate. However, the tragedies that had defined her life also shaped its end. Almost deaf, ill, and deeply depressed, Woolson, at fifty-three, was found dead (James believed by suicide) beneath her Venice apartment window on January 24, 1894.

Works by Constance Fenimore Woolson

SHORT FICTION

Castle Nowhere: Lake-Country Sketches, 1875

Rodman the Keeper: Southern Sketches, 1880

The Front Yard, and Other Italian Stories, 1895

For the Major, and Selected Short Stories, ed. Rayburn S. Moore, 1967

*Women Artists, Women Exiles: "Miss Grief" and Other Stories by
Constance Fenimore Woolson,* ed. Joan Myers Weimer, 1988

NOVELS

The Old Stone House, 1872

Anne, 1882

East Angels, 1886

Jupiter Lights, 1889

Horace Chase, 1894

POETRY

Two Women: 1862, 1877

LETTERS

Constance Fenimore Woolson, ed. Clare Benedict, 1930

Further Reading

Dean, Sharon. *Constance Fenimore Woolson: Homeward Bound.* Knoxville: University of Tennessee, 1995.

Gordon, Lyndall. *A Private Life of Henry James: Two Women and His Art.* London: Vintage, 1999.

James, Henry. "Miss Woolson." In *Partial Portraits.* London: Macmillan, 1888.

Kern, John Dwight. *Constance Fenimore Woolson: Literary Pioneer.* Philadelphia: University of Pennsylvania Press, 1934.

Moore, Rayburn S. *Constance F. Woolson.* New York: Twayne, 1963.

Rowe, Anne E. *The Idea of Florida in the American Literary Imagination.* Baton Rouge: Louisiana State University Press, 1986.

Torsney, Cheryl B. *Constance Fenimore Woolson: The Grief of Artistry.* Athens: University of Georgia Press, 1989.

————, ed. *Critical Essays on Constance Fenimore Woolson.* New York: G. K. Hall, 1992.

Felipa

Glooms of the live-oaks, beautiful-braided and woven
With intricate shades of the vines that, myriad cloven,
Clamber the forks of the multiform boughs.
                              . . . Green colonnades
Of the dim sweet woods, of the dear dark woods,
Of the heavenly woods and glades,
That run to the radiant marginal sand-beach within
        The wide sea-marshes of Glynn.
                              . . . Free
By a world of marsh that borders a world of sea.
Sinuous southward and sinuous northward the shimmering band
Of the sand-beach fastens the fringe of the marsh to the folds of the land.

Inward and outward to northward and southward the beach-lines linger
    and curl
As a silver-wrought garment that clings to and follows the firm, sweet
    limbs of a girl.
A league and a league of marsh-grass, waist-high, broad in the blade,
Green, and all of a height, and unflecked with a light or a shade.

            SIDNEY LANIER [1]

Christine and I found her there. She was a small, dark skinned, yellow-eyed child, the offspring of the ocean and the heats, tawny, lithe and wild, shy yet fearless—not unlike one of the little brown deer that bounded through the open reaches of the pine-barren [2] behind the house. She did not come to us—we came to her; we loomed into her life like genii from another world, and she was partly afraid and partly proud of us. For were we not her guests? proud thought! and, better still, were we not women? "I have only seen three women in all my life," said Felipa, inspecting us gravely, "and I like women. I am a woman too, although these clothes of the son of Pedro make me appear as a boy; I wear them on account of the boat and the hauling in of the fish. The son of Pedro being dead at a convenient age, and his clothes fitting me, what would you have? It was a chance not to be despised. But when I am grown I shall wear robes long and beautiful like the señora's." The little creature was dressed in a boy's suit of dark-blue linen, much the worse for wear, and torn.

"If you are a girl, why do you not mend your clothes?" I said.

"Do you mend, señora?"

"Certainly: all women sew and mend."

"The other lady?"

Christine laughed as she lay at ease upon the brown carpet of pine-needles, warm and aromatic after the tropic day's sunshine. "The child has divined me already, Catherine," she said.

Christine was a tall, lissome maid, with an unusually long stretch of arm, long sloping shoulders, and a long fair throat; her straight hair fell to her knees when unbound, and its clear flaxen hue had not one shade of gold, as her clear gray eyes had not one shade of blue. Her small, straight, rose-leaf lips parted over small, dazzlingly white teeth, and the outline of her face in profile reminded you of an etching in its distinctness, although

1. Poet (1842–81) from Macon, Ga.; "The Marshes of Glynn" (1878), which describes coastal Georgia, was one of his most famous works.

2. Pine forest in sandy soil.

it was by no means perfect according to the rules of art. Still, what a comfort it was, after the blurred outlines and smudged profiles many of us possess—seen to best advantage, I think, in church on Sundays, crowned with flower-decked bonnets, listening calmly serene to favorite ministers, unconscious of noses! When Christine had finished her laugh—and she never hurried anything—she stretched out her arm carelessly and patted Felipa's curly head. The child caught the descending hand and kissed the long white fingers.

It was a wild place where we were, yet not new or crude—the coast of Florida, that old-new land, with its deserted plantations, its skies of Paradise, and its broad wastes open to the changeless sunshine. The old house stood on the edge of the dry land, where the pine-barren ended and the salt-marsh[3] began; in front curved the tide-water river[4] that seemed ever trying to come up close to the barren and make its acquaintance, but could not quite succeed, since it must always turn and flee at a fixed hour, like Cinderella at the ball, leaving not a silver slipper behind, but purple driftwood and bright seaweeds, brought in from the Gulf Stream outside. A planked platform ran out into the marsh from the edge of the barren, and at its end the boats were moored; for, although at high tide the river was at our feet, at low tide it was far away out in the green waste somewhere, and if we wanted it we must go and seek it. We did not want it, however; we let it glide up to us twice a day with its fresh salt odors and flotsam of the ocean, and the rest of the time we wandered over the barrens or lay under the trees looking up into the wonderful blue above, listening to the winds as they rushed across from sea to sea. I was an artist, poor and painstaking. Christine was my kind friend. She had brought me South because my cough was troublesome, and here because Edward Bowne recommended the place. He and three fellow sportsmen were down at the Madre Lagoon, farther south; I thought it probable we should see him, without his three fellow sportsmen, before very long.

"Who were the three women you have seen, Felipa?" said Christine.

"The grandmother, an Indian woman of the Seminoles[5] who comes sometimes with baskets, and the wife of Miguel of the island. But they are all old, and their skins are curled: I like better the silver skin of the señora."

Poor little Felipa lived on the edge of the great salt-marsh alone with

3. Wetlands covered with salt-tolerant grasses and subject to tides.

4. River channel affected by ocean tides.

5. Independent Florida branch of the Creek tribe.

her grandparents, for her mother was dead. The yellow old couple were slow-witted Minorcans,[6] part pagan, part Catholic, and wholly ignorant; their minds rarely rose above the level of their orange-trees and their fish-nets. Felipa's father was a Spanish sailor, and, as he had died only the year before, the child's Spanish was fairly correct, and we could converse with her readily, although we were slow to comprehend the patois[7] of the old people, which seemed to borrow as much from the Italian tongue and the Greek as from its mother Spanish. "I know a great deal," Felipa remarked confidently, "for my father taught me. He had sailed on the ocean out of sight of land, and he knew many things. These he taught to me. Do the gracious ladies think there is anything else to know?"

One of the gracious ladies thought not, decidedly. In answer to my remonstrance, expressed in English, she said, "Teach a child like that, and you ruin her."

"Ruin her?"

"Ruin her happiness—the same thing."

Felipa had a dog, a second self—a great gaunt yellow creature of un-known breed, with crooked legs, big feet, and the name Drollo. What Drollo meant, or whether it was an abbreviation, we never knew; but there was a certain satisfaction in it, for the dog was droll: the fact that the Minorcan title, whatever it was, meant nothing of that sort, made it all the better. We never saw Felipa without Drollo. "They look a good deal alike," observed Christine—"the same coloring."

"For shame!" I said.

But it was true. The child's bronzed yellow skin and soft eyes were not unlike the dog's, but her head was crowned with a mass of short black curls, while Drollo had only his two great flapping ears and his low smooth head. Give him an inch or two more of skull, and what a creature a dog would be! For love and faithfulness even now what man can match him? But, although ugly, Felipa was a picturesque little object always, whether attired in boy's clothes or in her own forlorn bodice and skirt. Olive-hued and meager-faced, lithe and thin, she flew over the pine-barrens like a creature of air, laughing to feel her short curls toss and her thin childish arms buoyed up on the breeze as she ran, with Drollo, bark-

6. Descendants of settlers of Englishman Andrew Turnbull's failed colony at New Smyrna Beach, which brought 1,200 natives of Minorca, a Mediterranean island of Spain, to Florida in 1768.

7. A dialect spoken (not written) among more rural or less educated people.

ing behind. For she loved the winds, and always knew when they were coming—whether down from the north, in from the ocean, or across from the Gulf of Mexico: she watched for them, sitting in the doorway, where she could feel their first breath, and she taught us the signs of the clouds. She was a queer little thing: we used to find her sometimes dancing alone out on the barren in a circle she had marked out with pine-cones, and once she confided to us that she talked to the trees. "They hear," she said in a whisper; "you should see how knowing they look, and how their leaves listen."

Once we came upon her most secret lair in a dense thicket of thorn-myrtle[8] and wild smilax[9]—a little bower she had made, where was hidden a horrible-looking image formed of the rough pieces of saw-palmetto[10] grubbed up by old Bartolo from his garden. She must have dragged these fragments thither one by one, and with infinite pains bound them together with her rude withes[11] of strong marsh-grass, until at last she had formed a rough trunk with crooked arms and a sort of a head, the red hairy surface of the palmetto looking not unlike the skin of some beast, and making the creature all the more grotesque. This fetich[12] was kept crowned with flowers, and after this we often saw the child stealing away with Drollo to carry to it portions of her meals or a new-found treasure— a sea-shell, a broken saucer, or a fragment of ribbon. The food always mysteriously disappeared, and my suspicion is that Drollo used to go back secretly in the night and devour it, asking no questions and telling no lies: it fitted in nicely, however, Drollo merely performing the ancient part of the priests of Jupiter,[13] men who have been much admired. "What a little pagan she is!" I said.

"Oh, no, it is only her doll," replied Christine.

I tried several times to paint Felipa during these first weeks, but those eyes of hers always evaded me. They were, as I have said before, yellow— that is, they were brown with yellow lights—and they stared at you with the most inflexible openness. The child had the full-curved, half-open

8. Common evergreen shrub, covered with a wax used in scented candles.

9. Common thorny vine, with small flowers and black berries.

10. Shrub-like palms with fan-shaped leaves.

11. Binding material.

12. Fetish, an object regarded as magical.

13. Supreme Roman god; temple priests often consumed the offerings of the faithful.

mouth of the tropics, and a low Greek forehead. "Why isn't she pretty?" I said.

"She is hideous," replied Christine; "look at her elbows."

Now Felipa's arms *were* unpleasant: they were brown and lean, scratched and stained, and they terminated in a pair of determined little paws that could hold on like grim Death. I shall never forget coming upon a tableau one day out on the barren—a little Florida cow and Felipa, she holding on by the horns, and the beast with its small fore feet stubbornly set in the sand; girl pulling one way, cow the other; both silent and determined. It was a hard contest, but the girl won.

"And if you pass over her elbows, there are her feet," continued Christine languidly. For she was a sybaritic lover of the fine linens of life, that friend of mine—a pre-Raphaelite lady [14] with clinging draperies and a mediæval clasp on her belt. Her whole being rebelled against ugliness, and the mere sight of a sharp-nosed, light-eyed woman on a cold day made her uncomfortable.

"Have we not feet too?" I replied sharply.

But I knew what she meant. Bare feet are not pleasant to the eye nowadays, whatever they may have been in the days of the ancient Greeks; and Felipa's little brown insteps were half the time torn or bruised by the thorns of the chaparral.[15] Besides, there was always the disagreeable idea that she might step upon something cold and squirming when she prowled through the thickets knee-deep in the matted grasses. Snakes abounded, although we never saw them; but Felipa went up to their very doors, as it were, and rang the bell defiantly.

One day old Grandfather Bartolo took the child with him down to the coast: she was always wild to go to the beach, where she could gather shells and sea-beans,[16] and chase the little ocean-birds that ran along close to the waves with that swift gliding motion of theirs, and where she could listen to the roar of the breakers. We were several miles up the salt-marsh, and to go down to the ocean was quite a voyage to Felipa. She bade us good-by joyously; then ran back to hug Christine a second time, then to the boat again; then back.

14. The pre-Raphaelite Brotherhood of British artists, formed in 1848, were associated with a sensuous realism, often featuring ornately-dressed, beautiful, laconic women.

15. A dense stand of low, evergreen oaks.

16. Seeds that have drifted ashore, often polished and worn as jewelry or charms.

"I thought you wanted to go, child?" I said, a little impatiently; for I was reading aloud, and these small irruptions were disturbing.

"Yes," said Felipa, "I want to go; and still—Perhaps if the gracious señora would kiss me again—"

Christine only patted her cheek and told her to run away: she obeyed, but there was a wistful look in her eyes, and, even after the boat had started, her face, watching us from the stern, haunted me.

"Now that the little monkey has gone, I may be able at last to catch and fix a likeness of her," I said; "in this case a recollection is better than the changing quicksilver reality."

"You take it as a study of ugliness?"

"Do not be hard upon the child, Christine."

"Hard? Why, she adores me," said my friend, going off to her hammock under the tree.

Several days passed, and the boat returned not. I accomplished a fine amount of work, and Christine a fine amount of swinging in the hammock and dreaming. At length one afternoon I gave my final touch, and carried my sketch over to the pre-Raphaelite lady for criticism. "What do you see?" I said.

"I see a wild-looking child with yellow eyes, a mat of curly black hair, a lank little bodice, her two thin brown arms embracing a gaunt old dog with crooked legs, big feet, and turned-in toes."

"Is that all?"

"All."

"You do not see latent beauty, courage, and a possible great gulf of love in that poor wild little face?"

"Nothing of the kind," replied Christine decidedly. "I see an ugly little girl; that is all."

The next day the boat returned, and brought back five persons, the old grandfather, Felipa, Drollo, Miguel of the island, and—Edward Bowne.

"Already?" I said.

"Tired of the Madre, Kitty; thought I would come up here and see you for a while. I knew you must be pining for me."

"Certainly," I replied; "do you not see how I have wasted away?"

He drew my arm through his and raced me down the plank-walk toward the shore, where I arrived laughing and out of breath.

"Where is Christine?" he asked.

I came back into the traces [17] at once. "Over there in the hammock. You wish to go to the house first, I suppose?"

"Of course not."

"But she did not come to meet you, Edward, although she knew you had landed."

"Of course not, also."

"I do not understand you two."

"And of course not, a third time," said Edward, looking down at me with a smile. "What do peaceful little artists know about war?"

"Is it war?"

"Something very like it, Kitty. What is that you are carrying?"

"Oh! my new sketch. What do you think of it?"

"Good, very good. Some little girl about here, I suppose?"

"Why, it is Felipa!"

"And who is Felipa? Seems to me I have seen that old dog, though."

"Of course you have; he was in the boat with you, and so was Felipa; but she was dressed in boy's clothes, and that gives her a different look."

"Oh! that boy? I remember him. His name is Philip. He is a funny little fellow," said Edward calmly.

"Her name is Felipa, and she is not a boy or a funny little fellow at all," I replied.

"Isn't she? I thought she was both," replied Ned carelessly; and then he went off toward the hammock. I turned away, after noting Christine's cool greeting, and went back to the boat.

Felipa came bounding to meet me. "What is his name?" she demanded.

"Bowne."

"Buon—Buona; [18] I can not say it."

"Bowne, child—Edward Bowne."

"Oh! Eduardo; I know that. Eduardo—Eduardo—a name of honey."

She flew off singing the name, followed by Drollo carrying his mistress's palmetto basket in his big patient mouth; but when I passed the house a few moments afterward she was singing, or rather talking volubly of, another name—"Miguel," and "the wife of Miguel," who were apparently important personages on the canvas of her life. As it happened, I never really saw that wife of Miguel, who seemingly had no name of her own;

17. Ropes or chains used to harness a horse to a wagon; thus, to return to an onerous routine.
18. "Good" (It.).

but I imagined her. She lived on a sand-bar in the ocean not far from the mouth of our salt-marsh; she drove pelicans like ducks with a long switch, and she had a tame eagle; she had an old horse also, who dragged the drift-wood across the sand on a sledge, and this old horse seemed like a giant horse always, outlined as he was against the flat bar and the sky. She went out at dawn, and she went out at sunset, but during the middle of the burning day she sat at home and polished sea-beans, for which she obtained untold sums; she was very tall, she was very yellow, and she had but one eye. These items, one by one, had been dropped by Felipa at various times, and it was with curiosity that I gazed upon the original Miguel, the possessor of this remarkable spouse. He was a grave-eyed, yellow man, who said little and thought less, applying *cui bono?*[19] to mental much as the city man applies it to bodily exertion, and therefore achieving, I think, a finer degree of inanition. The tame eagle, the pelicans, were nothing to him; and, when I saw his lethargic, gentle countenance, my own curiosity about them seemed to die away in haze, as though I had breathed in an invisible opiate. He came, he went, and that was all; exit Miguel.

Felipa was constantly with us now. She and Drollo followed the three of us wherever we went—followed the two also whenever I staid behind to sketch, as I often staid, for in those days I was trying to catch the secret of the salt-marsh; a hopeless effort—I know it now. "Stay with me, Felipa," I said; for it was natural to suppose that the lovers might like to be alone. (I call them lovers for want of a better name, but they were more like haters; however, in such cases it is nearly the same thing.) And then Christine, hearing this, would immediately call "Felipa!" and the child would dart after them, happy as a bird. She wore her boy's suit now all the time, because the señora had said she "looked well in it." What the señora really said was, that in boy's clothes she looked less like a grasshopper. But this had been translated as above by Edward Bowne when Felipa suddenly descended upon him one day and demanded to be instantly told what the gracious lady was saying about her; for she seemed to know by intuition when we spoke of her, although we talked in English and mentioned no names. When told, her small face beamed, and she kissed Christine's hand joyfully and bounded away. Christine took out her handkerchief and wiped the spot.

"Christine," I said, "do you remember the fate of the proud girl who walked upon bread?"

19. "To whose benefit?" (Lat.).

"You think that I may starve for kisses some time?" said my friend, going on with the wiping.

"Not while I am alive," called out Edward from behind. His style of courtship *was* of the sledge-hammer sort sometimes. But he did not get much for it on that day; only lofty tolerance, which seemed to amuse him greatly.

Edward played with Felipa very much as if she was a rubber toy or a little trapeze performer. He held her out at arm's length in mid-air, he poised her on his shoulder, he tossed her up into the low myrtle-trees, and dangled her by her little belt over the claret-colored pools on the barren; but he could not frighten her; she only laughed and grew wilder and wilder, like a squirrel. "She has muscles and nerves of steel," he said admiringly.

"Do put her down; she is too excitable for such games." I said in French, for Felipa seemed to divine our English now. "See the color she has."

For there was a trail of dark red over the child's thin oval cheeks which made her look unlike herself. As she caught our eyes fixed upon her, she suddenly stopped her climbing and came and sat at Christine's feet. "Some day I shall wear robes like the señora's," she said, passing her hand over the soft fabric; "and I think," she added after some slow consideration, "that my face will be like the señora's too."

Edward burst out laughing. The little creature stopped abruptly and scanned his face.

"Do not tease her," I said.

Quick as a flash she veered around upon me. "He does not tease me," she said angrily in Spanish; "and, besides, what if he does? I like it." She looked at me with gleaming eyes and stamped her foot.

"What a little tempest!" said Christine.

Then Edward, man-like, began to explain. "You could not look much like this lady, Felipa," he said, "because you are so dark, you know."

"Am I dark?"

"Very dark; but many people are dark, of course; and for my part I always liked dark eyes," said this mendacious person.

"Do you like my eyes?" asked Felipa anxiously.

"Indeed I do: they are like the eyes of a dear little calf I once owned when I was a boy."

The child was satisfied, and went back to her place beside Christine. "Yes, I shall wear robes like this," she said dreamily, drawing the flowing drapery over her knees clad in the little linen trousers, and scanning the effect; "they would trail behind me—so." Her bare feet peeped out below the hem, and again we all laughed, the little brown toes looked so comical coming out from the silk and the snowy embroideries. She came down to reality again, looked at us, looked at herself, and for the first time seemed to comprehend the difference. Then suddenly she threw herself down on the ground like a little animal, and buried her head in her arms. She would not speak, she would not look up: she only relaxed one arm a little to take in Drollo, and then lay motionless. Drollo looked at us out of one eye solemnly from his uncomfortable position, as much as to say: "No use; leave her to me." So after a while we went away and left them there.

That evening I heard a low knock at my door. "Come in," I said, and Felipa entered. I hardly knew her. She was dressed in a flowered muslin[20] gown which had probably belonged to her mother, and she wore her grandmother's stockings and large baggy slippers; on her mat of curly hair was perched a high-crowned, stiff white cap adorned with a ribbon streamer; and her lank little neck, coming out of the big gown, was decked with a chain of large sea-beans, like exaggerated lockets. She carried a Cuban fan[21] in her hand which was as large as a parasol, and Drollo, walking behind, fairly clanked with the chain of sea-shells which she had wound around him from head to tail. The droll tableau and the supreme pride on Felipa's countenance overcame me, and I laughed aloud. A sudden cloud of rage and disappointment came over the poor child's face: she threw her cap on the floor and stamped on it; she tore off her necklace and writhed herself out of her big flowered gown, and, running to Drollo, nearly strangled him in her fierce efforts to drag off his shell chains. Then, a half-dressed, wild little phantom, she seized me by the skirts and dragged me toward the looking-glass. "You are not pretty either," she cried. "Look at yourself! look at yourself!"

"I did not mean to laugh at you, Felipa," I said gently; "I would not laugh at any one; and it is true I am not pretty, as you say. I can never be pretty, child; but, if you will try to be more gentle, I could teach you how to dress yourself so that no one would laugh at you again. I could make you a little bright-barred[22] skirt and a scarlet bodice: you could help, and that would teach you to sew. But a little girl who wants all this done for her must be quiet and good."

20. Light, inexpensive cotton.
21. Made from the leaf of a Cuban Royal Palm.
22. Striped in bright colors.

"I am good," said Felipa; "as good as everything."

The tears still stood in her eyes, but her anger was forgotten: she improvised a sort of dance around my room, followed by Drollo dragging his twisted chain, stepping on it with his big feet, and finally winding himself up into a knot around the chair-legs.

"Couldn't we make Drollo something too? dear old Drollo!" said Felipa, going to him and squeezing him in an enthusiastic embrace. I used to wonder how his poor ribs stood it: Felipa used him as a safety-valve for her impetuous feelings.

She kissed me good night, and then asked for "the other lady."

"Go to bed, child," I said; "I will give her your good night."

"But I want to kiss her too," said Felipa.

She lingered at the door and would not go; she played with the latch, and made me nervous with its clicking; at last I ordered her out. But on opening my door half an hour afterward there she was sitting on the floor outside in the darkness, she and Drollo, patiently waiting. Annoyed, but unable to reprove her, I wrapped the child in my shawl and carried her out into the moonlight, where Christine and Edward were strolling to and fro under the pines. "She will not go to bed, Christine, without kissing you," I explained.

"Funny little monkey!" said my friend, passively allowing the embrace.

"Me too," said Edward, bending down. Then I carried my bundle back satisfied.

The next day Felipa and I in secret began our labors: hers consisted in worrying me out of my life and spoiling material—mine in keeping my temper and trying to sew. The result, however, was satisfactory, never mind how we got there. I led Christine out one afternoon: Edward followed. "Do you like tableaux?" [23] I said. "There is one I have arranged for you."

Felipa sat on the edge of the low, square-curbed Spanish well, and Drollo stood behind her, his great yellow body and solemn head serving as a background. She wore a brown petticoat barred with bright colors, and a little scarlet bodice fitting her slender waist closely; a chemisette [24] of soft cream-color with loose sleeves covered her neck and arms, and set off the dark hues of her cheeks and eyes; and around her curly hair a

23. Nineteenth-century pastime of arranging people and settings to portray famous paintings or stories or exotic scenes.

24. "Small shirt" (Fr.); underblouse of linen or silk.

red scarf was twisted, its fringed edges forming a drapery at the back of the head, which, more than anything else, seemed to bring out the latent character of her face. Brown moccasins, red stockings, and a quantity of bright beads completed her costume.

"By Jove!" cried Edward, "the little thing is almost pretty."

Felipa understood this, and a great light came into her face: forgetting her pose, she bounded forward to Christine's side. "I am pretty, then?" she said with exultation; "I *am* pretty, then, after all? For now you yourself have said it—have said it."

"No, Felipa," I interposed, "the gentleman said it." For the child had a curious habit of confounding the two identities which puzzled me then as now. But this afternoon, this happy afternoon, she was content, for she was allowed to sit at Christine's feet and look up into her fair face unmolested. I was forgotten, as usual.

"It is always so," I said to myself. But cynicism, as Mr. Aldrich[25] says, is a small brass field-piece[26] that eventually bursts and kills the artilleryman. I knew this, having been blown up myself more than once; so I went back to my painting and forgot the world. Our world down there on the edge of the salt-marsh, however, was a small one: when two persons went out of it there was a vacuum.

One morning Felipa came sadly to my side. "They have gone away," she said.

"Yes, child."

"Down to the beach to spend all the day."

"Yes, I know it."

"And without me!"

This was the climax. I looked up. Her eyes were dry, but there was a hollow look of disappointment in her face that made her seem old; it was as though for an instant you caught what her old-woman face would be half a century on.

"Why did they not take me?" she said. "I am pretty now: she herself said it."

"They can not always take you, Felipa," I replied, giving up the point as to who had said it.

"Why not? I am pretty now: she herself said it," persisted the child. "In these clothes, you know: she herself said it. The clothes of the son of Pedro you will never see more: they are burned."

25. Thomas Bailey Aldrich (1836–1907), influential U.S. author.
26. Small wheel-mounted gun or cannon, more showy than effective.

"Burned?"

"Yes, burned," replied Felipa composedly. "I carried them out on the barren and burned them. Drollo singed his paw. They burned quite nicely. But they are gone, and I am pretty now, and yet they did not take me! What shall I do?"

"Take these colors and make me a picture," I suggested. Generally, this was a prized privilege, but to-day it did not attract; she turned away, and a few moments after I saw her going down to the end of the plank-walk, where she stood gazing wistfully toward the ocean. There she staid all day, going into camp with Drollo, and refusing to come to dinner in spite of old Dominga's calls and beckonings. At last the patient old grandmother went down herself to the end of the long walk where they were, with some bread and venison on a plate. Felipa ate but little, but Drollo, after waiting politely until she had finished, devoured everything that was left in his calmly hungry way, and then sat back on his haunches with one paw on the plate, as though for the sake of memory. Drollo's hunger was of the chronic kind; it seemed impossible either to assuage it or to fill him. There was a gaunt leanness about him which I am satisfied no amount of food could ever fatten. I think he knew it too, and that accounted for his resignation. At length, just before sunset, the boat returned, floating up the marsh with the tide, old Bartolo steering and managing the brown sails. Felipa sprang up joyfully; I thought she would spring into the boat in her eagerness. What did she receive for her long vigil? A short word or two; that was all. Christine and Edward had quarreled.

How do lovers quarrel ordinarily? But I should not ask that, for these were no ordinary lovers: they were extraordinary.

"You should not submit to her caprices so readily," I said the next day while strolling on the barren with Edward. (He was not so much cast down, however, as he might have been.)

"I adore the very ground her foot touches, Kitty."

"I know it. But how will it end?"

"I will tell you: some of these days I shall win her, and then—she will adore me."

Here Felipa came running after us, and Edward immediately challenged her to a race: a game of romps began. If Christine had been looking from her window she might have thought he was not especially disconsolate over her absence; but she was not looking. She was never looking out of anything or for anybody. She was always serenely content where she was. Edward and Felipa strayed off among the pine-trees, and gradually I lost sight of them. But as I sat sketching an hour afterward Edward came into view, carrying the child in his arms. I hurried to meet them.

"I shall never forgive myself," he said; "the little thing has fallen and injured her foot badly, I fear."

"I do not care at all," said Felipa; "I like to have it hurt. It is *my* foot, isn't it?"

These remarks she threw at me defiantly, as though I had laid claim to the member in question. I could not help laughing.

"The other lady will not laugh," said the child proudly. And in truth Christine, most unexpectedly, took up the *rôle* of nurse. She carried Felipa to her own room—for we each had a little cell opening out of the main apartment—and as white-robed Charity she shone with new radiance. "Shone" is the proper word; for through the open door of the dim cell, with the dark little face of Felipa on her shoulder, her white robe and skin seemed fairly to shine, as white lilies shine on a dark night. The old grandmother left the child in our care and watched our proceedings wistfully, very much as a dog watches the human hands that extract the thorn from the swollen foot of her puppy. She was grateful and asked no questions; in fact, thought was not one of her mental processes. She did not think much; she felt. As for Felipa, the child lived in rapture during those days in spite of her suffering. She scarcely slept at all—she was too happy: I heard her voice rippling on through the night, and Christine's low replies. She adored her beautiful nurse.

The fourth day came: Edward Bowne walked into the cell. "Go out and breathe the fresh air for an hour or two," he said in the tone more of a command than a request.

"The child will never consent," replied Christine sweetly.

"Oh, yes, she will; I will stay with her," said the young man, lifting the feverish little head on his arm and passing his hand softly over the bright eyes.

"Felipa, do you not want me?" said Christine, bending down.

"He stays; it is all the same," murmured the child.

"So it is.—Go, Christine," said Edward with a little smile of triumph.

Without a word Christine left the cell. But she did not go to walk; she came to my room, and, throwing herself on my bed, fell in a moment into a deep sleep, the reaction after her three nights of wakefulness. When she awoke it was long after dark, and I had relieved Edward in his watch.

"You will have to give it up," he said as our lily came forth at last with sleep-flushed cheeks and starry eyes shielded from the light. "The spell is broken; we have all been taking care of Felipa, and she likes one as well as the other."

Which was not true, in my case at least, since Felipa had openly derided my small strength when I lifted her, and beat off the sponge with which I attempted to bathe her hot face. "They" used no sponges, she said, only their nice cool hands; and she wished "they" would come and take care of her again. But Christine had resigned *in toto*.[27] If Felipa did not prefer her to all others, then Felipa should not have her; she was not a common nurse. And indeed she was not. Her fair face, ideal grace, cooing voice, and the strength of her long arms and flexible hands, were like magic to the sick, and—distraction to the well; the well in this case being Edward Bowne looking in at the door.

"You love them very much, do you not, Felipa?" I said one day when the child was sitting up for the first time in a cushioned chair.

"Ah, yes; it is so strong when they carry me," she replied. But it was Edward who carried her.

"He is very strong," I said.

"Yes; and their long soft hair, with the smell of roses in it too," said Felipa dreamily. But the hair was Christine's.

"I shall love them for ever, and they will love me for ever," continued the child. "Drollo too." She patted the dog's head as she spoke, and then concluded to kiss him on his little inch of forehead; next she offered him all her medicines and lotions in turn, and he smelled at them grimly. "He likes to know what I am taking," she explained.

I went on: "You love them, Felipa, and they are fond of you. They will always remember you, no doubt."

"Remember!" cried Felipa, starting up from her cushions like a Jack-in-a-box. "They are not going away? Never! never!"

"But of course they must go some time, for—"

But Felipa was gone. Before I could divine her intent she had flung herself out of her chair down on the floor, and was crawling on her hands and knees toward the outer room. I ran after her, but she reached the door before me, and dragging her bandaged foot behind her, drew herself toward Christine. "You are *not* going away! You are not! you are not!" she sobbed, clinging to her skirts.

Christine was reading tranquilly; Edward stood at the outer door mending his fishing-tackle. The coolness between them remained, unwarmed

27. "In all" or "completely" (Lat.).

by so much as a breath. "Run away, child; you disturb me," said Christine, turning over a leaf. She did not even look at the pathetic little bundle at her feet. Pathetic little bundles must be taught some time what ingratitude deserves.

"How can she run, lame as she is?" said Edward from the doorway.

"You are not going away, are you? Tell me you are not," sobbed Felipa in a passion of tears, beating on the floor with one hand, and with the other clinging to Christine.

"I am not going," said Edward. "Do not sob so, you poor little thing!"

She crawled to him, and he took her up in his arms and soothed her into stillness again; then he carried her out on the barren for a breath of fresh air.

"It is a most extraordinary thing how that child confounds you two," I said. "It is a case of color-blindness, as it were—supposing you two were colors."

"Which we are not," replied Christine carelessly. "Do not stray off into mysticism, Catherine."

"It is not mysticism; it is a study of character—"

"Where there is no character," replied my friend.

I gave it up, but I said to myself: "Fate, in the next world make me one of those long, lithe, light-haired women, will you? I want to see how it feels."

Felipa's foot was well again, and spring had come. Soon we must leave our lodge on the edge of the pine-barren, our outlook over the salt-marsh, with the river sweeping up twice a day, bringing in the briny odors of the ocean; soon we should see no more the eagles far above us or hear the night-cry of the great owls, and we must go without the little fairy flowers of the barren, so small that a hundred of them scarcely made a tangible bouquet, yet what beauty! what sweetness! In my portfolio were sketches and studies of the salt-marsh, and in my heart were hopes. Somebody says somewhere: "Hope is more than a blessing; it is a duty and a virtue." But I fail to appreciate preserved hope—hope put up in cans and served out in seasons of depression. I like it fresh from the tree. And so when I hope it *is* hope, and not that well-dried, monotonous cheerfulness which makes one long to throw the persistent smilers out of the window. Felipa danced no more on the barrens; her illness had toned her down; she seemed content to sit at our feet while we talked, looking up dreamily into our faces, but no longer eagerly endeavoring to comprehend. We were there; that was enough.

"She is growing like a reed," I said; "her illness has left her weak."

"-Minded," suggested Christine.

At this moment Felipa stroked the lady's white hand tenderly and laid her brown cheek against it.

"Do you not feel reproached?" I said.

"Why? Must we give our love to whoever loves us? A fine parcel of paupers we should all be, wasting our inheritance in pitiful small change! Shall I give a thousand beggars a half hour's happiness, or shall I make one soul rich his whole life long?"

"The latter," remarked Edward, who had come up unobserved.

They gazed at each other unflinchingly. They had come to open battle during those last days, and I knew that the end was near. Their words had been cold as ice, cutting as steel, and I said to myself, "At any moment." There would be a deadly struggle, and then Christine would yield. Even I comprehended something of what that yielding would be.

"Why do they hate each other so?" Felipa said to me sadly.

"Do they hate each other?"

"Yes, for I feel it here," she answered, touching her breast with a dramatic little gesture.

"Nonsense! Go and play with your doll, child." For I had made her a respectable, orderly doll to take the place of the ungainly fetich out on the barren.

Felipa gave me a look and walked away. A moment afterward she brought the doll out of the house before my very eyes, and, going down to the end of the dock, deliberately threw it into the water; the tide was flowing out, and away went my toy-woman out of sight, out to sea.

"Well!" I said to myself. "What next?"

I had not told Felipa we were going; I thought it best to let it take her by surprise. I had various small articles of finery ready as farewell gifts, which should act as sponges to absorb her tears. But Fate took the whole matter out of my hands. This is how it happened: One evening in the jasmine[28] arbor, in the fragrant darkness of the warm spring night, the end came; Christine was won. She glided in like a wraith, and I, divining at once what had happened, followed her into her little room, where I found her lying on her bed, her hands clasped on her breast, her eyes open and veiled in soft shadows, her white robe drenched with dew. I kissed her fondly—I never could help loving her then or now—and next I went

28. Favorite southern vine with small, fragrant flowers.

out to find Edward. He had been kind to me all my poor gray life; should I not go to him now? He was still in the arbor, and I sat down by his side quietly; I knew that the words would come in time. They came; what a flood! English was not enough for him. He poured forth his love in the rich-voweled Spanish tongue also; it has sounded doubly sweet to me ever since.

> "Have you felt the wool of the beaver?
> Or swan's down ever?
> Or have smelt the bud o' the brier?
> Or the nard[29] in the fire?
> Or ha' tasted the bag o' the bee?
> Oh so white, oh so soft, oh so sweet is she!"[30]

said the young lover; and I, listening there in the dark fragrant night, with the dew heavy upon me, felt glad that the old simple-hearted love was not entirely gone from our tired metallic world.

It was late when we returned to the house. After reaching my room I found that I had left my cloak in the arbor. It was a strong fabric; the dew could not hurt it, but it could hurt my sketching materials and various trifles in the wide inside pockets—*objets de luxe*[31] to me, souvenirs of happy times, little artistic properties that I hang on the walls of my poor studio when in the city. I went softly out into the darkness again and sought the arbor; groping on the ground I found, not the cloak, but— Felipa! She was crouched under the foliage, face downward; she would not move or answer.

"What is the matter, child?" I said, but she would not speak. I tried to draw her from her lair, but she tangled herself stubbornly still farther among the thorny vines, and I could not move her. I touched her neck; it was cold. Frightened, I ran back to the house for a candle.

"Go away," she said in a low hoarse voice when I flashed the light over her. "I know all, and I am going to die. I have eaten the poison things in your box,[32] and just now a snake came on my neck and I let him. He has bitten me, and I am glad. Go away; I am going to die."

I looked around; there was my color-case rifled and empty, and the

29. Aromatic Himalayan plant.

30. Lines from "Celebration of Charis," by British poet Ben Jonson (1572–1637).

31. "Objects of luxury" (Fr.); treasures.

32. Artists' supplies contained lead and arsenic.

other articles were scattered on the ground. "Good Heavens, child!" I cried, "what have you eaten?"

"Enough," replied Felipa gloomily. "I knew they were poisons; you told me so. And I let the snake stay."

By this time the household, aroused by my hurried exit with the candle, came toward the arbor. The moment Edward appeared Felipa rolled herself up like a hedgehog [33] again and refused to speak. But the old grandmother knelt down and drew the little crouching figure into her arms with gentle tenderness, smoothing its hair and murmuring loving words in her soft dialect.

"What is it?" said Edward; but even then his eyes were devouring Christine, who stood in the dark vine-wreathed doorway like a picture in a frame. I explained.

Christine smiled. "Jealousy," she said in a low voice. "I am not surprised."

But at the first sound of her voice Felipa had started up, and, wrenching herself free from old Dominga's arms, threw herself at Christine's feet. "Look at *me* so," she cried—"me too; do not look at him. He has forgotten poor Felipa; he does not love her any more. But *you* do not forget, señora; *you* love me—*you* love me. Say you do, or I shall die!"

We were all shocked by the pallor and the wild, hungry look of her uplifted face. Edward bent down and tried to lift her in his arms; but when she saw him a sudden fierceness came into her eyes; they shot out yellow light and seemed to narrow to a point of flame. Before we knew it she had turned, seized something, and plunged it into his encircling arm. It was my little Venetian dagger.

We sprang forward; our dresses were spotted with the fast-flowing blood; but Edward did not relax his hold on the writhing, wild little body he held until it lay exhausted in his arms. "I am glad I did it," said the child, looking up into his face with her inflexible eyes. "Put me down— put me down, I say, by the gracious señora, that I may die with the trailing of her white robe over me." And the old grandmother with trembling hands received her and laid her down mutely at Christine's feet.

Ah, well! Felipa did not die. The poisons racked but did not kill her, and the snake must have spared the little thin brown neck so despairingly offered to him. We went away; there was nothing for us to do but to go away

33. Nocturnal mammal that protects itself by rolling into a ball.

as quickly as possible and leave her to her kind. To the silent old grand-father I said: "It will pass; she is but a child."

"She is nearly twelve, señora. Her mother was married at thirteen."

"But she loved them both alike, Bartolo. It is nothing; she does not know."

"You are right, lady; she does not know," replied the old man slowly; "but *I* know. It was two loves, and the stronger thrust the knife."

Katharine (Sherwood Bonner) McDowell

(1849–1883)

BORN ON FEBRUARY 26, 1849, in the prosperous cotton town of Holly Springs in northern Mississippi, Sherwood Bonner's childhood was marked by material privilege, including formal education in Holly Springs and Montgomery, Alabama. Her father was an Irish immigrant who became a doctor; her mother, Mary Wilson, the daughter of wealthy southern planters. Her family's comfortable status was shattered by the Civil War as her hometown became the site of sixty Union and Confederate raids. The wartime hardships also hastened the death of her mother in 1865. But Bonner's powerful ambition was already manifest, and at fifteen she published her first story in a Boston journal, whose editor helped her to place other stories and later introduced her to an influential literary circle in Boston.

In 1871, Kate married fellow Mississippian Edward McDowell. Even with the birth later that year of their daughter, Lilian, the marriage soon foundered on McDowell's unsuccessful financial schemes and Kate's frustrated literary aspirations. In a move that would profoundly shape her career and reputation, Kate set out for Boston in 1873—without her husband or daughter, though she had planned that Lilian would join her later. Assisted by her first editor and her own determination, Kate was soon hired as an amanuensis by the aging but revered poet Henry Wadsworth Longfellow. Their flirtatious, though Platonic, affection for each other proved a lifelong source of support for Kate as well as the occasion for scandal, which was hardly ameliorated by her composition of a popular satire on Boston society in 1875. That same year under her new literary name, Sherwood Bonner, *Youth's Companion,* one of the nation's largest periodicals, published "Gran'mamy's [*sic*] Last Gift" on the front page of its July issue.

Though Bonner published several early romances when she was still a teenager and later experimented with the melodramatic formulas that brought fame to Bret Harte (Bonner attended Harte's 1873 Boston reading), the Gran'mammy story was noticeably fresh. With its use of black dialect, it incorporated both a black female type and a narrative feature that became standards of local color. Drawing on her intimate knowledge of southern domestic life and on her fond recollections of Molly Wilson, her childhood nurse, Bonner eventually published six Gran'mammy tales between 1875 and 1880, which she revised for *Dialect Tales* (1883), giving the mammy figure an even more prominent role. Despite Bonner's obvious affection for these characters, her stories do tend to caricature blacks for comic effect. Bonner's humor, often cited as her forte, also places her work in the rowdy Southwest tradition, which influenced early female humorists like Frances Whitcher and Marietta Holley as well as Bonner's contemporaries, Mary N. Murfree and Ruth M. Stuart.

Though Bonner's stories proved popular, she also supported herself with newspaper work and published a successful series of letters from Europe in 1876. Facing pressure from her family, Bonner attempted to reconcile with McDowell, but in 1877 again returned to Boston, this time with the manuscript of *Like unto Like,* published by *Harper's* in 1878 and dedicated to Longfellow. Bonner's only novel establishes the theme of sectional reconciliation that was to become a standard in southern local color and, two decades before Kate Chopin's *The Awakening,* subtly delineates the heroine's conflicts between marriage and selfhood. That same summer, a virulent epidemic of yellow fever struck the South, and Bonner raced home to rescue Lilian, whom she brought out safely, but not before she watched her father and brother die within hours of one another.

Though Bonner continued to write, financial pressures and the recognition that only divorce could help resolve her ambivalent social status began to take their toll. In 1880, she and Lilian moved to Illinois, where distant relatives enabled her to take advantage of the state's divorce laws. While there, Bonner composed a tartly comic serial romance, *The Valcours* (1881), and a number of children's stories, doubtless inspired by her renewed proximity to her daughter. She also wrote several fine vernacular tales set in the fundamentalist culture of southern Illinois; the first of this region, the stories aligned her with Indiana local colorists like Edward Eggleston and James Whitcomb Riley.

The discovery of a lump in her breast increased Bonner's anxious efforts to publish. She spent much of the next eighteen months resolutely writing and securing publication of her works, returning to Holly Springs just five months before her death on July 22, 1883. *Dialect Tales,* which includes the Gran'mammy stories and "Jack and the Mountain Pink," appeared three months before she died; *Suwanee River Tales* was published posthumously in 1884.

Bonner's fiction consistently reflects her genuine originality and her eagerness to cater to popular tastes. While her black dialect sketches and pioneering southern material reflect an innovative realism, many of her stories are melodramatic and imitate other successful writers like Cable and Murfree. But even Bonner's adaptations of others' materials exhibit her own inventive touch, such as the creation in "Jack and the Mountain Pink" of the sensuous and promiscuous mountain girl, a concept, that like her black dialect sketches, would be widely imitated. Bonner's scandalous independence almost superseded her literary reputation over the next half-century, but her work has recently received deserved appreciation for its lively ironic realism and impressive variety.

Works by Sherwood Bonner

Like unto Like, 1878, ed. Jane Turner Censer, 1997

Dialect Tales, 1883

Suwanee River Tales, 1884

Dialect Tales and Other Stories, ed. William L. Frank, 1990

A Sherwood Bonner Sampler, 1869–1884, ed. Anne Razey Gowdy, 2000

Further Reading

Biglane, Jean Nosser. "Sherwood Bonner: A Bibliography of Primary and Secondary Materials." *American Literary Realism, 1870–1910* 5 (1972): 39–60.

Frank, William L. *Sherwood Bonner (Catherine McDowell)*. Boston: Twayne, 1976.

McAlexander, Hubert H. *The Prodigal Daughter: A Biography of Sherwood Bonner*. 1981; Knoxville: University of Tennessee Press, 1999.

Gran'mammy

In our Southern home we were very fond of our old colored mammy, who had petted and scolded and nursed and coddled,—yes, and spanked us,— from the time we were born.

She was not a "black mammy," for her complexion was the color of clear coffee; and we did not call her "mammy," but "gran'mammy," because she had nursed our mother when a little delicate baby,—loving her foster child, I believe, more than her own, and loving us for our dear mother's sake.

She was all tenderness when we were wee toddlers, not more than able to clutch at the great gold hoops in her ears, or cling to her ample skirts like little burrs; but she showed a sharper side as we grew old enough to "bother round the kitchen," with inquisitive eyes and fingers and tongues. I regret to say that she sometimes called us "limbs,"[1] and would wonder, with many a groan and shake of the head, how we contrived to hold so much of the Evil One in our small frames.

"I never seed sich chillern in all my born days," she cried one day, when Ruth interrupted her in the midst of custard-making, to beg leave to get into the kettle of boiling soap that she might be clean once for all, and never need another bath; while Sam, on the other side, entreated that she would make three "points"[2] of gravy with the fried chicken for dinner. (Sam always came out strong on pronunciation; his very errors leaned to virtue's side.)[3]

"I clar to gracious," said poor gran'mammy, "you'll drive all de sense clean outen my head. How Miss Mary 'xpec's me ter git a dinner fitten fur white folks ter eat, wid you little onruly sinners *furever* under foot, is mo' dan I kin say. An' here's Leah an' Rachel,[4] my own gran'chillern, a no mo' use ter me dan two tar-babies!"

She looked very threatening as she shook her rolling-pin at her two idle grandchildren. They only grinned in an aggravating way; for to them as well as to us, the great wide kitchen, with its roomy fire-place, where the back-log glowed and the black kettle swung, was the pleasantest place in the world.

As gran'mammy grew older, her manner softened; her love was less fluctuating. It was she to whom we ran to tell of triumphs and sorrows; she, whose sympathy, ash-cakes,[5] and turnover-pies never failed us! It was she who hung over our sick-beds; who told us stories more beautiful than

---

1. Originally a "limb" of the body of Christ, or Christian; later "a limb of Lucifer," typically applied to mischievous children.

2. "Pints."

3. That is, his errors resulted from trying too hard (to be correct).

4. Sisters who were Jacob's wives (Genesis 29).

5. Cornmeal bread baked in hot ashes.

we read in any books; who sang to us old-fashioned hymns of praise and faith; and who talked to us with childlike simplicity of the God whom she loved.

During the troubled four years that swept like the hot breath of the simoon [6] over our country, she was true to the family. Her love, her courage, her faithful work, helped us to bear up under our heavy trials. And when the gentle mother whose life had been set to such sweet music that her spirit broke in the discords of dreadful war, sank out of life, it was in gran'mammy's arms that she died; and neither husband nor children mourned more tenderly for the beautiful life cut short.

Like most of her race, gran'mammy told a story well. Among the earliest that I remember, is one told to us when we were very small children, so complete, so naïve, so crowded with moral, as to deserve a chapter all to itself.

———— ✤ ————

Why Gran'mammy Didn't Like Pound-Cake

There had been a birthday party at our house, and, owing to a recent fit of illness, gran'mammy had been unable to take any part in the festivity. So the day after the party we piled up a basket with good things and started off, swinging it on a long pole, of which Ruth held one end and I the other. Gran'mammy's cabin was quite at the end of the negro quarter; a pretty log-house with roses growing over it and shaded by fine hickory trees. Evidently she was getting well fast; for we heard her singing. Long before we reached her house the swift wind bore to our ears these very queer words, sung to a see-saw tune:——

> "You may *back*-bite me
> Jes' as *much* as you please.
> Jes' gi' me deliverin' grace,
> An' I'll sail away
> On de golden seas.
> Jes' gi' me deliverin' grace!
> O Lord! han' down my crown!
> O Lord! han' *doown* my crown!"

6. "Simoom," a suffocating desert wind (i.e., the Civil War).

There sat gran'mammy, rocking back and forth in a great chair that Uncle Ned had made for her, warranted not to break down under her weight; for she was fat.

"Tell you what, I *tips* things I stan's on!" she used to say.

There was a legend in the family that our grandfather had bought our old mammy for her weight in silver dollars. She was a slim young girl then. She was worth her weight in gold now; but only a Bonanza[7] or a Golconda[8] man could have bought her.

"Lor, chillern!" she said, kissing us all round, "I's powerful glad ter see you. 'Pears like I gits lonesome wid on'y de birds an' dat little trash on de flo' fur company."

"Dat little trash on de flo'" consisted of half-a-dozen sprawling black babies, left in gran'mammy's charge, while their mothers were in the cotton field.

"We've brought you some of my birthday, grammy," said Sam, with an air of importance.

"So you did manage ter make out a party widout me!" cried gran'-mammy. "Well! well!" with innocent pride, "Becky is a tollerbul fust-class cook. I learnt her all she knows!"

We unpacked the basket,—turkey and jelly, and light bread, and wafers grey with sugar and rolled round in the most delicate curves, and fruit-cake and cup-cake, and a whole half of a pound-cake loaf.

"Why, chillern!" she cried with a start, "don't you know dat I don't love pound-cake?"

"Don't like pound-cake!" cried Sam, his eyes distended. "Well, I do!" And he took a great bite out of the loaf in an absent-minded sort of way.

"Why, gran'mammy?" said I, "why don't you?"

"I'll tell you why, chillern, an' let de warnin' sink inter you deep as a track inter de snow; but don't you let it melt away cause you lives in de sunshine!"[9]

So saying, gran'mammy lit a cob-pipe, settled herself comfortably and began:—

"Long time ago, my blessin's, I was a little gal. An' I wus a limb—I wus. Ole Mis', she had an *awful* time wid me. 'Pears as if imps hed possession o' me. Howmsoever, she kept a-b'arin' wid me, an' a-b'arin' wid me, till de time come when she couldn't bar *no mo*'. An' de way it happened

7. Literally, "fair weather" or "prosperity" (Fr., Sp.). Colloquial reference to a profitable mine.

8. A ruined city in India (1512–1687) known for its diamond trade.

9. "Don't forget the warning just because things are good now."

wus dis. Dar wus a pretty young lady in de nex' county from us who went an' got married. An' ole Mis' had a keard ter de weddin'.[10] Well now, as luck would have it, she wus took sick de very day ov de weddin'. She wus bilious I recollec', and jes' de color ov clover cream she wus! So she could n't go. An' she sont *me* — fur I wus her little maid — wid a gret basket ov jerponicas an' vi'lets an' geraniums. It wus winter, an' flowers wus skeerce; so dat wus a very pretty gif' for de young Miss dat wus about ter marry.

"Bless you, chillern! did n't I enjoy myse'f? I rid in a waggin ter de weddin', — for it wus a matter of ten mile or so in de country. An' when we got dar, all de groun's wus lighted wid pine knots[11] burnin' in forked sticks high as a man's head. Nothin' like dat beauty an' gorgeousness in dese days! Pooh! ef you had seen one weddin' like dat o' Miss Josephine Dandridge, you would n't roll off a log ter look at one now!

"Miss Josephine, she wus as white an' shinin' an' smilin' as an angel, but when she led off de dance, she blushed like a sweet rose. An' *sich* a weddin' supper! I et as much as I could fur de excitement; but my eyes was so eager to see all dat wus a-goin' on, an' my heart wus a-beatin' so fas' to de sound ov de music, dat I did n't do no manner of justice to de feast. More's de pity too! fur dat's one reason why I fell from grace de nex' day.

"Miss Josephine was gwine to her husband's house acrost de line of de State fur de *infair*.[12] Ever heard ov an *infair*, chillern? Well, dat's de gret, gret cillybration give by de young man's folks to de bridle an' de broom—"

"De bridle an' de broom?" echoed Sam, vaguely.

"In course, boy. What else should I call de young pa'r?" said gran'mammy, with severity.

"Well, in all de hurry of gittin' off, Miss Josephine writ a note to my ole Mis' a-thankin' her fur de flowers, an' a-sendin' her a big slice o' weddin'-cake; an' den she says:—

"'Why, ma! here's a poun'-cake dat has n't ben cut! S'pose we sen' it ter Mis' Rout',—dat was my Mis'.

"So, honeys, dey done up dat poun'-cake in silver paper, an' put it in a basket, an' give it to me wid dese words:—

"'Take dat to your mistis, Mariar.'

"'Yes'm,' says I.

"But lor, chillern! I wus a *limb!*

10. "Card to the wedding," invitation.

11. A stick of resinous pine, used for lighting.

12. "Infare," from *hin fahren* (Ger. "in going"); an early Scottish custom of celebrating the bride's moving into a new home.

"I tell you, I smelt dat poun'-cake all de way home, an' a v'ice, as close ter my ear as a flower in a young lady's hair, kep' sayin':

" 'Molly, you little goose, jes' *eat* dat cake. You'll never have sich anudder chance.'

"Ter be short wid it, chillern, I listened ter de v'ice, an' when I got home, I handed de slice o' weddin'-cake to Ole Mis', an' told her all about de weddin', lookin' as innercent as a lily; an' all de time wus dat poun'-cake hid away under de waggin seat.

"Jes' as soon as night fell, I stole up de stairs to ole Mis's room, an' I snuggled under de bed, an' I *et de poun'-cake!* De fust bite tasted as if all de stars had turned to cake an' was a-meltin' in my mouth; but to tell you de trufe,—an', Sam, you listen,—I had ter sort o' *push* de las' piece down.

"But eat it I did, to de las' crumb. Den I laid down, kind o' composed, an' went ter sleep. I was waked up by de mos' awful kind o' gripin' pain,— struck me somewhar inside like lightnin',—an' I jumped up an' screamed. Ole Mis', she came a-runnin' up,—seventy years ole do she wus,—an' says:—

" 'What's de matter, you little screech-owl?' She always called me by some pet-name, Ole Mis' did.

"An' seein' me all doubled up wid pain, she rings de bell, an' she says to little weakly Partridge, who answered it, 'Tell Uncle Dowdy to git on de fastest mule an' go fer de doctor, *quick!*'

"Den she turned ter me, a-squirmin' an' a-howlin' like a baby, on de flo', an' she says ter me, as still an' terrible as de pestilence:—

" 'What has you been eatin', Mariar?'

"It wasn't no use tryin' ter lie, my chillern; so I says, weak-like:—

" 'I *et* a whole poun'-cake dat Miss Josephine sent ter you.'

" 'I shall whip you for dat falsehood,' says Ole Mis', 'as soon as you is recovered. It is impossible dat a chile of your age could eat a whole poun'- cake. You might as well talk of a toad swallowin' a cat.'

"Den I give anudder screech, fur it seemed as if dat cake had turned to a cat, an' wus clawin' me.

"Arter about a million years o' sufferin', de doctor got dar; and he says:—

" 'Seems as if dis chile's stomach is been overloaded.'

"I jes' rolled my eyes up at him. I was tu fur gone ter speak.

"Well, he wrestled wid me *all night*, chillern; an' de nex' mornin' dar I wus, gaspin' like a fish out of water, but *saved*. Ole Mis', she handed de doctor somethin' folded up in an envelope, an' he went a-sailin' off. Den she looked at me. I wus powerful weak, so I went off kind o' faint-like.

"She nussed me like a baby; an' when I got well she never said one word ter me, excep' jes' dis:—

"'Mariar, you need n't ter come ter my Sunday-school class termorrer.'

"I bu'st out a-cryin' at dat, an' I said:—

"'Mis' Jane, I owns up. I et de cake, an' I'm a miserbel sinner; but if you will try me agin, I'll try to do a better part.'

"And den, honeys, she jes' knelt down, wid her little white han' on my head, and she prayed fur me, soft an' solemn.

"Well, I ain't never wanted to steal nothin' sence dat hour; an' I never has been able to look at a piece o' poun'-cake."

Silence.

"Anyhow," said Sam, "pound-cake is good."

"Yes, my boy," said our dear old gran'mammy; "but many a good thing is turned ter poison if you take it on de sly. You's mighty safe ter pend on dat ar trufe!"

———— ✣ ————

Jack and the Mountain Pink

Young Selden was bored. Who was not bored among the men? It was the tense summer of '78.[13] A forlorn band of refugees from the plague crowded a Nashville hotel. There was nothing for the men to do but to read the fever bulletins, play billiards in an insensate sort of way, and keep out of the way of the women crying over the papers.

Young Selden felt that another month of this sort of thing would leave him melancholy mad. So he jammed some things in a light bag and started off for a tramp over Cumberland Mountain.[14]

"I envy you," said a decrepit old gentleman, with whom he was shaking hands in good-bye. "I was brought up in the mountain country fifty years ago. Gay young buck I was! Go in my boy, and make love to a mountain pink![15] Ah, those jolly, barefooted, melting girls! No corsets, no back hair, no bangs, by Heaven!"

13. The year 1878−79 marked a devastating epidemic of yellow fever across the southern United States, with nearly sixteen thousand deaths. A tropical disease carried by mosquitoes, it causes high fever, hemorrhaging, and jaundice. Nashville's higher and cooler elevations offered some protection. Bonner lost her father and brother in this epidemic and wrote elsewhere about its effects on Holly Springs.

14. A scenic area about a hundred miles northeast of Nashville, whose important towns included Bloomington Springs and Cookeville.

15. A pink wildflower that blooms in early summer.

It was the afternoon of a hot September day. Young Selden had started that morning from Bloomington Springs in the direction of the Window Cliff—a ridge of rocks from which he had been told a very fine view could be obtained. The road grew rougher and wilder, seeming to lose itself in hills, stumps, and fields, and was as hard to trace out as a *Bazar*[16] pattern. He finally struck a foot-path leading to a log-cabin, where a very brown woman sat peacefully smoking in the door-way.

"Good-day," he said, taking off his hat.

The brown woman nodded in a friendly manner—the little short, meaning nod of the mountains, that serves, so to speak, as the pro-word of these silent folk. Young Selden inquired the way to Window Cliff.

"You carn't git thar 's the crow flies," she drawled, slowly, "but I reckin my daughter k'n g'long with yer."

"Aha!" thought Selden—"a mountain pink!"

"Take a cheer," said the mother, rising and going within. He seated himself on the steps, and made friends with a dog or two.

A young girl soon appeared, tying on a sun-bonnet. She greeted him with a nod, the reproduction of her mother's, and drawled, in the same tone, "Reckin you couldn't git tu Winder Clift 'thout somebody to show you the way."

"And you will be my guide?"

" 'F co'se."

They started off, young Selden talking airily. He soon felt, however, that he shouldn't make love to *this* mountain pink. To begin with, there was no pink about her. She was brown, like her mother.

"Coffee!" thought Selden, with a grim remembrance of a black, muddy liquid he had drunk a few nights before at a log-cabin, over which the very babies smacked their lips.

Her eyes had the melancholy of a cow's, without the ruminative expression that gives sufficient intellectuality to a cow's sad gaze. To put it tersely, they looked stupid. Her mouth curled down a little at each corner. Her hair was not visible under her pea-green sun-bonnet. Her dress of whitish linsey[17] was skimpy in its cut, and she wriggled in it as if it were a loose skin she was trying to get out of.

She was not a talker. She looked at Selden with big eyes and listened

16. *Harper's Bazaar,* founded in 1867, was a popular periodical that provided tissue-paper patterns for making fashionable clothing.

17. A coarse cloth of cotton and wool, here undyed.

impassively. He elicited from her that her name was Sincerity Hicks; that her mother was the widder Hicks, and there were no others in the family; that she had never been to school, but could read, only she had no books.

"Should you like some?"

"Dunno. 'Pears 's if thar's too much to do t' fool over books."

Perhaps because he had talked so much young Selden began to get out of breath. They had crossed a field, climbed a fence, and were descending a great hill, breaking a path as they walked. He panted, and could hardly keep up with Sincerity, though she seemed not to walk fast. But she got over the ground with a light-footed agility that aroused his envy. It looked easy, but, since he could not emulate her, he concluded that long practice had trained her walk to its perfection. He noticed, too, that she walked "parrot-footed," placing each new track in the impression of the other. Imitating this, awkwardly enough, he got on better.

Reaching the clear level at the bottom of the hill, he saw at a glance that he had penetrated to a wild and virginal heart of beauty. Like a rough water-fall melting into a silver-flowing river, the vexatious and shaggy hill sloped to a dreaming valley. Streams ran about, quietly as thoughts, over pale rocks. Calacanthus[18] bushes, speckled with their ugly little red blooms, filled the air with a fragrance like that of crushed strawberries. Up-springing from this low level of prettiness rose the glory of the valley— the lordly, the magnificent birch-trees. Their topmost boughs brushed against the cliffs that shut in the valley on the opposite side. How fine these cliffs were! They rose up almost perpendicularly, and, freed halfway of their height from the thick growth of underbrush, stood out in bare, bold picturesqueness. Window Cliffs! Aha! these were the windows. Two wide spaces, square and clean-blown, framing always a picture—now a bit of hard blue sky; other times pink flushes of sunrise, or the voluptuous moon and peeping eyes of stars.

"Want ter go t' the top?" inquired Sincerity.

"I—dunno," rejoined Selden, lazily. Truth was, he did not wish to move. He liked the vast shadows, the cool deeps, the singing tones of the valley. Then he was sure he had a blister on his heel. Still, to come so far—"How long a walk is it?"

"Oh, jest a little piece—'bout a quarter."

"Up and away, then!" cried young Selden.

A long "quarter" he found that walk. They crossed the valley, climbed

18. *Calycanthus floridus* or hairy allspice, flowers April–August.

a fence, and dropped into a corn-field to be hobbled over. Up and down those hideous little furrows—it was as sickening as tossing on a chopping sea. Selden stopped to rest. Sincerity, not a feather the worse, looked him over with mild patience.

"Lemme tote yo' haversack," she said.

"No, no," said the young man, with an honest blush. But he was reminded of a flask of brandy in his knapsack, of which he took a grateful swig.

"Now," said his guide, as, the corn-field crossed, they emerged into forest—"now we begins to climb the mountain."

Selden groaned. He had thought himself nearly on a level with the Window Cliff. To this day that climb is an excruciating memory to young Selden. He thought of

> "Johnny Schnapps,
> Who bust his shtraps,"

and wondered if the disaster was not suffered in going up a mountain. He felt himself melting away with heat. He knew that his face was blazing like a Christmas pudding, and dripping like a roast on a spit. He resigned the attempt to keep up with Sincerity. When they started on this excruciating tramp the droop of her pea-green sun-bonnet had seemed him abject; now he knew that it expressed only contempt—contempt for the weakling and the stranger.

But one gets to the top of most things by trying hard enough, and they gained at last the rough crags that commanded the valley.

Ah! the fair, grand State! There was a spot for a blind man to receive sight! The young man drew a long breath as he gazed over the bewitching expanse. All so fresh, so unbreathed-on, the only hints of human life the little log-cabins perched about, harmonious as birds' nests amid their surroundings.

Sincerity Hicks stood fanning herself with the green sun-bonnet. There was something pretty about her, now that this disfigurement was removed. But a mountain pink—what a pretty implication in the name!—no.

"So this is Window Cliff?" he said. "And is there any particular name for that ledge yonder?"

"'Tis called Devil's Chimney, 'nd the cut between is Long Hungry Gap."

"Long Hungry Gap?—where have I heard that famished name? Oh yes, some of Peters's scouts. You know Peters?"

"Yaas, I've heerd tell o' Jim Peters."

Sincerity's drawl was not quickened, but Selden was surprised to see a light leap into her eyes as suddenly as a witch through a key-hole.

"These fellows had a room next to mine at the Bloomington Hotel," Selden went on, "and the walls are like paper; so I heard all they said."

"And what d' they say?"

"Well, that the captain was up the country on a moonshine raid; but that they were on the track of something better—had heard of a 'powerful big still' up in Long Hungry Gap—and would mash it up as soon as the captain got back."

"D' they say when Peters wuz expected?"

"The next day."

Sincerity tied on her bonnet.

"Guess you kin find the way back," she remarked.

"Hello! what does this mean?"

"I've got somethin' t' attend to across' the mounting."

"I'll go with you."

Sincerity stopped and turned a serious face. "Likely 's not you'll git hurt."

"Oho! I'm *in*, if there's any chance of a scrimmage. Go ahead."

She did go ahead. If the path had been vexatious before, now it was revengeful and aggressive. In fact, there was no path. But Sincerity, like love, found out a way. Suddenly, like a comic mask popped on a friend's face, something sinister and strange burst upon them through the familiar woods. Or, rather, they burst upon it—a wild-cat still, securely sheltered under an innocent combination of rocks, ferns, and magnolia-trees.

Four or five wild-looking fellows sprang up, their hands on their rifles.

"None o' yo' shootin'," said Sincerity Hicks; "he's a friend."

"Sho' he ain't a spy? 'Cause if that's the case, mister, you'll stay in these woods face down."

"My impetuous moonshiner, I don't call myself the friend of you law-breakers, but I'm no spy. I brought the news to the faithful Sincerity of Captain Peters being on your track."

Hurried questions were asked and answered. Several resolute voices suggested to fight it out, but all seemed to await the decision of an old man they called Jack, who leaned against a tub, with a touching expression of meekness under unmerited ill-luck.

"No, boys," he said; "we ain't strong enough. But we'll run off what we can. Save the copper—we'll never git another so big an' satisfactory—an' the mash tun, an' as many of the tubs 's you can git off."

It was a transformation scene. Things seemed to fly to pieces all at once, like a bomb-shell. The great copper still was hoisted on the shoulders of two or three men; the worm, the mash tun, the coolers, were taken down with celerity, and the unlucky moonshiners made off through the woods.

"Reckin th' rest 'll have ter go," said Jack, pensively; "but tell you what, Sincerity Hicks, seems 's if I couldn't b'ar to have 'em git th' old sow an' her pigs." [19]

"Run 'em off."

"They're too young, honey. Come 'ere."

He led to a mimosa-tree [20] behind a rock; and under its sensitive shade reposed, like Father Nile, a portly porcine mother, overrun with little, pink, blind pigs.

"Ain't you got a spar' tub?" asked the girl.

His face lighted. "I catches," [21] he said, gently.

He brought an empty whiskey puncheon, and covered the bottom with straw. Then he lifted the pink pigs into it, assisted by Sincerity and the elegant Selden.

The mother squealed. "Stuff her mouth," ordered the old man.

Sincerity thrust an ear of corn into the open jaws.

"Now," said Jack, "I'll run briefly through the woods, a-toting this, an' the old sow she'll follow—"

"No, you don't, Jack Boddy!" said a quiet voice. "Smell o' that."

The ugly end of a rifle protruded itself. A Tennessee giant leaned against the rock. Peters? Of course it was Peters. What other man had that easy swagger, three feet of black beard, and as wide a grin in saying checkmate?

19. Pigs were fed the waste mash of cornmeal and other grains from liquor distillation to minimize the evidence of hidden stills. In the nineteenth and early twentieth centuries, moonshiners illegally produced liquor throughout the rugged mountains of the Southeast. The often violent policing by tax agents (revenuers) peaked during Reconstruction with two thousand arrests a year between 1875–80.

20. Originally Asian, a popular southern tree with feathery pink flowers.

21. "I understand."

Jack Boddy smiled innocently.

"Why, captain, you see me jest attendin' to a litter o' pigs o' mine."

"Yes, I see. An' my men is attendin' to some pigs o' yourn. Walk out, old 'coon."

Peters's scouts were destroying all that was left of the mountain still.

"Whar's the others?" asked one of the men.

"I run this here still all by myself," said Jack, with an air of ingenuous pride.

"What a lie!" said the captain. "Have you cut his copper boiler, boys?"

" 'Tain't here.

"Whar's your copper, Jack?"

"Gone to heaven," said Jack, rolling his eyes.

"You can't make anything out o' Jack Boddy," said a scout, grinning.

"Well, I've got you, anyhow," cried the captain.

"An' the oldest one in the business, Jim."

"An' I'll ketch the rest in time. Come on, boys. We'll stop at the widder Hicks's to-night. Can your mother put us up, Sissy?"

"Dunno," said Sincerity.

"Mighty know-nothin' all of a sudden." And turning to Selden: "You're a stranger, I see, mister. On the cirkit?" [22]

"Not at all; only a traveller. Climbed the Window Cliff, and stumbled over here."

" 'F you'd been in these parts a year or so ago," said an old man, relieving his mouth of the white whiskers he was chewing, "you'd 'a seen a sight o' stills. They were thick as weevils in flour. But a man of might arose in the land, and he cleared 'em out."

"Peters, I suppose?"

"Yessir—James Cook Peters, whose name ought to be Gideon, the Sword of the Lord; formerly an ignorant blacksmith of Tipper County, but advanced, by the grace of God an' the app'intment of gov'ment, to bust wild-cat stills, an' flood the earth with hot whiskey a-steamin' from the vats."

"Any—er—murderin' involved in the blacksmithin' trade?" inquired Jack Boddy, with a casual air of interest.

Captain Peters turned an angry red, but said nothing.

"Becaze," continued the artless old man, "it's a pretty bloody business

22. "Circuit riders" were itinerant ministers in a district.

you've took up now. How many men have you killed? Five, I b'lieve, with your own hand, an' twenty-one with yer men."

"It wuz a fair fight," said the captain. "I killed 'em honorable, an' wuz acquitted by the laws o' my country."

"And though their numbers should be seventy times seven," said the white-haired satellite of the captain, "and the land run with blood, this thing has got to be put a stop to."

"Look a-here, James Riggs," said Jack, "this here moonshinin' is jest like a wriggle-worm. Don't you know, howsoever many pieces you chop 'em into, a fresh head 'll grow, an' a new worm swim away? Tell you, you can't stop moonshinin' 's long's there's an honest man in Old Hickory's[23] State."

"The Lord commanded, and the sun stood still," said James Riggs; "'twon't be no harder job 'n that."

As they talked, they were descending the mountain. The noble Jack, alas! was handcuffed and guarded between two men. From time to time he scratched his head against the end of a rifle that was nearer his ear than some men would have liked. Evidently, though open to reproach, Mr. Boddy was a knight without fear.

The widow Hicks manifested no surprise at the coming of her guests. They found her with her hands plunged into a great tray of meal and water—enough to make hoe-cake for a regiment.

"Hurry up with supper, old woman," said Captain Peters. "I'm dead tired. I rid all last night, an' ain't slept for three nights runnin'."

At supper he could barely keep his eyes open.

"I'll turn in right off," he said.

There were some preliminaries to be gone through with—not of prayers or undressing, however. The captain eyed his prisoner thoughtfully, and remarked, "B'lieve they call you Slippery Jack?"

"I am kind of hard to hold," said Mr. Boddy, with a modest twinkle.

"So!"

Another moment, and Jack was tightly bound by a stout rope around the captain's own body. "I reckon you don't git away to-night."

"Dunno!" said Jack.

The cabin had two rooms. In one the widow, Sincerity, and Mr. James Riggs went to bed. Mr. Boddy and the captain occupied the one bed in the

23. Andrew Jackson (1767–1845), native of Tennessee, heroic general in the War of 1812 and seventh U.S. president, was affectionately nicknamed "Old Hickory" by his troops.

other. A third of it was offered young Selden, but he preferred a blanket and the floor. The scouts were divided, and guarded doors and windows.

Young Selden could not sleep. The wild novelty of the situation excited him, and his aching limbs made him toss uneasily. A little fire smouldered on the hearth, and big, shapeless shadows clutched at each other in the corners. Plenty of sounds broke the silence. The captain, happy in having made a Siamese twin of Slippery Jack, snored as if he were choking to death. The guards talked and jested roughly. A whippoor-will's three wild notes sounded just above the roof. He wondered if Jack was asleep. No; there was a slight alert movement of his body, and young Selden caught the gleam of a wild blue eye under a shaggy eyebrow. With perceptions sharpened, intensified, Selden waited for he knew not what. Mr. Boddy's eye rolled upward—and what! a wilder, brighter eye, a star, shone with answering ray through a crevice in the roof. The crevice widened; other stars stole in sight. Selden felt as if his senses were leaving him. Now the crevice was obscured; and now something shining, glimmering, and cold as the light of eye or star, protruded itself cautiously as peeping mouse through the hole in the roof. It was the point of an open knife.

Selden almost sprang to his feet. Was he to witness murder? But somehow he trusted Jack Boddy—and he waited.

The knife was affixed to a knotted rope. It soon dangled within reach of Mr. Boddy's hand. And the sly moonshiner, with a silent grin at the sleeping captain, cut the ropes that bound them together. Then hand over hand, lightly as a sailor, he climbed the rope, slipped through the opening, and was gone,

"Over the hills, and far away."[24]

Young Selden wanted to shout. But he contented himself with a quiet chuckle, and went to sleep.

He was awakened in the morning by blue-blaze swearing. The captain was foaming at the mouth, James Riggs was wiping his eyes with a spotted handkerchief, and the scouts were swearing by all that was blessed or damned that they had not closed their eyes.

"How is it with you, stranger?" said Captain Peters. "Did you see or hear anything?"

"Oh no. I slept straight through," said young Selden, with that cheerful readiness to lie that comes to great souls.

24. Line from "The Departure" by British poet Alfred, Lord Tennyson (1809–1892).

"Well, the devil must 'a helped him."

"Lor, boys," said the widow Hicks, with a slight twitch at the corners of her mouth, "you know Jack Boddy is a powerful cunnin' man—slippery as an eel."

"Jest let me get these hands on him once more—jes' *once* more!"

"S'pose you'd kill him, wouldn't you?" said the widow, sweetly. "Lor, now, I s'pose you don't make no more of killin' a man 'n I do of wringin' a chicken's neck?"

"Don't excite him," implored James Riggs; "he's powerful plagued over this misfortune."

"Come to breakfast," said the widow. "I won't make no laughin'-stawk of him 'f I can help it."

"Damnation!" said the captain.

As for Sincerity Hicks, she looked as stolid as a wooden Indian. Selden pressed some money in her hand at parting and whispered, "My dear girl, I was delighted; you climb like a cat."

"Guess this 'll be good for some blue beads," she said without moving a muscle; "I've been a-wantin' some a right smart while."

Young Selden shook with silent laughter as he strode away.

"A mountain pink!" he murmured. "Oh no, a bean stalk—a Cumberland bean stalk."

❧

Joel Chandler Harris

(1848–1908)

BORN ON DECEMBER 9, 1848, in Eatonton, Georgia, Joel Chandler Harris was the love child of Mary Harris, a respectable, unmarried woman who, at thirty-one, ran away from her home with an Irish day laborer. Deserted soon after her son's birth, the proud and educated Harris lived with her son in a one-room shed. With the exception of her sewing, their livelihood depended on the generosity of Eatonton citizens. Her son, a freckle-faced redhead, hid his sensitivity and shyness behind mischief-making and clowning. He would struggle throughout his lifetime with a speech impediment and a horror of public appearances. Even Mark Twain and George W. Cable could not later cajole a terrified Harris to become part of their lucrative public readings.

Unsuccessful in formal schooling, Harris devoured books and newspapers, particularly *The Countryman,* an ardently pro-Confederate and influential weekly published by Joseph Addison Turner at his nearby two-thousand-acre plantation, Turnwold. When Turner advertised for "a young white boy" to become an apprentice printer, the thirteen-year-old Harris seized the opportunity. The four years (1862–66) Harris lived at Turnwold changed his life and shaped his career. In *On the Plantation* (1892), Harris describes his Turnwold experiences and his early friendships with the storytelling slaves (Mink, Old George, and Aunt Crissy), who were the initial sources and inspiration for Harris's fictional Uncle Remus. Under Turner's tutelage, Harris became a neophyte journalist and acquired the information and values that would make him, like his mentor, a champion of southern life and literature. However, Turner's southern patriot dreams died with the arrival of Federal troops in 1864 and the failure of Turnwold and its newspaper two years later. While Harris was never fully separated from his vision of a loving, egalitarian, slaveholding Confederacy, his sympathy and his literary fame would rest with those who, like himself, learned to survive on the margins of white privilege and power.

After Turnwold, Harris's journalistic career evolved from typesetting and secretarial positions in Macon and New Orleans to service as an increasingly popular columnist, humorist, and editor in Forsyth and Savannah. Three years after his 1873 marriage to French Canadian Esther LaRose—a lifelong happy union with eight children—Harris moved to Atlanta to avoid a yellow-fever epidemic and there joined Henry Grady as associate co-editor of the *Atlanta Constitution*. The two men placed their differing visions in the service of the New South. Grady preached dramatic economic reform; Harris sought national reconciliation through sectional healing and the celebration of southern ways and literature.

In addition to his editorials, Harris wrote increasingly popular dialect sketches in the voice of an aging black man, who first appeared in the *Constitution* on October 26, 1876. A year later, with the publication of "Uncle Remus As a Rebel" (revised in *Songs and Sayings* as "A Story of the War"), Harris established his New South plantation "family" comprised of the vigorous Uncle Remus, his charming southern mistress, Miss Sally, and her beloved "Marse John" (a Union soldier). Other tales followed, including "The Story of Mr. Rabbit and Mr. Fox" (*Constitution*, July 20, 1879). Renamed "Uncle Remus Initiates the Little Boy," this story opened Harris's tremendously popular collection *Uncle Remus: His Songs and Sayings* (1880); the first printing sold ten thousand copies. As northern John becomes enamored of Sally and, through her, of the gentle South, so is their six-year-old son initiated into black folk wisdom and ways by Uncle Remus. Sitting in the flickering firelight of Uncle Remus's cabin, the boy begs for stories and asks questions as Remus beguiles him with tale after tale of the dancing, singing, smoking, tobacco-chewing trickster, Brer Rabbit. Harris also includes proverbs, songs, and myths like "Why the Negro Is Black." Its startling premise—that "Dey wuz a time w'en all de w'ite folks 'us black"—could only be tolerated from the safe distance that the now-venerated Harris had created with his dialect-speaking, faithful ex-slave. In the eight Uncle Remus books that followed, the little boy was eventually replaced by his son, but Brer Rabbit continued to fool creatures much stronger and less cunning than he. Based on African folktales that were retold in many areas of the South, stories like "The Wonderful Tar-Baby Story" and Brer Rabbit's brier-patch escape in

"How Mr. Rabbit Was Too Sharp for Mr. Fox" have become the stuff of American legend, emerging transformed in many forms, including Toni Morrison's *Tar Baby* (1981). In the southern local colorists' antebellum gallery of loyal blacks, Uncle Remus remains distinctive: energetic, sometimes overbearing, and always influential. Harris's stories of Uncle Remus create an antebellum climate of mutual trust, a gentle South of mostly beneficial race relations, one that northerners could respect, even admire.

Although the ten Uncle Remus collections (three published posthumously) constitute Harris's most familiar legacy, they were only part of his oeuvre. His distinguished and lengthy literary career spanned more than twenty-five years, producing essays, novels, a fictional autobiography, several collections of other middle-Georgia tales (featuring the spirited black woman Minervy Ann and former Confederate private and wisecracking philosopher Billy Sanders), as well as stories of freed blacks, the Civil War, and plain rural and mountain folk. Providing a sample of this lesser known but equally impressive work, "Where's Duncan?" (*Free Joe and Other Georgian Sketches* [1887]) exposes the violence, discord, and isolation of southern life that Harris often disguised with humor. The story's narrative ambiguity and surrealism (with its fiery destruction of an old white planter, his angry mulatta mistress, and their accuser) point toward the later work of southern modernists like William Faulkner and Eudora Welty.

After his retirement from the *Constitution* in 1900, Harris increased his commitment to writing, publishing additional tales and novels, including *Gabriel Tolliver: A Story of the Reconstruction* (1902). He was made a charter member of the American Academy of Folklore in 1889, awarded an honorary doctorate from Emory College, and became the only southerner invited to join the newly established American Academy of Arts and Letters. Three years before Harris's death, his ardent fan President Theodore Roosevelt praised Harris's vision of reconciliation as exulting "the South in the mind of every man who reads it [without] a flavor of bitterness toward any other part of the Union." Harris continued writing until his death on July 2, 1908, which was caused by complications related to cirrhosis of the liver. Even though Harris was a serious and influential regional writer and essayist, what Harris called "poor little stories" by a "dull reporter" with only "an old negro man [and] a little boy" established his contemporary fame and have lingered as the measure of his lasting influence.

Works by Joel Chandler Harris

Uncle Remus: His Songs and Sayings, 1880, ed. Robert Hemenway, 1982

Nights with Uncle Remus: Myths and Legends of the Old Plantation, 1883

Mingo and Other Sketches in Black and White, 1884

Free Joe and Other Georgian Sketches, 1887

Balaam and His Master and Other Sketches and Stories, 1891

Sister Jane: Her Friends and Acquaintances, 1896

The Chronicles of Aunt Minervy Ann, 1899

Gabriel Tolliver: A Story of the Reconstruction, 1902

Joel Chandler Harris, Editor and Essayist: Miscellaneous Literary, Political, and Social Writings, ed. Julia Collier Harris, 1931

The Complete Tales of Uncle Remus, ed. Richard Chase, 1955

Further Reading

Bickley, R. Bruce, Jr. *Joel Chandler Harris.* 1978; Athens: University of Georgia Press, 1987.

————, ed. *Critical Essays on Joel Chandler Harris.* Boston: G. K. Hall, 1981.

Bickley, R. Bruce, Jr., and Hugh T. Kennan. *Joel Chandler Harris: An Annotated Bibliography of Criticism.* Westport, Conn.: Greenwood Press, 1997.

Brasch, Walter M. *Brer Rabbit, Uncle Remus, and the "Cornfield-Journalist": The Tale of Joel Chandler Harris.* Macon, Ga.: Mercer University Press, 2000.

Brookes, Stella Brewer. *Joel Chandler Harris—Folklorist.* Athens: University of Georgia Press, 1950.

Cousins, Paul M. *Joel Chandler Harris: A Biography.* Baton Rouge: Louisiana State University Press, 1968.

Harris, Julia. *The Life and Letters of Joel Chandler Harris.* Boston: Houghton Mifflin, 1918.

Keenan, Hugh T., ed. *Dearest Chums and Partners: Joel Chandler Harris's Letters to His Children: A Domestic Biography.* Athens: University of Georgia Press, 1993.

————— ❧ —————

Uncle Remus Initiates the Little Boy

One evening recently, the lady whom Uncle Remus calls "Miss Sally" missed her little seven-year-old boy. Making search for him through the house and through the yard, she heard the sound of voices in the old man's cabin, and, looking through the window, saw the child sitting by Uncle Remus. His head rested against the old man's arm, and he was gazing with an expression of the most intense interest into the rough, weather-beaten face, that beamed so kindly upon him. This is what "Miss Sally" heard:

"Bimeby,[1] one day, arter Brer Fox bin doin' all dat he could fer ter ketch Brer Rabbit, en Brer Rabbit bin doin' all he could fer to keep 'im fum it, Brer Fox say to hisse'f dat he'd put up a game on Brer Rabbit, en he ain't mo'n got de wuds out'n his mouf twel Brer Rabbit come a lopin' up de big road, lookin' des ez plump, en ez fat, en ez sassy ez a Moggin hoss[2] in a barley-patch.

"'Hol' on dar, Brer Rabbit,' sez Brer Fox, sezee.[3]

"'I ain't got time, Brer Fox,' sez Brer Rabbit, sezee, sorter mendin' his licks.[4]

"'I wanter have some confab[5] wid you, Brer Rabbit,' sez Brer Fox, sezee.

"'All right, Brer Fox, but you better holler fum whar you stan'. I'm monstus full er fleas dis mawnin',' sez Brer Rabbit, sezee.

"'I seed Brer B'ar yistiddy,' sez Brer Fox, sezee, 'en he sorter rake me over de coals kaze you en me ain't make frens en live naberly, en I told 'im dat I'd see you.'

"Den Brer Rabbit scratch one year wid his off hinefoot sorter jub'usly,[6] en den he ups en sez, sezee:

"'All a settin',[7] Brer Fox. Spose'n you drap roun' ter-morrer en take din-ner wid me. We ain't got no great doin's at our house, but I speck de old 'oman en de chilluns kin sorter scramble roun' en git up sump'n fer ter stay yo' stummuck.'

"'I'm 'gree'ble, Brer Rabbit,' sez Brer Fox, sezee.

"'Den I'll 'pen' on you,' sez Brer Rabbit, sezee.

"Nex' day, Mr. Rabbit an' Miss Rabbit got up soon, 'fo' day, en raided on a gyarden like Miss Sally's out dar, en got some cabbiges en some roas'n

1. "By and by" or after a while.

2. "Morgan horse," a breed of trotting horses named after the original stallion's owner, Justin Morgan of New England.

3. "Says he."

4. Tending to his wounds or "licks."

5. "Confabulation" or chat.

6. "Dubiously."

7. "All (of that) is certain."

years, en some sparrer-grass,[8] en dey fix up a smashin' dinner. Bimeby one er de little Rabbits, playin' out in de backyard, come runnin' in hollerin', 'Oh, ma! oh, ma! I seed Mr. Fox a comin'!' En den Brer Rabbit he tuck de chilluns by der years en make um set down, en den him and Miss Rabbit sorter dally roun' waitin' for Brer Fox. En dey keep on waitin', but no Brer Fox ain't come. Atter 'while Brer Rabbit goes to de do', easy like, en peep out, en dar, stickin' fum behime de cornder, wuz de tip-een'er Brer Fox tail. Den Brer Rabbit shot de do' en sot down, en put his paws behime his years en begin fer ter sing:

> " 'De place wharbouts you spill de grease,
>   Right dar youer boun' ter slide,
> An' whar you fine a bunch er ha'r,
>   You'll sholy fine de hide.'

"Nex' day, Brer Fox sont word by Mr. Mink, en skuze hisse'f kaze he wuz too sick fer ter come, en he ax Brer Rabbit fer to come en take dinner wid him, en Brer Rabbit say he wuz 'gree'ble.

"Bimeby, w'en de shadders wuz at der shortes',[9] Brer Rabbit he sorter brush up en santer down ter Brer Fox's house, en w'en he got dar, he hear somebody groanin', en he look in de do' en dar he see Brer Fox settin' up in a rockin' cheer all wrop up wid flannil, en he look mighty weak. Brer Rabbit look all 'roun', he did, but he ain't see no dinner. De dishpan wuz settin' on de table, en close by wuz a kyarvin' knife.

" 'Look like you gwinter have chicken fer dinner, Brer Fox,' sez Brer Rabbit, sezee.

" 'Yes, Brer Rabbit, deyer nice, en fresh, en tender,' sez Brer Fox, sezee.

"Den Brer Rabbit sorter pull his mushtarsh, en say: 'You ain't got no calamus root,[10] is you, Brer Fox? I done got so now dat I can't eat no chicken 'ceppin she's seasoned up wid calamus root.' En wid dat Brer Rabbit lipt out er de do' and dodge 'mong de bushes, en sot dar watchin' fer Brer Fox; en he ain't watch long, nudder, kaze Brer Fox flung off de flannil en crope out er de house en got whar he could cloze in on Brer Rabbit, en bimeby Brer Rabbit holler out: 'Oh, Brer Fox! I'll des put yo' calamus root out yer on dish yer stump. Better come git it while hit's fresh,' and wid dat Brer Rabbit gallop off home. En Brer Fox ain't never kitch 'im yit, en w'at's mo', honey, he ain't gwineter."

8. Roasting ears of corn and asparagus.

9. "Shadows were at their shortest" (i.e., noon).

10. Sweet flag root, used for gastric discomfort.

The Wonderful Tar-Baby Story

"Didn't the fox *never* catch the rabbit, Uncle Remus?" asked the little boy the next evening.

"He come mighty nigh it, honey, sho's you born—Brer Fox did. One day atter Brer Rabbit fool 'im wid dat calamus root, Brer Fox went ter wuk en got 'im some tar, en mix it wid some turkentime, en fix up a contrapshun wat he call a Tar-Baby, en he tuck dish yer Tar-Baby en he sot 'er in de big road, en den he lay off in de bushes fer to see what de news wuz gwineter be. En he didn't hatter wait long, nudder, kaze bimeby here come Brer Rabbit pacin' down de road—lippity-clippity, clippity-lippity—dez ez sassy ez a jay-bird. Brer Fox, he lay low. Brer Rabbit come prancin' 'long twel he spy de Tar-Baby, en den he fotch up on his behime legs like he wus 'stonished. De Tar-Baby, she sot dar, she did, en Brer Fox, he lay low.

"'Mawnin'!' sez Brer Rabbit, sezee—'nice wedder dis mawnin',' sezee.

"Tar-Baby ain't sayin' nothin', en Brer Fox, he lay low.

"'How duz yo' sym'tums seem ter segashuate?'[11] sez Brer Rabbit, sezee.

"Brer Fox, he wink his eye slow, en lay low, en de Tar-Baby, she ain't sayin' nothin'.

"'How you come on, den? Is you deaf?' sez Brer Rabbit, sezee. 'Kaze if you is, I kin holler louder,' sezee.

"Tar-Baby stay still, en Brer Fox, he lay low.

"'Youer stuck up, dat's w'at you is,' says Brer Rabbit, sezee, 'en I'm gwineter kyore[12] you, dat's w'at I'm a gwineter do,' sezee.

"Brer Fox, he sorter chuckle in his stummick, he did, but Tar-Baby ain't sayin' nothin'.

"'I'm gwineter larn you howter talk ter 'specttubble fokes ef hit's de las' ack,' sez Brer Rabbit, sezee. 'Ef you don't take off dat hat en tell me howdy, I'm gwineter bus' you wide open,' sezee.

"Tar-Baby stay still, en Brer Fox, he lay low.

"Brer Rabbit keep on axin' 'im, en de Tar-Baby, she keep on sayin' nothin', twel present'y Brer Rabbit draw back wid his fis', he did, en blip he tuck 'er side er de head. Right dar's whar he broke his merlasses jug. His fis' stuck, en he can't pull loose. De tar hilt 'im. But Tar-Baby, she stay still, en Brer Fox, he lay low.

"'Ef you don't lemme loose, I'll knock you agin,' sez Brer Rabbit, sezee,

11. Combination of "situate" and "signify." "What are your symptoms?"

12. "Cure."

en wid dat he fotch 'er a wipe wid de udder han', en dat stuck. Tar-Baby, she ain't sayin' nothin', en Brer Fox, he lay low.

" 'Tu'n me loose, fo' I kick de natal stuffin' outen you,' sez Brer Rabbit, sezee, but de Tar-Baby, she ain't sayin' nothin'. She des hilt on, en den Brer Rabbit lose de use er his feet in de same way. Brer Fox, he lay low. Den Brer Rabbit squall out dat ef de Tar-Baby don't tu'n 'im loose he butt 'er cranksided.[13] En den he butted, en his head got stuck. Den Brer Fox, he sa'ntered fort', lookin' des ez innercent ez one er yo' mammy's mockin'-birds.

" 'Howdy, Brer Rabbit,' sez Brer Fox, sezee. 'You look sorter stuck up dis mawnin',' sezee, en den he rolled on de groun', en laughed en laughed twel he couldn't laugh no mo'. 'I speck you'll take dinner wid me dis time, Brer Rabbit. I done laid in some calamus root, en I ain't gwineter take no skuse,' sez Brer Fox, sezee."

Here Uncle Remus paused, and drew a two-pound yam out of the ashes.

"Did the fox eat the rabbit?" asked the little boy to whom the story had been told.

"Dat's all de fur de tale goes," replied the old man. "He mout, en den again he moutent. Some say Jedge B'ar come long en loosed 'im—some say he didn't. I hear Miss Sally callin'. You better run 'long."

— ✦ —

How Mr. Rabbit Was Too Sharp for Mr. Fox

"Uncle Remus," said the little boy one evening, when he had found the old man with little or nothing to do, "did the fox kill and eat the rabbit when he caught him with the Tar-Baby?"

"Law, honey, ain't I tell you 'bout dat?" replied the old darkey, chuckling slyly. "I 'clar ter grashus I ought er tole you dat, but old man Nod wuz ridin' on my eyeleds 'twel a leetle mo'n I'd a dis'member'd my own name, en den on to dat here come yo' mammy hollerin' atter you.

"W'at I tell you w'en I fus' begin? I tole you Brer Rabbit wuz a monstus soon[14] creetur; leas'ways dat's w'at I laid out fer ter tell you. Well, den, honey, don't you go en make no udder calkalashuns, kaze in dem days Brer

---

13. Nautical term meaning to lay over on one side, as in a ship too deep or narrow to stay upright under sail.

14. A "sooner" or person who gains advantage by getting ahead of others, especially settlers who moved onto government land before the official opening.

Rabbit en his fambly wuz at de head er de gang w'en enny racket wuz on han', en dar dey stayed. 'Fo' you begins fer ter wipe yo' eyes 'bout Brer Rabbit, you wait en see whar'bouts Brer Rabbit gwineter fetch up at. But dat's needer yer ner dar.

"W'en Brer Fox fine Brer Rabbit mixt up wid de Tar-Baby, he feel mighty good, en he roll on de groun' en laff. Bimeby he up'n say, sezee:

"'Well, I speck I got you dis time, Brer Rabbit, sezee; 'maybe I ain't, but I speck I is. You been runnin' roun' here sassin' atter me a mighty long time, but I speck you done come ter de een 'er de row. You bin cuttin' up yo' capers en bouncin' 'roun' in dis neighberhood ontwel[15] you come ter b'leeve yo'se'f de boss er de whole gang. En den youer allers some'rs whar you got no bizness,' sez Brer Fox, sezee. 'Who ax you fer ter come en strike up a 'quaintance wid dish yer Tar-Baby? En who stuck you up dar whar you iz? Nobody in de roun' worril.[16] You des tuck en jam yo'se'f on dat Tar-Baby widout waitin' fer enny invite,' sez Brer Fox, sezee, 'en dar you is, en dar you'll stay twel I fixes up a bresh-pile and fires her up, kaze I'm gwineter bobby-cue[17] you dis day, sho,' sez Brer Fox, sezee.

"Den Brer Rabbit talk mighty 'umble.

"'I don't keer w'at you do wid me, Brer Fox,' sezee, 'so you don't fling me in dat brier-patch. Roas' me, Brer Fox,' sezee, 'but don't fling me in dat brier-patch,' sezee.

"'Hit's so much trouble fer ter kindle a fier,' sez Brer Fox, sezee, 'dat I speck I'll hatter hang you,' sezee.

"'Hang me des ez high as you please, Brer Fox,' sez Brer Rabbit, sezee, 'but do fer de Lord's sake don't fling me in dat brier-patch,' sezee.

"'I ain't got no string,' sez Brer Fox, sezee, 'en now I speck I'll hatter drown you,' sezee.

"'Drown me des ez deep ez you please, Brer Fox,' sez Brer Rabbit, sezee, 'but do don't fling me in dat brier-patch,' sezee.

"'Dey ain't no water nigh,' sez Brer Fox, sezee, 'en now I speck I'll hatter skin you,' sezee.

"'Skin me, Brer Fox,' sez Brer Rabbit, sezee, 'snatch out my eyeballs, t'ar out my years by de roots, en cut off my legs,' sezee, 'but do please, Brer Fox, don't fling me in dat brier-patch,' sezee.

"Co'se Brer Fox wanter hurt Brer Rabbit bad ez he kin, so he cotch 'im

15. "Until."

16. "World."

17. "Barbecue."

by de behime legs en slung 'im right in de middle er de brier-patch. Dar wuz a considerbul flutter whar Brer Rabbit struck de bushes, en Brer Fox sorter hang 'roun' fer ter see w'at wuz gwineter happen. Bimeby he hear somebody call 'im, en way up de hill he see Brer Rabbit settin' cross-legged on a chinkapin[18] log koamin' de pitch outen his har wid a chip. Den Brer Fox know dat he bin swop off mighty bad. Brer Rabbit wuz bleedzed fer ter fling back some er his sass, en he holler out:

" 'Bred en bawn in a brier-patch, Brer Fox—bred en bawn in a brier-patch!' en wid dat he skip out des ez lively ez a cricket in de embers."

Where's Duncan?

Now, do you know you young people are mighty queer? Somebody has told you that he heard old man Isaiah Winchell a-gabbling about old times, and here you come fishing for what you call a story. Why, bless your soul, man, it is no story at all, just a happening, as my wife used to say. If you want me to tell what there is of it, there must be some understanding about it. You know what ought to be put in print and what ought to be left out. I would know myself, I reckon, if I stopped to think it all over; but there 's the trouble. When I get started, I just rattle along like a runaway horse. I'm all motion and no sense, and there 's no stopping me until I run over a stump or up against a fence. And if I tried to write it out, it would be pretty much the same. When I take a pen in my hand my mind takes all sorts of uncertain flights, like a pigeon with a hawk after it.

As to the affair you were speaking of, there's not much to tell, but it has pestered me at times when I ought to have been in my bed and sound asleep. I have told it a thousand times, and the rest of the Winchells have told it, thinking it was a very good thing to have in the family. It has been exaggerated, too; but if I can carry the facts to your ear just as they are in my mind, I shall be glad, for I want to get everything straight from the beginning.

Well, it was in 1826. That seems a long time ago to you, but it is no longer than yesterday to me. I was eighteen years old, and a right smart chunk of a boy for my age. While we were ginning and packing cotton our overseer left us, and my father turned the whole business over to me. Now, you may

18. Chinquapin, small chestnut tree; thus, a small log.

think that was a small thing, because this railroad business has turned your head, but, as a matter of fact, it was a very big thing. It fell to me to superintend the ginning and the packing of the cotton, and then I was to go to Augusta [19] in charge of two wagons. I never worked harder before nor since. You see we had no packing-screws nor cotton-presses in those days. The planter that was able to afford it had his gin, and the cotton was packed in round bales by a nigger who used something like a crowbar to do the packing. He trampled the lint cotton with his feet, and beat it down with his iron bar until the bagging was full, and then the bale weighed about three hundred pounds. Naturally you laugh at this sort of thing, but it was no laughing matter; it was hard work.

Well, when we got the cotton all prepared, we loaded the wagons and started for Augusta. We had n't got more than two miles from home, before I found that Crooked-leg Jake, my best driver, was drunk. He was beastly drunk. Where he got his dram, I could n't tell you to save my life, for it was against the law in those days to sell whiskey to a nigger. But Crooked-leg Jake had it and he was full of it, and he had to be pulled off of the mule and sent to roost on top of the cotton-bags. It was not a very warm roost either, but it was warm enough for a nigger full of whiskey.

This was not a good thing for me at all, but I had to make the best of it. Moreover, I had to do what I had never done before—I had to drive six mules, and there was only one rein to drive them with. This was the fashion, but it was a very difficult matter for a youngster to get the hang of it. You jerk, jerk, jerked, if you wanted the lead mule to turn to the right, and you pull, pull, pulled if you wanted her to go the left. While we were going on in this way, with a stubborn mule at the wheel and a drunken nigger on the wagon, suddenly there came out of the woods a thick-set, dark-featured, black-bearded man with a bag slung across his shoulder.

"Hello!" says he; "you must be a new hand."

"It would take a very old hand," said I, "to train a team of mules to meet you in the road."

"Now, there you have me," said he; and he laughed as if he were enjoying a very good joke.

"Who hitched up your team?" he asked.

"That drunken nigger," said I.

"To be sure," said he; "I might have known it. The lead-mule is on the off side."

19. Inland port and site of Georgia's earliest textile mills.

"Why, how do you know that?" I asked.

"My two eyes tell me," he replied, "they are pulling crossways." And with that, without asking anybody's permission, he unhitched the traces, unbuckled the reins and changed the places of the two front mules. It was all done in a jiffy, and in such a light-hearted manner that no protest could be made; and, indeed, no protest was necessary, for the moment the team started I could see that the stranger was right. There was no more jerking and whipping to be done. We went on in this way for a mile or more, when suddenly I thought to ask the stranger, who was trudging along good-humoredly by the side of the wagon, if he would like to ride. He laughed and said he would n't mind it if I would let him straddle the saddle-mule; and for my part I had no objections.

So I crawled up on the cotton and lay there with Crooked-leg Jake. I had been there only a short time when the nigger awoke and saw me. He looked scared.

"Who dat drivin' dem mules, Marse Isaiah?" he asked.

"I could n't tell you even if you were sober," said I. "The lead-mule was hitched on the off-side, and the man that is driving rushed out of the woods, fixed her right, and since then we have been making good time."

"Is he a sho' 'nuff w'ite man, Marse Isaiah?" asked Jake.

"Well, he looks like he is," said I; "but I 'm not certain about that."

With that Jake crawled to the front of the wagon, and looked over at the driver. After a while he came crawling back.

"Tell me what you saw," said I.

"Well, sir," said he, "I dunner whe'er dat man's a w'ite man or not, but he's a-settin' sideways on dat saddle-mule, en every time he chirps, dat lead-mule know what he talkin' about. Yasser. She do dat. Did you say he come outen de woods?"

"I don't know where he came from," said I. "He's there, and he's driving the mules."

"Yasser. Dat 's so. He 's dar sho', kaze I seed 'im wid my own eyes. He look like he made outen flesh en blood, en yit he mought be a ha'nt;[20] dey ain't no tellin'. Dem dar mules is gwine on mos' too slick fer ter suit me."

Well, the upshot of it was that the stranger continued to drive. He made himself useful during the day, and when night came, he made himself musical; for in the pack slung across his back was a fiddle, and in the manipulation of this instrument he showed a power and a mastery which are

20. "Haunt" or ghost.

given to few men to possess. I doubt whether he would have made much of a show on the stage, but I have heard some of your modern players, and none of them could approach him, according to my taste. I'll tell you why. They all seem to play the music for the music itself, but this man played it for the sake of what it reminded him of. I remember that when he took out his fiddle at night, as he invariably did if nobody asked him to, I used to shut my eyes and dream dreams that I have never dreamed since, and see visions that are given to few men to see. If I were younger I could describe it to you, but an old man like me is not apt at such descriptions.

We journeyed on, and, as we journeyed, we were joined by other wagons hauling cotton, until, at last, there was quite a caravan of them— twenty, at least, and possibly more. This made matters very lively, as you may suppose, especially at night, when we went into camp. Then there were scenes such as have never been described in any of the books that profess to tell about life in the South before the war. After the teams had been fed and supper cooked, the niggers would sing, dance and wrestle, and the white men would gather to egg them on, or sit by their fires and tell stories or play cards. Sometimes there would be a fight, and that was exciting; for in those days, the shotgun was mighty handy and the dirk [21] was usually within reach. In fact, there was every amusement that such a crowd of people could manage to squeeze out of such an occasion. In our caravan there were more than a dozen fiddlers, white and black, but not one of them that attracted as much attention as the stranger who drove my team. When he was in the humor he could entrance the whole camp; but it was not often that he would play, and it frequently happened that he and I would go to bed under our wagon while the rest of the teamsters were frolicking. I had discovered that he was a good man to have along. He knew just how to handle the mules, he knew all the roads, he knew just where to camp, and he knew how to keep Crooked-leg Jake sober. One night after we had gone to bed he raised himself on his elbow and said:

"To-morrow night, if I make no mistake, we will camp within a few miles of the Sandhills. There my journey ends, and yet you have never asked me my name."

"Well," said I, "you are a much older man than I am, and I had a notion that if you wanted me to know your name you would tell me. I had no more reason for asking it than you have for hiding it."

He lay over on his back and laughed.

21. Small dagger.

"You'll find out better than that when you are older," he said, and then he continued laughing—though whether it was what I said or his own thoughts that tickled him, I had no means of knowing.

"Well," he went on, after a while, "you are as clever a youngster as ever I met, and I've nothing to hide from you. My name is Willis Featherstone, and I am simply a vagabond, else you would never have seen me trudging along the public road with only a fiddle at my back; but I have a rich daddy hereabouts, and I'm on my way to see how he is getting along. Now," he continued, "I'll give you a riddle. If you can't unriddle it, it will unriddle itself. A father had a son. He sent him to school in Augusta, until he was fifteen. By that time, the father grew to hate the son, and one day, in a fit of anger, sold him to a nigger speculator."

"How could that be?" I asked.

"That is a part of the riddle," said he.

"Are you the son?"

"That is another part of the same riddle."

"Where was the son's mother?" I asked

"In the riddle—in the riddle," he replied.

I could not unriddle the riddle, but it seemed to hint at some such villainy as I had read about in the books in my father's library. Here was a man who had sold his son; that was enough for me. It gave me matter to dream on, and as I was a pretty heavy feeder in those days, my dreams followed hard on each other. But it is n't worth while to relate them here, for the things that actually happened were infinitely worse than any dream could be.

As Featherstone had foretold, we camped the next night not far from the Sandhills, where the rich people of Augusta went every summer to escape the heat and malaria of the city. We might have gone on and reached Augusta during the night, but both men and mules were tired, and of the entire caravan only one wagon went forward. I shall remember the place as long as I live. In a little hollow, surrounded by live-oaks—we call them water-oaks up here—was a very bold spring, and around and about was plenty of grass for the mules. It was somewhat dry, the time being November, but it made excellent forage. On a little hill beyond the spring was a dwelling-house. I came to have a pretty good view of it afterward, but in the twilight it seemed to be a very substantial building. It was painted white and had green blinds, and it sat in the midst of a beautiful grove of magnolias and cedars. I remember, too,—it is all impressed on my mind so vividly—that the avenue leading to the house was lined on each side with Lombardy poplars, and their spindling trunks stood clearly out against the sky.

While I was helping Featherstone unhitch and unharness the mules, he suddenly remarked:

"That's the place."

"What place?" I asked.

"The place the riddle tells about—where the son was sold by his father."

"Well," said I, by way of saying something, "what can't be cured must be endured."

"You are a very clever chap," he said, after a while. "In fact you are the best chap I have seen for many a long day, and I like you. I've watched you like a hawk, and I know you have a mother at home."

"Yes," said I, "and she's the dearest old mother you ever saw. I wish you knew her."

He came up to me, laid his hand on my shoulder, and looked into my face with an air I can never forget.

"That is the trouble," said he; "I don't know her. If I did I would be a better man. I never had much of a mother."

With that he turned away, and soon I heard him singing softly to himself as he mended a piece of the harness. All this time Crooked-leg Jake was cooking our supper beneath the live-oak trees. Other teamsters were doing the same, so that there were two dozen camp-fires burning brightly within an area of not more than a quarter of a mile. The weather was pleasant, too, and the whole scene struck me as particularly lively.

Crooked-leg Jake was always free-handed with his cooking. He went at it with a zest born of his own insatiate appetite, and it was not long before we were through with it; and while the other campers were fuming and stewing over their cooking, Jake was sitting by the fire nodding, and Featherstone was playing his fiddle. He never played it better than he did that night, and he played it a long time, while I sat listening. Meanwhile quite a number of the teamsters gathered around, some reclining in the leaves smoking their pipes, and others standing around in various positions. Suddenly I discovered that Featherstone had a new and an unexpected auditor. Just how I discovered this I do not know; it must have been proned in upon me, as the niggers say. I observed that he gripped the neck of his fiddle a little tighter, and suddenly he swung off from "Money-musk"[22] into one of those queer serenades which you have heard now and

22. "Money-musk," an eighteenth-century Scottish fiddle tune.

again on the plantation. Where the niggers ever picked up such tunes the Lord only knows, but they are heart-breaking ones.

Following the glance of Featherstone's eyes, I looked around; and I saw, standing within the circle of teamsters, a tall mulatto[23] woman. She was a striking figure as she stood there gazing with all her eyes, and listening with all her ears. Her hair was black and straight as that of an Indian, her cheeks were sunken, and there was that in her countenance that gave her a wolfish aspect. As she stood there rubbing her skinny hands together and moistening her thin lips with her tongue, she looked like one distraught. When Featherstone stopped playing, pretending to be tuning his fiddle, the mulatto woman drew a long breath, and made an effort to smile. Her thin lips fell apart and her white teeth gleamed in the firelight like so many fangs. Finally she spoke, and it was an ungracious speech:—

"Ole Giles Featherstone, up yonder—he's my marster—he sont me down here an' tole me to tell you-all dat, bein's he got some vittles lef' over fum dinner, he'll be glad ef some un you would come take supper 'long wid 'im. But, gentermens"—here she lowered her voice, giving it a most tragic tone—"you better not go, kaze he ain't got nothin' up dar dat 's fittin' ter eat—some cole scraps an' de frame uv a turkey. He scrimps hisse'f, an' he scrimps me, an' he scrimps eve'ybody on de place, an' he 'll scrimp you-all ef you go dar. No, gentermens, ef you des got corn-bread an' bacon you better stay 'way."

Whatever response the teamsters might have made was drowned by Featherstone's fiddle, which plunged suddenly into the wild and plaintive strains of a plantation melody. The mulatto woman stood like one entranced; she caught her breath, drew back a few steps, stretched forth her ebony arms, and cried out:—

"Who de name er God is dat man?"

With that Featherstone stopped his playing, fixed his eyes on the woman, and exclaimed:—

"Where's Duncan?"

For a moment the woman stood like one paralyzed. She gasped for breath, her arms jerked convulsively, and there was a twitching of the muscles of her face pitiful to behold; then she rushed forward and fell on her knees at the fiddler's feet, hugging his legs with her arms.

"Honey, who is you?" she cried in a loud voice. "In de name er de Lord, who is you! Does you know me? Say, honey, does you?"

23. An individual born of one black parent and one white parent.

Featherstone looked at the writhing woman serenely.

"Come, now," he said, "I ask you once more, *Where's Duncan?*"

His tone was most peculiar: it was thrilling, indeed, and it had a tremendous effect on the woman. She rose to her feet, flung her bony arms above her head, and ran off into the darkness, screaming:—

"He sold 'im!—he sold Duncan! He sold my onliest boy!"

This she kept on repeating as she ran, and her voice died away like an echo in the direction of the house on the hill. There was not much joking among the teamsters over this episode, and somehow there was very little talk of any kind. None of us accepted the invitation. Featherstone put his fiddle in his bag, and walked off toward the wagons, and it was not long before everybody had turned in for the night.

I suppose I had been asleep an hour when I felt some one shaking me by the shoulder. It was Crooked-leg Jake.

"Marse Isaiah," said he, "dey er cuttin' up a mighty rippit[24] up dar at dat house on de hill. I 'spec' somebody better go up dar."

"What are they doing?" I asked him drowsily.

"Dey er cussin' an' gwine on scan'lous. Dat ar nigger 'oman, she's a-cussin' out de white man, an' de white man, he's a-cussin' back at her."

"Where's Featherstone?" I inquired, still not more than half awake.

"Dat what make me come atter you, suh. Dat white man what bin 'long wid us, he's up dar, an' it look like ter me dat he's a-aggin' de fuss on. Dey gwine ter be trouble up dar, sho ez you er born."

"Bosh!" said I, "the woman's master will call her up, give her a strapping, and that will be the end of it."

"No, suh! no, suh!" exclaimed Jake, "dat ar nigger 'oman done got dat white man hacked. Hit's des like I tell you, mon!"

I drove Jake off to bed, turned over on my pallet, and was about to go to sleep again, when I heard quite a stir in the camp. The mules and horses were snorting and tugging at their halters, the chickens on the hill were cackling, and somewhere near, a flock of geese was screaming. Just then Crooked-leg Jake came and shook me by the shoulder again. I spoke to him somewhat sharply, but he did n't seem to mind it.

"What I tell you, Marse Isaiah?" he cried. "Look up yonder! Ef dat house ain't afire on top, den Jake 's a liar!"

I turned on my elbow, and, sure enough, the house on the hill was outlined in flame. The hungry, yellow tongues of fire reached up the corners

24. A "ripping" or violent fight.

and ran along the roof, lapping the shingles, here and there, as if blindly searching for food. They found it, too, for by the time I reached the spot, and you may be sure I was not long getting there, the whole roof was in a blaze. I had never seen a house on fire before, and the sight of it made me quake; but in a moment I had forgotten all about the fire, for there, right before my eyes, was a spectacle that will haunt me to my dying day. In the dining-room—I suppose it must have been the dining-room, for there was a sideboard with a row of candles on it—I saw the mulatto woman (the same that had acted so queerly when Featherstone had asked her about Duncan) engaged in an encounter with a gray-haired white man. The candles on the sideboard and the flaring flames without lit up the affair until it looked like some of the spectacles I have since seen in theatres, only it was more terrible.

It was plain that the old man was no match for the woman, but he fought manfully for his life. Whatever noise they made must have been drowned by the crackling and roaring of the flames outside; but they seemed to be making none except a snarling sound when they caught their breath, like two bull-dogs fighting. The woman had a carving-knife in her right hand, and she was endeavoring to push the white man against the wall. He, on his side, was trying to catch and hold the hand in which the woman held the knife, and was also making a frantic effort to keep away from the wall. But the woman had the advantage; she was younger and stronger, and desperate as he was, she was more desperate still.

Of course, it is a very easy matter to ask why some of my companions or myself did n't rush to the rescue. I think such an attempt was made; but the roof of the house was ablaze and crackling from one end to the other, and the heat and smoke were stifling. The smoke and flames, instead of springing upward, ranged downward, so that before anything could be done, the building appeared to be a solid sheet of fire; but through it all could be seen the writhing and wrestling of the nigger woman and the white man. Once, and only once, did I catch the sound of a voice; it was the voice of the nigger woman; she had her carving-knife raised in the air in one hand, and with the other she had the white man by the throat.

"*Where's Duncan?*" she shrieked.

If the man had been disposed to reply, he had no opportunity, for the woman had no sooner asked the question than she plunged the carving knife into his body, not only once, but twice. It was a sickening sight, indeed, and I closed my eyes to avoid seeing any more of it; but there was no need of that, for the writhing and struggling bodies of the two fell to the floor and so disappeared from sight.

Immediately afterward there was a tremendous crash. The roof had fallen in, and this was followed by an eruption of sparks and smoke and flame, accompanied by a violent roaring noise that sounded like the culmination of a storm. It was so loud that it aroused the pigeons on the place, and a great flock of them began circling around the burning building. Occasionally one more frightened than the rest would dart headlong into the flames, and it was curious to see the way it disappeared. There would be a fizz and a sputter, and the poor bird would be burnt harder than a crackling. I observed this and other commonplace things with unusual interest—an interest sharpened, perhaps, by the fact that there could be no hope for the two human beings on whom the roof had fallen.

Naturally, you will want to ask me a great many questions. I have asked them myself a thousand times, and I've tried to dream the answers to them while I sat dozing here in the sun, but when I dream about the affair at all, the fumes of burning flesh seem to fill my nostrils. Crooked-leg Jake insisted to the day of his death that the man who had driven our team sat in a chair in the corner of the dining-room, while the woman and the man were fighting, and seemed to be enjoying the spectacle. It may be so. At any rate none of us ever saw him again. As for the rest, you know just as much about it as I do.

Mary Noailles Murfree
(Charles Egbert Craddock)

(1850–1922)

BORN JANUARY 24, 1850, ON Grantland, her family's cotton plantation near Murfreesboro, Tennessee (a town named to honor her great-grandfather), the young Mary Noailles Murfree enjoyed all the advantages of education and wealth. Fanny Priscilla Dickinson, her highly cultured mother, brought the first piano to Tennessee and taught her daughters music and singing. William Law Murfree, her father, was a distinguished lawyer, linguist, and published author. Mary was the middle of three children; her older sister, Fanny, became her lifelong companion while her younger brother, William, eventually established a law practice in St. Louis. Having moved to Nashville in 1857 so that the senior William might further his legal practice and his daughters might attend the Nashville Female Academy, the family personally escaped the ravages of the Civil War; however, their Grantland home and their cotton plantation were destroyed. Murfree later recalled the devastation in her postwar novel, *Where the Battle Was Fought* (1884). Under the tutelage of her father, who actively encouraged her writing, Mary read British authors Sir Walter Scott, William Thackeray, and Charles Dickens and learned Spanish, Latin, and French. At sixteen, she enrolled for two years in a prestigious finishing school for girls. In 1872, the family relocated to the newly rebuilt Grantland, and, literally on the ashes of the old South, Murfree began to write and publish.

Very early, she began to draw her material from the dialect and customs of the Cumberland mountaineers with whom she had interacted every summer of her girlhood. Commencing when she was five, she and Fanny had spent fifteen summers at her family's Beersheba Springs cottage in the Tennessee mountains. Briefly paralyzed from a childhood illness that left her lame, Murfree appeared to understand those who were "t'other" and differently abled. On horseback, she and Fanny explored the mountain settlements and enjoyed the mountaineers' hospitality. Her faithful rendering of southern Appalachian dialect, her graphic descriptions, and her romantic plots won her immediate popularity. After publishing two *Lippincott's Magazine* pieces with plantation settings under the pseudonym R. Emmet Dembry (1874, 1875), Murfree, using the new pen name Charles Egbert Craddock, published her first mountain tale, "Dancin' Party at Harrison's Cove," in the *Atlantic Monthly* (1878). "Dancin' Party" established the competing perspectives fundamental to Murfree's mountain tales: the observations of genteel visitors who stand apart from the customs, rivalries, and antics of the mountain settlements and the vernacular reports of the mountaineers who live them. The titular star of "The Star in the Valley," published in the *Atlantic* six months later, serves as an emblem for these shifting vantage points. Even though Murfree privileges her outsider protagonist and his "literary" language, she also deftly reveals his condescension and passivity just as she lauds her mountain heroine's (and star's) courage, clan allegiance, and "common humanity."

"The Star in the Valley" joined seven other stories in the collection *In the Tennessee Mountains* (1884), published three years after the Murfree family relocated to St. Louis, where the younger William had built a thriving legal practice. The collection catapulted Murfree to national attention and has remained her most distinguished accomplishment. Critics, believing its author to be a male, praised this vigorously masculine fiction, and when her novel *The Prophet of the Great Smoky Mountains* was serialized in 1885, reviewers mistakenly applauded the popular work as her father's. Accompanied by her father and sister, Murfree traveled to Boston to introduce herself to publishers and to reveal that Charles Egbert Craddock was an elegant, small, southern lady. The formal announcement was made at a dinner party to the astonished delight of Annie Fields, among others. The Murfrees enjoyed three months of Boston social engagements; Fields, Sarah Orne Jewett, and Celia Thaxter warmly welcomed this talented southerner as a literary sister. Buoyed by this support and by the enthusiastic reception of her work, Murfree entered an intensively productive period, writing six volumes of mountain stories (two directed toward young people) and her first Civil War novel. The 1880s were the zenith of her literary career. Even though she remained a prolific writer, publishing twenty-five books in her lifetime, she never regained the literary reputation she achieved with her Tennessee mountain material.

Because of the elder William's deteriorating health, the family returned to Grantland in 1890, where her father, her literary mentor and ardent champion, died two years later. Murfree recognized that the local-color market was waning, and she, like local colorists George W. Cable and Thomas Nelson Page, turned to the regional, historical romance. She meticulously researched the Tennessee colonial frontier for three novels, including *The Story of Old Fort Loudon* (1899) and the short-story collection *The Frontiersmen* (1904). She also wrote juvenile fiction, which had been lucrative for her earlier, including *The Champion* (1902), which drew on her St. Louis experiences. After turning briefly to the Civil War in *The Storm Centre* (1905), she returned once more to the Tennessee mountain material, producing eight stories and a novel, *The Windfall* (1907). Her final regional subject, the Mississippi Delta, generated two novels: *The Fair Mississippian* (1908) and *The Story of Duciehurst* (1914).

Single all her life, Murfree considered Fanny her closest companion, and after their mother's death in 1902, the sisters moved to Murfreesboro, where they lived the remainder of their lives. For the next two decades, Murfree, no longer popular or successful, struggled to make a sufficient income. In 1910 her longtime publisher refused her offer of additional fiction. In 1912, the year in which she was elected state regent of the Daughters of the American Revolution, she sold her fifteen-book publication rights for the small sum of a thousand dollars. Although she was awarded an honorary degree by the University of the South in 1922, Murfree, by then blind and confined to a wheelchair, was unable to attend the ceremony. She died soon afterward, on July 31, 1922, in Murfreesboro.

Works by Mary Noailles Murfree

SHORT FICTION

In the Tennessee Mountains, 1884, ed. Nathalia Wright, 1970

The Mystery of Witchface Mountain, and Other Stories, 1895

The Phantoms of the Foot-Bridge, and Other Stories, 1895

The Young Mountaineers, 1897

The Bushwhackers and Other Stories, 1899

The Frontiersmen, 1904

The Raid of the Guerilla, and Other Stories, 1912

NOVELS

Where the Battle Was Fought, 1884

Down the Ravine, 1885

The Prophet of the Great Smoky Mountains, 1885

In the Clouds, 1886

The Story of Keedon Bluffs, 1887

The Despot of Broomsedge Cove, 1888

In the 'Stranger People's' Country, 1891

The Juggler, 1897

The Story of Old Fort Loudon, 1899

The Champion, 1902

A Spectre of Power, 1903

The Amulet, 1906

The Windfall, 1907

The Fair Mississippian, 1908

The Ordeal: A Mountain Romance of Tennessee, 1912

The Story of Duciehurst: A Tale of the Mississippi, 1914

Further Reading

Carleton, Reese M. "Mary Noailles Murfree (1850–1922): An Annotated Bibliography," *American Literary Realism, 1870–1910* 7 (autumn 1974): 293–378.

Cary, Richard. *Mary N. Murfree.* New York: Twayne, 1967.

Parks, Edd Winfield. *Charles Egbert Craddock.* Chapel Hill: University of North Carolina Press, 1941.

The Star in the Valley

He first saw it in the twilight of a clear October evening. As the earliest planet[1] sprang into the sky, an answering gleam shone red amid the glooms in the valley. A star too it seemed. And later, when the myriads of the fairer, whiter lights of a moonless night were all athrob in the great concave vault bending to the hills, there was something very impressive in that solitary star of earth, changeless and motionless beneath the ever-changing skies.

Chevis never tired of looking at it. Somehow it broke the spell that

---

1. The evening star, usually Venus, named for the Roman goddess of love.

draws all eyes heavenward on starry nights. He often strolled with his ci-gar at dusk down to the verge of the crag, and sat for hours gazing at it and vaguely speculating about it. That spark seemed to have kindled all the soul and imagination within him, although he knew well enough its pro-saic source, for he had once questioned the gawky mountaineer whose ser-vices he had secured as guide through the forest solitudes during this hunt-ing expedition.

"That thar spark in the valley?" Hi Bates had replied, removing the pipe from his lips and emitting a cloud of strong tobacco smoke. "Tain't nuthin' but the light in Jerry Shaw's house, 'bout haffen mile from the foot of the mounting. Ye pass that thar house when ye goes on the Chris-tel road, what leads down the mounting off the Back-bone. That's Jerry Shaw's house,—that's what it is. He's a blacksmith, an' he kin shoe a horse toler'ble well when he ain't drunk, ez he mos'ly is."

"Perhaps that is the light from the forge," suggested Chevis.

"That thar forge ain't run more 'n half the day, let 'lone o' nights. I hev never hearn tell on Jerry Shaw a-workin' o' nights,—nor in the daytime nuther, ef he kin git shet of it. No sech no 'count critter 'twixt hyar an' the Settlemint."

So spake Chevis's astronomer. Seeing the star even through the prosaic lens of stern reality did not detract from its poetic aspect. Chevis never failed to watch for it. The first faint glinting in the azure evening sky sent his eyes to that red reflection suddenly aglow in the valley; even when the mists rose above it and hid it from him, he gazed at the spot where it had disappeared, feeling a calm satisfaction to know that it was still shining beneath the cloud-curtain. He encouraged himself in this bit of sentimen-tality. These unique eventide effects seemed a fitting sequel to the pictur-esque day, passed in hunting deer, with horn and hounds, through the gor-geous autumnal forest; or perchance in the more exciting sport in some rocky gorge with a bear at bay and the frenzied pack around him; or in the idyllic pleasures of bird-shooting with a thoroughly-trained dog; and coming back in the crimson sunset to a well-appointed tent and a smok-ing supper of venison or wild turkey,—the trophies of his skill. The vague dreaminess of his cigar and the charm of that bright bit of color in the night-shrouded valley added a sort of romantic zest to these primitive en-joyments, and ministered to that keen susceptibility of impressions which Reginald Chevis considered eminently characteristic of a highly wrought mind and nature.

He said nothing of his fancies, however, to his fellow sportsman, Ned Varney, nor to the mountaineer. Infinite as was the difference between these two in mind and cultivation, his observation of both had convinced him that they were alike incapable of appreciating and comprehending his delicate and dainty musings. Varney was essentially a man of this world; his mental and moral conclusions had been adopted in a calm, mercantile spirit, as giving the best return for the outlay, and the market was not liable to fluctuations. And the mountaineer could go no further than the prosaic fact of the light in Jerry Shaw's house. Thus Reginald Chevis was wont to sit in contemplative silence on the crag until his cigar was burnt out, and afterward to lie awake deep in the night, listening to the majestic lyric welling up from the thousand nocturnal voices of these mountain wilds.

During the day, in place of the red light a gauzy little curl of smoke was barely visible, the only sign or suggestion of human habitation to be seen from the crag in all the many miles of long, narrow valley and parallel tiers of ranges. Sometimes Chevis and Varney caught sight of it from lower down on the mountain side, whence was faintly distinguishable the little log-house and certain vague lines marking a rectangular inclosure; near at hand, too, the forge, silent and smokeless. But it did not immediately occur to either of them to theorize concerning its inmates and their lives in this lonely place; for a time, not even to the speculative Chevis. As to Varney, he gave his whole mind to the matter in hand,—his gun, his dog, his game,—and his note-book was as systematic and as romantic as the ledger at home.

It might be accounted an event in the history of that log-hut when Reginald Chevis, after riding past it eighty yards or so, chanced one day to meet a country girl walking toward the house. She did not look up, and he caught only an indistinct glimpse of her face. She spoke to him, however, as she went by, which is the invariable custom with the inhabitants of the sequestered nooks among the encompassing mountains, whether meeting stranger or acquaintance. He lifted his hat in return, with that punctilious courtesy which he made a point of according to persons of low degree. In another moment she had passed down the narrow sandy road, overhung with gigantic trees, and, at a deft, even pace, hardly slackened as she traversed the great log extending across the rushing stream, she made her way up the opposite hill, and disappeared gradually over its brow.

The expression of her face, half-seen though it was, had attracted his attention. He rode slowly along, meditating. "Did she go into Shaw's house, just around the curve of the road?" he wondered. "Is she Shaw's daughter, or some visiting neighbor?"

That night he looked with a new interest at the red star, set like a jewel in the floating mists of the valley.

"Do you know," he asked of Hi Bates, when the three men were seated, after supper, around the camp-fire, which sent lurid tongues of flame and a thousand bright sparks leaping high in the darkness, and illumined the vistas of the woods on every side, save where the sudden crag jutted over the valley,—"Do you know whether Jerry Shaw has a daughter,—a young girl?"

"Ye-es," drawled Hi Bates, disparagingly, "he hev."

A pause ensued. The star in the valley was blotted from sight; the rising mists had crept to the verge of the crag; nay, in the undergrowth fringing the mountain's brink, there were softly clinging white wreaths.

"Is she pretty?" asked Chevis.

"Waal, no, she ain't," said Hi Bates, decisively. "She 's a pore, no 'count critter." Then he added, as if he were afraid of being misapprehended, "Not ez thar is any harm in the gal, ye onderstand. She 's a mighty good, saft-spoken, quiet sort o' gal, but she 's a pore, white-faced, slim little critter. She looks like she hain't got no sort 'n grit in her. She makes me think o' one o' them slim little slips o' willow every time nor I sees her. She hain't got long ter live, I reckon," he concluded, dismally.

Reginald Chevis asked him no more questions about Jerry Shaw's daughter.

Not long afterward, when Chevis was hunting through the deep woods about the base of the mountain near the Christel road, his horse happened to cast a shoe. He congratulated himself upon his proximity to the forge, for there was a possibility that the blacksmith might be at work; according to the account which Hi Bates had given of Jerry Shaw's habits, there were half a dozen chances against it. But the shop was at no great distance, and he set out to find his way back to the Christel road, guided by sundry well-known landmarks on the mountain side: certain great crags hanging above the tree-tops, showing in grander sublimity through the thinning foliage, or beetling bare and grim; a dismantled and deserted hovel, the red-berried vines twining amongst the rotting logs; the full flow of a tumultuous stream making its last leap down a precipice eighty feet high, with yeasty, maddening waves below and a rainbow-crowned crystal sheet above. And here again the curves of the woodland road. As the sound of the falling water grew softer and softer in the distance, till it was hardly more than a drowsy murmur, the faint vibrations of a far-off anvil rang upon the air. Welcome indeed to Chevis, for however enticing might be the long rambles through the redolent October woods with dog and gun, he had no mind to tramp up the mountain to his tent, five miles distant, leading the resisting horse all the way. The afternoon was so clear and so still that the metallic sound penetrated far through the quiet forest. At every curve of the road he expected to see the log-cabin with its rail fence, and beyond the low-hanging chestnut-tree, half its branches resting upon the roof of the little shanty of a blacksmith's shop. After many windings a sharp turn brought him full upon the humble dwelling, with its background of primeval woods and the purpling splendors of the western hills. The chickens were going to roost in a stunted cedar-tree just without the door; an incredibly old man, feeble and bent, sat dozing in the lingering sunshine on the porch; a girl, with a pail on her head, was crossing the road and going down a declivity toward a spring which bubbled up in a cleft of the gigantic rocks that were piled one above another, rising to a great height. A mingled breath of cool, dripping water, sweet-scented fern, and pungent mint greeted him as he passed it. He did not see the girl's face, for she had left the road before he went by, but he recognized the slight figure, with that graceful poise acquired by the prosaic habit of carrying weights upon the head, and its lithe, swaying beauty reminded him of the mountaineer's comparison,—a slip of willow.

And now, under the chestnut-tree, in anxious converse with Jerry Shaw, who came out hammer in hand from the anvil, concerning the shoe to be put on Strathspey's[2] left fore-foot, and the problematic damage sustained since the accident. Chevis's own theory occupied some minutes in expounding, and so absorbed his attention that he did not observe, until the horse was fairly under the blacksmith's hands, that, despite Jerry Shaw's unaccustomed industry, this was by no means a red-letter day in his habitual dissipation. He trembled for Strathspey, but it was too late now to interfere. Jerry Shaw was in that stage of drunkenness which is greatly accented by an elaborate affectation of sobriety. His desire that Chevis should consider him perfectly sober was abundantly manifest in his rigidly steady gait, the preternatural gravity in his bloodshot eyes, his sparingness of speech, and the earnestness with which he enunciated the acquiescent formulæ which had constituted his share of the conversation. Now and then,

2. Named for a lively Scottish dance.

controlling his faculties by a great effort, he looked hard at Chevis to discover what doubts might be expressed in his face concerning the genuineness of this staid deportment; and Chevis presently found it best to affect too. Believing that the blacksmith's histrionic attempts in the *rôle* of sober artisan were occupying his attention more than the paring of Strathspey's hoof, which he held between his knees on his leather apron, while the horse danced an animated measure on the other three feet, Chevis assumed an appearance of indifference, and strolled away into the shop. He looked about him, carelessly, at the horseshoes hanging on a rod in the rude aperture that served as window, at the wagon-tires, the plowshares, the glowing fire of the forge. The air within was unpleasantly close, and he soon found himself again in the door-way.

"Can I get some water here?" he asked, as Jerry Shaw reentered, and began hammering vigorously at the shoe destined for Strathspey.

The resonant music ceased for a moment. The solemn, drunken eyes were slowly turned upon the visitor, and the elaborate affectation of sobriety was again obtrusively apparent in the blacksmith's manner. He rolled up more closely the blue-checked homespun sleeve from his corded hammer-arm, twitched nervously at the single suspender that supported his copper-colored jeans trousers, readjusted his leather apron hanging about his neck, and, casting upon Chevis another glance, replete with a challenging gravity, fell to work upon the anvil, every heavy and well-directed blow telling with the precision of machinery.

The question had hardly been heard before forgotten. At the next interval, when he was going out to fit the horse, Chevis repeated his request.

"Water, did ye say?" asked Jerry Shaw, looking at him with narrowing eyelids, as if to shut out all other contemplation that he might grapple with this problem. "Thar 's no fraish water hyar, but ye kin go yander ter the house and ax fur some; or," he added, shading his eyes from the sunlight with his broad, blackened hand, and looking at the huge wall of stone beyond the road, "ye kin go down yander ter the spring, an' ax that thar gal fur a drink."

Chevis took his way, in the last rays of sunshine, across the road and down the declivity in the direction indicated by the blacksmith. A cool gray shadow fell upon him from the heights of the great rocks, as he neared them; the narrow path leading from the road grew dank and moist, and presently his feet were sunk in the still green and odorous water-loving weeds, the clumps of fern, and the pungent mint. He did not notice the soft verdure; he did not even see the beautiful vines that hung from earth-filled niches among the rocks, and lent to their forbidding aspect something of a smiling grace; their picturesque grouping, where they had fallen apart to show this sparkling fountain of bright up-springing water, was all lost upon his artistic perceptions. His eyes were fixed on the girl standing beside the spring, her pail filled, but waiting, with a calm, expectant look on her face, as she saw him approaching.

No creature could have been more coarsely habited: a green cotton dress, faded to the faintest hue; rough shoes, just visible beneath her skirts; a dappled gray and brown calico sun-bonnet, thrown aside on a moss-grown boulder near at hand. But it seemed as if the wild nature about her had been generous to this being toward whom life and fortune had played the niggard. There were opaline lights in her dreamy eyes which one sees nowhere save in sunset clouds that brood above dark hills; the golden sun-beams, all faded from the landscape, had left a perpetual reflection in her bronze hair; there was a subtle affinity between her and other pliant, swaying, graceful young things, waving in the mountain breezes, fed by the rain and the dew. She was hardly more human to Chevis than certain lissome little woodland flowers, the very names of which he did not know,— pure white, star-shaped, with a faint green line threading its way through each of the five delicate petals;[3] he had seen them embellishing the banks of lonely pools, or growing in dank, marshy places in the middle of the unfrequented road, where perhaps it had been mended in a primitive way with a few rotting rails.

"May I trouble you to give me some water?" asked Chevis, prosaically enough. She neither smiled nor replied. She took the gourd from the pail, dipped it into the lucent depths of the spring, handed it to him, and stood awaiting its return when he should have finished. The cool, delicious water was drained, and he gave the gourd back. "I am much obliged," he said.

"Ye're welcome," she replied, in a slow, singing monotone. Had the autumn winds taught her voice that melancholy cadence?

Chevis would have liked to hear her speak again, but the gulf between his station and hers—so undreamed of by her (for the differences of caste are absolutely unknown to the independent mountaineers), so patent to him—could be bridged by few ideas. They had so little in common that for a moment he could think of nothing to say. His cogitation suggested only the inquiry, "Do you live here?" indicating the little house on the other side of the road.

3. Wood anemone or starflower.

"Yes," she chanted in the same monotone, "I lives hyar."

She turned to lift the brimming pail. Chevis spoke again: "Do you always stay at home? Do you never go anywhere?"

Her eyes rested upon him, with a slight surprise looking out from among their changing lights. "No," she said, after a pause; "I hev no call to go nowhar ez I knows on."

She placed the pail on her head, took the dappled sun-bonnet in her hand, and went along the path with the assured, steady gait and the graceful backward poise of the figure that precluded the possibility of spilling a drop from the vessel.

He had been touched in a highly romantic way by the sweet beauty of this little woodland flower. It seemed hard that so perfect a thing of its kind should be wasted here, unseen by more appreciative eyes than those of bird, or rabbit, or the equally uncultured human beings about her; and it gave him a baffling sense of the mysterious injustice of life to reflect upon the difference in her lot and that of others of her age in higher spheres. He went thoughtfully through the closing shadows to the shop, mounted the re-shod Strathspey, and rode along the rugged ascent of the mountain, gravely pondering on worldly inequalities.

He saw her often afterward, although he spoke to her again but once. He sometimes stopped as he came and went on the Christel road, and sat chatting with the old man, her grandfather, on the porch, sunshiny days, or lounged in the barn-like door of Jerry Shaw's shop talking to the half-drunken blacksmith. He piqued himself on the readiness with which he became interested in these people, entered into their thoughts and feelings, obtained a comprehensive idea of the machinery of life in this wilderness,—more complicated than one could readily believe, looking upon the changeless face of the wide, unpopulated expanse of mountain ranges stretching so far beneath that infinite sky. They appealed to him from the basis of their common humanity, he thought, and the pleasure of watching the development of the common human attributes in this peculiar and primitive state of society never palled upon him. He regarded with contempt Varney's frivolous displeasure and annoyance because of Hi Bates's utter insensibility to the difference in their social position, and the necessity of either acquiescing in the supposititious equality or dispensing with the invaluable services of the proud and independent mountaineer; because of the *patois*[4] of the untutored people, to hear which, Varney

4. A dialect spoken (not written) among more rural or less educated people.

was wont to declare, set his teeth on edge; because of their narrow prejudices, their mental poverty, their idle shiftlessness, their uncouth dress and
appearance. Chevis flattered himself that he entertained a broader view.
He had not even a subacute idea that he looked upon these people and their
inner life only as picturesque bits of the mental and moral landscape; that
it was an æsthetic and theoretical pleasure their contemplation afforded
him; that he was as far as ever from the basis of common humanity.

Sometimes while he talked to the old man on the sunlit porch, the "slip
o' willow" sat in the door-way, listening too, but never speaking. Sometimes he would find her with her father at the forge, her fair, ethereal face
illumined with an alien and fluctuating brilliancy, shining and fading as
the breath of the fire rose and fell. He came to remember that face so well
that in a sorry sketch-book, where nothing else was finished, there were
several laborious pages lighted up with a faint reflection of its beauty. But
he was as much interested perhaps, though less poetically, in that massive
figure, the idle blacksmith. He looked at it all from an ideal point of view.
The star in the valley was only a brilliant,[5] set in the night landscape, and
suggested a unique and pleasing experience.

How should he imagine what luminous and wistful eyes were turned
upward to where another star burned,—the light of his campfire on the
crag; what pathetic, beautiful eyes had learned to watch and wait for that
red gleam high on the mountain's brow,—hardly below the stars in heaven
it seemed! How could he dream of the strange, vague, unreasoning trouble with which his idle comings and goings had clouded that young life,
a trouble as strange, as vague, as vast, as the limitless sky above her.

She understood him as little. As she sat in the open door-way, with the
flare of the fire behind her, and gazed at the red light shining on the crag,
she had no idea of the heights of worldly differences that divided them,
more insurmountable than precipices and flying chutes of mountain torrents, and chasms and fissures of the wild ravine: she knew nothing of the
life he had left, and of its rigorous artificialities and gradations of wealth
and estimation. And with a heart full of pitiable unrealities she looked up
at the glittering simulacrum of a star on the crag, while he gazed down on
the ideal star in the valley.

The weeks had worn deep into November. Chevis and Varney were
thinking of going home; indeed, they talked of breaking camp day after
to-morrow, and saying a long adieu to wood and mountain and stream.

5. Diamond.

They had had an abundance of good sport and a surfeit of roughing it. They would go back to town and town avocations invigorated by their holiday, and taking with them a fresh and exhilarating recollection of the forest life left so far behind.

It was near dusk, on a dull, cold evening, when Chevis dismounted before the door of the blacksmith's little log-cabin. The chestnut-tree hung desolate and bare on the eaves of the forge; the stream rushed by in swift gray whirlpools under a sullen gray sky; the gigantic wall of broken rocks loomed gloomy and sinister on the opposite side of the road,—not so much as a withered leaf of all their vines clung to their rugged surfaces. The mountains had changed color: the nearest ranges were black with the myriads of the grim black branches of the denuded forest; far away they stretched in parallel lines, rising tier above tier, and showing numberless gradations of a dreary, neutral tint, which grew ever fainter in the distance, till merged in the uniform tone of the sombre sky.

Indoors it was certainly more cheerful. A hickory fire dispensed alike warmth and light. The musical whir of a spinning-wheel added its unique charm. From the rafters depended numberless strings of bright red pepperpods and ears of pop-corn; hanks of woolen and cotton yarn; bunches of medicinal herbs; brown gourds and little bags of seeds. On rude shelves against the wall were ranged cooking utensils, drinking vessels, etc., all distinguished by that scrupulous cleanliness which is a marked feature of the poor hovels of these mountaineers, and in striking contrast to the poor hovels of lowlanders. The rush-bottomed chairs, drawn in a semicircle before the rough, ill-adjusted stones which did duty as hearth, were occupied by several men, who seemed to be making the blacksmith a prolonged visit; various members of the family were humbly seated on sundry inverted domestic articles, such as wash-tubs, and splint-baskets made of white oak. There was circulating among Jerry Shaw's friends a flat bottle, facetiously denominated "tickler," readily emptied, but as readily replenished from a keg in the corner. Like the widow's cruse of oil,[6] that keg was miraculously never empty. The fact of a still near by in the wild ravine might suggest a reason for its perennial flow. It was a good strong article of apple-brandy, and its effects were beginning to be distinctly visible.

Truly the ethereal woodland flower seemed strangely incongruous with these brutal and uncouth conditions of her life, as she stood at a little dis-

---

6. A widow shares her last meal with Elijah and is rewarded with an unending supply of flour and oil (1 Kings 17:8–24).

tance from this group, spinning at her wheel. Chevis felt a sudden sharp pang of pity for her when he glanced toward her; the next instant he had forgotten it in his interest in her work. It was altogether at variance with the ideas which he had hitherto entertained concerning that humble hand-icraft. There came across him a vague recollection from his city life that the peasant girls of art galleries and of the lyric stage were wont to sit at the wheel. "But perhaps they were spinning flax," he reflected. This spin-ning was a matter of walking back and forth with smooth, measured steps and graceful, undulatory motion; a matter, too, of much pretty gesticu-lation,—the thread in one hand, the other regulating the whirl of the wheel. He thought he had never seen attitudes so charming.

Jerry Shaw hastened to abdicate and offer one of the rush-bottomed chairs with the eager hospitality characteristic of these mountaineers,— a hospitality that meets a stranger on the threshold of every hut, presses upon him, ungrudgingly, its best, and follows him on his departure with protestations of regret out to the rickety fence. Chevis was more or less known to all of the visitors, and after a little, under the sense of familiar-ity and the impetus of the apple-brandy, the talk flowed on as freely as before his entrance. It was wilder and more antagonistic to his principles and prejudices than anything he had hitherto heard among these people, and he looked on and listened, interested in this new development of a phase of life which he had thought he had sounded from its lowest note to the top of its compass. He was glad to remain; the scene had impressed his cultivated perceptions as an interior by Teniers[7] might have done, and the vehemence and lawlessness of the conversation and the threats of violence had little reality for him; if he thought about the subject under discussion at all, it was with a reassuring conviction that before the plans could be carried out the already intoxicated mountaineers would be helplessly drunk. Nevertheless, he glanced ever and anon at the young girl, loath that she should hear it, lest its virulent, angry bitterness should startle her. She was evidently listening, too, but her fair face was as calm and untroubled as one of the pure white faces of those flower-stars of his early stay in the mountains.

"Them Peels ought n't ter be let live!" exclaimed Elijah Burr, a gi-gantic fellow, arrayed in brown jeans, with the accompaniments of knife, powder-horn, etc., usual with the hunters of the range; his gun stood, with

7. David Teniers, the Elder (1592−1649), and his son David (1610−1690) were Flemish paint-ers and engravers.

those of the other guests, against the wall in a corner of the room. "They ought n't ter be let live, an' I'd top off all three of 'em fur the skin an' horns of a deer."

"That thar is a true word," assented Jerry Shaw. "They oughter be run down an' kilt,—all three o' them Peels."

Chevis could not forbear a question. Always on the alert to add to his stock of knowledge of men and minds, always analyzing his own inner life and the inner life of those about him, he said, turning to his intoxicated host, "Who are the Peels, Mr. Shaw,—if I may ask?"

"Who air the Peels?" repeated Jerry Shaw, making a point of seizing the question. "They air the meanest men in these hyar mountings. Ye might hunt from Copperhead Ridge ter Clinch River,[8] an' the whole spread o' the valley, an' never hear tell o' no sech no 'count critters."

"They ought n't ter be let live!" again urged Elijah Burr. "No man ez treats his wife like that dad-burned scoundrel Ike Peel do oughter be let live. That thar woman is my sister an' Jerry Shaw's cousin,—an' I shot him down in his own door year afore las'. I shot him ter kill; but somehow 'nother I war that shaky, an' the cussed gun hung fire a-fust, an' that thar pore wife o' his'n screamed an' hollered so, that I never done nuthin' arter all but lay him up for four month an' better for that thar pore critter ter nuss. He 'll see a mighty differ nex' time I gits my chance. An' 't ain't fur off," he added threateningly.

"Would n't it be better to persuade her to leave him?" suggested Chevis pacifically, without, however, any wild idea of playing peacemaker between fire and tow.[9]

Burr growled a fierce oath, and then was silent.

A slow fellow on the opposite side of the fireplace explained: "Thar's whar all the trouble kem from. She would n't leave him, fur all he treated her awful. She said ez how he war mighty good ter her when he war n't drunk. So 'Lijah shot him."

This way of cutting the Gordian knot of domestic difficulties might have proved efficacious but for the shakiness induced by the thrill of fraternal sentiment, the infusion of apple-brandy, the protest of the bone of contention, and the hanging fire of the treacherous gun. Elijah Burr could remember no other failure of aim for twenty years.

"He won't git shet of me that easy agin!" Burr declared, with another

8. Two small communities in eastern Tennessee, about one hundred miles apart.
9. Loose fibers of flax or hemp and thus easily ignited.

pull at the flat tickler. "But ef it hed n't hev been fur what happened las' week, I mought hev let him off fur awhile," he continued, evidently actuated by some curiously distorted sense of duty in the premises. "I oughter hev kilt him afore. But now the cussed critter is a gone coon. Dadburn the whole tribe!"

Chevis was desirous of knowing what had happened last week. He did not, however, feel justified in asking more questions. But apple-brandy is a potent tongue-loosener, and the unwonted communicativeness of the stolid and silent mountaineers attested its strength in this regard. Jerry Shaw, without inquiry, enlightened him.

"Ye see," he said, turning to Chevis, " 'Lijah he thought ez how ef he could git that fool woman ter come ter his house, he could shoot Ike fur his meanness 'thout botherin' of her, an' things would all git easy agin. Waal, he went thar one day when all them Peels, the whole lay-out, war gone down ter the Settlemint ter hear the rider preach,[10] an' he jes' run away with two of the brats,—the littlest ones, ye onderstand,—a-thinkin' he mought tole her off from Ike that thar way. We hearn ez how the pore critter war nigh on ter distracted 'bout 'em, but Ike never let her come arter 'em. Leastways, she never kem. Las' week Ike kem fur 'em hisself,— him an' them two cussed brothers o' his'n. All 'Lijah's folks war out 'n the way; him an' his boys war off a-huntin', an' his wife hed gone down ter the spring, a haffen mile an' better, a-washin' clothes; nobody war ter the house 'ceptin' them two chillen o' Ike's. An' Ike an' his brothers jes' tuk the chillen away, an' set fire ter the house; an' time 'Lijah's wife got thar, 't war nuthin' but a pile o' ashes. So, we've determinated ter go up yander ter Laurel Notch, twenty mile along the ridge of the mounting, ter-night, an' wipe out them Peels,—'kase they air a-goin' ter move away. That thar wife o' Ike's, what made all the trouble, hev fretted an' fretted at Ike till he hev determinated ter break up an' wagon across the range ter Kaintucky, whar his uncle lives in the hills thar. Ike hav gin his cornsent ter go jes' ter pleasure her, 'kase she air mos' crazed ter git Ike away whar 'Lijah can't kill him. Ike's brothers is a-goin', too. I hearn ez how they 'll make a start at noon ter-morrer."

"They 'll never start ter Kaintucky ter-morrer," said Burr, grimly. "They 'll git off, afore that, fur hell, stiddier Kaintucky. I hev been a-tryin' ter make out ter shoot that thar man ever sence that thar gal war married ter him, seven year ago,—seven year an' better. But what with her a-foolin'

10. Circuit rider, or itinerant minister.

round, an' a-talkin', an' a-goin' on like she war distracted—she run right 'twixt him an' the muzzle of my gun wunst, or I would hev hed him that time fur sure—an' somehow 'nother that critter makes me so shaky with her ways of goin' on that I feel like I hain't got good sense, an' can't git no good aim at nuthin'. Nex' time, though, thar 'll be a differ. She ain't a-goin' ter Kaintucky along of him ter be beat fur nuthin' when he 's drunk."

It was a pitiable picture presented to Chevis's open-eyed imagination,—this woman standing for years between the two men she loved: holding back her brother from his vengeance of her wrongs by that subtle influence that shook his aim; and going into exile with her brute of a husband when that influence had waned and failed, and her wrongs were supplemented by deep and irreparable injuries to her brother. And the curious moral attitude of the man: the strong fraternal feeling that alternately nerved and weakened his revengeful hand.

"We air goin' thar 'bout two o'clock ter-night," said Jerry Shaw, "and wipe out all three o' them Peels,—Ike an' his two brothers."

"They ought n't ter be let live," reiterated Elijah Burr, moodily. Did he speak to his faintly stirring conscience, or to a woeful premonition of his sister's grief?

"They 'll all three be stiff an' stark afore daybreak," resumed Jerry Shaw. "We air all kin ter 'Lijah, an' we air goin' ter holp him top off them Peels. Thar's ten of us an' three o' them, an' we won't hev no trouble 'bout it. An' we 'll bring that pore critter, Ike's wife, an' her chillen hyar ter stay. She 's welcome ter live along of us till 'Lijah kin fix some sort 'n place fur her an' the little chillen. Thar won't be no trouble a-gittin' rid of the men folks, ez thar is ten of us an' three o' them, an' we air goin' ter take 'em in the night."

There was a protest from an unexpected quarter. The whir of the spinning-wheel was abruptly silenced. "I don't see no sense," said Celia Shaw, her singing monotone vibrating in the sudden lull,—"I don't see no sense in shootin' folks down like they war nuthin' better nor bear, nor deer, nor nuthin' wild. I don't see no sense in it. An' I never did see none."

There was an astonished pause.

"Shet up, Cely! Shet up!" exclaimed Jerry Shaw, in mingled anger and surprise. "Them folks ain't no better nor bear, nor sech. They hain't got no right ter live,—them Peels."

"No, that they hain't!" said Burr.

"They is powerful no 'count critters, I know," replied the little woodland flower, the firelight bright in her opaline eyes and on the flakes of burnished gold gleaming in the dark masses of her hair. "They is always a-hangin' round the still an' a-gittin' drunk; but I don't see no sense in a-huntin' 'em down an' a-killin' 'em off. 'Pears ter me like they air better nor the dumb ones. I don't see no sense in shootin' 'em."

"Shet up, Cely! Shet up!" reiterated Shaw.

Celia said no more. Reginald Chevis was pleased with this indication of her sensibility; the other women—her mother and grandmother—had heard the whole recital with the utmost indifference, as they sat by the fire monotonously carding cotton. She was beyond her station in sentiment, he thought. However, he was disposed to recant this favorable estimate of her higher nature when, twice afterward, she stopped her work, and, filling the bottle from the keg, pressed it upon her father, despite her unfavorable criticism of the hangers-on of stills. Nay, she insisted. "Drink some more," she said. "Ye hain't got half enough yit." Had the girl no pity for the already drunken creature? She seemed systematically trying to make him even more helpless than he was.

He had fallen into a deep sleep before Chevis left the house, and the bottle was circulating among the other men with a rapidity that boded little harm to the unconscious Ike Peel and his brothers at Laurel Notch, twenty miles away. As Chevis mounted Strathspey he saw the horses of Jerry Shaw's friends standing partly within and partly without the blacksmith's shop. They would stand there all night, he thought. It was darker when he commenced the ascent of the mountain than he had anticipated. And what was this driving against his face,—rain? No, it was snow. He had not started a moment too soon. But Strathspey, by reason of frequent travel, knew every foot of the way, and perhaps there would only be a flurry. And so he went on steadily up and up the wild, winding road among the great, bare, black trees and the grim heights and chasms. The snow fell fast,—so fast and so silently, before he was half-way to the summit he had lost the vague companionship of the sound of his horse's hoofs, now muffled in the thick carpet so suddenly flung upon the ground. Still the snow fell, and when he had reached the mountain's brow the ground was deeply covered, and the whole aspect of the scene was strange. But though obscured by the fast-flying flakes, he knew that down in the bosom of the white valley there glittered still that changeless star.

"Still spinning, I suppose," he said to himself, as he looked toward it and thought of the interior of the log-cabin below. And then he turned into the tent to enjoy his cigar, his æsthetic reveries, and a bottle of wine.

But the wheel was no longer awhirl. Both music and musician were gone. Toiling along the snow-filled mountain ways; struggling with the fierce gusts of wind as they buffeted and hindered her, and fluttered derisively among her thin, worn, old garments; shivering as the driving flakes came full into the pale, calm face, and fell in heavier and heavier wreaths upon the dappled calico sun-bonnet; threading her way through unfrequented woodland paths, that she might shorten the distance; now deftly on the verge of a precipice, whence a false step of those coarse, rough shoes would fling her into unimaginable abysses below; now on the sides of steep ravines, falling sometimes with the treacherous, sliding snow, but never faltering; tearing her hands on the shrubs and vines she clutched to help her forward, and bruised and bleeding, but still going on; trembling more than with the cold, but never turning back, when a sudden noise in the terrible loneliness of the sheeted woods suggested the close proximity of a wild beast, or perhaps, to her ignorant, superstitious mind, a supernatural presence,—thus she journeyed on her errand of deliverance.

Her fluttering breath came and went in quick gasps; her failing limbs wearily dragged through the deep drifts; the cruel winds untiringly lashed her; the snow soaked through the faded green cotton dress to the chilled white skin,—it seemed even to the dull blood coursing feebly through her freezing veins. But she had small thought for herself during those long, slow hours of endurance and painful effort. Her pale lips moved now and then with muttered speculations: how the time went by; whether they had discovered her absence at home; and whether the fleeter horsemen were even now ploughing their way through the longer, winding mountain road. Her only hope was to outstrip their speed. Her prayer—this untaught being!—she had no prayer, except perhaps her life, the life she was so ready to imperil. She had no high, cultured sensibilities to sustain her. There was no instinct stirring within her that might have nerved her to save her father's, or her brother's, or a benefactor's life. She held the creatures that she would have died to warn in low estimation, and spoke of them with reprobation and contempt. She had known no religious training, holding up forever the sublimest ideal. The measureless mountain wilds were not more infinite to her than that great mystery. Perhaps, without any philosophy, she stood upon the basis of a common humanity.

When the silent horsemen, sobered by the chill night air and the cold snow, made their cautious approach to the little porch of Ike Peel's log-hut at Laurel Notch, there was a thrill of dismayed surprise among them to discover the door standing half open, the house empty of its scanty furniture and goods, its owners fled, and the very dogs disappeared; only, on the rough stones before the dying fire, Celia Shaw, falling asleep and waking by fitful starts.

"Jerry Shaw swore ez how he would hev shot that thar gal o' his'n,—that thar Cely," Hi Bates said to Chevis and Varney the next day, when he recounted the incident, "only he did n't think she hed her right mind; a-walkin' through this hyar deep snow full fifteen mile,—it's fifteen mile by the short cut ter Laurel Notch,—ter git Ike Peel's folks off 'fore 'Lijah an' her dad could come up an' settle Ike an' his brothers. Leastways, 'Lijah an' the t'others, fur Jerry hed got so drunk he could n't go; he war dead asleep till ter-day, when they kem back a-fotchin' the gal with 'em. That thar Cely Shaw never did look ter me like she hed good sense, nohow. Always looked like she war queer an' teched in the head." [11]

There was a furtive gleam of speculation on the dull face of the mountaineer when his two listeners broke into enthusiastic commendation of the girl's high heroism and courage. The man of ledgers swore that he had never heard of anything so fine, and that he himself would walk through fifteen miles of snow and midnight wilderness for the honor of shaking hands with her. There was that keen thrill about their hearts sometimes felt in crowded theatres, responsive to the cleverly simulated heroism of the boards; or in listening to a poet's mid-air song; or in looking upon some grand and ennobling phase of life translated on a great painter's canvas.

Hi Bates thought that perhaps they too were a little "teched in the head."

There had fallen upon Chevis a sense of deep humiliation. Celia Shaw had heard no more of that momentous conversation than he; a wide contrast was suggested. He began to have a glimmering perception that despite all his culture, his sensibility, his yearnings toward humanity, he was not so high a thing in the scale of being; that he had placed a false estimate upon himself. He had looked down on her with a mingled pity for her dense ignorance, her coarse surroundings, her low station, and a dilettante's delight in picturesque effects, and with no recognition of the moral splendors of that star in the valley. A realization, too, was upon him that fine feelings are of most avail as the motive power of fine deeds.

He and his friend went down together to the little log-cabin. There had been only jeers and taunts and reproaches for Celia Shaw from her own people. These she had expected, and she had stolidly borne them. But she listened to the fine speeches of the city-bred men with a vague wonderment on her flower-like face,—whiter than ever to-day.

11. "Touched in the head," that is, mentally impaired.

"It was a splendid—a noble thing to do," said Varney, warmly.

"I shall never forget it," said Chevis, "it will always be like a sermon to me."

There was something more that Reginald Chevis never forgot: the look on her face as he turned and left her forever; for he was on his way back to his former life, so far removed from her and all her ideas and imaginings. He pondered long upon that look in her inscrutable eyes,—was it suffering, some keen pang of despair?—as he rode down and down the valley, all unconscious of the heart-break he left behind him. He thought of it often afterward; he never penetrated its mystery.

He heard of her only once again. On the eve of a famous day, when visiting the outposts of a gallant corps, Reginald Chevis happened to recognize in one of the pickets the gawky mountaineer who had been his guide through those autumnal woods so far away. Hi Bates was afterward sought out and honored with an interview in the general's tent; for the accidental encounter had evoked many pleasant reminiscences in Chevis's mind, and among other questions he wished to ask was what had become of Jerry Shaw's daughter.

"She 's dead,—long ago," answered Hi Bates. "She died afore the winter war over the year ez ye war a-huntin' thar. She never hed good sense ter my way o'thinkin', nohow, an' one night she run away, an' walked 'bout fifteen mile through a big snow-storm. Some say it settled on her chist. Anyhow, she jes' sorter fell away like afterward, an' never held up her head good no more. She always war a slim little critter, an' looked like she war teched in the head."

There are many things that suffer unheeded in those mountains: the birds that freeze on the trees; the wounded deer that leaves its cruel kind to die alone; the despairing, flying fox with its pursuing train of savage dogs and men. And the jutting crag whence had shone the camp-fire she had so often watched—her star, set forever—looked far over the valley beneath, where in one of those sad little rural graveyards she had been laid so long ago.

But Reginald Chevis has never forgotten her. Whenever he sees the earliest star spring into the evening sky, he remembers the answering red gleam of that star in the valley.

(Patrick) Lafcadio Hearn
(1850–1904)

LAFCADIO HEARN'S BIRTH NAME reflects his dual heritage as the second son of an Irish surgeon-major in the British army, C. B. Hearn, and a Greek woman, Rosa Tessima, whom he married shortly before his son's birth on June 27, 1850, on the island of Leucadia. Eventually abandoned by both parents, Hearn grew up in the care of a wealthy Irish aunt, who sent him to Catholic boarding schools in England, where a schoolyard accident caused the loss of sight in one eye. He later studied in a school near Rouen, France, but ran off to Paris after only two years. When his aunt's fortune failed, he set out at nineteen for Cincinnati, where a family acquaintance helped him to find work assisting a printer. Within a few years, "Paddy" Hearn was well established as a reporter, particularly of sensational crimes and the seamier sides of Cincinnati life. In 1874 he contracted an illegal marriage with Hattie Foley, an attractive young former slave. The relationship did not last, and, dismissed in 1877 from the *Cincinnati Enquirer* as a result of the liaison, Hearn set out for New Orleans.

Now using the name Lafcadio, Hearn was deeply attracted by the city, especially its Creole and African life. After a difficult start, he soon became one of the best-known writers for the local papers, first the *New Orleans Item* and later the *Times-Democrat*, for which he wrote hundreds of editorials, translations of French literature, impressionistic sketches of local life, surreal tales which he called "Fantastics," and even some of the first cartoons published in a southern newspaper. Hearn was well received by the New Orleans literary community. Though he disagreed with George W. Cable's progressive racial views, he admired Cable's writing and shared with him a profound interest in the folklore and idiosyncratic dialects of Louisiana. The short explanation, "Why Crabs are Boiled Alive," which appeared in the *New Orleans Item* (1879), reflects the ethnological interests that led to two successful 1885 publications: the recipe collection *La Cuisine Créole* and a dictionary of African-Creole proverbs, *Gombo Zhêbes*.

Although Hearn derived his contemporary reputation through newspaper sketches and translations, the numerous collections of his work (many of them gathered posthumously) reveal the range of his eclectic talent: prose poems, folktales of Asia, African America, and the Caribbean, translations of French fiction, philosophy, brief dialect sketches of local life, and ghost stories, like "A Creole Mystery" (*New Orleans Item*, 1880). The latter observes characters and situations as through a half-open door, but in that glimpse it deftly captures the dark face of an elusive city.

Hearn's talent lay more in his sensuous scene-painting and careful observation than in plotting; he rarely tells much of a story. His two novellas, the much-admired *Chita: A Memory of Last Island* (1888), which recounts a violent Gulf Coast hurricane of 1856, and *Youma* (1890), based on his two-year residence in Martinique, richly evoke the atmosphere of sea and untamed spaces, although character and plot are left almost wholly in the service of impressions. Hearn's fascination with language and its effects give his writings a very modernist flavor, and his best work achieves what many local-color writers were attempting: to capture the spirit of a place in words.

After nearly a decade in New Orleans, Hearn traveled to the French West Indies and then, in 1890, settled in Japan. In 1891, he married Setsu Koizumi, a twenty-two-year-old daughter of a renowned Samurai family, and together they raised three sons and a daughter. A much-beloved university professor, Hearn eventually became a Japanese citizen, assumed the name of Koizumi ("Little Spring") Yakumo, and embraced Buddhism. His many works on Japanese life and culture gave him prominence in the West as an interpreter of Japanese society, just as the United States was beginning its own imperial adventures in the Pacific. Amidst increasing financial difficulties, Hearn died on September 26, 1904, in Tokyo and four days later became the first foreigner to be buried in Japan with Buddhist rites.

Works by (Patrick) Lafcadio Hearn

Stray Leaves from Strange Literature, 1884

Gombo Zhêbes: Little Dictionary of Creole Proverbs, 1885

Chita: A Memory of Last Island, 1888, ed. Arlin Turner, 1969

Youma, the Story of a West Indian Slave, 1890

Karma, 1890

Glimpses of Unfamiliar Japan, 2 vols., 1894

Gleanings in Buddha-Fields, 1897

Exotics and Retrospectives, 1898

Fantastics and Other Fancies, ed. Charles Woodward Hutson, 1914

The Writings of Lafcadio Hearn, Koizumi Edition, 16 vols., 1923

Creole Sketches, ed. Charles Woodward Hutson, 1924

The Selected Writings of Lafcadio Hearn, ed. Henry Goodman, intro. Malcolm Cowley, 1949

Inventing New Orleans: Writings of Lafcadio Hearn, ed. S. Frederick Starr, 2001.

Further Reading

Bisland, Elizabeth. *The Life and Letters of Lafcadio Hearn.* 2 vols. Boston: Houghton Mifflin, 1906.

Frisby, James R., Jr. "New Orleans Writers and the Negro: George Washington Cable, Grace King, Ruth McEnery Stuart, Kate Chopin, and Lafcadio Hearn, 1870–1900." Ph.D. diss., Emory University, 1972.

Murray, Paul. *A Fantastic Journey: The Life and Literature of Lafcadio Hearn.* Ann Arbor: University of Michigan Press, 1993.

Roskelly, Hephzibah. "Cultural Translator: Lafcadio Hearn." In *Literary New Orleans: Essays and Meditations.* Ed. Richard S. Kennedy. Baton Rouge: Louisiana State University Press, 1992.

Stevenson, Elizabeth. *Lafcadio Hearn.* New York: Macmillan, 1961.

Why Crabs Are Boiled Alive

And for why you not have of crab? Because one must dem boil 'live? It is all vat is of most beast to tell so. How you make for dem kill so you not dem boil? You not can cut dem de head off, for dat dey have not of head. You not can break to dem de back, for dat dey not be only all back. You not can dem bleed until dey die, for dat dey not have blood. You not can stick to dem troo de brain, for dat dey be same like you—dey not have of brain.

A Creole Mystery

They came together from Havana,[1] mistress and servant. The mistress had a strange and serpentine sort of beauty;—the litheness of a snake in every movement;—the fascination of an ophidian;—and great eyes that flamed like black opals. One felt on meeting her that the embraces of lianas[2] and of ivy were less potent to fetter than hers—and to fetter forever. Her voice was remarkably sweet, but had strangely deep tones in it;—and her laugh caused a feeling of unpleasant surprise. It was a mocking, weird, deep laugh, uttered without any change of features; there was no smile, no movement of the facial muscles; the lips simply opened and the laugh came pealing from her white throat, while the eyes, large, brilliant, and sinister with mockery, fixed themselves with motionless lids upon the face of the person present. But she seldom laughed.

None knew who she was. She was a mystery to the French people of the quarter. Her rooms were luxuriously furnished and hung in blue satin. At long intervals strangers called upon her—men of olivaceous complexion and hair tropically black with dead-blue lights in it. They spoke only in Spanish; and their interviews lasted far into the night. Sometimes they seemed to be gay. Gossipy people said they heard the popping of champagne corks; and a perfume of Havana tobacco floated out of the windows and hung about the shrubbery that enshrouded the veranda. Sometimes, however, there were sinister sounds as of men's voices raised in anger, and at intervals the deep laugh of the mysterious woman, long and loud and clear, and vibrant with mockery.

The servant was a mulattress,[3] tall and solidly constructed as a caryatid[4] of bronze. She was not less of a mystery than her mistress. She spoke French and Spanish with equal facility, but these only on rare occasions. Generally no mute in the seraglio of a Sultan[5] could be more silent or more impassible. She never smiled. She never gossiped. She never seemed

1. Capital of Cuba, which in 1879 was in the midst of a fifty-year war for independence from Spain.

2. Binding tropical vines.

3. A female mulatto, a person having one white and one black parent.

4. A sculpture of a woman functioning as a column.

5. The closed residence of the wives and children of a Persian king. Often guarded by eunuchs, the sequestered women were a popular and exotic figure for Victorians.

to hear or to see; yet she saw and heard all. Only a strange face could attract her attention—for a brief moment, during which she gazed upon it with an indescribable look that seemed potent enough to burn what it touched. It was a look that made its living object feel that his face was photographed in her brain and would be equally vivid there fifty years after. The foreigners who came were received by her in silence and without scrutiny. Their faces were doubtless familiar. None of them ever spoke to her. She seemed to be more than a Doppelgänger,[6] and to appear in five or six different rooms at the same time. Nothing could transpire unperceived by her; though she seemed never to look at anything. Her feet were never heard. She moved like a phantom through the house, opening and closing doors noiselessly as a ghost. She always suddenly appeared when least expected. When looked for, she was never to be found. Her mistress never called her. When needed, she appeared to rise suddenly from the floor, like those Genii[7] of Arabian fables summoned by a voiceless wish. She never played with the children; and these hushed their voices when she glided by them in silence. With a subtle intelligence seemingly peculiar to her, she answered questions before they were fully asked. She never seemed to sleep. Persons who visited the house were as certain to meet her at the entrance three hours before sunrise as at any other hours. She appeared to be surprised at nothing, and to anticipate everything. She was even a greater mystery, if possible, than her mistress.

At last the swarthy foreigners called more frequently and the interviews grew stormier. It was said that sometimes the conversations were held in Catalan;[8] and that when Catalan was spoken there were angrier words and wickeder laughing. And one night the interviews were so terrible that all the old-fashioned French folks in the quarter put their heads out of the windows to listen. There were sounds as of broken glass and passionate blows given to the mahogany table. And the strange laughter suddenly ceased.

Next morning the postman calling to deliver a registered letter found the rooms empty. The spectral servant was gone. The sinister mistress was gone. The furniture was all there; and the only records of the night's mys-

6. "Double walker" (Ger.), the ghostlike double of a living person, invoking both uncanny practices like voudou and the emerging field of psychology or "alienism."

7. "Jinn," Islamic spirits capable of assuming any living form for good or evil.

8. The language of Catalonia, a region of northeastern Spain bordering France, noted for its rebellious and hardy spirit.

tery were two broken glasses and stains of wine on the rich carpet. The bed had been undisturbed. The clock still ticked on its marble pedestal. The wind moved the blue silk hangings. A drowsy perfume of woman lingered in the rooms like incense. The wardrobes retained their wealth of silks and laces. The piano remained open. A little Angora cat[9] was playing with a spool of silk under the table. A broken fan lay on the luxuriously padded rocking-chair; and a bouquet of camellias[10] lay dying upon the mantelpiece.

The letter was never delivered. The rooms remained as they were, until mould and dust came to destroy the richness of their upholstery. The strangers never came back, nor did any ever hear what became of them. The mystery remains unexplained. The letter remains in the dead-letter office. But I would like to open it and find out what is in it;—would n't you?

9. Originally from Ankara (Angora), Turkey, and prized for its singular shape and long hair.

10. Delicate, winter-blooming southern flower, ranging from white and pink to red.

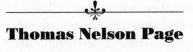

Thomas Nelson Page

(1853–1922)

AMONG THE NINETEENTH-CENTURY plantation apologists, none was more ardent, respected, or popular than Thomas Nelson Page. Born in his family's ancestral Virginia home, Oakland (about forty miles from Richmond), on April 23, 1853, Page was raised by prosperous parents in an elegant household served by purportedly faithful and "happily" enslaved retainers. Among his distinguished Nelson forebears were a signer of the Declaration of Independence and two Virginia governors. In *Two Little Confederates* (1888), based on Page's memories of his own blessed childhood, the young hero plays with plantation slave boys, admires the wisdom he gains from his family's older servants, and witnesses his uncle and father, who had opposed secession, set out for the Civil War. For a time Page attended Washington College (now Washington and Lee University) when former Confederate general Robert E. Lee was president. A reluctant student, he left without a degree, but soon became interested in law. Supplementing his meager postwar income by tutoring a relative's children, he received his law degree from the University of Virginia in 1874 and established a law practice in Richmond where he enjoyed professional and social success. Gaining a reputation as a genial raconteur, Page was called on to write addresses, obituaries, and news accounts for the Richmond paper. Although he soon had poetry published in a national magazine, Page's preferred pose for many years was as a lawyer for whom writing was a delightful sideline.

His first national publication was "Uncle Gabe's White Folks" (1876), a dialect poem modeled on the popular plantation verse of Irwin Russell. In "Marse Chan," his first published short story, Page transferred Uncle Gabe's sentimental nostalgia to the faithful Channing servant Sam, who yearningly declares those golden Old South days "de bes' Sam ever see." Written in 1881 and published three years later by *Century*, "Marse Chan" became an immediate sensation and secured its author's role as the premier spokesperson for a gentler, nobler Old South filled with courageous and courteous white aristocrats, who were loved by womanly paragons of virtue and deservedly adored by their former slaves. In the face of the profound and alienating changes of postbellum life, these noble men and their adoring retainers yearn for "de good old times" before the war. Two years later Page pursued similar material in two more stories: "Unc' Edinburgh's Drowndin': A Plantation Echo" *(Harper's)* and "Meh Lady" *(Century)*. These three tales joined others in the 1887 publication of *In Ole Virginia*. A wildly popular collection, *In Ole Virginia* was reprinted in six Scribner's editions (1892, 1896, 1910, 1916, 1928) and one London edition (1901).

Considered by influential editor Richard Watson Gilder "an exquisite story" of "an interesting and complete society," "Unc' Edinburgh's Drowndin'" is, as its subtitle reflects, an echo of better times and of properly defined race relations. In lieu of what many viewed as unsavory industrialization, Page offered in such stories an idealized agrarian past. Dangerously imbalanced racial relations became in Page's hands a chivalric hierarchy in which black slaves were safe, protected, and joyfully subservient to their virtuous white masters. In this mythic structure, women also vigorously embraced their supportive roles. Page became a publishing sensation as he reclaimed in fiction the distinction, elegance, and white privilege to which he had been born.

Page's financial affairs flourished as richly as his literary reputation, and he became a welcome national and international speaker. However, in 1888 his wife, Anne Seldom Bruce, whom he had married just after the publication of "Marse Chan," died unexpectedly, and Page retired briefly from public life. In 1893 he married the wealthy widow Florence Lathrop Field, a society woman and continental traveler, whose gift of Impressionistic paintings on the occasion of their marriage formed the basic collection of the Art Institute of Chicago. Her affluence and social standing offered Page, already a distinguished literary figure, even greater prominence and influence. At his wife's urging, the Pages established residence in Washington, D.C., where they entertained U.S. and international political figures and generously supported many artists and writers. His financial and personal life secure, Page again devoted himself to writing and produced two best-sellers: his Reconstruction novel *Red Rock* (1898) and his fictional vision for the New South, *Gordon Keith* (1903). He described his conservative view of racial relations in *The Negro: The Southerner's Prob-*

lem (1904) and gathered his essays on antebellum Virginia in 1908 as *The Old Dominion: Her Making and Her Manners.* His only urban novel, *John Marvel, Assistant,* an account of late-nineteenth-century corruption and greed, was published in 1909.

Page's literary contributions were celebrated with a Yale University honorary degree in 1901, and southern contemporaries, like Grace King, credited him with the creation of the post–Civil War market for southern material. The end of his serious writing career was signaled by Scribner's, which published all of Page's writing to date in its Plantation Edition (1906–12). Page became increasingly interested in politics, and his support of Woodrow Wilson in 1912 resulted in his being appointed Ambassador to Italy in 1913. Poet, essayist, fiction writer, philanthropist, diplomat, Page lived many of the virtues he extolled. Grieving over the sudden death of his wife in 1921, Page died at Oakland a year later on November 1, 1922.

Works by Thomas Nelson Page

SHORT FICTION

In Ole Virginia: or, Marse Chan and Other Stories, 1887, ed. Kimball King, 1969

Elsket, and Other Stories, 1891

The Burial of the Guns, and Other Stories, 1894

Pastime Stories, 1894

NOVELS

Two Little Confederates, 1888

On Newfound River, 1891

Red Rock: A Chronicle of Reconstruction, 1898

Gordon Keith, 1903

Bred in the Bone, 1904

John Marvel, Assistant, 1909

The Red Riders, 1924

SOCIAL HISTORY AND ESSAYS

The Old South: Essays Social and Political, 1892

Social Life in Old Virginia Before the War, 1897

The Negro: The Southerner's Problem, 1904

The Old Dominion: Her Making and Her Manners, 1908

Further Reading

Gross, Theodore L. *Thomas Nelson Page*. New York: Twayne, 1967.

Longest, George C. *Three Virginia Writers: Mary Johnston, Thomas Nelson Page, and Amelie Rives Troubetzkoy: A Reference Guide*. Boston: G. K. Hall, 1978.

MacKethan, Lucinda Hardwick. *The Dream of Arcady: Place and Time in Southern Literature*. Baton Rouge: Louisiana State University Press, 1980.

Page, Rosewell. *Thomas Nelson Page: A Memoir of a Virginia Gentleman*. New York: C. Scribner Sons, 1923.

Unc' Edinburg's Drowndin'

A PLANTATION ECHO

"Well, suh, dat's a fac—dat's what Marse George al'ays said. 'Tis hard to spile Christmas anyways."

The speaker was "Unc' Edinburg," the driver from Werrowcoke, where I was going to spend Christmas; the time was Christmas Eve, and the place the muddiest road in eastern Virginia—a measure which, I feel sure, will, to those who have any experience, establish its claim to distinction.

A half-hour before he had met me at the station, the queerest-looking, raggedest old darky conceivable, brandishing a cedar-staffed whip of enormous proportions in one hand, and clutching in the other a calico letter-bag with a twisted string; and with the exception of a brief interval of temporary suspicion on his part, due to the unfortunate fact that my luggage consisted of only a hand-satchel instead of a trunk, we had been steadily progressing in mutual esteem.

"Dee's a boy standin' by my mules; I got de ker'idge heah for you," had been his first remark on my making myself known to him. "Mistis say as how you might bring a trunk."

I at once saw my danger, and muttered something about "a short visit," but this only made matters worse.

"Dee don' nobody nuver pay short visits dyah," he said decisively, and I fell to other tactics.

"You couldn' spile Christmas den noways," he repeated, reflectingly, while his little mules trudged knee-deep through the mud. " 'Twuz Christmas den, sho' 'nough," he added, the fires of memory smouldering, and then, as they blazed into sudden flame, he asserted positively: "Dese heah free-issue niggers don' know what Christmas is. Hawg meat an' pop crackers don' meck Christmas. Hit tecks ole times to meck a sho'-'nough, tyahin'-down[1] Christmas. Gord! I's seen 'em'! But de wuss Christmas I ever seen tunned out de best in de een," he added, with sudden warmth, "an' dat wuz de Christmas me an' Marse George an' Reveller all got drownded down at Braxton's Creek. You's hearn 'bout dat?"

As he was sitting beside me in solid flesh and blood, and looked as little ethereal in his old hat and patched clothes as an old oak stump would have done, and as Colonel Staunton had made a world-wide reputation when he led his regiment through the Chickahominy thickets against McClellan's intrenchments,[2] I was forced to confess that I had never been so favored, but would like to hear about it now; and with a hitch of the lap blanket under his outside knee, and a supererogatory jerk of the reins, he began:

"Well, you know, Marse George was jes' eighteen when he went to college. I went wid him, 'cause me an' him wuz de same age; I was born like on a Sat'day in de Christmas, an' he wuz born in de new year on a Chuesday, an' my mammy nussed us bofe at one breast. Dat's de reason maybe huccome we took so to one nurr. He sutney set a heap o' sto' by me; an' I 'ain' nuver see nobody yit wuz good to me as Marse George."

The old fellow, after a short reverie, went on:

"Well, we growed up togerr, jes as to say two stalks in one hill. We cotch ole hyahs[3] togerr, an' we hunted 'possoms togerr, an' 'coons. Lord! he wuz a climber! I 'member a fight he had one night up in de ve'y top of a big poplar tree wid a 'coon, whar he done gone up after, an' he flung he hat over he head; an' do' de varmint leetle mo' tyah him all to pieces, he fotch him down dat tree 'live; an' me an' him had him at Christmas. 'Coon meat mighty good when dee fat, you know?"

As this was a direct request for my judgment, I did not have the moral

1. "Tearing-down" (i.e., rollicking).

2. In May–June 1862, Union general George B. McClellan (1826–85) fought against Confederate troops alongside the flooded Chickahominy River in northern Virginia, in an unsuccessful effort to capture Richmond.

3. "Hares."

courage to raise an issue, although my views on the subject of 'coon meat are well known to my family; so I grunted something which I doubt not he took for assent, and he proceeded:

"Dee warn' nuttin he didn' lead the row in; he wuz the bes' swimmer I ever see, an' he handled a skiff same as a fish handle heself. An' I wuz wid him constant; wherever you see Marse George, dyah Edinburg sho', jes' like he shadow. So twuz, when he went to de university; 'twarn' nuttin would do but I got to go too. Master he didn' teck much to de notion, but Marse George wouldn' have it no urr way, an' co'se mistis she teck he side. So I went 'long as he body-servant[4] to teck keer on him an' help meck him a gent'man. An' he wuz, too. From time he got dyah tell he cum 'way he wuz de head man.

"Dee warn' but one man dyah didn' compliment him, an' dat wuz Mr. Darker. But he warn' nuttin! not dat he didn' come o' right good fambly—'cep' dee politics;[5] but he wuz sutney pitted,[6] jes' like sometimes you see a weevly runty pig in a right good litter. Well, Mr. Darker he al'ays 'ginst Marse George; he hate me an' him bofe, an' he sutney act mischeevous todes us; 'cause he know he warn' as we all. De Stauntons dee wuz de popularitiest folks in Virginia; an' dee wuz high-larnt besides. So when Marse George run for de medal, an' wuz to meck he gret speech, Mr. Darker he speak 'ginst him. Dat's what Marse George whip him 'bout. 'Ain' nobody nuver told you 'bout dat?"

I again avowed my misfortune; and although it manifestly aroused new doubts, he worked it off on the mules, and once more took up his story:

"Well, you know, dee had been speakin' 'ginst one nurr ev'y Sat'dy night; an' ev'ybody knowed Marse George wuz de bes' speaker, but dee give him one mo' sho', an' dee was bofe gwine spread deeselves, an' dee wuz two urr gent'mens also gwine speak. An' dat night when Mr. Darker got up he meck sich a fine speech ev'ybody wuz s'prised; an' some on 'em say Mr. Darker done beat Marse George. But shuh! I know better'n dat; an' Marse George face look so curious; but, suh, when he riz I knowed der wuz somen gwine happen—I wuz leanin' in de winder. He jes' step out in front an' throwed up he head like a horse wid a rank kyurb[7] on him, and den he begin; an' twuz jes like de river when hit gits out de bank. He

4. Manservant or valet.

5. Period euphemism for views on slavery.

6. "Certainly pitted" or pock-marked.

7. "Rank curb," a bit with a chin chain to keep "in rank" or restrain a difficult horse.

swep' ev'ything. When he fust open he mouf I knowed twuz comin'; he face wuz pale, an' he wuds tremble like a fiddle-string, but he eyes wuz blazin', an' in a minute he wuz jes reshin'. He voice soun' like a bell; an' he jes wallered dat turr[8] man, an' wared him out; an' when he set down dee all yelled an' hollered so you couldn' heah you' ears. Gent'mans, twuz royal!

"Den dee tuck de vote, an' Marse George got it munanimous, an' dee all hollered agin, all 'cep' a few o' Mr. Darker's friends. An' Mr. Darker he wuz de second. An' den dee broke up. An' jes den Marse George walked thoo de crowd straight up to him, an' lookin' him right in de eyes, says to him, 'You stole dat speech you made to-night.' Well, suh, you ought to 'a hearn 'em; hit soun' like a mill-dam. You couldn' heah nuttin 'cep' roarin', an' you couldn' see nuttin 'cep' shovin'; but, big as he wuz, Marse George beat him; an' when dee pulls him off, do' he face wuz mighty pale, he stan' out befo' 'em all, dem whar wuz 'ginst him, an' all, jes as straight as an arrow, an' say: 'Dat speech wuz written an' printed years ago by some-body or nurr in Congress, an' this man stole it; had he beat me only, I should not have said one word; but as he has beaten others, I shall show him up!' Gord, suh, he voice wuz clear as a game rooster. I sutney wuz proud on him.

"He did show him up, too, but Mr. Darker ain' wait to see it; he lef' dat night. An' Marse George he wuz de populariti est gent'man at dat univer-sity. He could handle dem students dyah same as a man handle a hoe.

"Well, twuz de next Christmas we meet Miss Charlotte an' Nancy. Mr. Braxton invite we all to go down to spen' Christmas wid him at he home. An' sich a time as we had!

"We got dyah Christmas Eve night—dis very night—jes befo' supper, an' jes natchelly froze to death," he pursued, dealing in his wonted hyper-bole, "an' we jes had time to git a apple toddy or two when supper was ready, an' wud come dat dee wuz waitin' in de hall. I had done fix Marse George up gorgeousome, I tell you; and when he walk down dem stairs in dat swaller-tail coat, an' dem paten'-leather pumps on, dee warn nay one dyah could tetch him; he looked like he own 'em all. I jes rest my mind. I seen him when he shake hands wid 'em all roun', an' I say, 'Um-m-m! he got 'em.'

"But he ain' teck noticement o' none much tell Miss Charlotte come. She didn' live dyah, had jes come over de river dat evenin' from her home,

8. "T'other" or "the other."

'bout ten miles off, to spen' Christmas like we all, an' she come down de stairs jes as Marse George finish shakin' hands. I seen he eye light on her as she come down de steps smilin', wid her dim blue dress trainin' behind her, an' her little blue foots peepin' out so pretty, an' holdin' a little hank-cher, lookin' like a spider-web, in one hand, an' a gret blue fan in turr, spread out like a peacock tail, an' jes her roun' arms an' th'oat white, an' her gret dark eyes lightin' up her face. I say, 'Dyah 'tis!' and when de old Cun'l stan' aside an' interduce 'em, an' Marse George step for'ard an' meck he gran' bow, an' she sort o' swing back an' gin her curtchy, wid her dress sort o' dammed up 'ginst her, an' her arms so white, an' her face sort o' sunsetty, I say, 'Yes, Lord! Edinburg, dyah you mistis.' Marse George look like he think she done come right down from de top o' de blue sky an' bring piece on it wid her. He ain' nuver took he eyes from her dat night. Dee glued to her, mun! an' she—well, do' she mighty rosy, an' look mighty unconsarned, she sutney ain' hender him. Hit look like kyarn nobody else tote dat fan an' pick up dat hankcher skusin o' him; an' after supper, when dee all playin' blindman's-buff in de hall—I don' know how twuz—but do' she jes as nimble as a filly, an' her ankle jes as clean, an' she kin git up her dress an' dodge out de way o' ev'ybody else, somehow or nurr she kyarn help him ketchin' her to save her life; he al'ays got her corndered; an' when dee'd git fur apart, dat ain' nuttin, dee jes as sure to come togerr agin as water is whar you done run you hand thoo. An' do' he kiss ev'ybody else under de mistletow, 'cause dee be sort o' cousins, he ain' nuver kiss her, nor nobody else ain't nurr, 'cep' de old Cun'l. I wuz standin' down at de een de hall wid de black folks, an' I notice it 'tic'lar, 'cause I done meck de 'quaintance o' Nancy; she wuz Miss Charlotte's maid; a mighty likely young gal she wuz den, an' jes as impident as a fly. She see it too, do' she ain' 'low it.

"Fust thing I know I seen a mighty likely light-skinned gal standin' dyah by me, wid her hyah mos' straight as white folks, an' a mighty good frock on, an' a clean apron, an' her hand mos' like a lady, only it brown, an' she keep on 'vidin her eyes twix me an' Miss Charlotte; when I watchin' Miss Charlotte she watchin' me, an' when I steal my eye 'roun' on her she noticin' Miss Charlotte; an' presney I sort o' sidle 'longside her, an' I say, 'Lady, you mighty sprightly to-night.' An' she say she 'bleeged to be sprightly, her mistis look so good; an' I ax her which one twuz, an' she tell me, 'Dat queen one over dyah,' an' I tell her dee's a king dyah too, she got her eye set for; an' when I say her mistis tryin' to set her cap for Marse George, she fly up, an' say she an' her mistis don' have to set dee cap for nobody; *dee* got to set dee cap an' all de clo'es for dem, an' den dee ain' gwine cotch 'em, 'cause dee ain' studyin' 'bout no up-country folks whar dee ain' nobody know nuttin 'bout.

"Well, dat oudaciousness so aggrivate me, I lite into dat nigger right dyah. I tell her she ain' been nowhar 'tall ef she don' know we all; dat we wuz de bes' of quality, de ve'y top de pot; an' den I tell her 'bout how gret we wuz; how de ker'idges wuz al'ays hitched up night an' day, an' niggers jes thick as weeds; an' how Unc' Torm he wared he swaller-tail ev'y day when he wait on de table; and Marse George he won' wyah a coat mo'n once or twice anyways, to save you life. Oh! I sutney 'stonish dat nigger, 'cause I wuz teckin up for de fambly, an' I meck out like dee use gold up home like urr folks use wood, an' sow silver like urr folks sow wheat; an' when I got thoo dee wuz all on 'em listenin', an' she 'lowed dat Marse George he were ve'y good, sho 'nough, ef twarn for he nigger; but I ain' tarrifyin' myself none 'bout dat, 'cause I know she jes projickin,[9] an' she couldn' help bein' impident ef you wuz to whup de frock off her back.

"Jes den dee struck up de dance. Dee had wheel de pianer out in de hall, and somebody say Jack Forester had come cross de river, an' all on 'em say dee must' git Jack; an' presney he come in wid he fiddle, grinnin' and scrapin', 'cause he wuz a notable fiddler, do' I don' think he wuz equal to we all's Tubal, an' I know he couldn' tech Marse George, 'cause Marse George wuz a natchel fiddler, jes like 'coons is natchel pacers, an' mules an womens is natchel kickers. Howsomever, he sutney jucked a jig sweet, an' when he shake dat bow you couldn' help you foot switchin' a leetle—not ef you wuz a member of de chutch. He was a mighty sinful man, Jack wuz, an' dat fiddle had done drawed many souls to torment.

"Well, in a minute dee wuz all flyin', an' Jack he wuz rockin' like boat rockin' on de water, an' he face right shiny, an' he teef look like ear o' corn he got in he mouf, an' he big foot set 'way out keepin' time, an' Marse George he was in de lead row dyah too; ev'y chance he git he tunned Miss Charlotte—'petchel motion, right hand across, an' cauliflower, an' croquette[10]—dee croquette plenty o' urrs,[11] but I notice dee ain' nuver fail to tun one nurr, an' ev'y tun he gin she wrappin' de chain roun' him; once when dee wuz 'prominadin-all' down we all's een o' de hall, as he tunned

9. Fooling with, playing around.

10. Edinburgh proceeds to mention or garble several dance calls, or steps, including "perpetual motion," "promenade all," and "wrap the chain."

11. "Others."

her somebody step on her dress an' to' it. I heah de screech o' de silk, an' Nancy say, 'O Lord!' den she say, 'Nem mine! now I'll git it!' an' dee stop for a minute for Marse George to pin 't up, while turrers went on, an' Marse George wuz down on he knee, an' she look down on him mighty sweet out her eyes, an' say, 'Hit don' meck no difference,' an' he glance up an' cotch her eye, an', jes 'dout a wud, he tyah a gret piece right out de silk an' slipt it in he bosom, an' when he got up, he say, right low, lookin' in her eyes real deep, 'I gwine wyah dis at my weddin',' an' she jes look sweet as candy; an' ef Nancy ever wyah dat frock I ain' see it.

"Den presney dee wuz talkin' 'bout stoppin'. De ole Cun'l say hit time to have prars, an' dee wuz beggin' him to wait a leetle while; an' Jack Forester lay he fiddle down nigh Marse George, an' he picked 't up an' drawed de bow 'cross it jes to try it, an' den jes projickin' he struck dat chune 'bout 'You'll ermember me.' [12] He hadn' mo'n tech de string when you coulda' heah a pin drap. Marse George he warn noticin', an' he jes lay he face on de fiddle, wid he eyes sort o' half shet, an' drawed her out like he'd do some nights at home in de moonlight on de gret porch, tell on a sudden he looked up an' cotch Miss Charlotte eye leanin' for'ards so earnest, an' all on 'em list'nin', an' he stopt, an' dee all clapt dee hands, an' he sudney drapt into a jig. Jack Forester ain' had to play no mo' dat night. Even de ole Cun'l ketched de fever, an' he stept out in de flo' in he long-tail coat an' high collar, an' knocked 'em off de 'Snow-bud on de Ash-bank,' an' 'Chicken in de Bread-tray,' [13] right natchel.

"Oh, he could jes plank 'em down!

"Oh, dat wuz a Christmas like you been read 'bout! An' twuz hard to tell which gittin cotch most, Marse George or me; 'cause dat nigger she jes as confusin' as Miss Charlotte. An' she sutney wuz sp'ilt [14] dem days; ev'y nigger on dat place got he eye on her, an' she jes az oudacious an' aggrivatin as jes womens kin be.

"Dees monsus 'ceivin' [15] critters, womens is, jes as onreliable as de hind-leg of a mule; a man got to watch 'em all de time; you kyarn break 'em like you kin horses.

"Now dat off mule dyah" (indicating, by a lazy but not light lash of his

12. "You'll Remember Me," lyric from a popular opera, *The Bohemian Girl* (1843), by Irish composer Michael William Balfe.

13. Popular fiddle tunes.

14. "Spoiled."

15. "Monstrous deceiving."

whip the one selected for his illustration), "dee ain' no countin' on her at all; she go 'long all day, or maybe a week, jes dat easy an' sociable, an' fust thing you know you ain' know nuttin. She done knock you brains out; dee ain' no 'pendence to be placed in 'em 'tall, suh; she jes as sweet as a kiss one minute, an' next time she come out de house she got her head up in de air, an' her ears backed, an' goin' 'long switchin' herself like I ain' good 'nough for her to walk on.

" 'Fox-huntin's?' oh, yes, suh, ev'y day mos'; an' when Marse George didn' git de tail, twuz 'cause twuz a bobtail fox—you heah me! He play de fiddle for he pastime, but he fotched up in de saddle—dat he cradle!

"De fust day dee went out I heah Nancy quoilin [16] 'bout de tail layin' on Miss Charlotte dressin'-table gittin' hyahs over ev'ything.

"One day de ladies went out too, Miss Charlotte 'mongst 'em, on Miss Lucy gray myah Switchity, an' Marse George he rid Mr. Braxton's chestnut Willful.

"Well, suh, he stick so close to dat gray myah, he leetle mo' los' dat fox; but, Lord! he know what he 'bout—he monsus 'ceivin' 'bout dat— he know de way de fox gwine jes as well he know heself; an' all de time he leadin' Miss Charlotte whar she kin heah de music, but he watchin' him too, jes as narrow as a ole hound. So, when de fox tun de head o' de creek, Marse George had Miss Charlotte on de aidge o' de flat, an' he de fust man see de fox tun down on turr side wid de hounds right rank after him. Dat sort o' set him back, 'cause by rights de fox ought to 'a double an' come back dis side: he kyarn git out dat way; an' two or three gent'mens dee had see it too, an' wuz jes layin de horses to de groun' to git roun' fust, 'cause de creek wuz heap too wide to jump, an' wuz 'way over you head, an hit cold as Christmas, sho 'nough; well, suh, when dee tunned, Mr. Clarke he wuz in de lead (he wuz ridin' for Miss Charlotte too), an' hit fyah set Marse George on fire; he ain' said but one wud, 'Wait,' an' jes set de chestnut's head straight for de creek, whar de fox comin' wid he hyah up on he back, an' de dogs ravlin mos' on him.

"De ladies screamed, an' some de gent'mens hollered for him to come back, but he ain' mind; he went 'cross dat flat like a wild-duck; an' when he retch de water he horse try to flinch, but dat hand on de bridle, an' dem rowels [17] in he side, an' he 'bleeged to teck it.

"Lord! suh, sich a screech as dee set up! But he wuz swimmin' for life,

16. "Squalling."
17. Spurs.

an' he wuz up de bank an' in de middle o' de dogs time dee tetched old
Gray Jacket; an' when Mr. Clarke got dyah Marse George wuz stan'in'
holdin' up de tail for Miss Charlotte to see, turr side de creek, an' de hounds
wuz wallerin' all over de body, an' I don' think Mr. Clarke done got up wid
'em yit.

"He cotch de fox, an' he cotch some'n else besides, in my 'pinion, 'cause
when de ladies went upstairs dat night Miss Charlotte had to wait on de
steps for a glass o' water, an' couldn' nobody git it but Marse George; an'
den when she tell him goodnight over de banisters, he couldn' say it good
enough; he got to kiss her hand; an' she ain' do nuttin but jes peep upstairs
ef anybody dyah lookin'; an' when I come thoo de do' she juck her hand
'way an' run upstairs jes as farst as she could. Marse George look at me sort
o' laughin', an' say: 'Confound you! Nancy couldn' been very good to you.'
An' I say, 'She le' me squench my thirst a leetle kissin' her hand'; an' he
sort o' laugh an' tell me to keep my mouf shet.

"But dat ain' de on'y time I come on 'em. Dee al'ays gittin' corndered;
an' de evenin' befo' we come 'way I wuz gwine in thoo de conservity, an'
dyah dee wuz sort o' hide 'way. Miss Charlotte she wuz settin' down, an'
Marse George he wuz leanin' over her, got her hand to he face, talkin'
right low an' lookin' right sweet, an' she ain' say nuttin; an' presney he
drapt on one knee by her, an' slip he arm roun' her, an' try to look in her
eyes, an' she so 'shamed to look at him she got to hide her face on he shoulder, an' I slipt out.

"We come 'way next mornin'. When marster heah 'bout it he didn't
teck to de notion at all, 'cause her pa—dat is, he warn' her own pa, 'cause
he had married her ma when she wuz a widder after Miss Charlotte pa
died—an' he politics warn' same as ourn. 'Why, you kin never stand him,
suh,' he said to Marse George. 'We won't mix any mo'n fire and water; you
ought to have found that out at college; dat fellow Darker is his son.'

"Marse George he say he know dat; but he on'y de step-brurr of de
young lady, an' ain' got a drap o' her blood in he veins, an' he didn' know
it when he meet her, an' anyhow hit wouldn' meck any diffence; an' when
de mistis see how sot Marse George is on it she teck he side, an' dat fix it;
'cause when ole mistis warn marster to do a thing, hit jes good as done. I
don' keer how much he rar roun' an' say he ain' gwine do it, you jes well
go 'long an' put on you hat; you gwine see him presney doin' it jes peaceable as a lamb. She tun him jes like she got bline-bridle [18] on him, an' he
ain' nuver know it.

18. Blind-bridle, a form of blinders, to calm a skittish horse.

"So she got him jes straight as a string. An' when de time come for Marse George to go, marster he mo' consarned 'bout it 'n Marse George; he ain' say nuttin 'bout it befo'; but now he walkin' roun' an' roun' axin mistis mo' questions 'bout he cloes an' he horse an' all; an' dat mornin' he gi' him he two Sunday razors, an' gi' me a pyah o' boots an' a beaver hat, 'cause I wuz gwine wid him to kyar he portmanteau, an' git he shavin' water, sense marster say ef he wuz gwine marry a Locofoco,[19] he at least must go like a gent'man; an' me an' Marse George had done settle it 'twixt us, cause we al'ays set bofe we traps on de same hyah parf.[20]

"Well, we got 'em, an' when I ax dat gal out on de wood-pile dat night, she say bein' as her mistis gwine own me, an' we bofe got to be in de same estate, she reckon she ain' nuver gwine to be able to git shet o' me; an' den I clamp her. Oh, she wuz a beauty!"

A gesture and guffaw completed the recital of his conquest.

"Yes, suh, we got 'em sho!" he said presently. "Dee couldn' persist us; we crowd 'em into de fence an' run 'em off dee foots.

"Den come de 'gagement; an' ev'ything wuz smooth as silk. Marse George an' me wuz ridin' over dyah constant, on'y we nuver did git over bein' skeered when we wuz ridin' up dat turpentine[21] road facin' all dem winders. Hit 'pear like ev'ybody in de wull 'mos' wuz lookin' at us.

"One evenin' Marse George say, 'Edinburg, d' you ever see as many winders p'intin' one way in you life? When I git a house,' he say, 'I gwine have all de winders lookin' turr way.'

"But dat evenin', when I see Miss Charlotte come walkin' out de gret parlor wid her hyah sort o' rumpled over her face, an' some yaller roses on her bres, an' her gret eyes so soft an' sweet, an' Marse George walkin' 'long hinst her, so peaceable, like she got chain roun' him, I say, 'Winders ain' nuttin.'

"Oh, twuz jes like holiday all de time! An' den Miss Charlotte come over to see mistis, an' of co'se she bring her maid wid her, 'cause she 'bleeged to have her maid, you know, an' dat wuz de bes' of all.

"Dat evenin', 'bout sunset, dee come drivin' up in de big ker'idge, wid de gret hyah trunk stropped on de seat behind, an' Nancy she settin' by Billy, an' Marse George settin' inside by he rose-bud, 'cause he had done gone down to bring her up; an' marster he done been drest in he blue coat

19. Literally, a friction match. Radical antebellum Democrats, associated in the South with liberal attitudes toward slavery.

20. "Path."

21. Turpentine, a product of pine trees, was a major source of revenue.

an' yaller westket[22] ever sence dinner, an' walkin' roun', watchin' up de road all de time, an' tellin' de mistis he reckon dee ain' comin', an' old mistis she try to pacify him, an' she come out presney drest, an' rustlin' in her stiff black silk an' all; an when de ker'idge come in sight, ev'ybody wuz runnin'; an' when dee draw up to de do', Marse George he help her out an' in'duce her to marster an' ole mistis; an' marster he start to meck her a gret bow, an' she jes put up her mouf like a little gal to be kissed, an' dat got him. An' mistis teck her right in her arms an' kiss her twice, an' de servants dee wuzz all peepin' an' grinnin'.

"Ev'ywhar you tun you see a nigger teef, 'cause dee all warn see de young mistis whar good 'nough for Marse George.

"Dee ain' gwine be married tell de next fall, 'count o' Miss Charlotte bein' so young; but she jes good as b'longst to we all now; an' ole marster and mistis dee jes as much in love wid her as Marse George. Hi! dee warn pull de house down an' buil' it over for her! An' ev'y han' on de place he peepin' to try to git a look at he young mistis whar he gwine b'longst to. One evenin' dee all on 'em come roun' de porch an' send for Marse George, an' when he come out, Charley Brown (he al'ays de speaker, 'cause he got so much mouf, kin' talk pretty as white folks), he say dee warn interduce to de young mistis, an' pay dee bespects to her; an' presney Marse George lead her out on de porch laughin' at her, wid her face jes rosy as a winesop apple,[23] an' she meck 'em a beautiful bow, an' speak to 'em ev'y one, Marse George namin' de names; an' Charley Brown he meck her a pretty speech, an' tell her we mighty proud to own her; an' one o'dem impident gals ax her to gin her dat white frock when she git married; an' when she say, 'Well, what am I goin' wear?' Sally say, 'Lord, honey, Marse George gwine dress you in pure gol'!' an' she look up at him wid sparks flashin' out her eyes, while he look like dat ain' good 'nough for her. An' so twuz, when she went 'way, Sally Marshall got dat frock, an' proud on it I tell you.

"Oh, yes; he sutney mindin' her tender. Hi! when she go to ride in evenin' wid him, de ain' no horse-block good 'nough for her! Marse George got to have her step in he hand; an' when dee out walkin' he got de umbrellar holdin' 't over her all de time, he so feared de sun 'll kiss her; an' dee walk so slow down dem walks in de shade you got to sight 'em by a tree to tell ef dee movin' 'tall. She use' to look like she used to it too, I tell

22. Weskit or waistcoat, men's vest.
23. Winesap, a variety of red apple.

you, 'cause she wuz quality, one de white-skinned ones; an' she'd set in dem big cheers, wid her little foots on de cricket[24] whar Marse George al'ays set for her, he so feared dee'd tetch de groun', jes like she on her throne; an' ole marster he'd watch her mos' edmirin as Marse George; an' when she went 'way, hit sutney was lonesome. Hit look like daylight gone wid her. I don' know which I miss mos', Miss Charlotte or Nancy.

"Den Marse George was 'lected to de Legislature, an' old Jedge Darker run for de Senator, an' Marse George vote gin him and beat him. An' dat commence de fuss; an' den dat man gi' me de whuppin', an' dat breck 'tup an' breck he heart.

"You see, after Marse George wuz 'lected ('lections wuz 'lections dem days; dee warn' no baitgode[25] 'lections, wid ev'y sort o' wurrms squirmin' up 'ginst one nurr, wid piece o' paper d' ain' know what on, drappin' in a chink; didn' nuttin but gent'mens vote den, an' dee took dee dram, an' vote out loud, like gent'mens)—well, arter Marse George wuz 'lected, de parties wuz jes as even balanced as stilyuds,[26] an' wen dee ax Marse George who wuz to be de Senator, he vote for de Whig, 'ginst de old jedge, an' dat beat him, of co'se. An' dee ain' got sense to know he 'bleeged to vote wid he politics. Dat he principle; he kyarn vote for Locofoco, I don' keer ef he is Miss Charlotte pa, much less her step-pa. Of co'se de old jedge ain' speak to him arter dat, nur is Marse George ax him to. But who dat gwine s'pose women-folks got to put dee mouf in too? Miss Charlotte she write Marse George a letter dat pester him mightily; he set up all night answerin' dat letter, an' he mighty solemn, I tell you. An' I wuz gittin' right grewjousome myself, 'cause I studyin' 'bout dat gal down dyah whar I done gi' my wud to, an' when dee ain' no letters come torectly hit hard to tell which one de anxiouser, me or Marse George. Den presney I so 'straughted[27] 'long o' it I ax Aunt Haly 'bouten it: (She know all sich things, 'cause she 'mos' a hunderd years ole, an' seed evil sperits, an' got skoripins up her chimley, an' knowed conjure);[28] an' she ax me what wuz de signication,[29] an' I tell her I ain' able nuther to eat nor to sleep, an' dat gal come foolin'

24. Small, low stool.

25. "Bait" and "goad", suggesting promises made by politicians to win elections.

26. "Steelyard" or scales.

27. "Distraught."

28. African-based practice, using spells as well as roots and herbs for spiritual and physical healing.

29. "Situation" and "signification," that is, signs and symptoms.

'long me when I sleep jes as natchel as ef I see her sho 'nough. An' she say I done conjured; dat de gal done tricked me.

"Oh, Gord! dat skeered me!

"You white folks, marster, don' believe nuttin like dat; y' all got too much sense, 'cause y' all kin read; but niggers dee ain' know no better, an' I sutney wuz skeered, 'cause Aunt Haly say my coffin done seasoned, de planks up de chimley.

"Well, I got so bad Marse George ax me 'bout it, an' he sort o' laugh an' sort o' cuss, an' he tell Aunt Haly ef she don' stop dat foolishness skeerin' me he'll sell her an' tyah her ole skoripin house down. Well, co'se he jes talkin', an' he ax me next day how'd I like to go an' see my sweetheart. Gord, suh, I got well torectly. So I set off next evenin', feelin' jes big as ole marster, wid my pass[30] in my pocket, which I warn' to show nobody 'douten I 'bleeged to, 'cause Marse George didn' warn nobody to know he le' me go. An' den dat rascallion[31] teck de shut off my back. But ef Marse George didn' pay him de wuth o' it!

"I done git 'long so good, too.

"When Nancy see me she sutney wuz 'stonished. She come roun' de cornder in de back yard whar I settin' in Nat's do' (he wuz de gardener), wid her hyah all done ontwist, an' breshed out mighty fine, an' a clean ap'on wid fringe on it, meckin' out she so s'prised to see me (whar wuz all a lie, 'cause some on 'em done notify her I dyah), an' she say, 'Hi! what dis black nigger doin' heah?'

"An' I say, 'Who you callin' nigger, you impident, kercumber-faced thing, you?' Den we shake hands, an' I tell her Marse George done set me free — dat I done buy myself; dat's de lie I done lay off to tell her.

"An when I tole her dat, she bust out laughin', an' say, well, I better go 'long 'way, den, dat she don' warn no free nigger to be comp'ny for her. Dat sort o' set me back, an' I tell her she kickin' 'fo' she spurred, dat I ain' got her in my mine; I got a nurr gal at home whar grievin' 'bout me dat ve'y minute. An' after I tell her all sich lies as dat presney she ax me ain' I hongry; an' ef dat nigger didn' git her mammy to gi' me de bes' supter! Umm-m! I kin mos' tas'e it now. Wheat bread off de table, an' zerves,[32] an' fat bacon, tell I couldn' put a nurr moufful nowhar sep'n I'd teck my hat. Dat night I tote Nancy water for her, an' I tell her all about ev'ything, an'

30. Slaves away from their home plantation without a letter of permission were subject to arrest, punishment, and even death.
31. "Rapscallion," rascal.
32. "Preserves" or jelly.

she jes sweet as honey. Next mornin', do', she done sort o' tunned some, an'
ain' so sweet. You know how milk gits sort o' bonny-clabberish? An' when
she see me she 'gin to 'buse me—say I jes' tryin' to fool her, an' all de time
got nurr wife at home, or gittin' ready to git one, for all she know, an' she
ain' know wherr Marse George ain' jes 'ceivin' as I is; an' nem mine, she
got plenty warn marry her; an' as to Miss Charlotte, she got de whole wull;
Mr. Darker he ain' got nobody in he way now, dat he deah all de time, an'
ain' gwine West no mo'. Well, dat aggrivate me so I tell her ef she say dat
'bout Marse George I gwine knock her; an' wid dat she got so oudacious I
meck out I gwine 'way, an' lef' her, an' went up todes de barn; an' up dyah,
fust thing I know, I come across dat ar man Mr. Darker. Soon as he see me
he begin to cuss me, an' he ax me what I doin' on dat land, an' I tell him
'Nuttin'.' An' he say, well, he gwine gi'me some'n; he gwine teach me to
come prowlin' round gent'men's houses. An' he meck me go in de barn an'
teck off my shut, an' he beat me wid he whup tell de blood run out my back.
He sutney did beat me scandalous, 'cause he done hate me an' Marse George
ever since we wuz at college togurr. An' den he say: 'Now you git right off
dis land. Ef either you or you marster ever put you foot on it, you'll git de
same thing agin.' An' I tell you, Edinburg he come way, 'cause he sutney
had worry me. I ain' stop to see Nancy or nobody; I jes come 'long, shakin'
de dust, I tell you. An' as I come 'long de road I pass Miss Charlotte walkin'
on de lawn by herself, an' she call me: 'Why, hi! ain' dat Edinburg?'

"She look so sweet, an' her voice soun' so cool, I say, 'Yes'm; how you do,
missis?' An' she say, she ve'y well, an' how I been, an' whar I gwine? I tell
her I ain' feelin' so well, dat I gwine home. 'Hi!' she say, 'is anybody treat
you bad?' An' I tell her, 'Yes'm.' An' she say, 'Oh! Nancy don' mean nuttin
by dat; dat you mus'n mine what womens say, an' do, 'cause dee feel sorry
for it next minute; an' sometimes dee kyarn help it, or maybe hit you fault;
an' anyhow, you ought to be willin' to overlook it; an' I better go back an'
wait till to-morrow—ef—ef I ain' bleeged to git home to-day.'

"She got mighty mixed up in de een part o' dat, an' she looked mighty
anxious 'bout me an' Nancy; an' I tell her, 'No'm, I 'bleeged to git home.'

"Well, when I got home Marse George he warn know all dat gwine on;
but I mighty sick—dat man done beat me so; an he ax me what de marter,
an' I upped an' tell him.

"Gord! I nuver see a man in sich a rage. He call me in de office an' meck
me teck off my shut, an' he fyah bust out cryin'. He walked up an' down
dat office like a caged lion. Ef he had got he hand on Mr. Darker den, he'd
'a kilt him, sho!

"He wuz most 'stracted. I don't know what he'd been ef I'd tell him what Nancy tell me. He call for Peter to get he horse torectly, an' he tell me to go an' git some'n from mammy to put on my back, an' to go to bed torectly, an' not to say nuttin to nobody, but to tell he pa he'd be away for two days, maybe; an' den he got on Reveller an' galloped 'way hard as he could, wid he jaw set farst, an' he heaviest whup clamped in he hand. Gord! I wuz most hopin' he wouldn' meet dat man, 'cause I feared ef he did he'd kill him; an' he would, sho, ef he had meet him right den; dee say he leetle mo' did when he fine him next day, an' he had done been ridin' den all night; he cotch him at a sto' on de road, an' dee say he leetle mo' cut him all to pieces; he drawed a weepin[33] on Marse George, but Marse George wrench it out he hand an' flung it over de fence; an' when dee got him 'way he had weared he whup out on him; an' he got dem whelps on him now, ef he ain' dead. Yes, suh, he ain' let nobody else do dat he ain' do heself, sho!

"Dat done de business!

"He sont Marse George a challenge, but Marse George sont him wud he'll cowhide him agin ef he ever heah any mo' from him, an' he ain't. Dat perrify him, so he shet he mouf. Den come he ring an' all he pictures an' things back—a gret box on 'em, and not a wud wid 'em. Marse George, I think he know'd dee wuz comin', but dat ain' keep it from huttin' him, 'cause he done been 'gaged to Miss Charlotte, an' got he mine riveted to her; an' do' befo' dat dee had stop writin', an' a riff done git 'twixt 'em, he ain' satisfied in he mine dat she ain't gwine 'pologizee—I know by Nancy; but now he got de confirmation dat he done for good, an' dat de gret gulf fixed 'twixt him an' Aberham bosom.[34] An', Gord, suh, twuz torment, sho 'nough! He ain' say nuttin 'bout it, but I see de light done pass from him, an' de darkness done wrap him up in it. In a leetle while you wouldn' a knowed him.

"Den ole mistis died.

"B'lieve me, ole marster he 'most much hut by Miss Charlotte as Marse George. He meck a 'tempt to buy Nancy for me, so I find out arterward, an' write Jedge Darker he'll pay him anything he'll ax for her, but he letter wuz sont back 'dout any answer. He sutney was mad 'bout it—he say he'd horsewhip him as Marse George did dat urr young puppy, but ole mistis wouldn' le' him do nuttin, and den he grieve heself to death. You see

33. "Weapon."

34. In one of Jesus' parables, a rich man in hell is separated by a "great chasm" from the poor man sitting in "Abraham's bosom" or heaven (Luke 16:19–27).

he mighty ole, anyways. He nuver got over ole mistis' death. She had been failin' a long time, an' he ain' tarry long 'hinst her; hit sort o' like breckin' up a holler—de ole 'coon goes 'way soon arter dat; an' marster nuver could pin he own collar or buckle he own stock—mistis she al'ays do dat; an' do' Marse George do de bes' he kin, an' mighty willin', he kyarn handle pin like a woman; he hand tremble like a p'inter dog; an' anyways he ain' ole mistis. So ole marster foller her dat next fall, when dee wuz gittin in de corn, an' Marse George he ain' got nobody in de wull left; he all alone in dat gret house, an' I wonder sometimes he ain' die too, 'cause he sutney wuz fond o' old marster.

"When ole mistis wuz dyin', she tell him to be good to ole marster, an' patient wid him, 'cause he ain' got nobody but him now (ole marster he had jes step out de room to cry); an' Marse George he lean over an' kiss her an' promise her faithful he would. An' he sutney wuz tender wid him as a woman; an' when ole marster die, he set by him an' hol' he hand an' kiss him sorf, like he wuz ole mistis.

"But, Gord! twuz lonesome arter dat, an' Marse George eyes look wistful, like he al'ays lookin' far 'way.

"Aunt Haly say he see harnts[35] whar walk 'bout in de gret house. She say dee walk dyah constant of nights sence ole marster done alterate de rooms from what dee wuz when he gran'pa buil' 'em, an' dat dee huntin' for dee ole chambers an' kyarn git no rest 'cause dee kyarn fine 'em. I don't know how dat wuz. I know Marse George *he* used to walk about heself mightily of nights. All night long, all night long, I'd heah him tell de chickens crowin' dee second crow, an' some mornin's I'd go dyah an' he ain' even rumple de bed. I thought sho he wuz gwine die, but I suppose he done 'arn he days to be long in de land, an' dat save him. But hit sutney wuz lonesome, an' he nuver went off de plantation, an' he got older an' older, tell we all thought he wuz gwine die.

"An' one day come jes befo' Christmas, 'bout nigh two year after marster die, Mr. Braxton ride up to de do'. He had done come to teck Marse George home to spen' Christmas wid him. Marse George warn git out it, but Mr. Braxton won' teck no disapp'intment; he say he gwine baptize he boy, an' he done name him after Marse George (he had marry Marse George cousin, Miss Peggy Carter, an' he vite Marse George to de weddin', but he wouldn' go, do' I sutney did want him to go, 'cause I heah Miss Charlotte was nominated to marry Mr. Darker, an' I warn know what

35. "Haunts" or spirits.

done 'come o' dat bright-skinned nigger gal, whar I used to know down dyah); an' he say Marse George got to come an' stan' for him, an' gi' him a silver cup an' a gol' rattle. So Marse George he finally promise to come an' spend Christmas Day, an' Mr. Braxton went 'way next mornin', an' den hit tun in an' rain so I feared we couldn' go, but hit cler off de day befo' Christmas Eve an' tun cold. Well, suh, we ain' been nowhar for so long I wuz skittish as a young filly; an den you know twuz de same ole place.

"We didn' git dyah till supper-time, an 'twuz a good one too, 'cause seventy miles dat cold a weather hit whet a man's honger jes like a whetstone.

"Dey sutney wuz glad to see we all. We rid roun' by de back yard to gi' Billy de horses, an' we see dee wuz havin' gret fixin's; an' den we went to de house, jest as some o' de folks run in an' tell 'em we wuz come. When Marse George stept in de hall, dee all clustered roun' him like dee gwine hug him, dee faces fyah dimplin' wid pleasure, an' Miss Peggy she jes reched up and teck him in her arms an' hug him.

"Dee tell me in de kitchen dat dee wuz been 'spectin' of Miss Charlotte over to spend Christmas too, but de river wuz so high dee s'pose dee couldn' git cross. Chile, dat sutney disapp'int me!

"Well, after supper de niggers had a dance. Hit wuz down in de washhouse, an' de table wuz set in de carpenter shop jes' by. Oh, hit sutney wuz beautiful! Miss Lucy an' Miss Ailsy dee had superintend ev'ything wid dee own hands. So dee wuz down dyah wid dee ap'ons up to dee chins, an' dee had de big silver strandeliers out de house, two on each table, an' some o' ole mistis's best damas'[36] tablecloths, an' ole marster's gret bowl full o' eggnog; hit look big as a mill-pond settin' dyah in de cornder; an' dee had flowers out de greenhouse on de table, an' some o' de chany out de gret house, an' de dinin'-room cheers set roun' de room. Oh! oh! nuttin warn too good for niggers dem times; an' de little niggers wuz runnin' roun' right 'stracted, squealin' an' peepin' an' gittin in de way onder you foots; an' de mens dee wuz totin' in de wood—gret hickory logs, look like stock whar you gwine saw—an' de fire so big hit look like you gwine kill hawgs, 'cause hit sutney wuz cold dat night. Dis nigger ain' nuver gwine forgit it! Jack Forester he had come 'cross de river to lead de fiddlers, an' he say he had to put he fiddle onder he coat an' poke he bow in he breeches leg to keep de strings from poppin', an' dat de river would freeze over sho ef twarn so high; but twuz jes snortin', an' he had hard wuk to git over in he

36. "Damask," a fine patterned fabric.

skiff, an' Unc' Jeems say he ain' gwine come out he boat-house no mo' dat night——he done tempt Providence often 'nough for one day.

"Den ev'ything wuz ready, an' de fiddlers got dee dram[37] an' chuned up, an' twuz lively, I tell you! Twuz jes as thick in dyah as blackberries on de blackberry bush, 'cause ev'y gal on de plantation wuz dyah shakin' her foot for some young buck, an' back-steppin' for to go 'long. Dem ole sleepers wuz jes a-rockin', an' Jack Forester he wuz callin' de figgers[38] for to wake 'em up. I warn' dancin', 'cause I done got 'ligion an 'longst to de chutch sence de trouble done tech us up so rank; but I tell you my foots wuz pintedly eechchin for a leetle sop on it, an' I had to come out to keep from crossin' 'em onst, anyways. Den, too, I had a tetch o' misery in my back, an' I lay off to git a tas'e o' dat egg-nog out dat big bowl, wid snow-drift on it, from Miss Lucy——she al'ays mighty fond o' Marse George; so I slip into de carpenter shop, an' ax her kyarn I do nuttin for her, an' she laugh an' say, yes, I kin drink her health, an' gi' me a gret gobletful, an' jes den de white folks come in to 'spec' de tables, Marse George in de lead, an' dee all fill up dee glasses an' pledge dee health, an' all de servants', an' a merry Christmas; an' den dee went in de wash-house to see de dancin', an' maybe to teck a hand deeself, 'cause white folks' 'ligion ain' like niggers', you know; dee got so much larnin dee kin dance, an' fool de devil too. An' I stay roun' a little while, an' den went in de kitchen to see how supper gittin' on, 'cause I wuz so hongry when I got dyah I ain' able to eat 'nough at one time to 'commodate it, an' de smell o' de tuckeys an' de gret saddlers o' mutton in de tin-kitchens[39] wuz mos' 'nough by deeself to feed a right hongry man; an' dyah wuz a whole parcel o' niggers cookin' an' tunnin' 'bout for life, an' dee faces jes as shiny as ef dee done bas'e 'em wid gravy; an' dyah, settin' back in a cheer out de way, wid her clean frock up off de flo', wuz dat gal! I sutney did feel curiosome.

"I say, 'Hi! name o' Gord! whar'd you come from?' She say 'Oh, Marster! ef heah ain' dat free nigger agin!' An' ev'ybody laughed.

"Well, presney we come out, cause Nancy warn see de dancin', an' we stop a leetle while 'hind de cornder out de wind while she tell me 'bout ev'thing. An' she say dat's all a lie she tell me dat day 'bout Mr. Darker and

---

37. A measured drink of liquor.

38. "Calling the figures," announcing the dance steps.

39. Short-legged tin cylinder that is placed in front of a fireplace providing access to roasting meat.

Miss Charlotte; an' he done gone 'way now for good 'cause he so low down an' wuthless dee kyarn nobody stand him; an' all he warn marry Miss Charlotte for is to git her niggers. But Nancy say Miss Charlotte nuver could abide him; he so 'sateful, 'spressly sence she fine out what a lie he told 'bout Marse George. You know, Mr. Darker he done meck 'em think Marse George sont me dyah to fine out ef he done come home, and den dat he fall on him wid he weepin' when he ain' noticin' him, an' sort o' out de way too, an' git two urr mens to hold him while he beat him, all 'cause he in love wid Miss Charlotte. D'you ever, ever heah sich a lie? An' Nancy say, do' Miss Charlotte ain' b'lieve it all togerr, hit look so reasonable she done le' de ole jedge an' her ma, who wuz 'pending on what she heah, 'duce her to send back he things; an' dee ain' know no better not tell after de ole jedge die; den dee fine out 'bout dee whuppin me, an' all; an' den Miss Charlotte know huccome I ain' gwine stay dat day; an' she say dee was sutney outdone 'bout it, but it too late den; an' Miss Charlotte kyarn do nuttin but cry 'bout it, an' dat she did, pintedly, 'cause she done lost Marse George, an' done 'stroy he life; an' she nuver keer 'bout nobody else sep Marse George, Nancy say. Mr. Clarke he hangin' on, but Miss Charlotte she done tell him pintedly she ain' nuver gwine marry nobody. An' dee jes done come, she say, 'cause dee had to go 'way roun' by de rope ferry 'long o' de river bein' so high, an' dee ain' know tell dee done git out de ker'idge an' in de house dat we all wuz heah; an' Nancy say she glad dee ain', 'cause she 'feared ef dee had, Miss Charlotte wouldn' 'a come.

"Den I tell her all 'bout Marse George, 'cause I know she 'bleeged to tell Miss Charlotte. Twuz powerful cold dyah, but I ain' mine dat, chile. Nancy she done had to wrop her arms up in her ap'on an' she kyarn meck no zistance, 'tall, an' dis nigger ain' keerin' nuttin 'bout cold den.

"An' jes den two ladies come out de carpenter shop 'an went 'long to de wash-house, an' Nancy say, 'Dyah Miss Charlotte now'; an' twuz Miss Lucy an' Miss Charlotte; an' we heah Miss Lucy coaxin' Miss Charlotte to go, tellin' her she kin come right out; an' jes den dee wuz a gret shout, an' we went in hinst 'em. Twuz Marse George had done teck de fiddle, an' ef he warn' natchelly layin' hit down! he wuz up at de urr een o' de room, 'way from we all, 'cause we wuz at de do', nigh Miss Charlotte whar she wuz standin' 'hind some on 'em, wid her eyes on him mighty timid, like she hidin' from him, an' ev'y nigger in de room wuz on dat flo'. Gord! suh, dee wuz grinnin' so dee warn' a toof in dat room you couldn' git you tweezers on; an' you couldn' heah a wud, dee so proud o' Marse George playin' for 'em.

"Well, dee danced tell you couldn' tell which wuz de clappers an' which de back-steppers;[40] de whole house look like it wuz rockin'; an' presney somebody say supper, an' dat stop 'em, an' dee wuz a spell for a minute, an' Marse George standin' dyah wid de fiddle in he hand. He face wuz tunned away, an' he wuz studyin'—studyin' 'bout dat urr Christmas so long ago— an' sudney he face drapt down on de fiddle, an' he drawed de bow 'cross de strings, an' dat chune 'bout 'You'll ermember me' begin to whisper right sorf. Hit begin so low ev'ybody had to stop talkin' an' hold dee mouf to heah it; an Marse George he ain' know nuttin 'bout it, he done gone back, an' standin' dyah in de gret hall playin' it for Miss Charlotte, whar done come down de steps wid her little blue foots an' gret fan, an' standin' dyah in her dim blue dress an' her fyah arms, an' her gret eyes lookin' in he face so earnest, whar he ain' gwine nuver speak to no mo'. I see it by de way he look—an' de fiddle wuz jes pleadin'. He drawed it out jes as fine as a stran' o' Miss Charlotte's hyah.

"Hit so sweet, Miss Charlotte, mun, she couldn' stan' it; she made to de do'; an' jes while she watchin' Marse George to keep him from seein' her he look dat way, an' he eyes fall right into hern.

"Well, suh, de fiddle drapt down on de flo'—perlang!—an' he face wuz white as a sycamore limb.

"Dee say twuz a swimmin' in de head he had; an' Jack say de whole fid- dle warn' wuff de five dollars.

"Me an Nancy followed 'em tell dee went in de house, an' den we come back to de shop whar de supper wuz gwine on, an' got we all supper an' a leetle sop o' dat yaller gravy out dat big bowl, an' den we all rejourned to de wash-house agin, an' got onder de big bush o' misseltow whar hangin' from de jice,[41] an' ef you ever see scufflin', dat's de time.

"Well, me an' she had jes done lay off de whole Christmas, when wud come dat Marse George want he horses.

"I went, but it sutney breck me up; an' I wonder whar de name o' Gord Marse George gwine sen' me dat cold night, an' jes as I got to de do' Marse George an' Mr. Braxton come out, an' I know torectly Marse George wuz gwine 'way. I seen he face by de light o' de lantern, an' twuz set jes rigid as a rock.

"Mr. Braxton he wuz baiggin him to stay; he tell him he ruinin' he life,

40. The uninhibited dancers ("clappers") and the religious "back-steppers" who, by dancing, were back-stepping into sin.

41. Joists.

dat he sho dee's some mistake, an' twill be all right. An' all de answer Marse George meck wuz to swing heself up in de saddle, an' Reveller he look like he gwine fyah 'stracted. He al'ays mighty fool anyways, when he git cold, dat horse wuz.

"Well, we come 'long 'way, an' Mr. Braxton an' two mens come down to de river wid lanterns to see us cross, 'cause twuz dark as pitch, sho 'nough.

"An' jes 'fo' I started I got one o' de mens to hol' my horses, an' I went in de kitchen to git warm, an' dyah Nancy wuz. An' she say Miss Charlotte upstairs cryin' right now, 'cause she think Marse George gwine cross de river 'count o' her, an' she whimper a little herself when I tell her good-by. But twuz too late den.

"Well, de river wuz jes natchelly b'ilin', an' hit soun' like a mill-dam roarin' by; an' when we got dyah Marse George tunned to me an' tell me he reckon I better go back. I ax him whar he gwine, an' he say, 'Home.' 'Den I gwine wid you,' I says. I wuz mighty skeered, but me an' Marse George wuz boys togerr; an' he plunged right in, an' I after him.

"Gord! twuz cold as ice; an' we hadn' got in befo' bofe horses wuz swim-min' for life. He holler to me to byah de myah head up de stream; an' I did try, but what's a nigger to dat water! Hit jes pick me up an' dash me down like I ain' no mo'n a chip, an' de fust thing I know I gwine down de stream like a piece of bark, an' water washin' all over me. I knowed den I gone, an' I hollered for Marse George for help. I heah him answer me not to git skeered, but to hold on; but de myah wuz lungin' an' de water wuz all over me like ice, an' den I washed off de myah back, and got drownded.

"I 'member comin' up, an' hollerin' agin for help, but I know den 'tain' no use, dee ain' no help den, an' I got to pray to Gord, an' den some'n hit me an' I went down agin' an'—de next thing I know I wuz in de bed, an' I heah 'em talkin' 'bout wherr I dead or not, an' I ain' know myself tell I taste de whiskey dee po'rin' down my jugular.

"An den dee tell me 'bout how when I hollered Marse George tun back an' struck out for me for life, an' how jes as I went down de last time he cotch me an' helt on to me tell we wash down to whar de bank corve, an dyah de current wuz so rapid hit yuck him off Reveller back, but he helt on to de reins tell de horse lunge so he hit him wid he fo' foot an' breck he collar-bone, an' den he had to let him go, an' jes helt on to me; an' den we wash up agin de bank an' cotch in a tree, an' de mens got dyah quick as dee could, an' when dee retched us Marse George wuz holdin' on to me, an' had he arm wropped round' a limb, an' we wuz lodged in de crotch, an' bofe jes as dead as a nail; an' de myah she got out, but Reveller he wuz drowned, wid his foot cotch in de rein an' de saddle tunned onder he side; an' dee ain' know wherr Marse George ain' dead too, 'cause he not only drownded, but he lef' arm broke up nigh de shoulder.

"An' dee say Miss Charlotte she 'mos' 'stracted; dat de fust thing anybody know 'bout it wuz when de servants bust in de hall an' holler, an' say Marse George an' me bofe done washed 'way an' drownded, an' dat she drapt down dead on de flo', an' when dee bring her to she 'low to Miss Lucy dat she de 'casion on he death; an' dee say dat when de mens wuz totin' him in de house, an' wuz shufflin' de feets not to make no noise, an' a little piece o' wet blue silk drapt out he breast whar somebody picked up an' gin Miss Lucy, Miss Charlotte breck right down agin; an' some on 'em say she sutney did keer for him; an' now when he layin' upstairs dyah dead, hit too late for him ever to know it.

"Well, suh, I couldn't teck it in dat Marse George and Reveller wuz dead, an' jes den somebody say Marse George done comin' to an' dee gi' me so much whiskey I went to sleep.

"An' next mornin' I got up an' went to Marse George room, an' see him layin' dyah in de bed, wid he face so white an' he eyes so tired-lookin', an' he ain' know me no mo' 'n ef he nuver see me, an' I couldn' stan' it; I jes drap down on de flo' an' bust out cryin'. Gord! suh, I couldn' help it, 'cause Reveller wuz drownded, an' Marse George he wuz mos' gone.

"An' he came nigher goin' yit, 'cause he had sich a strain, an' been so long in de water, he heart done got numbed, an' he got 'lirium, an' all de time he thought he tryin' to git 'cross de river to see Miss Charlotte, an' hit so high he kyarn git dyah.

"Hit sutney wuz pitiful to see him layin' dyah tossin' an' pitchin', not knowin' whar he wuz, tell it teck all Mr. Braxton an' me could do to keep him in de bed, an' de doctors say he kyarn hol' out much longer.

"An' all dis time Miss Charlotte she wuz gwine 'bout de house wid her face right white, an' Nancy say she don' do nuttin all day long in her room but cry an' say her pra'rs, prayin' for Marse George, whar dyin' upstairs by 'count o' not knowin' she love him, an' I tell Nancy how he honin' all de time to see her, an' how he constant cravin' her name.

"Well, so twuz, tell he mos' done wyah heself out; an' jes lay dyah wid his face white as de pillow, an' he gret pitiful eyes rollin' 'bout so restless, like he still lookin' for her whar he all de time callin' her name, an' kyarn git 'cross dat river to see.

"An' one evenin' 'bout sunset he 'peared to be gwine; he weaker'n he been at all, he ain' able to scuffle no mo', an' jes layin' dyah so quiet, an' presney he say, lookin' mighty wistful:

"'Edinburg, I'm goin' to-night; ef I don' git 'cross dis time, I'll gin't up.'

"Mr. Braxton wuz standin' nigh de head o' de bed, an' he say, 'Well, by Gord! he *shell* see her!'—jes so. An' he went out de room, an' to Miss Charlotte do', an' call her, an' tell her she got to come, ef she don't, he'll die dat night; an' fust thing I know, Miss Lucy bring Miss Charlotte in, wid her face right white, but jes as tender as a angel's, an' she come an' stan' by de side de bed, an' lean down over him an' call he name, 'George!'—jes so.

"An' Marse George he ain' answer; he jes look at her study for a minute, an' den he forehead got smooth, an' he tun he eyes to me, an' say, 'Edinburg, I'm 'cross.'"

Grace King

(1852–1932)

BORN IN NEW ORLEANS ON November 29, 1852, Grace King was the daughter of prominent lawyer William Woodson King, whose Confederate sympathies forced him into exile when federal forces took over the city early in the war. His resourceful and intrepid wife, Sarah Ann Miller, managed to slip out of the occupied city with seven children, five servants, and her mother in order to meet him at their plantation near New Iberia about eighty miles away. That period not only provoked King's desire at age ten to become a writer but also deeply shaped her imaginative and emotional experience. When the King family returned to New Orleans in 1866, it was no longer wealthy. The bitterness of remaking their lives as members of a defeated faction in an impoverished city created a underlying sense of grievance that inflects much of King's writing.

Although the Kings were forced into unfamiliar working-class neighborhoods, their daughters still received fine educations, first at the Institut St. Louis for upper-class white girls and then as private pupils of Boston-bred Heloise Cenas, with whom King studied French. Though a Protestant minority in a pervasively Catholic culture, the Kings also quickly regained access to the social life of the New Orleans elite. Even after William King's death in 1881, an event that further reduced their financial circumstances, Sarah King maintained a genteel and hospitable household, known for its excellent dining and clever guests. King recalled her mother as a "charming raconteuse," a skill shared by her "Grandmamma," whose tales of her own Huguenot childhood in Georgia shaped King's love of storytelling.

The Cotton Centennial Exposition of 1884, intended to resuscitate New Orleans's lagging economy, proved a major turning point in King's life. It brought to the city Julia Ward Howe, who revived the Pan-Gnostic Society, a women's club for which King's essay, "The Heroines of Fiction," marked her first appearance in print. It also provided the occasion for King's meeting *Century Magazine* editor Richard Watson Gilder at the exclusive Pickwick Club during the carnival season. When Gilder challenged New Orleans's resentful treatment of George W. Cable (whose work *Century* had published), King retorted that Cable had "stabbed the city in the back . . . to please the Northern press" by his "preference for colored people over white." Taking Gilder's dare that someone should then write "better" of Creole life, that same night King began "Monsieur Motte," based on her days at the Institut St. Louis. Elaborating the devotion of a former slave for her young white mistress, the story (submitted anonymously to *Century*) was rejected. However, another carnival acquaintance, *Harper's* editor Charles Dudley Warner, helped her to publish it in the *New Princeton Review* (1886). Warner also introduced King to a prominent circle of writers living in New England, including noted feminist Isabel Hooker, Annie Fields, Sarah Orne Jewett, Mary Wilkins Freeman, and Samuel and Olivia Clemens. The Clemenses, particularly Olivia, remained lifelong friends.

King enjoyed immediate success with her fiction. "Monsieur Motte" and its sequels constituted her first collection, *Monsieur Motte* (1888), followed by *Tales of a Time and Place* (1892), many of which appeared first in *Harper's. Balcony Stories* (1893), the fourteen-story collection from which all of the present selections are taken, contains work acclaimed by her contemporaries and recognized today as among her finest. The brief preface, "The Balcony," evokes the deepest strength of King's fiction: its insistence on hearing the (unheard) voices of women. Critics have increasingly taken note of King's focus on the unjust displacement of women in a world governed by the negligence and/or indifference of men. Throughout her stories, women are simultaneously disappointed and constrained by the promise of male protection. Such a perspective closely parallels King's broader identification as a cultivated southern aristocrat overruled and supplanted by brash northern ideologies of race and commerce, a point of view whose poignancy and indignation struck a chord with her readers. That sense of aggrieved resignation informs "La Grande Demoiselle," in which a woman of enormous prewar wealth and pride endures a fall so abject that marriage to a misogynist "mushroom" of a man seems preferable to teaching black children. Similarly, "The Little Convent Girl," who, after her father's death, travels down the river to meet her mysterious mother, prefers death to the humiliating fate awaiting her when she learns that she is "colored." In both stories, King's conservative notions of race and class are indisputable; however, they are unsettled by her empathy for the powerlessness of all women in controlling their destinies. One marker of that complexity is her finely ironic and often impressionistic prose. King's well-crafted stories, which rely on French phrases rather than extensive dialect to convey regional differences, also depend less on plot than on skillful portraiture, the development of relationships, and subtle shifts in awareness to create their effects. In these qualities, King's fiction anticipates the work of modernists like Anton Chekhov and Katherine Mansfield.

Though King consciously identifies with the privileges of her class and race, she often focuses on women at the margins. She once observed that "white as well as black women have a sad showing in what some people call romance." King thus richly expresses the conflicts felt by white southern women writers as they tried to maintain their regional (and racist) allegiances along with their feminist and realist perspectives.

King never married, but she traveled to Europe several times, staying in Paris for extended periods, where in 1891 she befriended writer and critic Marie-Thérèse Blanc (Thomas Bentzon) and busied herself researching at the Bibliothèque Nationale for materials for her historical studies of early Louisiana. As her careful research suggests, King was a fine scholar, publishing several highly readable works of biography and history, including her best-known, *New Orleans, the Place and the People* (1895). After the publication of *Balcony Stories,* she focused extensively on history, although she later wrote two short novels, *The Pleasant Ways of St. Médard* (1916), an impressionistic and surprisingly subtle tale of Reconstruction life, and *La Dame de Sainte Hermine* (1924), a less successful historical novel of early Louisiana.

Her literary accomplishments and her social grace combined to make King the grande dame of New Orleans literature. In 1904, one of her surviving brothers purchased a residence for her and his other two unmarried sisters. The Greek revival house on Coliseum Street became a pleasant stopping place for many visiting writers and intellectuals, who benefited from the Kings' gracious hospitality. King received a number of tributes, among them election as a fellow of the Royal Society of Arts and Sciences in England, an honorary degree from Tulane University, and the Officier de l'Instruction Publique, awarded by the French consul in a ceremony at her house in 1918. King continued to work and travel throughout the last decade of her life, finishing the proofs of her rather polite and anecdotal autobiography, *Memories of a Southern Woman of Letters*, just a few months before her death. Suffering complications following a stroke, King died peacefully on January 14, 1932, attended by her devoted sisters. Her native city, grateful for her loyalty and proud of her achievements, publicly mourned the loss of one of its most able interpreters.

Works by Grace King

FICTION

Monsieur Motte, 1888

Tales of a Time and Place, 1892

Balcony Stories, 1893

The Pleasant Ways of St. Médard, 1916

La Dame de Sainte Hermine, 1924

Grace King of New Orleans: A Selection of Her Writings, ed. Robert Bush, 1973

SOCIAL HISTORY

Jean-Baptiste Le Moine, Sieur de Bienville, 1892

New Orleans: The Place and the People, 1895

Stories from Louisiana History, 1905

Creole Families of New Orleans, 1921

Memories of a Southern Woman of Letters, 1932, rpt. 1971

Further Reading

Bush, Robert. *Grace King: A Southern Destiny*. Baton Rouge: Louisiana State University Press, 1983.

Coleman, Linda S. "At Odds: Race and Gender in Grace King's Short Fiction." In *Louisiana Women Writers: New Essays and a Comprehensive Bibliography*. Ed. Dorothy H. Brown and Barbara C. Ewell. Baton Rouge: Louisiana State University Press, 1992.

Juncker, Clara. "Grace King: Woman as Artist." *The Southern Literary Journal* 20 (1987).

Kirby, David. *Grace King*. New York: Twayne, 1980.

Robinson, Lori. "'Why, Why Do We Not Write Our Side': Gender and Southern Self-Representation in Grace King's *Balcony Stories*." In *Breaking Boundaries:*

New Perspectives on Women's Regional Writing. Ed. Sherrie A. Inness and Diana Royer. Iowa City: University of Iowa Press, 1997.

Taylor, Helen. "The Case of Grace King." *The Southern Review* 18.4 (1982).

The Balcony

There is much of life passed on the balcony in a country where the summer unrolls in six moon-lengths, and where the nights have to come with a double endowment of vastness and splendor to compensate for the tedious, sun-parched days.

And in that country the women love to sit and talk together of summer nights, on balconies, in their vague, loose, white garments,—men are not balcony sitters,—with their sleeping children within easy hearing, the stars breaking the cool darkness, or the moon making a show of light— oh, such a discreet show of light!—through the vines. And the children inside, waking to go from one sleep into another, hear the low, soft mother-voices on the balcony, talking about this person and that, old times, old friends, old experiences; and it seems to them, hovering a moment in wakefulness, that there is no end of the world or time, or of the mother-knowledge; but, illimitable as it is, the mother-voices and the mother-love and protection fill it all,—with their mother's hand in theirs, children are not afraid even of God,—and they drift into slumber again, their little dreams taking all kinds of pretty reflections from the great unknown horizon outside, as their fragile soap-bubbles take on reflections from the sun and clouds.

Experiences, reminiscences, episodes, picked up as only women know how to pick them up from other women's lives,— or other women's destinies, as they prefer to call them,—and told as only women know how to relate them; what God has done or is doing with some other woman whom they have known— that is what interests women once embarked on their own lives,—the embarkation takes place at marriage, or after the marriageable time,— or, rather, that is what interests the women who sit of summer nights on balconies. For in those long-moon countries life is open and accessible, and romances seem to be furnished real and gratis, in order to save, in a languor-breeding climate, the ennui of reading and writing books. Each woman has a different way of picking up and relating her stories, as each one selects different pieces, and has a personal way of playing them on the piano.

Each story *is* different, or appears so to her; each has some unique and peculiar pathos in it. And so she dramatizes and inflects it, trying to make the point visible to her apparent also to her hearers. Sometimes the pathos and interest to the hearers lie only in this—that the relater has observed it, and gathered it, and finds it worth telling. For do we not gather what we have not, and is not our own lacking our one motive? It may be so, for it often appears so.

And if a child inside be wakeful and precocious, it is not dreams alone that take on reflections from the balcony outside: through the half-open shutters the still, quiet eyes look across the dim forms on the balcony to the star-spangled or the moon-brightened heavens beyond; while memory makes stores for the future, and germs are sown, out of which the slow, clambering vine of thought issues, one day, to decorate or hide, as it may be, the structures or ruins of life.

The Little Convent Girl

She was coming down on the boat from Cincinnati, the little convent girl. Two sisters had brought her aboard. They gave her in charge of the captain, got her a state-room, saw that the new little trunk was put into it, hung the new little satchel up on the wall, showed her how to bolt the door at night, shook hands with her for good-by (good-bys have really no significance for sisters), and left her there. After a while the bells all rang, and the boat, in the awkward elephantine fashion of boats, got into midstream. The chambermaid found her sitting on the chair in the state-room where the sisters had left her, and showed her how to sit on a chair in the saloon.[1] And there she sat until the captain came and hunted her up for supper. She could not do anything of herself; she had to be initiated into everything by some one else.

She was known on the boat only as "the little convent girl." Her name, of course, was registered in the clerk's office, but on a steamboat no one thinks of consulting the clerk's ledger. It is always the little widow, the fat madam, the tall colonel, the parson, etc. The captain, who pronounced by the letter, always called her the little con*vent* girl. She was the beau-ideal[2]

1. Common or public room on a steamboat.
2. "The perfection of beauty" (Fr.), or ideal instance.

of the little convent girl. She never raised her eyes except when spoken to. Of course she never spoke first, even to the chambermaid, and when she did speak it was in the wee, shy, furtive voice one might imagine a just-budding violet to have; and she walked with such soft, easy, carefully cal-culated steps that one naturally felt the penalties that must have secured them—penalties dictated by a black code of deportment.[3]

She was dressed in deep mourning. Her black straw hat was trimmed with stiff new crape,[4] and her stiff new bombazine[5] dress had crape collar and cuffs. She wore her hair in two long plaits fastened around her head tight and fast. Her hair had a strong inclination to curl, but that had been taken out of it as austerely as the noise out of her footfalls. Her hair was as black as her dress; her eyes, when one saw them, seemed blacker than either, on account of the bluishness of the white surrounding the pupil. Her eyelashes were almost as thick as the black veil which the sisters had fastened around her hat with an extra pin the very last thing before leav-ing. She had a round little face, and a tiny pointed chin; her mouth was slightly protuberant from the teeth, over which she tried to keep her lips well shut, the effort giving them a pathetic little forced expression. Her complexion was sallow, a pale sallow, the complexion of a brunette bleached in darkened rooms. The only color about her was a blue taffeta ribbon from which a large silver medal of the Virgin hung over the place where a breastpin should have been. She was so little, so little, although she was eighteen, as the sisters told the captain; otherwise they would not have permitted her to travel all the way to New Orleans alone.

Unless the captain or the clerk remembered to fetch her out in front, she would sit all day in the cabin, in the same place, crocheting lace, her spool of thread and box of patterns in her lap, on the handkerchief spread to save her new dress. Never leaning back—oh, no! always straight and stiff, as if the conventual back board[6] were there within call. She would eat only convent fare at first, notwithstanding the importunities of the waiters, and the jocularities of the captain, and particularly of the clerk.

3. The rules for proper behavior, with a glance at the *Code Noir* or Black Code, which was is-sued in 1724 by the French monarchy to govern the interactions of blacks and whites in Loui-siana, but which influenced legislation well into the nineteenth century.

4. Thin fabric with a wrinkly surface; black crepe was a common nineteenth-century trim for mourning clothes.

5. Twill blend of wool and cotton or silk.

6. Stiff board worn by girls to straighten posture, originally a medieval practice.

Every one knows the fund of humor possessed by a steamboat clerk, and what a field for display the table at meal-times affords. On Friday she fasted rigidly, and she never began to eat, or finished, without a little Latin movement of the lips and a sign of the cross. And always at six o'clock of the evening she remembered the angelus,[7] although there was no church bell to remind her of it.

She was in mourning for her father, the sisters told the captain, and she was going to New Orleans to her mother. She had not seen her mother since she was an infant, on account of some disagreement between the parents, in consequence of which the father had brought her to Cincinnati, and placed her in the convent. There she had been for twelve years, only going to her father for vacations and holidays. So long as the father lived he would never let the child have any communication with her mother. Now that he was dead all that was changed, and the first thing that the girl herself wanted to do was to go to her mother.

The mother superior had arranged it all with the mother of the girl, who was to come personally to the boat in New Orleans, and receive her child from the captain, presenting a letter from the mother superior, a facsimile of which the sisters gave the captain.

It is a long voyage from Cincinnati to New Orleans, the rivers doing their best to make it interminable, embroidering themselves *ad libitum*[8] all over the country. Every five miles, and sometimes oftener, the boat would stop to put off or take on freight, if not both. The little convent girl, sitting in the cabin, had her terrible frights at first from the hideous noises attendant on these landings—the whistles, the ringings of the bells, the running to and fro, the shouting. Every time she thought it was shipwreck, death, judgment, purgatory;[9] and her sins! her sins! She would drop her crochet, and clutch her prayer-beads from her pocket, and relax the constraint over her lips, which would go to rattling off prayers with the velocity of a relaxed windlass.[10] That was at first, before the captain took to

7. The girl observes a number of Roman Catholic religious practices indicating particular devotion. Fasting on Friday was customary among the very devout, while the "angelus" is a prayer recited at six in the morning, noon, and six at night and signaled by ringing bells; it recalls the angel's announcement to Mary that she will bear the Christ.

8. "At (their) pleasure" (Lat.).

9. In Roman Catholicism, a temporary place of punishment to purge lesser sins before entering heaven.

10. A device for raising an object by turning a crank. If the crank is released, the object drops.

fetching her out in front to see the boat make a landing. Then she got to liking it so much that she would stay all day just where the captain put her, going inside only for her meals. She forgot herself at times so much that she would draw her chair a little closer to the railing, and put up her veil, actually, to see better. No one ever usurped her place, quite in front, or intruded upon her either with word or look; for every one learned to know her shyness, and began to feel a personal interest in her, and all wanted the little convent girl to see everything that she possibly could.

And it was worth seeing—the balancing and *chasséeing*[11] and waltzing of the cumbersome old boat to make a landing. It seemed to be always attended with the difficulty and the improbability of a new enterprise; and the relief when it did sidle up anywhere within rope's-throw of the spot aimed at! And the roustabout[12] throwing the rope from the perilous end of the dangling gang-plank! And the dangling roustabouts hanging like drops of water from it—dropping sometimes twenty feet to the land, and not infrequently into the river itself. And then what a rolling of barrels, and shouldering of sacks, and singing of Jim Crow[13] songs, and pacing of Jim Crow steps; and black skins glistening through torn shirts, and white teeth gleaming through red lips, and laughing, and talking and—bewildering! entrancing! Surely the little convent girl in her convent walls never dreamed of so much unpunished noise and movement in the world!

The first time she heard the mate—it must have been like the first time woman ever heard man—curse and swear, she turned pale, and ran quickly, quickly into the saloon, and—came out again? No, indeed! not with all the soul she had to save, and all the other sins on her conscience. She shook her head resolutely, and was not seen in her chair on deck again until the captain not only reassured her, but guaranteed his reassurance. And after that, whenever the boat was about to make a landing, the mate would first glance up to the guards, and if the little convent girl was sitting there he would change his invective to sarcasm, and politely request the colored gentlemen not to hurry themselves—on no account whatever; to take their time about shoving out the plank; to send the rope ashore by post-office—write him when it got there; begging them not to strain their backs; calling them mister, colonel, major, general, prince, and your

11. "Sashay," a gliding dance step.

12. Wharf laborer, usually young and daring.

13. Late-century term for the laws of racial segregation, it also (as here) was applied generally to African-American people and their culture.

royal highness, which was vastly amusing. At night, however, or when the little convent girl was not there, language flowed in its natural curve, the mate swearing like a pagan to make up for lost time.

The captain forgot himself one day: it was when the boat ran aground in the most unexpected manner and place, and he went to work to express his opinion, as only steamboat captains can, of the pilot, mate, engineer, crew, boat, river, country, and the world in general, ringing the bell, first to back, then to head, shouting himself hoarser than his own whistle—when he chanced to see the little black figure hurrying through the chaos on the deck; and the captain stuck as fast aground in midstream as the boat had done.

In the evening the little convent girl would be taken on the upper deck, and going up the steep stairs there was such confusion, to keep the black skirts well over the stiff white petticoats; and, coming down, such blushing when suspicion would cross the unprepared face that a rim of white stocking might be visible; and the thin feet, laced so tightly in the glossy new leather boots, would cling to each successive step as if they could never, never make another venture; and then one boot would (there is but that word) hesitate out, and feel and feel around, and have such a pause of helpless agony as if indeed the next step must have been wilfully removed, or was nowhere to be found on the wide, wide earth.

It was a miracle that the pilot ever got her up into the pilot-house; but pilots have a lonely time, and do not hesitate even at miracles when there is a chance for company. He would place a box for her to climb to the tall bench behind the wheel, and he would arrange the cushions, and open a window here to let in air, and shut one there to cut off a draft, as if there could be no tenderer consideration in life for him than her comfort. And he would talk of the river to her, explain the chart, pointing out eddies, whirlpools, shoals, depths, new beds, old beds, cut-offs, caving banks, and making banks, as exquisitely and respectfully as if she had been the River Commission.

It was his opinion that there was as great a river as the Mississippi flowing directly under it—an underself of a river, as much a counterpart of the other as the second story of a house is of the first; in fact, he said they were navigating through the upper story. Whirlpools were holes in the floor of the upper river, so to speak; eddies were rifts and cracks. And deep under the earth, hurrying toward the subterranean stream, were other streams, small and great, but all deep, hurrying to and from that great mother-stream underneath, just as the small and great overground streams hurry to and from their mother Mississippi. It was almost more than the little convent girl could take in: at least such was the expression of her eyes; for they opened as all eyes have to open at pilot stories. And he knew as much of astronomy as he did of hydrology, could call the stars by name, and define the shapes of the constellations; and she, who had studied astronomy at the convent, was charmed to find that what she had learned was all true. It was in the pilot-house, one night, that she forgot herself for the first time in her life, and stayed up until after nine o'clock. Although she appeared almost intoxicated at the wild pleasure, she was immediately overwhelmed at the wickedness of it, and observed much more rigidity of conduct thereafter. The engineer, the boiler-men, the firemen, the stokers, they all knew when the little convent girl was up in the pilot-house: the speaking-tube became so mild and gentle.

With all the delays of river and boat, however, there is an end to the journey from Cincinnati to New Orleans. The latter city, which at one time to the impatient seemed at the terminus of the never, began, all of a sudden, one day to make its nearingness felt; and from that period every other interest paled before the interest in the imminence of arrival into port, and the whole boat was seized with a panic of preparation, the little convent girl with the others. Although so immaculate was she in person and effects that she might have been struck with a landing, as some good people might be struck with death, at any moment without fear of results, her trunk was packed and repacked, her satchel arranged and rearranged, and, the last day, her hair was brushed and plaited and smoothed over and over again until the very last glimmer of a curl disappeared. Her dress was whisked, as if for microscopic inspection; her face was washed; and her finger-nails were scrubbed with the hard convent nail-brush, until the disciplined little tips ached with a pristine soreness. And still there were hours to wait, and still the boat added up delays. But she arrived at last, after all, with not more than the usual and expected difference between the actual and the advertised time of arrival.

There was extra blowing and extra ringing, shouting, commanding, rushing up the gangway and rushing down the gangway. The clerks, sitting behind tables on the first deck, were plied, in the twinkling of an eye, with estimates, receipts, charges, countercharges, claims, reclaims, demands, questions, accusations, threats, all at topmost voices. None but steamboat clerks could have stood it. And there were throngs composed of individuals every one of whom wanted to see the captain first and at once: and those who could not get to him shouted over the heads of the others; and as usual he lost his temper and politeness, and began to do what he termed "hustle."

"Captain! Captain!" a voice called him to where a hand plucked his sleeve, and a letter was thrust toward him. "The cross, and the name of the convent." He recognized the envelop of the mother superior. He read the duplicate of the letter given by the sisters. He looked at the woman—the mother—casually, then again and again.

The little convent girl saw him coming, leading some one toward her. She rose. The captain took her hand first, before the other greeting, "Good-by, my dear," he said. He tried to add something else, but seemed undetermined what. "Be a good little girl——" It was evidently all he could think of. Nodding to the woman behind him, he turned on his heel, and left.

One of the deck-hands was sent to fetch her trunk. He walked out behind them, through the cabin, and the crowd on deck, down the stairs, and out over the gangway. The little convent girl and her mother went with hands tightly clasped. She did not turn her eyes to the right or left, or once (what all passengers do) look backward at the boat which, however slowly, had carried her surely over dangers that she wot not of. All looked at her as she passed. All wanted to say good-by to the little convent girl, to see the mother who had been deprived of her so long. Some expressed surprise in a whistle; some in other ways. All exclaimed audibly, or to themselves, "Colored!"

It takes about a month to make the round trip from New Orleans to Cincinnati and back, counting five days' stoppage in New Orleans. It was a month to a day when the steamboat came puffing and blowing up to the wharf again, like a stout dowager after too long a walk; and the same scene of confusion was enacted, as it had been enacted twelve times a year, at almost the same wharf for twenty years; and the same calm, a death calmness by contrast, followed as usual the next morning.

The decks were quiet and clean; one cargo had just been delivered, part of another stood ready on the levee to be shipped. The captain was there waiting for his business to begin, the clerk was in his office getting his books ready, the voice of the mate could be heard below, mustering the old crew out and a new crew in; for if steamboat crews have a single principle,—and there are those who deny them any,—it is never to ship twice in succession on the same boat. It was too early yet for any but roustabouts, marketers, and church-goers; so early that even the river was still partly mist-covered; only in places could the swift, dark current be seen rolling swiftly along.

"Captain!" A hand plucked at his elbow, as if not confident that the mere calling would secure attention. The captain turned. The mother of the little convent girl stood there, and she held the little convent girl by the hand. "I have brought her to see you," the woman said. "You were so kind—and she is so quiet, so still, all the time, I thought it would do her a pleasure."

She spoke with an accent, and with embarrassment; otherwise one would have said that she was bold and assured enough.

"She don't go nowhere, she don't do nothing but make her crochet and her prayers, so I thought I would bring her for a little visit of 'How d' ye do' to you."

There was, perhaps, some inflection in the woman's voice that might have made known, or at least awakened, the suspicion of some latent hope or intention, had the captain's ear been fine enough to detect it. There might have been something in the little convent girl's face, had his eye been more sensitive—a trifle paler, maybe, the lips a little tighter drawn, the blue ribbon a shade faded. He may have noticed that, but—And the visit of "How d' ye do" came to an end.

They walked down the stairway, the woman in front, the little convent girl—her hand released to shake hands with the captain—following, across the bared deck, out to the gangway, over to the middle of it. No one was looking, no one saw more than a flutter of white petticoats, a show of white stockings, as the little convent girl went under the water.

The roustabout dived, as the roustabouts always do, after the drowning, even at the risk of their good-for-nothing lives. The mate himself jumped overboard; but she had gone down in a whirlpool. Perhaps, as the pilot had told her whirlpools always did, it may have carried her through to the underground river, to that vast, hidden, dark Mississippi that flows beneath the one we see; for her body was never found.

La Grande Demoiselle

That was what she was called by everybody as soon as she was seen or described.[14] Her name, besides baptismal titles, was Idalie Sainte Foy Mortemart des Islets.[15] When she came into society, in the brilliant little world of New Orleans, it was the event of the season, and after she came in, what-

14. "The noble young lady" (Fr.).

15. St. Foy ("St. Faith" [Fr.]) was a young medieval martyr, who inspired the "Song of St. Foy" ("Chanson de Sainte Foi"). Mortemart is an old French surname, which literally means "death-market," while "des islets" means "of the little islands." "Consolation à Idalie sur la mort d'un parent," a poem by Tristan L'Hermite (1601–1655), who was rediscovered in the late nineteenth century, might also have inspired King.

ever she did became also events. Whether she went, or did not go; what she said, or did not say; what she wore, and did not wear—all these became important matters of discussion, quoted as much or more than what the president said, or the governor thought. And in those days, the days of '59,[16] New Orleans was not, as it is now, a one-heiress place, but it may be said that one could find heiresses then as one finds type-writing girls now.[17]

Mademoiselle Idalie received her birth, and what education she had, on her parents' plantation, the famed old Reine [18] Sainte Foy place, and it is no secret that, like the ancient kings of France, her birth exceeded her education.

It was a plantation, the Reine Sainte Foy, the richness and luxury of which are really well described in those perfervid pictures of tropical life, at one time the passion of philanthropic imaginations, excited and exciting over the horrors of slavery. Although these pictures were then often accused of being purposely exaggerated, they seem now to fall short of, instead of surpassing, the truth. Stately walls, acres of roses, miles of oranges, unmeasured fields of cane, colossal sugar-house—they were all there, and all the rest of it, with the slaves, slaves, slaves everywhere, whole villages of negro cabins. And there were also, most noticeable to the natural, as well as to the visionary, eye—there were the ease, idleness, extravagance, self-indulgence, pomp, pride, arrogance, in short the whole enumeration, the moral *sine qua non*,[19] as some people considered it, of the wealthy slaveholder of aristocratic descent and tastes.

What Mademoiselle Idalie cared to learn she studied, what she did not she ignored; and she followed the same simple rule untrammeled in her eating, drinking, dressing, and comportment generally; and whatever discipline may have been exercised on the place, either in fact or fiction, most assuredly none of it, even so much as in a threat, ever attainted her sacred person. When she was just turned sixteen, Mademoiselle Idalie made up her mind to go into society. Whether she was beautiful or not, it is hard to say. It is almost impossible to appreciate properly the beauty of the rich, the very rich. The unfettered development, the limitless choice of accessories, the confidence, the self-esteem, the sureness of expression, the sim-

16. Before the onset of the Civil War, 1861−65.

17. Alluding to the entrance in the 1890s of many middle-class women into the workforce, in contrast to their (idealized) prewar status.

18. "Queen" (Fr.).

19. "Without which not" or "essential condition" (Lat.).

plicity of purpose, the ease of execution—all these produce a certain effect of beauty behind which one really cannot get to measure length of nose, or brilliancy of eye. This much can be said: there was nothing in her that positively contradicted any assumption of beauty on her part, or credit of it on the part of others. She was very tall and very thin with small head, long neck, black eyes, and abundant straight black hair,—for which her hair-dresser deserved more praise than she,—good teeth, of course, and a mouth that, even in prayer, talked nothing but commands; that is about all she had *en fait d'ornements*,[20] as the modistes[21] say. It may be added that she walked as if the Reine Sainte Foy plantation extended over the whole earth, and the soil of it were too vile for her tread. Of course she did not buy her toilets in New Orleans. Everything was ordered from Paris, and came as regularly through the custom-house as the modes and robes to the milliners. She was furnished by a certain house there, just as one of a royal family would be at the present day. As this had lasted from her layette up to her sixteenth year, it may be imagined what took place when she determined to make her début. Then it was literally, not metaphorically, *carte blanche*,[22] at least so it got to the ears of society. She took a sheet of note-paper, wrote the date at the top, added, "I make my début in November," signed her name at the extreme end of the sheet, addressed it to her dressmaker in Paris, and sent it.

It was said that in her dresses the very handsomest silks were used for linings, and that real lace was used where others put imitation,—around the bottoms of the skirts, for instance,—and silk ribbons of the best quality served the purposes of ordinary tapes; and sometimes the buttons were of real gold and silver, sometimes set with precious stones. Not that she ordered these particulars, but the dressmakers, when given *carte blanche* by those who do not condescend to details, so soon exhaust the outside limits of garments that perforce they take to plastering them inside with gold, so to speak, and, when the bill goes in, they depend upon the furnishings to carry out a certain amount of the contract in justifying the price. And it was said that these costly dresses, after being worn once or twice, were cast aside, thrown upon the floor, given to the negroes—anything to get them out of sight. Not an inch of the real lace, not one of the jeweled buttons, not a scrap of ribbon, was ripped off to save. And it was said that if

20. "Of actual ornamentation" (Fr.).
21. Milliners or fashionable dress makers (Fr.).
22. "Blank check" or without limit to expense (Fr.).

she wanted to romp with her dogs in all her finery, she did it; she was known to have ridden horseback, one moonlight night, all around the plantation in a white silk dinner-dress flounced with Alençon.[23] And at night, when she came from the balls, tired, tired to death as only balls can render one, she would throw herself down upon her bed in her tulle skirts,—on top, or not, of the exquisite flowers, she did not care,—and make her maid undress her in that position; often having her bodices cut off her, because she was too tired to turn over and have them unlaced.

That she was admired, raved about, loved even, goes without saying. After the first month she held the refusal of half the beaux of New Orleans. Men did absurd, undignified, preposterous things for her; and she? Love? Marry? The idea never occurred to her. She treated the most exquisite of her pretenders no better than she treated her Paris gowns, for the matter of that. She could not even bring herself to listen to a proposal patiently; whistling to her dogs, in the middle of the most ardent protestations, or jumping up and walking away with a shrug of the shoulders, and a "Bah!"

Well! Every one knows what happened after '59. There is no need to repeat. The history of one is the history of all. But there was this difference—for there is every shade of difference in misfortune, as there is every shade of resemblance in happiness. Mortemart des Islets went off to fight. That was natural; his family had been doing that, he thought, or said, ever since Charlemagne.[24] Just as naturally he was killed in the first engagement. They, his family, were always among the first killed; so much so that it began to be considered assassination to fight a duel with any of them. All that was in the ordinary course of events. One difference in their misfortunes lay in that after the city was captured, their plantation, so near, convenient, and rich in all kinds of provisions, was selected to receive a contingent of troops—a colored company. If it had been a colored company raised in Louisiana it might have been different; and these negroes mixed with the negroes in the neighborhood,—and negroes are no better than whites, for the proportion of good and bad among them,— and the officers were always off duty when they should have been on, and on when they should have been off.

One night the dwelling caught fire. There was an immediate rush to save the ladies. Oh, there was no hesitation about that! They were seized

23. Valuable lace of ornate patterns on tulle (net), originally made in Alençon in northwest France.

24. Charles the Great, king of the Franks and Roman emperor, 742–814.

in their beds, and carried out in the very arms of their enemies; carried away off to the sugar-house, and deposited there. No danger of their doing anything but keep very quiet and still in their *chemises de nuit*,[25] and their one sheet apiece, which was about all that was saved from the conflagration—that is, for them. But it must be remembered that this is all hearsay. When one has not been present, one knows nothing of one's own knowledge; one can only repeat. It has been repeated, however, that although the house was burned to the ground, and everything in it destroyed, wherever, for a year afterward, a man of that company or of that neighborhood was found, there could have been found also, without search-warrant, property that had belonged to the Des Islets. That is the story; and it is believed or not, exactly according to prejudice.

How the ladies ever got out of the sugar-house, history does not relate; nor what they did. It was not a time for sociability, either personal or epistolary. At one offensive word your letter, and you, very likely, examined; and Ship Island [26] for a hotel, with soldiers for hostesses! Madame Des Islets died very soon after the accident—of rage, they say; and that was about all the public knew.

Indeed, at that time the society of New Orleans had other things to think about than the fate of the Des Islets. As for *la grande demoiselle,* she had prepared for her own oblivion in the hearts of her female friends. And the gentlemen,—her *preux chevaliers*,[27]—they were burning with other passions than those which had driven them to her knees, encountering a little more serious response than "bahs" and shrugs. And, after all, a woman seems the quickest thing forgotten when once the important affairs of life come to men for consideration.

It might have been ten years according to some calculations, or ten eternities,—the heart and the almanac never agree about time,—but one morning old Champigny (they used to call him Champignon) [28] was walking along his levee front,[29] calculating how soon the water would come

25. "Nightgowns" (Fr.).

26. Island twelve miles off the Mississippi coast, which served as a notorious Union prison after its recapture from Confederate troops in 1862.

27. "Valiant knights" (Fr.).

28. "Mushroom," also "wig stand" (Fr.).

29. As early as 1760, France decreed that property along the Mississippi River be divided into narrow perpendicular strips, thus assuring a dense population with an interest in maintaining the levees as flood protection.

over, and drown him out, as the Louisianians say. It was before a seven-o'clock breakfast, cold, wet, rainy, and discouraging. The road was knee-deep in mud, and so broken up with hauling, that it was like walking upon waves to get over it. A shower poured down. Old Champigny was hurry-ing in when he saw a figure approaching. He had to stop to look at it, for it was worth while. The head was hidden by a green barege[30] veil, which the showers had plentifully besprinkled with dew; a tall, thin figure. Figure! No; not even could it be called a figure: straight up and down, like a finger or a post; high-shouldered, and a step—a step like a plowman's. No um-brella; no—nothing more, in fact. It does not sound so peculiar as when first related—something must be forgotten. The feet—oh, yes, the feet—they were like waffle-irons, or frying-pans, or anything of that shape.

Old Champigny did not care for women—he never had; they simply did not exist for him in the order of nature. He had been married once, it is true, about a half century before; but that was not reckoned against the existence of his prejudice, because he was *célibataire*[31] to his finger-tips, as any one could see a mile away. But that woman *intrigué'd* him.

He had no servant to inquire from. He performed all of his own do-mestic work in the wretched little cabin that replaced his old home. For Champigny also belonged to the great majority of the *nouveaux pauvres*.[32] He went out into the rice-field, where were one or two hands that worked on shares with him, and he asked them. They knew immediately; there is nothing connected with the parish that a field-hand does not know at once. She was the teacher of the colored public school some three or four miles away. "Ah," thought Champigny, "some Northern lady on a mission." He watched to see her return in the evening, which she did, of course; in a blinding rain. Imagine the green barege veil then; for it remained always down over her face.

Old Champigny could not get over it that he had never seen her before. But he must have seen her, and, with his abstraction and old age, not have noticed her, for he found out from the negroes that she had been teaching four or five years there. And he found out also—how, is not important—that she was Idalie Sainte Foy Mortemart des Islets. *La grande demoiselle!* He had never known her in the old days, owing to his uncomplimentary

30. A sheer veil of cotton or silk and wool.

31. "Celibate" or "bachelor" (Fr.).

32. "New poor," pun on *nouveaux riches* ("the newly rich"), disparagingly regarded as osten-tatious.

attitude toward women, but he knew of her, of course, and of her family. It should have been said that his plantation was about fifty miles higher up the river, and on the opposite bank to Reine Sainte Foy. It seemed terrible. The old gentleman had had reverses of his own, which would bear the telling, but nothing was more shocking to him than this—that Idalie Sainte Foy Mortemart des Islets should be teaching a public colored school for—it makes one blush to name it—seven dollars and a half a month. For seven dollars and a half a month to teach a set of—well! He found out where she lived, a little cabin—not so much worse than his own, for that matter—in the corner of a field; no companion, no servant, nothing but food and shelter. Her clothes have been described.

Only the good God himself knows what passed in Champigny's mind on the subject. We know only the results. He went and married *la grande demoiselle*. How? Only the good God knows that too. Every first of the month, when he goes to the city to buy provisions, he takes her with him—in fact, he takes her everywhere with him.

Passengers on the railroad know them well, and they always have a chance to see her face. When she passes her old plantation *la grande demoiselle* always lifts her veil for one instant—the inevitable green barege veil. What a face! Thin, long, sallow, petrified! And the neck! If she would only tie something around the neck! And her plain, coarse cottonade[33] gown! The negro women about her were better dressed than she.

Poor old Champignon! It was not an act of charity to himself, no doubt cross and disagreeable, besides being ugly. And as for love, gratitude!

33. Coarse cotton fabric resembling wool, used for work clothes.

Mollie E. Moore Davis

(1844?–1909)

MARY EVALINA MOORE, the second of nine children, was born on April 12, 1844 (or 1852), to an Alabama woman, Marian Crutchfield, and her young doctor-husband, John Moore from Massachusetts. Mary spent the first years of her life near Talladega, Alabama. In 1855, to improve its failing fortunes, the family set out by wagon to central Texas and settled into what was to be a hardscrabble life, supported by a rented farm and her father's country medical practice.

Though Mary received little formal schooling, her talent was manifest early. When she was sixteen, she published a poem in the Tyler, Texas, newspaper as "Mollie Evelyn Moore," a name change that reflected a life-long consciousness about her public persona. Moore's early poems, about nature, family and southern patriotism, earned her a regional reputation that attracted the attention of E. H. Cushing, owner-editor of the *Houston Telegraph*. The Cushings invited Moore for a visit in 1862, and, over the next five years, she lived with them for extended periods. Hungry for culture and education, Moore made eager use of the intellectual opportunities and gracious lifestyle that the Cushings' wealth provided. Cushing helped produce her first volume, *Minding the Gap and Other Poems* (1867), and by 1869 she had begun to develop a national reputation and was profiled in two standard anthologies of southern writers. "Counsel," a poem about separation written in 1872, was reprinted well into the twentieth century.

Meanwhile, the income from her writing was becoming essential to her hard-pressed family, especially after her mother's death in 1867. Cushing helped Moore secure a salaried position as a weekly contributor to the Galveston newspaper. There she met Thomas E. Davis, a former Confederate officer and Galveston tobacco dealer, whom she married in 1874. After his business failed in 1875, they both worked for newspapers for several years. In 1879 Major Davis accepted an editorial position at the *New Orleans Times Picayune*.

Though the Davises were not affluent, Mollie quickly set about crafting a life that would become both a benchmark and magnet for the literary set of New Orleans. Inspired by the romantic tales of her new friend and fellow journalist George W. Cable, she took up residence in the then-unfashionable French Quarter. The Davises eventually settled on Royal Street, where her Friday afternoons became a popular and prestigious gathering place for both local and visiting writers and artists, including Cable, Lafcadio Hearn, Ruth Stuart, Grace King, Hamlin Garland, Kate Chopin, a number of women poets, and Eliza Jane Nicholson, who was the first female publisher of a major U.S. newspaper. Soon after the move to New Orleans, Davis began to write children's fiction, publishing black dialect tales and stories of frontier Texas and becoming a regular contributor to national magazines. In 1884 she published her first short story for an adult audience in a national journal (the Chicago *Courier*), and for the following decade her fiction and poetry appeared with some regularity in many of the nation's most reputable journals.

Although many of Davis's most authentic stories are set on her childhood's Texas frontier, her most popular work drew on New Orleans's romantic environs. Particularly successful were sketches eventually published in her first book of prose, *In War Times at La Rose Blanche* (1888). Its romantic evocation of antebellum plantation life seemed to be thinly veiled autobiography, a mistake Davis never corrected, evidently quite content to erase the vexation of her early poverty as well as the accurate date of her birth. A later novel with a similar setting, *Jaconetta: Her Loves* (1901), confirmed these public misapprehensions.

After 1895 Davis increasingly turned to the novel as her genre of choice, publishing seven before her death in 1909. *The Queen's Garden* (1900) and *The Little Chevalier* (1903) capitalize on the popularity of plantation fiction, whereas *The Wire Cutters* (1899) makes effective use of its Texas setting and characters. Although Davis typically used conventional materials in her fiction, she also broached riskier themes. Two of her last novels, *The Price of Silence* (1907) and the posthumous *Ships of Desire* (1955), offer relatively complex portraits of interracial romance. As in "A Bamboula," collected in *An Elephant's Track and Other Stories* (1897), Davis invokes the mysteries of heredity to hint at darker realities than its love plot might suggest. The intricate dance of the story's tangled relationships, like the African *bamboula*, reflects the hidden complexities of southern race and gender with surprising directness.

Afflicted with ill health throughout much of her adult life, Davis began to suffer the early symptoms of cancer in 1903, the year her beloved niece (whom she had adopted in 1886) was married. She alternated between writing and withdrawal during the final years of her life, with pain finally forcing her to daily doses of morphine. She died on New Year's Day, 1909.

Works by Mollie E. Moore Davis

Minding the Gap and Other Poems, 1867

In War Times at La Rose Blanche, 1888

Under the Man-Fig, 1895

An Elephant's Track and Other Stories, 1897

The Wire-Cutters: A Novel, 1899

The Queen's Garden, 1900

Jaconetta: Her Loves, 1901

The Little Chevalier, 1903

Keren-Happuch and I: In Two Parts, 1907

The Price of Silence, 1907

Selected Poems of Mollie Moore Davis, ed. Grace King, 1927

The Ships of Desire, 1955

Further Reading

Brady, Patricia. "Mollie Moore Davis: A Literary Life." In *Louisiana Women Writers: New Essays and a Comprehensive Bibliography.* Ed. Dorothy H. Brown and Barbara C. Ewell. Baton Rouge: Louisiana State University Press, 1992.

Sneller, Judy E. "Saints, Hell-Raisers, and Other 'Typical Texans': Frontier Women and the Humor of Mollie Moore Davis." *Journal of the American Studies Association of Texas* 25 (1994).

Wilkinson, Clyde W. "The Broadening Stream: The Life and Literary Career of Mollie E. Moore Davis." Ph.D. diss., University of Illinois, 1947.

A Bamboula

Francis Underwood glanced about him as the train whizzed away, leaving him the sole occupant of the narrow platform upon which he had alighted. His smaller luggage lay at his feet, but his traveling-trunk was nowhere in sight. The few idlers—a couple of sallow-faced, shock-headed crackers [1] and a squad of noisy negro lads—who had collected about the little way-station while the train made its momentary halt, had disappeared. He walked to the end of the platform, where a dozen or more turpentine barrels stood on end, their contents oozing from the rifts in their sun-warped sides, and cast his eyes over the green flat, which was bounded in every direction by low, red, pine-clad hills. The dim haze of an early autumn afternoon hung in the pine-tops; a thin spiral of smoke arose from the chimney of the single cabin within range of vision; a rickety buggy, over whose sagging top fluttered the loose end of a woman's veil, was just turning the distant bend of a road. There were no other visible signs of life. The perplexed traveler strode back to the dingy waiting-room and looked in. The tripping click of the telegraph in the cubby beyond and a familiar opening in the thin board partition indicated the occasional presence, at least, of operator and agent; but the individual who combined these two functions was in momentary eclipse.

Underwood thrust his hands into his pockets and meditated, frowning impatiently.

"De telegraph is boun' fer ter clickety-click, sah," said a voice over his shoulder; "she jes keep er-talkin' ter herse'f in yander same ez ef de boss was 'longside her ter write her down."

The young man turned quickly and found himself face to face with a negro, who held a carriage-whip in one hand, and in the other his own bag, top-coat, and umbrella.

"Scuse me, sah," the speaker continued, removing his hat. "I reckin you mus' be Mist' Onderwood?"

Underwood nodded assent.

"Dey's lookin' fer you at Pine Needles, Mist' Onderwood. Step dis way, sah. Yo' trunk is gone on in de cyart. But I ain' been able ter fetch up de cay'age ontwel de ingine stop her fool screechin', 'caze my hosses is kinder res'less."

He led the way as he spoke to a light trap,[2] which had been driven up noiselessly, and was waiting near the steps of the low platform.

Underwood settled himself comfortably on the cushioned seat, and

1. Shock-headed: a thick mass of unruly hair, as in a sheaf or "shock" of grain. Crackers: derogative term for poor whites, alluding either to their "cracking" of corn for consumption or to the whips ("crackers") common among rural southern herdsmen.

2. Lightweight, two-wheeled passenger carriage.

turned a gaze of wondering admiration on his conductor, who stood with a hand on the glossy flank of one of the horses respectfully awaiting orders. He was himself of unusual height, slenderly proportioned, but with an athletic frame and well-knit muscles, which contradicted a rather boyish face, laughing blue eyes, and a sensitive mouth, whose weakness was not wholly concealed by a light, drooping mustache. But he seemed suddenly dwarfed. The negro towered like a giant above the tall mulatto[3] who held the bridles of the horses. His large head, crowned with a bush of crisp, wiry curls, was set squarely upon shoulders of enormous breadth. Underwood examined almost with awe the broad chest and massive limbs; the latter were straight and well formed; the powerful wrist, indeed, and the hand, with its long fingers, perfect nails, and outward-curving palm, might have served for a sculptor's model. He was jet-black. His square-jawed face was beardless. His long, brown eyes had the melancholy softness characteristic of his race; the lips were thick, and the cheek-bones prominent, but the nose was straight and shapely, giving a curious and unexpected dignity to an otherwise typical negro physiognomy. He spoke the uncouth *patois*[4] of the quarters, but his bearing was that of one who held a position of trust and confidence.

He was clad in a sort of homely livery of dark-blue flannel—a blouse, whose open collar exposed his full throat, and loose trousers held in at the waist by a broad leather belt.

Underwood waved his hand as he concluded his brief, half-unconscious inspection, and the black colossus took a seat beside him, the mulatto stepped aside, and the handsome bays sprang forward at the loosening of the reins. The road wound gradually up long, sloping hills, dipping now and then into a moist hollow, where the sturdy underbrush and the jungle-like growth of trees were aflame under the first light touches of the frost. A few belated spikes of goldenrod nodded by the road-side, and an occasional cluster of dim purple asters shone against the background of a fallen pine; but the Indian-pipe—precursor of winter—was already thrusting its waxen crook through the dark mould on the sheltered slopes. The hill-sides were brown with pine-needles. The sky, in the waning sunlight, was a fine, soft purple; the plumy tops of the lofty pines seemed to melt into it far overhead; the warm air was charged with aromatic odors. Underwood bared his head, and expanded his lungs with an idle sense of

3. Offspring of a white parent and a black parent.

4. Dialect that is spoken (not written) among more rural and less educated people.

well-being. His eyes followed dreamily the flight of a hawk across the sky. A faint smile curved his lips.

"Dar's a molly cottontail!"[5] suddenly exclaimed the negro. A rabbit sped across the road a few paces in front of the horses and scurried up a ridge, her gray ears laid back and her white bit of a tail in the air. "Dat's bad luck, Mist' Onderwood!"

Underwood recalled a half-forgotten superstition. "Not for me," he said, gayly. "I carry a rabbit foot in my pocket! What is your name— boy?" he continued, stumbling over the last word, quizzically conscious of its inappropriateness.

"Marcas, sah," returned the "boy," promptly. "Dey calls me Blue-gum Marc," he added, with a side glance at the questioner and a suppressed chuckle.

"Blue-gum Marc?" echoed Underwood, interrogatively.

The giant opened his mouth, drawing back his thick lips, and pointed significantly to a double row of glistening white teeth, set in gums of a dark leaden blue. "Dat's de reason, sah," he said, lightly. "I's a blue-gum nigger. An' dey 'lows ef I git mad at anybody, an' bite de pusson, dat bite gwine ter be wusser 'n rattlesnake pizen! Der ain' no whiskey in de jug dat kin heal up de bite of a blue-gum nigger!"

He threw back his head and laughed with a keen enjoyment of his own words.

"Have you ever tried it?" asked Underwood, carelessly.

"Who? Me? Gawd-a-mighty!—*no sah!*" A sudden spasm of terror swept over the ebon face. "No, sah," he repeated, relapsing into decorous mirth. "I 'ain' never had no call ter bite anybody yit."

The horses shied violently as he concluded.

"What in de name o' Gawd is de matter wid you, Dandy? Whoa, Jim!" he ejaculated, tightening his grasp on the reins, and peering to right and left with a frown on his forehead. Underwood saw the frown melt suddenly, and a light leap into the dark eyes. He followed the direction of his gaze; his own heart beat tumultuously, and the blood surged into his cheeks.

The glade through which they were passing was filled with the uncertain shadows of a fast-gathering twilight, though the slanting beams of the sun still illuminated the crest of the hills. A little stream, whose rippling murmur filled the silence, ran obliquely across the road and widened into a broad pool in the thicket beyond. The half-dried reeds on the margin,

5. Small rabbit with a white puff-tail; a rabbit crossing the road was bad luck.

and the overhanging trees with their festooning vines, were mirrored in the clear brown depths of this waveless tarn.[6] A woman was standing on the farther side, her tall, lithe figure outlined by the pale glimmer of her gown. One hand, which held a cluster of vivid red leaves, hung at her side; the other was arched above her brows as she leaned forward in a listening attitude. As they whirled past, Underwood caught the gleam of a bare, tawny wrist, and the glow of a pair of large, lustrous eyes.

"Who was that?" he demanded, abruptly.

"S'lome,"[7] responded his companion, with affected indifference. "She Miss Cecil's own maid," he added, after a pause.

"I thought at first that it was Miss Cecil herself," said Underwood, glancing back over his shoulder.

"S'lome do look lak—" the negro checked himself and averted his face, flecking Dandy's arched neck with the whip-tassel.

Something in his tone struck the young man at his side; he drew the lap-robe closer about his knees, for the air was growing chill, and remained silent until Marcas sprang to the ground to open the boundary gate of Pine Needles, Miss Cecil Berkeley's fine old country place.

"How old are you, Marc?" he asked, struck anew by the negro's noble physical proportions.

"Twenty-five, come Christmas, sah. Bawn jes inside o' freedom. Hit's mighty liftin' ter be bawn free, an' ter be raise' up free, Mist' Onderwood," he went on, resuming his seat and taking the reins from Underwood's hands. "But my old daddy 'ain' had no call ter complain whilse *he* was a slave."

"Where—" began Underwood.

"My daddy was a Affican prince—" the fine nostrils dilated and the broad chest heaved. "Colonel Berkeley bought him out'n a slave-pen in Charl's'n, wher he was dyin' lak a dog, an' fotch him home. An' fum dat day twel de day he died he had de treatments of a genterman at Pine Needles. Dere wa'n't a drap o' blood in his body dat he wouldn't ha' spill' fer de Berkeleys! An' dat huccome I 'ain' never lef' Miss Cecil, Mist' Onderwood. 'Caze dat ole Affican prince is layin' out yander in de fam'ly buryin' groun' 'longside o' ole marster an' ole mis'; an' who gwine ter tek keer o' Miss Cecil ef I go?"

6. Small clear lake, often suggestive of magic.

7. Salome's dance for Herod's birthday won the granting of any wish. She ordered John the Baptist's head on a platter after consulting her mother, Herodias, who was angry with him for blocking her marriage to her brother-in-law, Herod (Matt. 14:6–11, Mark 6:21–28).

Underwood, moved by the simplicity and earnestness of the speaker, laid his hand on the brawny arm next to him, and opened his lips to speak. But Marcas shrank from the light touch. Underwood felt the firm flesh quiver beneath his fingers. "He knows that I have come to carry away his young mistress, and he is jealous," he thought, smiling with pardonable exultation.

His eyes roved curiously over the broad park. The kind of table-land, from which the pine hills sloped away to the west and north, was covered with noble woodland trees, through whose trunks, in passing, he caught glimpses of orchards, vineyards, and fields. It was his first visit to Pine Needles, and he looked out eagerly for the house. A last turn of the smooth road brought it in view—a large, rambling country-house, embowered in greenery, with wide galleries, slanting roof, and square, red-brick chimneys.

"Yander's Miss Cecil, er-waitin'!" said Marcas, pointing with his whip. Underwood barely had time to catch the flutter of light garments through the foliage before the horses were drawn up beneath the veranda where she stood.

She came down the steps with outstretched hands. "Welcome to Pine Needles, Francis," she said, with a sort of shy pride. "This is my cousin, Mrs. Garland," she added, presenting the small, alert-looking personage who filled the agreeable office of companion to the young heiress.

Cecil Berkeley offered a pleasing contrast to the man upon whom she was about to bestow the ownership of herself and the Berkeley estates. She was tall and slender, with hair and brows of an almost startling blackness, and dark eyes in which a smouldering fire seemed to dwell; her high-bred oval face was singularly delicate in its outlines. There was a pliant softness in her movements and a hint of strength in her firm white chin and perfect mouth. She flushed as her lover's ardent eyes met hers in the fading light.

"Welcome to Pine Needles!" she cried again, springing lightly up the steps.

Underwood had not finished relating the common-place details of his southward journey when the soft fall of unshod feet sounded on the polished floor; a shadowy form glided across the dim-lit room in which they were seated, and bent over Miss Berkeley's chair. He felt, rather than saw, that it was the woman whom he had seen an hour before standing on the edge of the dark pool in the hollow.

"Thank you, S'lome," said her mistress, in a tone of affectionate familiarity, taking the leaves, whose color was lost in the semi-darkness. The quadroon[8] bent her shapely head, and passed from the room as silently as she had entered it.

That night they sat late before a blazing pine-knot fire in the snug library. The hands of the slow-ticking old clock on the mantel pointed almost to midnight when the guest arose to bid his hostess good-night. As he opened the door a strain of music fell upon his ears, accompanied with a burst of noisy laughter.

Cecil smiled in reply to his questioning look. "Uncle Darius is fiddling on the kitchen gallery," she said, "and the negroes are doubtless dancing there, late as it is. Come, let us take a peep at them."

She led the way down the wide hall, and out upon a small vine-hung porch in the rear of the dining-room. The night was clear and still. The grassy yard and the garden beyond were bathed in the tranquil light of a full moon. But an enormous fig-tree, whose branches brushed the low eaves, swathed the long kitchen gallery in dense shadow, save where, from an open door, a broad glare of red light streamed across it. Uncle Darius, lean and brown, sat just within the doorway, fiddling with all his might, his chair tilted against the wall, his gray head thrown back, his big bare foot keeping time on the floor. Aunt Peggy, the old black cook, dozed on a stool beside him. A confused mass of dark forms were dimly visible in the shadow, lying about the floor, lounging on the low steps, squatting against the wall. Here and there a dusky face, a bare foot, an out-thrust arm, gleamed strangely in the muddy light. Lindy, big-limbed and black, and Mushmelon Joe, small, wizened, and wiry, sank on their heels against the door-posts, breathless and exhausted after a prolonged "break-down,"[9] as the invisible spectators drew aside the leafy curtain and looked out.

"I ain' gwine ter play nary 'nother tune ternight," declared Uncle Darius, bringing his chair legs down with a thump. "De chickens is fair crowin fer day now." But as a tall figure stepped noiselessly from the darkness into the shaft of light, he tucked his fiddle under his chin again with a whoop. "Now you gwine ter see *dancin*'!" he shouted, flourishing his bow. "Blue-gum Marc gwine ter teach the niggers how ter raek down de cotton row!"

Marc swayed his huge body from side to side rhythmically, then paused. "Ain' you gwine ter raek down de cotton row 'long o' me, S'lome?" he demanded, turning his face towards a group of women at the farther end of the gallery.

8. Offspring of a white parent and a mulatto (one who is half black and half white).

9. Noisy, country folk dance.

"No," drawled a low, musical voice there.

"Den you can ontie de fiddle-strings, Unc' Darius," said Marc, joining good-naturedly in the loud laugh at his own expense.

Underwood bent forward, straining his eyes in the darkness. But Aunt Peggy had already shut the kitchen door, and a moment later they all trooped away, singing, to the negro settlement in the pines, which had replaced the old-time quarters.

II

One morning about ten days later Miss Berkeley came out of the house alone and walked slowly across the lawn. Her step was listless; her eyes were downcast; her cheek had lost its brilliant color. She seated herself on a rustic bench under a low-branched oak, and opened the book which she held in her hand. But her gaze wandered absently from the printed page. It fell at length upon Marcas, who was moving to and fro among the flower-beds, whistling joyously. He carried a small garden hoe, and the splint basket on his arm was heaped with tufts of violets. His face brightened as his eyes caught those of his young mistress. He took off his hat and came over to where she was sitting.

"Hit's edzackly de weather ter transplan', Miss Cecil," he said; "de groun' is dat meller an' sof'——"

"Marcas," she interrupted, imperiously, leaning her head against the dark tree-trunk and looking fixedly at him, "is it true that you carry poison in your teeth like a rattlesnake?"

"Lawd-a-mussy, Miss Cecil!" he cried, falling back a step or two in his amazement. "I dunno. Yes, 'm. I 'ain' never projecked[10] none wi' dat foolishness. But my ole daddy useter *say* so, en' I reckin a Affican prince oughter *know!*"

Her eyes dropped on her book, and he returned with a bewildered air to his work. She watched him abstractedly as he placed the moist roots one by one deftly in the ground, and patted the loose earth about them with a large, open palm.

"The dwarf-marigolds are nearly all gone," she remarked, after a long silence.

"Yes, 'm," assented Marc, glancing at a triangular plot in the center of the lawn, where a few small yellow flowers shone on their low stalks.

"S'lome has been gathering them——" she went on, musingly, and as if speaking to herself.

10. Played around with; here, something dangerous.

"S'lome do hone a'ter yeller, dat's a fac'!" he commented, with a pleased laugh.

"—for Mr. Underwood," she concluded, in a monotonous tone.

The negro rose slowly to his feet. A sombre fire shot into his eyes. He stood for a moment silently looking down at her. Then he dropped again to his knees and drew the basket to him.

She went away presently, leaving the book, which had slipped from her lap, lying face downward in the yellowing grass.

He watched her furtively until she entered the house. Then, without a glance at the overturned basket and neglected tools, he passed across the grounds, leaped the low fence, and plunged into the silent reaches of the pines.

That night when the mistress of Pine Needles came down from her own room, whither, under pretext of a headache, she had withdrawn after the mid-afternoon country dinner, she found the house wearing an unwonted air of festivity.

"Ah, there you are at last, Cecil dear!" cried Mrs. Garland, bustling into the hall to meet her. "Everything is waiting for you. I've arranged what Uncle Darius calls a *speckle-tickle*[11] for your Mr. Underwood," she added, dropping her voice.

She drew the girl into the long parlor, whose polished floor reflected the clustered lights in the old-fashioned crystal chandeliers. Wax tapers burned softly in the tall silver candelabra on the mantel; roses were stuffed in the wide-mouthed vases; the furniture was pushed against the wall; a couple of quaint high-backed chairs were placed side by side in the broad curve of the bow-window.

"You and Francis are to sit here, like the king and queen in a play," said Mrs. Garland, gayly. "Don't lift an eyebrow, Cecil, pray, if you recognize the contents of your own armoires and jewel-cases."

Cecil sank into the chair with a wan smile. She looked frail and almost ghost-like in her trailing white gown. Underwood, who seemed possessed by a sort of reckless gayety, seated himself beside her. He wore pinned upon the lapel of his coat a small yellow flower.

There was a moment of almost painful silence. Then Mrs. Garland, leaning on the back of her cousin's chair, touched a small silver bell. The heavy portière[12] which draped the entrance to the library was pushed

11. "Spectacle."

12. Curtain hung in a doorway, often replacing the door.

aside, and Uncle Darius, arrayed in an antiquated blue coat with brass buttons, light trousers, and ruffled shirt-front, entered pompously, fiddle in hand, and seated himself on the edge of a chair. Mushmelon Joe, Scip, 'Riah, Sara-Wetumpka—a motley gang of field hands and house servants—swarmed in after him. They ranged themselves, grinning and nudging each other, about him, and began to pat a subdued accompaniment to his music. At a scarcely perceptible signal from the fiddler, Lindy bounced into the room. A scarlet sash was wound turbanwise about her kinky head, and an Oriental shawl draped her blue cotton skirt. The black arms and neck were encircled with strings of many-colored beads. She looked preternaturally solemn as she dropped her arms and began the heavy "hoe-down" [13] for which she was famous in the settlement; but a broad grin presently stole over her face; her glistening eyeballs rolled from side to side; the perspiration streamed from her forehead.

"Wire down de crack, nigger, wire down de crack!" [14] exhorted Uncle Darius. "Pick up dem battlin' sticks [15] you calls yo' feet, gal, an' tromp in de flo'!"

"She sho is made de flat o' her foot *talk* ter de fiddle," remarked Mushmelon Joe, as she executed a last breathless whirl, and retired giggling into the admiring circle of clappers.

The clear tinkle of the little bell echoed on the air. Blue-gum Marc appeared suddenly in a doorway that gave upon a side gallery, and, folding his arms on his breast, leaned his great bulk against the frame. At the same moment S'lome stepped from behind the portière.

An involuntary exclamation burst from Underwood. Cecil closed her eyes, dazzled by the wild and barbaric beauty of the tawny creature before her.

She wore a short, close-clinging skirt and sleeveless bodice of pale, shimmering yellow satin; a scarf of silver gauze girdled her slender waist, and was knotted below her swelling hips. Her slim brown ankles and shapely feet were bare. Bands and coils of gold wreathed her naked arms; a jewelled chain clasped her throat; a glittering butterfly, with quivering outspread wings, was set in the crinkly mass of black hair above her forehead. Her eyelids were down-cast, their long fringes sweeping her bronze-like cheeks. A curious light, defiant and disdainful, played over her face

13. Jig-like dance, modeled after digging potatoes or cultivating down a row of corn with a hoe.
14. "Wear down the crack" (in the floor), that is, dance harder.
15. Battens or slats, often used to beat the dust from rugs.

as she stood motionless, with her arms hanging loosely at her sides, while Uncle Darius played the first bars of the *bamboula*[16] which had been brought by Marcas's father from the heart of Africa.

The music was low and monotonous—a few constantly recurring notes, which at first vexed the ear, and then set the blood on fire.

The girl hardly appeared to move; there was a languid swaying of the hips from side to side, and an almost imperceptible yet rhythmic stir of the feet. But as the music gradually quickened its time, a thrill seemed to pass along her sinuous limbs, and a subtle passion pervaded her movements; her arms were tossed voluptuously above her head; her breast heaved; a seductive fire burned in her half-closed amber eyes; the sound of her light feet on the floor resembled the whir of wings.

The negroes, huddled mute and breathless against the wall, gazed at her with wide, fascinated eyes. Suddenly, as if moved by some mysterious and irresistible impulse, they rushed forward and closed in a circle around the flashing figure, whirling about her with strange evolutions and savage cries.

. . . A powerful, penetrating odor thickened the air. . . .

Underwood had started from his seat; he stood as if transfixed, breathing heavily, his arms unconsciously extended, his eyes aflame, and the veins in his forehead swollen almost to bursting. Marcas, curiously impassive in the doorway, kept his gaze fixed steadily, not upon the dancer, but upon his young mistress, who leaned back in her chair, faint and dizzy, the rose-tint on her cheek fading to a death-like pallor.

The movement of the *bamboula* became by degrees less rapid; the panting circle opened and fell back. S'lome paused, and stretched her arms slowly upward with the supple grace of a young panther. She looked full at Underwood, and her lips parted in an exultant smile.

The blood surged into Miss Berkeley's white cheeks; she lifted her head haughtily; her nostrils quivered; her eyes met those of Marcas for an instant, then rested, flashing, upon S'lome, decked for triumph, as it were, in her own hereditary jewels.

With a roar like that of a wild beast, Marcas leaped across the room. His hand fell with a vise-like grasp upon the gleaming shoulder of the quadroon; he stooped with a second ferocious cry, and buried his teeth deep

16. African dance, accompanied by the "bamboula," a small drum or tambourine made from a large bamboo joint. Popular among blacks in the nineteenth century, the dance begins slowly and builds to a sexualized frenzy.

in the smooth flesh of the rounded arm. A single agonizing shriek pierced the sudden stillness; before it had ended he had caught the slight form in one hand, and bearing her high above his head he bounded through the open door end disappeared in the darkness.

Underwood, heedless of the terrified confusion and wild clamor which reigned around, was springing after him, when he felt a hand upon his arm. "For Heaven's sake come and help me, Francis," said Mrs. Garland; "Cecil has fainted!"

III

The next afternoon Miss Berkeley passed through a small gate into the pine woods which stretched away to the south, forming a part of her own domain. She walked slowly along the well-worn path, halting now and again with an air of indecision. Once she stooped mechanically and plucked a yellow daisy which grew in a drift of warm brown pine-needles, but cast it from her with a gesture of loathing. Her black garments gave her an appearance of uncommon height. Her face was livid, her lips compressed, her dark eyes dull and suffering. She turned at length into the narrow lane which led to the negro settlement. As she drew near the outermost cabin she saw Underwood standing in the shadow of a scrubby pine that overhung the picket-fence. Aunt Peggy, the mistress of the cabin, was leaning over the low gate; her arms were uplifted, as if in entreaty or adjuration.

He started at sight of the approaching figure, and walked rapidly forward. He had a white flower in his hand. His face was turned away, and for a moment it seemed as if he were about to pass his betrothed without a greeting. But as she stepped aside he paused, and said, abruptly:

"I am going away, Cecil. I—I think it is best." His eyes were fixed upon the althea [17] blossom which he was twirling awkwardly in his fingers.

"You are quite right," she returned, coldly; "it is best."

She left him without another word. He lingered a moment, gazing irresolutely after her, then struck into the beaten road that led to the railway station.

Aunt Peggy had come out of the gate. "Miss Cecil, honey," she said, hoarsely, "dis ain' no place fer de likes o' you! Go back ter de house, chile—go back!" she entreated. "Mist' Onderwood yander he's been here, off an' on, 'mos' all day. But I ain' dassen [18] ter lef him go inter de cabin.

17. Rose of sharon, a common purple or white southern flower.

18. "Dassent," dare not.

I ax him fer Gawd's sake ef he ain' mek enough trebble a'ready 'd'out showin' hisself wher' Blue-gum Marc kin see him. He say he wan' ter see *S'lome!* My Gawd! I gin him a althy flower fum offin de corpse, an' saunt him erway. Doan go in de cabin, Miss Cecil!" she panted, following her mistress into the little dooryard, and laying hold of the folds of her gown. "Blue-gum Marc is in de cabin. He ain' never lef' de gal sence he pizen her. Nobody dassen ter go er-nigh him 'cep'n' me, an' he ain' lef *me* tech her, not even ter put on de grave-close. He say he gwine ter kill the pusson dat steps inside dat cabin do'. De mo'ners is 'bleedge' ter mo'n in Lindy's cabin yander. Fer Gawd's sake, Miss Cecil—fer Gawd's—"

Cecil put the old woman gently aside and pushed open the cabin door. The little room had been hastily put in order. The large four-posted bed was spread with white; the bare floor was swept clean; the pine table, piled with blue-rimmed dishes, was placed in the chimney-corner. Uncle Darius's fiddle hung in its accustomed place on the wall, with his Sunday coat on a nail beneath it. The level rays of a setting sun came in at the single window; a light breeze moved the white curtains to and fro.

The dead girl was lying in the center of the room on a rude bier, her head resting on a pillow. She was still clad in the fantastic costume in which she had danced the night before; the gold bands and jewelled ornaments sparkled in the red light which streamed over her. Her eyes were closed; their silken lashes made a black line against the dusky pallor of her cheeks. Her lips were slightly parted, and an inscrutable smile seemed to hover about their corners. One arm was laid across her breast, a fold of silver gauze was drawn over the purpling wound just below the shoulder; the other arm hung to the floor, the closed hand grasping the filigree chain which she had torn, in the death agony, from her neck. A few white altheas were scattered on her bosom, and some sprigs of lavender and rue[19] were lying on the rough boards about her bare feet and ankles. A short, large-handled, keen-bladed knife was laid across the pillow above her head. She looked like a savage queen asleep on her primitive couch.

Marcas sat by the head of the bier. His body was erect and rigid; his powerful hands rested on his knees; his feet were drawn close together; his head was turned towards the dead girl, showing his curiously fine profile. It was the attitude and pose of the Pharaoh of the Egyptian monuments.

He did not move as Cecil entered the room. She stood for a second as motionless as the dead and the watcher of the dead, with her hands clasped

19. Fragrant, medicinal herbs.

before her, the fingers interlocked. Then she stumbled across the floor, and halted at the foot of the bier.

The buzzing of some bees about the pots of flowering moss on the window-sill filled the silence with a low, droning sound. The wail of the mourners in Lindy's cabin came in fitfully, softened by the distance.

"Miss Cecil," he said, presently, without turning his head or lifting his heavy eyelids, "I jes' waited fer de tu'n o' yo' eye, 'caze I didn' know which you was gwine ter p'int out fust—S'lome or *him*. De knife is fer *him*, soon ez de gal is onder groun'."

Cecil shuddered and put out her hands.

"Doan fret, Miss Cecil," he went on, in the same sombre tone. "No stranger ain' gwine ter turn de rosy cheek o' Colonel Berkeley's chile white ez cotton—*an' live!* Not whilse de blood o' de ole Affican prince is hot in de vein o' his son!" His voice shook with sudden rage as he concluded; his breast rose and fell spasmodically. When he spoke again, it was almost in a whisper, strangely soft and musical: "S'lome! *S'lome!* I doan 'member de time, Miss Cecil, when I 'ain' been lovin' S'lome! Fum de day when she wa'n't ez high ez de pretty-by-nights[20] in Aun' Peggy's do'-yard I is had my heart sot on her. . . . She was swif' ez a fiel'-lark, Miss Cecil, an' her eyes is ez sof' ez de eyes of a dove when she look at me an' say she ain' gwine ter love nobody 'cep'n' me ez long ez she is 'bove de groun'. . . . She is de onlies' one in de settlemint dat ain' 'feard o' de pizen in de gum o' Blue-gum Marc . . . dat's de fam'ly blood in her . . . de Berkeley blood—"

Cecil Berkeley threw up her arms convulsively and sank to her knees; her forehead pressed the feet of the dead girl, and she shivered as if the chill of death had passed from them into her own benumbed veins.

20. Tropical American night-blooming flower, *mirabilis jalapa*, or "four o'clock."

Charles W. Chesnutt

(1855–1932)

THE SON OF ANDREW JACKSON CHESNUTT and Anne Maria Sampson, free blacks who had emigrated from Fayetteville, North Carolina, Charles W. Chesnutt was born on June 20, 1858, in Cleveland, Ohio. When he was eight, his family returned to Fayetteville, where Chesnutt attended a Freedmen's Bureau school. At fourteen he became a teacher in Charlotte, North Carolina, returning once again to Fayetteville in 1877 to become an instructor in the new State Colored Normal School. Appointed principal the next year, he was able to marry his fiancée, Susan Perry. At twenty-two Chesnutt dedicated himself to "the elevation [and moral education] of whites" and to the eradication of "the unjust spirit of caste which is so insidious as to pervade a whole nation." Faced by constant discrimination and longing for greater opportunities than the South afforded, he moved his family (which now included three children) north and, after a brief stay in New York, settled in Cleveland in 1884.

First working as a court reporter, Chesnutt eventually established a successful legal stenography firm. In 1877 he passed the Ohio bar examination (with the highest score) and published his first noteworthy piece of fiction, "The Goophered Grapevine," in the *Atlantic Monthly*. Drawing on Joel Chandler Harris's popular black storyteller, Chesnutt subtly transformed Uncle Remus into the consummate trickster Julius McAdoo, who employed his tales (eventually numbering fourteen) to secure himself some form of personal or economic advantage. Urged on by George W. Cable, who had become a friend and mentor after reading Chesnutt's second Uncle Julius story in 1888, Chesnutt turned with energy to his writing.

Chesnutt published his seven-story Uncle Julius collection, *The Conjure Woman*, in March 1899. "The Goophered Grapevine" opens the collection, but "Dave's Neckliss," which had appeared in the *Atlantic* ten years earlier, is omitted, perhaps because it unmasks the psychological destruction inherent in white cruelty and black duplicity. The broad humor of the conjured (bewitched) scuppernong vine and the ham-stealing Henry of Chesnutt's first story are replaced with the madness of honorable, literate Dave and his grisly ham necklace. Though the Uncle Julius stories were intended to entertain, they also revealed the distressing situation of blacks, whose identities remained vulnerable both to self-betrayal and white complicity.

The collection's publication stimulated speculation about Chesnutt's heritage. Even though he had made his ancestry clear to his editors in 1891, Chesnutt's lineage had remained a quiet secret. Most readers had assumed he was white (just as some readers, ironically, had once assumed Harris was black). The fact of his African American heritage was soon confirmed in a review of this much-acclaimed volume, and Chesnutt became a national celebrity. The resulting notoriety hastened the publication of *The Wife of His Youth and Other Stories of the Color Line* in time for the December 1899 Christmas market. These non-dialect stories permitted him greater freedom to illuminate the complex issues surrounding the color line and to use settings as diverse as contemporary Ohio and the antebellum South. The nine collected stories, among them "The Passing of Grandison," are often laced with sentimentality and melodrama, but their plots consistently reflect the trials of racial injustice, discrimination, and miscegenation. In contrast to the faithful "Negro" so essential to Old South apologists like Thomas Nelson Page, Chesnutt offers complex images of emancipated black life and explores the white-defined standards that blacks are measured against. The humor of "The Passing of Grandison" draws on plantation nostalgia, but Chesnutt also exposes the absurdities of slavery (and, by extension, whites' views of black people) as well as the pretenses necessary to survive and subvert such subjugations. That same year, Chesnutt wrote a short biography of Frederick Douglass. Its publication thrust Chesnutt into prominence as a black spokesperson, a role he energetically accepted throughout the rest of his life.

Comparing Chesnutt to distinguished international and American authors, William Dean Howells enthusiastically praised both of Chesnutt's short-story collections. Encouraged, Chesnutt devoted himself full-time to what he considered a more serious genre than the short story. His first novel, *The House Behind the Cedars* (1900), explored the temptations of "passing" as white. His next, *The Marrow of Tradition* (1901), often considered his finest work, was based on the 1898 race riots in Wilmington, North Carolina, and juxtaposes white hostility against the compassionate behavior of a mulatto physician and his wife. Dismayed by the limited public interest these problem novels attracted, Chesnutt created a white protagonist for *The Colonel's Dream* (1905), which chronicles the well-intentioned racial and economic remedies of an ex-Confederate officer, who has returned to North Carolina after making his fortune in the north. His dream fails because in the Jim Crow South, as the Colonel (and, lamentably, Chesnutt himself) finally realizes, "standards of right and wrong had been confused by the race issue." Indeed, while Chesnutt's ambitious and courageous novel received little attention, Thomas Dixon's antagonistic *The Clansman*, published the same year, became a best-seller.

An increasingly influential Cleveland citizen, Chesnutt continued to write, although his later years were devoted to managing his prosperous stenographic practice and vigorously advocating for social justice. Although few white readers knew his work until the latter part of the twentieth century, black editors and authors have continuously admired Chesnutt. Acknowledging his influential contributions as a pioneer critic, scholar, citizen, and writer, the NAACP awarded him the prestigious Spingarn Medal in 1928. Chesnutt died unexpectedly but peacefully five years later at his home on November 15, 1932. He left six novels, unpublished and mostly unfinished, at his death.

Works by Charles W. Chesnutt

Mandy Oxendine: A Novel, ca. 1897, ed. Charles Hackenberry, 1997

The Conjure Woman, and Other Conjure Tales, 1899,
ed. Richard H. Brodhead, 1993

The Wife of His Youth and Other Stories of the Color Line, 1899

Frederick Douglass, 1899

The House Behind the Cedars, 1900

The Marrow of Tradition, 1901

Colonel's Dream, 1905

The Quarry, ca. 1928, ed. Dean McWilliams, 1999

Paul Marchand, F.M.C., ca. 1928, ed. Dean McWilliams, 1999

The Short Fiction of Charles W. Chesnutt, ed. Sylvia Lyons Render, 1974

The Collected Stories of Charles W. Chesnutt, ed. William L. Andrews, 1992

The Journals of Charles W. Chesnutt, ed. Richard H. Brodhead, 1993

"To Be an Author": Letters of Charles W. Chesnutt, 1889–1905,
ed. Joseph R. McElrath and Robert C. Leitz, 1997

Further Reading

Andrews, William L. *The Literary Career of Charles W. Chesnutt.* Baton Rouge: Louisiana State University Press, 1980.

Chesnutt, Helen M. *Charles Waddell Chesnutt, Pioneer of the Color Line.* Chapel Hill: University of North Carolina Press, 1952.

Duncan, Charles. *The Absent Man: The Narrative Craft of Charles W. Chesnutt.* Athens: Ohio University Press, 1998.

Ellison, Curtis W., and Eugene W. Metcalf Jr. *Charles W. Chesnutt: A Reference Guide.* Boston: G. K. Hall, 1977.

Heermance, J. Noel. *Charles W. Chesnutt: America's First Great Black Novelist.* Hamden, Conn.: Archon Books, 1974.

Keller, Frances Richardson. *An American Crusade: The Life of Charles Waddell Chesnutt.* Provo, Utah: Brigham Young University Press, 1978.

Pickens, Ernestine Williams. *Charles Chesnutt and the Progressive Movement.* New York: Pace University Press, 1994.

Render, Sylvia Lyons. *Charles W. Chesnutt.* Boston: Twayne, 1980.

Wonham, Henry B. *Charles W. Chesnutt: A Study of the Short Fiction.* New York: Twayne, 1998.

The Goophered Grapevine

Some years ago my wife was in poor health, and our family doctor, in whose skill and honesty I had implicit confidence, advised a change of climate. I shared, from an unprofessional standpoint, his opinion that the raw winds, the chill rains, and the violent changes of temperature that characterized the winters in the region of the Great Lakes tended to aggravate my wife's difficulty, and would undoubtedly shorten her life if she remained exposed to them. The doctor's advice was that we seek, not a temporary place of sojourn, but a permanent residence, in a warmer and more equable climate. I was engaged at the time in grape-culture in northern Ohio, and, as I liked the business and had given it much study, I decided to look for some other locality suitable for carrying it on. I thought of sunny France, of sleepy Spain, of Southern California, but there were objections to them all. It occurred to me that I might find what I wanted in some one of our own Southern States. It was a sufficient time after the war for conditions in the South to have become somewhat settled; and I was enough of a pioneer to start a new industry, if I could not find a place where grape-culture had been tried. I wrote to a cousin who had gone into the turpentine business in central North Carolina. He assured me, in response to my inquiries, that no better place could be found in the South than the State and neighborhood where he lived; the climate was perfect for health, and, in conjunction with the soil, ideal for grape-culture; labor was cheap, and land could be bought for a mere song. He gave us a cordial invitation to come and visit him while we looked into the matter. We accepted the invitation, and after several days of leisurely travel, the last hundred miles of which were up a river on a sidewheel steamer,[1] we reached our destination, a quaint old town, which I shall call Patesville,[2] because, for one reason, that is not its name. There was a red brick market-house in the public square, with a tall tower, which held a four-faced clock that struck the hours, and from which there pealed out a curfew at nine o'clock. There were two or three hotels, a court-house, a jail, stores, offices, and all the appurtenances of a county seat and a commercial emporium; for while Patesville numbered only four or five thousand inhabitants, of all shades of complexion, it was one of the principal towns in North Carolina, and had a considerable trade in cotton and naval stores.[3] This business activity was not immediately apparent to my unaccustomed eyes. Indeed, when I first saw the town, there brooded over it a calm that seemed almost sabbatic in its restfulness, though I learned later on that underneath its somnolent exterior the deeper currents of life—love and hatred, joy and despair, ambition and avarice, faith and friendship—flowed not less steadily than in livelier latitudes.

We found the weather delightful at that season, the end of summer, and were hospitably entertained. Our host was a man of means and evidently regarded our visit as a pleasure, and we were therefore correspondingly at our ease, and in a position to act with the coolness of judgment desirable in making so radical a change in our lives. My cousin placed a horse and buggy at our disposal, and himself acted as our guide until I became somewhat familiar with the country.

I found that grape-culture, while it had never been carried on to any great extent, was not entirely unknown in the neighborhood. Several plant-

1. Passenger boat with a steam-driven paddle wheel mounted on one side, designed for shallow river conditions.

2. Fayetteville, North Carolina.

3. Pine-tree products, especially pitch, resin, and turpentine, used to build and maintain ships.

ers thereabouts had attempted it on a commercial scale, in former years, with greater or less success; but like most Southern industries, it had felt the blight of war and had fallen into desuetude.

I went several times to look at a place that I thought might suit me. It was a plantation of considerable extent, that had formerly belonged to a wealthy man by the name of McAdoo. The estate had been for years involved in litigation between disputing heirs, during which period shift-less cultivation had well-nigh exhausted the soil. There had been a vine-yard of some extent on the place, but it had not been attended to since the war, and had lapsed into utter neglect. The vines—here partly supported by decayed and broken-down trellises, there twining themselves among the branches of the slender saplings which had sprung up among them— grew in wild and unpruned luxuriance, and the few scattered grapes they bore were the undisputed prey of the first comer. The site was admirably adapted to grape-raising; the soil, with a little attention, could not have been better; and with the native grape, the luscious scuppernong,[4] as my main reliance in the beginning, I felt sure that I could introduce and cul-tivate successfully a number of other varieties.

One day I went over with my wife to show her the place. We drove out of the town over a long wooden bridge that spanned a spreading mill-pond, passed the long whitewashed fence surrounding the county fair-ground, and struck into a road so sandy that the horse's feet sank to the fetlocks. Our route lay partly up hill and partly down, for we were in the sand-hill county;[5] we drove past cultivated farms, and then by abandoned fields grown up in scrub-oak and short-leaved pine, and once or twice through the solemn aisles of the virgin forest, where the tall pines, well-nigh meet-ing over the narrow road, shut out the sun, and wrapped us in cloistral solitude. Once, at a cross-roads, I was in doubt as to the turn to take, and we sat there waiting ten minutes—we had already caught some of the na-tive infection of restfulness—for some human being to come along, who could direct us on our way. At length a little negro girl appeared, walking straight as an arrow, with a piggin[6] full of water on her head. After a little patient investigation, necessary to overcome the child's shyness, we learned what we wished to know, and at the end of about five miles from the town reached our destination.

We drove between a pair of decayed gateposts—the gate itself had long

4. The silvery-green Muscadine grape, southern native plant.

5. Sandy region of central North Carolina, characterized by grasses, shrubs, and long-leaf pines.

6. Small wooden pail with handles formed by two staves extended above the rim.

since disappeared—and up a straight sandy lane, between two lines of
rotting rail fence, partly concealed by jimsonweeds and briers, to the open
space where a dwelling-house had once stood, evidently a spacious mansion, if we might judge from the ruined chimneys that were still standing, and the brick pillars on which the sills rested. The house itself, we had
been informed, had fallen a victim to the fortunes of war.

We alighted from the buggy, walked about the yard for a while, and
then wandered off into the adjoining vineyard. Upon Annie's complain-
ing of weariness I led the way back to the yard, where a pine log, lying
under a spreading elm, afforded a shady though somewhat hard seat. One
end of the log was already occupied by a venerable-looking colored man.
He held on his knees a hat full of grapes, over which he was smacking his
lips with great gusto, and a pile of grapeskins near him indicated that the
performance was no new thing. We approached him at an angle from the
rear, and were close to him before he perceived us. He respectfully rose as
we drew near, and was moving away, when I begged him to keep his seat.

"Don't let us disturb you," I said. "There is plenty of room for us all."

He resumed his seat with somewhat of embarrassment. While he had
been standing, I had observed that he was a tall man, and, though slightly
bowed by the weight of years, apparently quite vigorous. He was not entirely black, and this fact, together with the quality of his hair, which was
about six inches long and very bushy, except on the top of his head, where
he was quite bald, suggested a slight strain of other than negro blood.
There was a shrewdness in his eyes, too, which was not altogether African,
and which, as we afterwards learned from experience, was indicative of a
corresponding shrewdness in his character. He went on eating the grapes,
but did not seem to enjoy himself quite so well as he had apparently done
before he became aware of our presence.

"Do you live around here?" I asked, anxious to put him at his ease.

"Yas, suh. I lives des ober yander, behine de nex' san'-hill, on de Lumberton plank-road." [7]

"Do you know anything about the time when this vineyard was cultivated?"

"Lawd bless you, suh, I knows all about it. Dey ain' na'er a man in dis
settlement w'at won' tell you ole Julius McAdoo 'uz bawn en raise' on dis

7. First laid in North Carolina in the 1850s, plank-road paving typically consisted of stringers
down the roadsides crossed by sixteen-foot wood planks. Lumberton is about thirty miles
south of Fayetteville.

yer same plantation. Is you de Norv'n gemman w'at's gwine ter buy de ole vimya'd?"

"I am looking at it," I replied; "but I don't know that I shall care to buy unless I can be reasonably sure of making something out of it."

"Well, suh, you is a stranger ter me, en I is a stranger ter you, en we is bofe strangers ter one anudder, but 'f I 'uz in yo' place, I would n' buy dis vimya'd."

"Why not?" I asked.

"Well, I dunno whe'r you b'lieves in cunj'in' [8] er not,—some er de w'ite folks don't, er says dey don't,—but de truf er de matter is dat dis yer ole vimya'd is goophered."

"Is what?" I asked, not grasping the meaning of this unfamiliar word.

"Is goophered,—cunju'd, bewitch'."

He imparted this information with such solemn earnestness, and with such an air of confidential mystery, that I felt somewhat interested, while Annie was evidently much impressed, and drew closer to me.

"How do you know it is bewitched?" I asked.

"I would n' spec' fer you ter b'lieve me 'less you know all 'bout de fac's. But ef you en young miss dere doan' min' lis'nin' ter a ole nigger run on a minute er two w'ile you er restin', I kin 'splain to you how it all happen'."

We assured him that we would be glad to hear how it all happened, and he began to tell us. At first the current of his memory—or imagination— seemed somewhat sluggish; but as his embarrassment wore off, his language flowed more freely, and the story acquired perspective and coherence. As he became more and more absorbed in the narrative, his eyes assumed a dreamy expression, and he seemed to lose sight of his auditors, and to be living over again in monologue his life on the old plantation.

"Ole Mars Dugal' McAdoo," he began, "bought dis place long many years befo' de wah, en I 'member well w'en he sot out all dis yer part er de plantation in scuppernon's. De vimes growed monst'us fas', en Mars Dugal' made a thousan' gallon er scuppernon' wine eve'y year.

"Now, ef dey's an'thing a nigger lub, nex' ter 'possum, en chick'n, en watermillyums, it's scuppernon's. Dey ain' nuffin dat kin stan' up side'n de scuppernon' fer sweetness; sugar ain't a suckumstance ter scuppernon'. W'en de season is nigh 'bout ober, en de grapes begin ter swivel up des a little wid de wrinkles er ole age,—w'en de skin git sof' en brown,—den

8. "Conjuring." Conjure is an African-based spiritual, healing, and spell-working practice that uses roots, herbs, and/or artifacts from the person being conjured.

de scuppernon' make you smack yo' lip en roll yo' eye en wush fer mo'; so I reckon it ain' very 'stonishin' dat niggers lub scuppernon'.

"Dey wuz a sight er niggers in de naberhood er de vimya'd. Dere wuz ole Mars Henry Brayboy's niggers, en ole Mars Jeems McLean's niggers, en Mars Dugal's own niggers; den dey wuz a settlement er free niggers en po' buckrahs,[9] down by de Wim'l'ton Road,[10] en Mars Dugal' had de only vimya'd in de naberhood. I reckon it ain' so much so nowadays, but befo' de wah, in slab'ry times, a nigger did n' mine goin' fi' er ten mile in a night, w'en dey wuz sump'n good ter eat at de yuther een'.

"So atter a w'ile Mars Dugal' begin ter miss his scuppernon's. Co'se he 'cuse' de niggers er it, but dey all 'nied it ter de las'. Mars Dugal' sot spring guns en steel traps, en he en de oberseah[11] sot up nights once't er twice't, tel one night Mars Dugal'—he 'uz a monst'us keerless man—got his leg shot full er cow-peas. But somehow er nudder dey could n' nebber ketch none er de niggers. I dunner how it happen, but it happen des like I tell you, en de grapes kep' on a-goin' des de same.

"But bimeby ole Mars Dugal' fix' up a plan ter stop it. Dey wuz a cun-juh 'oman livin' down 'mongs' de free niggers on de Wim'l'ton Road, en all de darkies fum Rockfish ter Beaver Crick[12] wuz feared er her. She could wuk de mos' powerfulles' kin' er goopher,—could make people hab fits, er rheumatiz, er make 'em des dwinel away en die; en dey say she went out ridin' de niggers at night, fer she wuz a witch 'sides bein' a cunjuh 'oman. Mars Dugal' hearn 'bout Aun' Peggy's doin's, en begun ter 'flect whe'r er no he could n' git her ter he'p him keep de niggers off 'n de grapevimes. One day in de spring er de year, ole miss pack' up a basket er chick'n en poun'-cake, en a bottle er scuppernon' wine, en Mars Dugal' tuk it in his buggy en driv ober ter Aun' Peggy's cabin. He tuk de basket in, en had a long talk wid Aun' Peggy.

"De nex' day Aun' Peggy come up ter de vimya'd. De niggers seed her slippin' 'roun', en dey soon foun' out what she 'uz doin' dere. Mars Dugal' had hi'ed her ter goopher de grapevimes. She sa'ntered 'roun' 'mongs' de vimes, en tuk a leaf fum dis one, en a grape-hull fum dat one, en a grape-seed fum anudder one; en den a little twig fum here, en a little pinch er

9. "Buckra," white people (sometimes derogatory); Ibo or Efik word for "demon, powerful being."

10. Wilmington, about a hundred miles southeast.

11. "Overseer": plantation manager of work gangs, usually white.

12. Beaver Creek and Rockfish are small communities about fifteen miles apart.

dirt fum dere,—en put it all in a big black bottle, wid a snake's toof en a speckle' hen's gall en some ha'rs fum a black cat's tail, en den fill' de bottle wid scuppernon' wine. W'en she got de goopher all ready en fix', she tuk'n went out in de woods en buried it under de root uv a red oak tree, en den come back en tole one er de niggers she done goopher de grapevimes, en a'er a nigger w'at eat dem grapes 'ud be sho ter die inside'n twel' mont's.

"Atter dat de niggers let de scuppernon's 'lone, en Mars Dugal' did n' hab no 'casion ter fine no mo' fault; en de season wuz mos' gone, w'en a strange gemman stop at de plantation one night ter see Mars Dugal' on some business; en his coachman, seein' de scuppernon's growin' so nice en sweet, slip 'roun' behine de smoke-house, en et all de scuppernon's he could hole. Nobody did n' notice it at de time, but dat night, on de way home, de gemman's hoss runned away en kill' de coachman. W'en we hearn de noos, Aun' Lucy, de' cook, she up'n say she seed de strange nigger eat'n' er de scuppernon's behine de smokehouse; en den we knowed de goopher had b'en er wukkin'. Den one er de nigger chilluns runned away fum de quarters one day, en got in de scuppernon's, en died de nex' week. W'ite folks say he die' er de fevuh, but de niggers knowed it wuz de goopher. So you k'n be sho de darkies did n' hab much ter do wid dem scuppernon' vimes.

"W'en de scuppernon' season 'uz ober fer dat year, Mars Dugal' foun' he had made fifteen hund'ed gallon er wine; en one er de niggers hearn him laffin' wid de oberseah fit ter kill, en sayin' dem fifteen hund'ed gallon er wine wuz monst'us good intrus' on de ten dollars he laid out on de vimya'd. So I 'low ez he paid Aun' Peggy ten dollars fer to goopher de grapevimes.

"De goopher did n' wuk no mo' tel de nex' summer, w'en 'long to'ds de middle er de season one er de fiel' han's died; en ez dat lef' Mars Dugal' sho't er han's, he went off ter town fer ter buy anudder. He fotch de noo nigger home wid 'im. He wuz er ole nigger, er de color er a gingy-cake, en ball ez a hossapple on de top er his head. He wuz a peart[13] ole nigger, do', en could do a big day's wuk.

"Now it happen dat one er de niggers on de nex' plantation, one er ole Mars Henry Brayboy's niggers, had runned away de day befo', en tuk ter de swamp, en ole Mars Dugal' en some er de yuther nabor w'ite folks had gone out wid dere guns en dere dogs fer ter he'p 'em hunt fer de nigger; en de han's on our own plantation wuz all so flusterated dat we fuhgot ter

13. "Pert," that is, lively, energetic.

tell de noo han' 'bout de goopher on de scuppernon' vimes. Co'se he smell de grapes en see de vimes, an atter dahk de fus' thing he done wuz ter slip off ter de grapevimes 'dout sayin' nuffin ter nobody. Nex' mawnin' he tole some er de niggers 'bout de fine bait [14] er scuppernon' he et de night befo'.

"W'en dey tole 'im 'bout de goopher on de grapevimes, he 'uz dat tarrified dat he turn pale, en look des like he gwine ter die right in his tracks. De oberseah come up en axed w'at 'uz de matter; en w'en dey tole 'im Henry be'n eatin' er de scuppernon's, en got de goopher on 'im, he gin Henry a big drink er w'iskey, en 'low dat de nex' rainy day he take 'im ober ter Aun' Peggy's, en see ef she would n' take de goopher off'n him, seein' ez he did n' know nuffin erbout it tel he done et de grapes.

"Sho nuff, it rain de nex' day, en de oberseah went ober ter Aun' Peggy's wid Henry. En Aun' Peggy say dat bein' ez Henry did n' know 'bout de goopher, en et de grapes in ign'ance er de conseq'ences, she reckon she mought be able fer ter take de goopher off'n him. So she fotch out er bottle wid some cunjuh medicine in it, en po'd some out in a go'd [15] fer Henry ter drink. He manage ter git it down; he say it tas'e like whiskey wid sump'n bitter in it. She 'lowed dat 'ud keep de goopher off 'n him tel de spring; but w'en de sap begin ter rise in de grapevimes he ha' ter come en see her ag'in, en she tell him w'at e's ter do.

"Nex' spring, w'en de sap commence' ter rise in de scuppernon' vime, Henry tuk a ham one night. Whar'd he git de ham? *I* doan know; dey wa'n't no hams on de plantation 'cep'n' w'at 'uz in de smoke-house, but *I* never see Henry 'bout de smoke-house. But ez I wuz a-sayin', he tuk de ham ober ter Aun' Peggy's; en Aun' Peggy tole 'im dat w'en Mars Dugal' begin ter prune de grapevimes, he mus' go en take'n scrape off de sap whar it ooze out'n de cut een's er de vimes, en 'n'int his ball head wid it; en ef he do dat once't a year de goopher would n' wuk agin 'im long ez he done it. En bein' ez he fotch her de ham, she fix' it so he kin eat all de scuppernon' he want.

"So Henry 'n'int his head wid de sap out'n de big grapevime des ha'f way 'twix' de quarters en de big house, en de goopher nebber wuk agin him dat summer. But de beatenes' thing you eber see happen ter Henry. Up ter dat time he wuz ez ball ez a sweeten' 'tater, but des ez soon ez de young leaves begun ter come out on de grapevimes, de ha'r begun ter grow out on Henry's head, en by de middle er de summer he had de bigges'

14. Meal, supper (archaic English).

15. "Gourd," the dried and hollowed-out shell of a squash-like fruit, used as a drinking vessel.

head er ha'r on de plantation. Befo' dat, Henry had tol'able good ha'r 'roun' de aidges, but soon ez de young grapes begun ter come, Henry's ha'r begun to quirl all up in little balls, des like dis yer reg'lar grapy ha'r, en by de time de grapes got ripe his head look des like a bunch er grapes. Combin' it did n' do no good; he wuk at it ha'f de night wid er Jim Crow,[16] en think he git it straighten' out, but in de mawnin' de grapes 'ud be dere des de same. So he gin it up, en tried ter keep de grapes down by havin' his ha'r cut sho't.

"But dat wa'n't de quares' thing 'bout de goopher. When Henry come ter de plantation, he wuz gittin' a little ole an stiff in de j'ints. But dat summer he got des ez spry en libely ez any young nigger on de plantation; fac', he got so biggity dat Mars Jackson, de oberseah, ha' ter th'eaten ter whip 'im, ef he did n' stop cuttin' up his didos[17] en behave hisself. But de mos' cur'ouses' thing happen' in de fall, when de sap begin ter go down in de grapevimes. Fus', when de grapes 'uz gethered, de knots begun ter straighten out'n Henry's ha'r; en w'en de leaves begin ter fall, Henry's ha'r 'mence' ter drap out; en when de vimes 'uz bar', Henry's head wuz baller'n it wuz in de spring, en he begin ter git ole en stiff in de j'ints, ag'in, en paid no mo' 'tention ter de gals dyoin' er de whole winter. En nex' spring, w'en he rub de sap on agin, he got young ag'in, en so soopl[18] en libely dat none er de young niggers on de plantation could n' jump, ner dance, ner hoe ez much cotton ez Henry. But in de fall er de year his grapes 'mence' ter straighten out, en his j'ints ter git stiff, en his ha'r drap off, en de rheuma-tiz begin ter wrastle wid 'im.

"Now, ef you'd 'a' knowed ole Mars Dugal' McAdoo, you'd 'a' knowed dat it ha' ter be a mighty rainy day when he could n' fine sump'n fer his niggers ter do, en it ha' ter be a mighty little hole he could n' crawl thoo, en ha' ter be a monst'us cloudy night when a dollar git by him in de dahk-ness; en w'en he see how Henry git young in de spring en ole in de fall, he 'lowed ter hisse'f ez how he could make mo' money out'n Henry dan by wukkin' him in de cotton-fiel'. Long de nex' spring, atter de sap 'mence' ter rise, en Henry 'n'int 'is head en sta'ted fer ter git young en soopl, Mars Dugal' up 'n tuk Henry ter town, en sole 'im fer fifteen hunder' dollars.

16. Wooden brush with short, wire bristles resembling a carding "comb" used to untangle wool for spinning. The term Jim Crow, originally from an antebellum minstrel show, was generally applied to African American people and culture and later to the postwar laws of segregation.

17. "Pranks" (Irish); fool around or cut capers.

18. "Supple."

Co'se de man w'at bought Henry did n' know nuffin 'bout de goopher, en Mars Dugal' did n' see no 'casion fer ter tell 'im. Long to'ds de fall, w'en de sap went down, Henry begin ter git ole ag'in same ez yuzhal, en his noo marster begin ter git skeered les'n he gwine ter lose his fifteen-hunder'-dollar nigger. He sent fer a mighty fine doctor, but de med'cine did n' 'pear ter do no good; de goopher had a good holt. Henry tole de doctor 'bout de goopher, but de doctor des laff at 'im.

"One day in de winter Mars Dugal' went ter town, en wuz santerin' 'long de Main Street, when who should he meet but Henry's noo marster. Dey said 'Hoddy,' en Mars Dugal' ax 'im ter hab a seegyar; en atter dey run on awhile 'bout de craps en de weather, Mars Dugal' ax 'im, sorter keerless, like ez ef he des thought of it,—

"'How you like de nigger I sole you las' spring?'

"Henry's marster shuck his head en knock de ashes off'n his seegyar.

"'Spec' I made a bad bahgin when I bought dat nigger. Henry done good wuk all de summer, but sence de fall set in he 'pears ter be sorter pinin' away. Dey ain' nuffin pertickler de matter wid 'im—leastways de doctor say so—'cep'n' a tech er de rheumatiz; but his ha'r is all fell out, en ef he don't pick up his strenk mighty soon, I spec' I'm gwine ter lose 'im.'

"Dey smoked on awhile, en bimeby ole mars say, 'Well, a bahgin's a bahgin, but you en me is good fren's, en I doan wan' ter see you lose all de money you paid fer dat nigger; en ef w'at you say is so, en I ain't 'sputin' it, he ain't wuf much now. I 'spec's you wukked him too ha'd dis summer, er e'se de swamps down here don't agree wid de san'-hill nigger. So you des lemme know, en ef he gits any wusser I'll be willin' ter gib yer five hund'ed dollars fer 'im, en take my chances on his livin'.'

"Sho 'nuff, when Henry begun ter draw up wid de rheumatiz en it look like he gwine ter die fer sho, his noo marster sen' fer Mars Dugal', en Mars Dugal' gin him what he promus, en brung Henry home ag'in. He tuk good keer uv 'im dyoin' er de winter,—give 'im w'iskey ter rub his rheumatiz, en terbacker ter smoke, en all he want ter eat,—'caze a nigger w'at he could make a thousan' dollars a year off'n did n' grow on eve'y huckle-berry bush.

"Nex' spring, w'en de sap ris en Henry's ha'r commence' ter sprout, Mars Dugal' sole 'im ag'in, down in Robeson County dis time; en he kep' dat sellin' business up fer five year er mo. Henry nebber say nuffin 'bout de goopher ter his noo marsters, 'caze he know he gwine ter be tuk good keer uv de nex' winter, w'en Mars Dugal' buy him back. En Mars Dugal' made 'nuff money off'n Henry ter buy anudder plantation ober on Beaver Crick.

"But 'long 'bout de een' er dat five year dey come a stranger ter stop at de plantation. De fus' day he 'uz dere he went out wid Mars Dugal' en spent all de mawnin' lookin' ober de vimya'd, en atter dinner dey spent all de evenin' playin' kya'ds. De niggers soon 'skiver' dat he wuz a Yankee, en dat he come down ter Norf C'lina fer ter l'arn de w'ite folks how to raise grapes en make wine. He promus Mars Dugal' he c'd make de grapevimes b'ar twice't ez many grapes, en dat de noo winepress 'he wuz a-sellin' would make mo' d'n twice't ez many gallons er wine. En ole Mars Dugal' des drunk it all in, des 'peared ter be bewitch' wid dat Yankee. W'en de darkies see dat Yankee runnin' 'roun' de vimya'd en diggin' under de grapevimes, dey shuk dere heads, en 'lowed dat dey feared Mars Dugal' losin' his min'. Mars Dugal' had all de dirt dug away fum under de roots er all de scuppernon' vimes, an' let 'em stan' dat away fer a week er mo'. Den dat Yankee made de niggers fix up a mixtry er lime en ashes en manyo,[19] en po' it 'roun' de roots er de grapevimes. Den he 'vise Mars Dugal' fer ter trim de vimes close't, en Mars Dugal' tuck 'n done eve'ything de Yankee tole him ter do. Dyoin' all er dis time, mind yer, dis yer Yankee wuz libbin' off'n de fat er de lan', at de big house, en playin' kya'ds wid Mars Dugal' eve'y night; en dey say Mars Dugal' los' mo'n a thousan' dollars dyoin' er de week dat Yankee wuz a-ruinin' de grapevimes.

"W'en de sap ris nex' spring, ole Henry 'n'inted his head ez yuzhal, en his ha'r 'mence' ter grow des de same ez it done eve'y year. De scuppernon' vimes growed monst's fast, en de leaves wuz greener en thicker dan dey eber be'n dyoin' my remem'ance; en Henry's ha'r growed out thicker dan eber, en he 'peared ter git younger 'n younger, en soopler 'n soopler; en seein' ez he wuz sho't er han's dat spring, havin' tuk in consid'able noo groun', Mars Dugal' 'cluded he wouldn' sell Henry 'tel he git de crap in en de cotton chop'. So he kept Henry on de plantation.

"But 'long 'bout time fer de grapes ter come on de scuppernon' vimes, dey 'peared ter come a change ober 'em; de leaves withered en swivel' up, en de young grapes turn' yaller, en bimeby eve'ybody on de plantation could see dat de whole vimya'd wuz dyin'. Mars Dugal' tuk'n water de vimes en done all he could, but 't wa'n' no use: dat Yankee had done bus' de watermillyum. One time de vimes picked up a bit, en Mars Dugal' 'lowed dey wuz gwine ter come out ag'in; but dat Yankee done dug too close under de roots, en prune de branches too close ter de vime, en all dat lime en ashes done burn' de life out'n de vimes, en dey des kep' a-with'in' en a-swivelin'.

19. Manure.

"All dis time de goopher wuz a-wukkin'. When de vimes sta'ted ter wither, Henry 'mence' ter complain er his rheumatiz; en when de leaves begin ter dry up, his ha'r 'mence' ter drap out. When de vimes fresh' up a bit, Henry 'd git peart ag'in, en when de vimes wither' ag'in, Henry 'd git ole ag'in, en des kep' gittin' mo' en mo' fitten fer nuffin; he des pined away, en pined away, en finely tuk ter his cabin; en when de big vime whar he got de sap ter 'n'int his head withered en turned yaller en died, Henry died too,—des went out sorter like a cannel. Dey didn't 'pear ter be nuffin de matter wid 'im, 'cep'n' de rheumatiz, but his strenk des dwinel' away 'tel he did n' hab ernuff lef' ter draw his bref. De goopher had got de under holt, en th'owed Henry dat time fer good en all.

"Mars Dugal' tuk on might'ly 'bout losin' his vimes en his nigger in de same year; en he swo' dat ef he could git holt er dat Yankee he'd wear 'im ter a frazzle, en den chaw up de frazzle; en he'd done it, too, for Mars Dugal' 'uz a monst'us brash man w'en he once git started. He sot de vimya'd out ober ag'in, but it wuz th'ee er fo' year befo' de vimes got ter b'arin' any scuppernon's.

"W'en de wah broke out, Mars Dugal' raise' a comp'ny, en went off ter fight de Yankees. He say he wuz mighty glad dat wah come, en he des want ter kill a Yankee fer eve'y dollar he los' 'long er dat grape-raisin' Yankee. En I spec' he would 'a' done it, too, ef de Yankees had n' s'picioned sump'n, en killed him fus'. Atter de s'render ole miss move' ter town, de niggers all scattered 'way fum de plantation, en de vimya'd ain' be'n cultervated sence."

"Is that story true?" asked Annie doubtfully, but seriously, as the old man concluded his narrative.

"It's des ez true ez I'm a-settin' here, miss. Dey's a easy way ter prove it: I kin lead de way right ter Henry's grave ober yander in de plantation buryin'-groun'. En I tell yer w'at, marster, I would n' 'vise you to buy dis yer ole vimya'd, 'caze de goopher's on it yit, en dey ain' no tellin' w'en it's gwine ter crap out."

"But I thought you said all the old vines died."

"Dey did 'pear ter die, but a few un 'em come out ag'in, en is mixed in 'mongs' de yuthers. I ain' skeered ter eat de grapes, 'caze I knows de old vimes fum de noo ones; but wid strangers dey ain' no tellin' w'at mought happen. I would n' 'vise yer ter buy dis vimya'd."

I bought the vineyard, nevertheless, and it has been for a long time in a thriving condition, and is often referred to by the local press as a striking illustration of the opportunities open to Northern capital in the development of Southern industries. The luscious scuppernong holds first rank among our grapes, though we cultivate a great many other varieties, and our income from grapes packed and shipped to the Northern markets is quite considerable. I have not noticed any developments of the goopher in the vineyard, although I have a mild suspicion that our colored assistants do not suffer from want of grapes during the season.

I found, when I bought the vineyard, that Uncle Julius had occupied a cabin on the place for many years, and derived a respectable revenue from the product of the neglected grapevines. This, doubtless, accounted for his advice to me not to buy the vineyard, though whether it inspired the goopher story I am unable to state. I believe, however, that the wages I paid him for his services as coachman, for I gave him employment in that capacity, were more than an equivalent for anything he lost by the sale of the vineyard.

Dave's Neckliss

"Have some dinner, Uncle Julius?" said my wife.

It was a Sunday afternoon in early autumn. Our two women-servants had gone to a camp-meeting[20] some miles away, and would not return until evening. My wife had served the dinner, and we were just rising from the table, when Julius came up the lane, and, taking off his hat, seated himself on the piazza.[21]

The old man glanced through the open door at the dinner-table, and his eyes rested lovingly upon a large sugar-cured ham, from which several slices had been cut, exposing a rich pink expanse that would have appealed strongly to the appetite of any hungry Christian.

"Thanky, Miss Annie," he said, after a momentary hesitation. "I dunno ez I keers ef I does tas'e a piece er dat ham, ef yer'll cut me off a slice un it."

"No," said Annie, "I won't. Just sit down to the table and help yourself; eat all you want, and don't be bashful."

Julius drew a chair up to the table, while my wife and I went out on the piazza. Julius was in my employment; he took his meals with his own family, but when he happened to be about our house at meal-times, my wife never let him go away hungry.

I threw myself into a hammock, from which I could see Julius through an open window. He ate with evident relish, devoting his attention chiefly

20. Spirited religious revival meeting held outdoors and lasting several days.
21. Verandah or porch.

to the ham, slice after slice of which disappeared in the spacious cavity of his mouth. At first the old man ate rapidly, but after the edge of his appetite had been taken off he proceeded in a more leisurely manner. When he had cut the sixth slice of ham (I kept count of them from a lazy curiosity to see how much he *could* eat) I saw him lay it on his plate; as he adjusted the knife and fork to cut it into smaller pieces, he paused, as if struck by a sudden thought, and a tear rolled down his rugged cheek and fell upon the slice of ham before him. But the emotion, whatever the thought that caused it, was transitory, and in a moment he continued his dinner. When he was through eating, he came out on the porch, and resumed his seat with the satisfied expression of countenance that usually follows a good dinner.

"Julius," I said, "you seemed to be affected by something a moment ago. Was the mustard so strong that it moved you to tears?"

"No, suh, it wa'n't de mustard; I wuz studyin' 'bout Dave."

"Who was Dave, and what about him?" I asked.

The conditions were all favorable to story-telling. There was an autumnal languor in the air, and a dreamy haze softened the dark green of the distant pines and the deep blue of the Southern sky. The generous meal he had made had put the old man in a very good humor. He was not always so, for his curiously undeveloped nature was subject to moods which were almost childish in their variableness. It was only now and then that we were able to study, through the medium of his recollection, the simple but intensely human inner life of slavery. His way of looking at the past seemed very strange to us; his view of certain sides of life was essentially different from ours. He never indulged in any regrets for the Arcadian[22] joyousness and irresponsibility which was a somewhat popular conception of slavery; his had not been the lot of the petted house servant, but that of the toiling field-hand. While he mentioned with a warm appreciation the acts of kindness which those in authority had shown to him and his people, he would speak of a cruel deed, not with the indignation of one accustomed to quick feeling and spontaneous expression, but with a furtive disapproval which suggested to us a doubt in his own mind as to whether he had a right to think or to feel, and presented to us the curious psychological spectacle of a mind enslaved long after the shackles had been struck off from the limbs of its possessor. Whether the sacred name of liberty ever set his soul aglow with a generous fire; whether he had more

22. From Arcadia, a region of Greece poetically identified with rustic inhabitants.

than the most elementary ideas of love, friendship, patriotism, religion—things which are half, and the better half, of life to us; whether he even realized, except in a vague, uncertain way, his own degradation, I do not know. I fear not; and if not, then centuries of repression had borne their legitimate fruit. But in the simple human feeling, and still more in the undertone of sadness, which pervaded his stories, I thought I could see a spark which, fanned by favoring breezes and fed by the memories of the past, might become in his children's children a glowing flame of sensibility, alive to every thrill of human happiness or human woe.

"Dave use' ter b'long ter my old marster," said Julius; "he wuz raise' on dis yer plantation, en I kin 'member all erbout 'im, fer I wuz old 'nuff ter chop cotton w'en it all happen'. Dave wuz a tall man, en monst'us strong: he could do mo' wuk in a day den any yuther two niggers on de plantation. He wuz one er dese yer solemn kine er men, en nebber run on wid much foolishness, like de yuther darkies. He use' ter go out in de woods en pray; en w'en he hear de han's on de plantation cussin' en gwine on wid dere dancin' en foolishness, he use' ter tell 'em 'bout religion en jedgmen'-day, w'en dey would haf ter gin account fer eve'y idle word en all dey yuther sinful kyarin's-on.

"Dave had l'arn' how ter read de Bible. Dey wuz a free nigger boy in de settlement w'at wuz monst'us smart, en could write en cipher, en wuz alluz readin' books er papers. En Dave had hi'ed dis free boy fer ter l'arn 'im how ter read. Hit wuz 'g'in' de law, but co'se none er de niggers did n' say nuffin ter de w'ite folks 'bout it. Howsomedever, one day Mars Walker—he wuz de oberseah [23]—foun' out Dave could read. Mars Walker wa'n't nuffin but a po' bockrah,[24] en folks said he could n' read ner write hisse'f, en co'se he did n' lack ter see a nigger w'at knowed mo' d'n he did; so he went en tole Mars Dugal'. Mars Dugal' sont fer Dave, en ax' 'im 'bout it.

"Dave did n't hardly knowed w'at ter do; but he could n' tell no lie, so he 'fessed he could read de Bible a little by spellin' out de words. Mars Dugal' look' mighty solemn.

"'Dis yer is a se'ious matter,' sezee; 'it 's 'g'in' de law ter l'arn niggers how ter read, er 'low 'em ter hab books. But w'at yer l'arn out'n dat Bible, Dave?'

"Dave wa'n't no fool, ef he wuz a nigger, en sezee:—

23. "Overseer": plantation manager of work gangs, usually white.

24. "Buckra" (sometimes derogatory), white people; Ibo or Efik word for "demon, superior being."

"'Marster, I l'arns dat it 's a sin fer ter steal, er ter lie, er fer ter want w'at doan b'long ter yer; en I l'arns fer ter love de Lawd en ter 'bey my marster.'

"Mars Dugal' sorter smile' en laf' ter hisse'f, like he 'uz might'ly tickle' 'bout sump'n, en sezee:

"'Doan 'pear ter me lack readin' de Bible done yer much harm, Dave. Dat 's w'at I wants all my niggers fer ter know. Yer keep right on readin', en tell de yuther han's w'at yer be'n tellin' me. How would yer lack fer ter preach ter de niggers on Sunday?'

"Dave say he'd be glad fer ter do w'at he could. So Mars Dugal' tole de oberseah fer ter let Dave preach ter de niggers, en tell 'em w'at wuz in de Bible, en it would he'p ter keep 'em fum stealin' er runnin' erway.

"So Dave 'mence' ter preach, en done de han's on de plantation a heap er good, en most un 'em lef' off dey wicked ways, en 'mence' ter love ter hear 'bout God, en religion, en de Bible; en dey done dey wuk better, en did n' gib de oberseah but mighty little trouble fer ter manage 'em.

"Dave wuz one er dese yer men w'at did n' keer much fer de gals— leastways he did n' 'tel Dilsey come ter de plantation. Dilsey wuz a mon-st'us peart, good-lookin', gingybread-colored gal—one er dese yer high-steppin' gals w'at hol's dey heads up, en won' stan' no foolishness fum no man. She had b'long' ter a gemman over on Rockfish,[25] w'at died, en whose 'state ha' ter be sol' fer ter pay his debts. En Mars Dugal' had be'n ter de oction, en w'en he seed dis gal a-cryin' en gwine on 'bout bein' sol' erway fum her ole mammy, Aun' Mahaly, Mars Dugal' bid 'em bofe in, en fotch 'em ober ter our plantation.

"De young nigger men on de plantation wuz des wil' atter Dilsey, but it did n' do no good, en none un 'em could n' git Dilsey fer dey junesey,[26] 'tel Dave 'mence' fer ter go roun' Aun' Mahaly's cabin. Dey wuz a fine-lookin' couple, Dave en Dilsey wuz, bofe tall, en well-shape', en soopl'.[27] En dey sot a heap by one ernudder. Mars Dugal' seed 'em tergedder one Sunday, en de nex' time he seed Dave atter dat, sezee:

"'Dave, w'en yer en Dilsey gits ready fer ter git married, I ain' got no rejections. Dey 's a poun' er so er chawin'-terbacker up at de house, en I reckon yo' mist'iss kin fine a frock en a ribbin er two fer Dilsey. Youer bofe good niggers, en yer neenter be feared er bein' sol' 'way fum one ernud-der long ez I owns dis plantation; en I 'spec's ter own it fer a long time yit.'

25. Small stream southeast of Fayetteville.
26. Sweetheart.
27. "Supple."

"But dere wuz one man on de plantation w'at did n' lack ter see Dave en Dilsey tergedder ez much ez ole marster did. W'en Mars Dugal' went ter de sale whar he got Dilsey en Mahaly, he bought ernudder han', by de name er Wiley. Wiley wuz one er dese yer shiny-eyed, double-headed little niggers, sha'p ez a steel trap, en sly ez de fox w'at keep out'n it. Dis yer Wiley had be'n pesterin' Dilsey 'fo' she come ter our plantation, en had nigh 'bout worried de life out'n her. She did n' keer nuffin fer im, but he pestered her so she ha' ter th'eaten ter tell her marster fer ter make Wiley let her 'lone. W'en he come ober to our place it wuz des ez bad, 'tel bimeby Wiley seed dat Dilsey had got ter thinkin' a heap 'bout Dave, en den he sorter hilt off aw'ile, en purten' lack he gin Dilsey up. But he wuz one er dese yer 'ceitful niggers, en w'ile he wuz laffin' en jokin' wid de yuther han's 'bout Dave en Dilsey, he wuz settin' a trap fer ter ketch Dave en git Dilsey back fer hisse'f.

"Dave en Dilsey made up dere min's fer ter git married long 'bout Christmas time, w'en dey 'd hab mo' time fer a weddin'. But 'long 'bout two weeks befo' dat time ole mars 'mence' ter lose a heap er bacon. Eve'y night er so somebody 'ud steal a side er bacon, er a ham, er a shoulder, er sump'n, fum one er de smoke'ouses. De smoke'ouses wuz lock', but somebody had a key, en manage' ter git in some way er 'nudder. Dey 's mo' ways 'n one ter skin a cat, en dey 's mo' d'n one way ter git in a smoke-'ouse— leastways dat 's w'at I hearn say. Folks w'at had bacon fer ter sell did n' hab no trouble 'bout gittin' rid un it. Hit wuz 'g'in de law fer ter buy things fum slabes; but Lawd! dat law did n' 'mount ter a hill er peas. Eve'y week er so one er dese yer big covered waggins would come 'long de road, peddlin' terbacker en w'iskey. Dey wuz a sight er room in one er dem big waggins, en it wuz monst'us easy fer ter swop off bacon fer sump'n ter chew er ter wa'm yer up in de wintertime. I s'pose de peddlers did n' knowed dey wuz breakin' de law, caze de niggers alluz went at night, en stayed on de dark side er de waggin; en it wuz mighty hard fer ter tell *w'at* kine er folks dey wuz.

"Atter two er th'ee hund'ed er meat had be'n stole', Mars Walker call all de niggers up one ebenin', en tol' 'em dat de fus' nigger he cot stealin' bacon on dat plantation would git sump'n fer ter 'member it by long ez he lib'. En he say he'd gin fi' dollars ter de nigger w'at 'skiver' de rogue. Mars Walker say he s'picion' one er two er de niggers, but he could n' tell fer sho, en co'se dey all 'nied it w'en he 'cuse 'em un it.

"Dey wa'n't no bacon stole' fer a week er so, 'tel one dark night w'en somebody tuk a ham fum one er de smoke'ouses. Mars Walker des cusst awful w'en he foun' out de ham wuz gone, en say he gwine ter sarch all de niggers' cabins; w'en dis yer Wiley I wuz tellin' yer 'bout up'n say he s'pi-cion' who tuk de ham, fer he seed Dave comin' 'cross de plantation fum to'ds de smoke'ouse de night befo'. W'en Mars Walker hearn dis fum Wi-ley, he went en sarch' Dave's cabin, en foun' de ham hid under de flo'.

"Eve'ybody wuz 'stonish'; but dere wuz de ham. Co'se Dave 'nied it ter de las', but dere wuz de ham. Mars Walker say it wuz des ez he 'spected: he did n' b'lieve in dese yer readin' en prayin' niggers; it wuz all 'pocrisy, en sarve' Mars Dugal' right fer 'lowin' Dave ter be readin' books w'en it wuz 'g'in' de law.

"W'en Mars Dugal' hearn 'bout de ham, he say he wuz might'ly 'ceived en disapp'inted in Dave. He say he would n' nebber hab no mo' confer-dence in no nigger, en Mars Walker could do des ez he wuz a mineter wid Dave er any er de res' er de niggers. So Mars Walker tuk'n tied Dave up en gin 'im forty;[28] en den he got some er dis yer wire clof w'at dey uses fer ter make sifters out'n, en tuk'n wrap' it roun' de ham en fasten it terged-der at de little een'. Den he tuk Dave down ter de blacksmif shop, en had Unker Silas, de plantation blacksmif, fasten a chain ter de ham, en den fasten de yuther een' er de chain roun' Dave's neck. En den he says ter Dave, sezee:—

"'Now, suh, yer ' 'll wear dat neckliss fer de nex' six mont's; en I 'spec's yer ner none er de yuther niggers on dis plantation won' steal no mo' ba-con dyoin' er dat time.'

"Well, it des 'peared ez if fum dat time Dave did n' hab nuffin but trou-ble. De niggers all turnt ag'in' 'im, caze he be'n de 'casion er Mars Dugal' turnin' 'em all ober ter Mars Walker. Mars Dugal' wa'n't a bad marster hisse'f, but Mars Walker wuz hard ez a rock. Dave kep' on sayin' he did n' take de ham, but none un 'em did n' b'lieve 'im.

"Dilsey wa'n't on de plantation w'en Dave wuz 'cused er stealin' de ba-con. Ole mist'iss had sont her ter town fer a week er so fer ter wait on one er her darters w'at had a young baby, en she did n' fine out nuffin 'bout Dave's trouble 'tel she got back ter de plantation. Dave had patien'ly en-dyoed de finger er scawn, en all de hard words w'at de niggers pile' on 'im, caze he wuz sho' Dilsey would stan' by 'im, en would n' b'lieve he wuz a rogue, ner none er de yuther tales de darkies wuz tellin' 'bout 'im.

"W'en Dilsey come back fum town, en got down fum behine de buggy

28. Forty lashes with a whip.

whar she b'en ridin' wid ole mars, de fus' nigger 'ooman she met says ter her—

"'Is yer seed Dave, Dilsey?'

"'No, I ain' seed Dave,' says Dilsey.

"'Yer des oughter look at dat nigger; reckon yer would n' want 'im fer yo' junesey no mo'. Mars Walker cotch 'im stealin' bacon, en gone en fasten' a ham roun' his neck, so he can't git it off'n hisse'f. He sut'nly do look quare.' En den de 'ooman bus' out laffin' fit ter kill herse'f. W'en she got thoo laffin' she up'n tole Dilsey all 'bout de ham, en all de yuther lies w'at de niggers be'n tellin' on Dave.

"W'en Dilsey started down ter de quarters, who should she meet but Dave, comin' in fum de cotton-fiel'. She turnt her head ter one side, en purten' lack she did n' seed Dave.

"'Dilsey!' sezee.

"Dilsey walk' right on, en did n' notice 'im.

"'*Oh*, Dilsey!'

"Dilsey did n' paid no 'tention ter 'im, en den Dave knowed some er de niggers be'n tellin' her 'bout de ham. He felt monst'us bad, but he 'lowed ef he could des git Dilsey fer ter listen ter 'im for a minute er so, he could make her b'lieve he did n' stole de bacon. It wuz a week er two befo' he could git a chance ter speak ter her ag'in; but fine'ly he cotch her down by de spring one day, en sezee:—

"'Dilsey, w'at fer yer won' speak ter me, en purten' lack yer doan see me? Dilsey, yer knows me too well fer ter b'lieve I'd steal, er do dis yuther wick'ness de niggers is all layin' ter me—yer *knows* I would n' do dat, Dilsey. Yer ain' gwine back on yo' Dave, is yer?'

"But w'at Dave say did n' hab no 'fec' on Dilsey. Dem lies folks b'en tellin' her had p'isen' her min' 'g'in' Dave.

"'I doan wanter talk ter no nigger,' says she, 'w'at be'n whip' fer stealin', en w'at gwine roun' wid sich a lookin' thing ez dat hung roun' his neck. I's a 'spectable gal, *I* is. W'at yer call dat, Dave? Is dat a cha'm fer to keep off witches, er is it a noo kine er neckliss yer got?'

"Po' Dave did n' knowed w'at ter do. De las' one he had 'pended on fer ter stan' by 'im had gone back on 'im, en dey did n' 'pear ter be nuffin mo' wuf libbin' fer. He could n' hol' no mo' pra'r-meetin's, fer Mars Walker would n' 'low 'im ter preach, en de darkies would n' 'a' listen' ter 'im ef he had preach.' He did n' eben hab his Bible fer ter comfort hisse'f wid, fer Mars Walker had tuk it erway fum 'im en burnt it up, en say ef he ketch any mo' niggers wid Bibles on de plantation he 'd do 'em wuss'n he done Dave.

"En ter make it still harder fer Dave, Dilsey tuk up wid Wiley. Dave could see him gwine up ter Aun' Mahaly's cabin, en settin' out on de bench in de moonlight wid Dilsey, en singin' sinful songs en playin' de banjer. Dave use' ter scrouch down behine de bushes, en wonder w'at de Lawd sen' 'im all dem tribberlations fer.

"But all er Dave's yuther troubles wa'n't nuffin side er dat ham. He had wrap' de chain roun' wid a rag, so it did n' hurt his neck; but w'eneber he went ter wuk, dat ham would be in his way; he had ter do his task, howsomedever, des de sam ez ef he did n' hab de ham. W'eneber he went ter lay down, dat ham would be in de way. Ef he turn ober in his sleep, dat ham would be tuggin' at his neck. It wuz de las' thing he seed at night, en de fus' thing he seed in de mawnin'. W'eneber he met a stranger, de ham would be de fus' thing de stranger would see. Most un 'em would 'mence' ter laf, en whareber Dave went he could see folks p'intin' at him, en year 'em sayin':—

" 'W'at kine er collar dat nigger got roun' his neck?' er, ef dey knowed 'im, 'Is yer stole any mo' hams lately?' er 'W'at yer take fer yo' neckliss, Dave?' er some joke er 'nuther 'bout dat ham.

"Fus' Dave did n' mine it so much, caze he knowed he had n' done nuffin. But bimeby he got so he could n' stan' it no longer, en he'd hide hisse'f in de bushes w'eneber he seed anybody comin', en alluz kep' hisse'f shet up in his cabin atter he come in fum wuk.

"It wuz monst'us hard on Dave, en bimeby, w'at wid dat ham eberlastin' en etarnally draggin' roun' his neck, he 'mence' fer ter do en say quare things, en make de niggers wonder ef he wa'n't gittin' out'n his mine. He got ter gwine roun' talkin' ter hisse'f, en singin' cornshuckin' songs, en laffin' fit ter kill 'bout nuffin. En one day he tole one er de niggers he had 'skivered a noo way fer ter raise hams,—gwine ter pick 'em off'n trees, en save de expense er smoke'ouses by kyoin' 'em in de sun. En one day he up'n tole Mars Walker he got sump'n pertickler fer ter say ter 'im; en he tuk Mars Walker off ter one side, en tole 'im he wuz gwine ter show 'im a place in de swamp whar dey wuz a whole trac' er lan' covered wid ham-trees.

"W'en Mars Walker hearn Dave talkin' dis kine er fool-talk, en w'en he seed how Dave wuz 'mencin' ter git behine in his wuk, en w'en he ax' de niggers en dey tole 'im how Dave be'n gwine on, he 'lowed he reckon' he'd punish' Dave ernuff, en it mou't do mo' harm den good fer ter keep de ham on his neck any longer. So he sont Dave down ter de blacksmif-shop en had de ham tuk off. Dey wa'n't much er de ham lef' by dat time, fer de sun had melt all de fat, en de lean had all swivel' up, so dey wa'n't but th'ee er fo' poun's lef'.

"W'en de ham had be'n tuk off'n Dave, folks kinder stopped talkin' 'bout 'im so much. But de ham had be'n on his neck so long dat Dave had sorter got use' ter it. He look des lack he'd los' sump'n fer a day er so atter de ham wuz tuk off, en did n' 'pear ter know w'at ter do wid hisse'f; en fine'ly he up'n tuk'n tied a lighterd-knot[29] ter a string, en hid it under de flo' er his cabin, en w'en nobody wuz n' lookin' he'd take it out en hang it roun' his neck, en go off in de woods en holler en sing; en he allus tied it roun' his neck w'en he went ter sleep. Fac', it 'peared lack Dave done gone clean out'n his mine. En atter a w'ile he got one er de quarest notions you eber hearn tell un. It wuz 'bout dat time dat I come back ter de plantation fer ter wuk,—I had be'n out ter Mars Dugal's yuther place on Beaver Crick for a mont' er so. I had hearn 'bout Dave en de bacon, en 'bout w'at wuz gwine on on de plantation; but I did n' b'lieve w'at dey all say 'bout Dave, fer I knowed Dave wa'n't dat kine er man. One day atter I come back, me'n Dave wuz choppin' cotton tergedder, w'en Dave lean' on his hoe, en motion' fer me ter come ober close ter 'im; en den he retch' ober en w'ispered ter me.

" 'Julius,' sezee, 'did yer knowed yer wuz wukkin' long yer wid a ham?'

"I could n' 'magine w'at he meant. 'G'way fum yer, Dave,' says I. 'Yer ain' wearin' no ham no mo'; try en fergit 'bout dat; 't ain' gwine ter do yer no good fer ter 'member it.'

" 'Look a-yer, Julius,' sezee, 'kin yer keep a secret?'

" 'Co'se I kin, Dave,' says I. 'I doan go roun' tellin' people w'at yuther folks says ter me.'

" 'Kin I trus' yer, Julius? Will yer cross yo' heart?'

"I cross' my heart. 'Wush I may die ef I tells a soul,' says I.

"Dave look' at me des lack he wuz lookin' thoo me en 'way on de yuther side er me, en sezee:—

" 'Did yer knowed I wuz turnin' ter a ham, Julius?'

"I tried ter 'suade Dave dat dat wuz all foolishness, en dat he ought n't ter be talkin' dat-a-way,—hit wa'n't right. En I tole 'im ef he'd des be patien', de time would sho'ly come w'en eve'ything would be straighten' out, en folks would fine out who de rale rogue wuz w'at stole de bacon. Dave

29. Likely "lighter knot," a pine knot used to start a fire.

'peared ter listen ter w'at I say, en promise' ter do better, en stop gwine on dat-a-way; en it seem lack he pick' up a bit w'en he seed dey wuz one pusson did n' b'lieve dem tales 'bout 'im.

"Hit wa'n't long atter dat befo' Mars Archie McIntyre, ober on de Wimbleton road, 'mence' ter complain 'bout somebody stealin' chickens fum his hen-'ouse. De chickens kep' on gwine, en at las' Mars Archie tole de han's on his plantation dat he gwine ter shoot de fus' man he ketch in his hen-'ouse. In less'n a week atter he gin dis warnin', he cotch a nigger in de hen-'ouse, en fill' 'im full er squir'l-shot. W'en he got a light, he 'skivered it wuz a strange nigger; en w'en he call' one er his own sarven's, de nigger tole 'im it wuz our Wiley. W'en Mars Archie foun' dat out, he went ober ter our plantation fer ter tell Mars Dugal' he had shot one er his niggers, en dat he could sen' ober dere en git w'at wuz lef'-un 'im.

"Mars Dugal' wuz mad at fus'; but w'en he got ober dere en hearn how it all happen', he did n' hab much ter say. Wiley wuz shot so bad he wuz sho' he wuz gwine ter die, so he up'n says ter ole marster:—

"'Mars Dugal,' sezee, 'I knows I's be'n a monst'us bad nigger, but befo' I go I wanter git sump'n off'n my mine. Dave did n' steal dat bacon w'at wuz tuk out'n de smoke-'ouse. I stole it all, en I hid de ham under Dave's cabin fer ter th'ow de blame on him—en may de good Lawd fergib me fer it.'

"Mars Dugal' had Wiley tuk back ter de plantation, en sont fer a doctor fer ter pick de shot out'n 'im. En de ve'y nex' mawnin' Mars Dugal' sont fer Dave ter come up ter de big house; he felt kinder sorry fer de way Dave had be'n treated. Co'se it wa'n't no fault er Mars Dugal's, but he wuz gwine ter do w'at he could fer ter make up fer it. So he sont word down ter de quarters fer Dave en all de yuther han's ter 'semble up in de yard befo' de big house at sun-up nex' mawnin'.

"Yearly in de mawnin' de niggers all swarm' up in de yard. Mars Dugal' wuz feelin' so kine dat he had brung up a bairl er cider, en tole de niggers all fer ter he'p deyselves.

"All de han's on de plantation come but Dave; en bimeby, w'en it seem lack he wa'n't comin', Mars Dugal' sont a nigger down ter de quarters ter look fer 'im. De sun wuz gittin' up, en dey wuz a heap er wuk ter be done, en Mars Dugal' sorter got ti'ed waitin'; so he up'n says:—

"'Well, boys en gals, I sont fer yer all up yer fer ter tell yer dat all dat 'bout Dave's stealin' er de bacon wuz a mistake, ez I s'pose yer all done hearn befo' now, en I 's mighty sorry it happen'. I wants ter treat all my niggers right, en I wants yer all ter know dat I sets a heap by all er my han's w'at is hones' en smart. En I want yer all ter treat Dave des lack yer did befo' dis thing happen', en mine w'at he preach ter yer; fer Dave is a good nigger, en has had a hard row ter hoe. En de fus' one I ketch sayin' anythin' 'g'in' Dave, I'll tell Mister Walker ter gin 'im forty. Now take ernudder drink er cider all roun', en den git at dat cotton, fer I wanter git dat Persimmon Hill trac' all pick' ober ter-day.'

"W'en de niggers wuz gwine 'way, Mars Dugal' tole me fer ter go en hunt up Dave, en bring 'im up ter de house. I went down ter Dave's cabin, but could n' fine 'im dere. Den I look' roun' de plantation, en in de aidge er de woods, en 'long de road; but I could n' fine no sign er Dave. I wuz 'bout ter gin up de sarch, w'en I happen' fer ter run 'cross a foot-track w'at look' lack Dave's. I had wukked 'long wid Dave so much dat I knowed his tracks: he had a monst'us long foot, wid a holler instep, w'ich wuz sump'n skase 'mongs' black folks. So I follered dat track 'cross de fiel' fum de quarters 'tel I get ter de smoke-'ouse. De fus' thing I notice' wuz smoke comin' out'n de cracks: it wuz cu'ous, caze dey had n' be'n no hogs kill' on de plantation fer six mont' er so, en all de bacon in de smoke-'ouse wuz done kyoed. I could n' 'magine fer ter sabe my life w'at Dave wuz doin' in dat smoke-'ouse. I went up ter de do' en hollered:—

"'Dave!'

"Dey did n' nobody answer. I did n' wanter open de do', fer w'ite folks is monst'us pertickler 'bout dey smoke-'ouses; en ef de oberseah had a-come up en cotch me in dere, he mou't not wanter b'lieve I wuz des lookin' fer Dave. So I sorter knock at de do' en call' out ag'in:—

"'O Dave, hit's me—Julius! Doan be skeered. Mars Dugal' wants yer ter come up ter de big house,—he done 'skivered who stole de ham.'

"But Dave did n' answer. En w'en I look' roun' ag'in en did n' seed none er his tracks gwine way fum de smoke-'ouse, I knowed he wuz in dere yit, en I wuz 'termine' fer ter fetch 'im out; so I push de do' open en look in.

"Dey wuz a pile er bark burnin' in de middle er de flo', en right ober de fier, hangin' fum one er de rafters, wuz Dave; dey wuz a rope roun' his neck, en I did n' haf ter look at his face mo' d'n once fer ter see he wuz dead.

"Den I knowed how it all happen'. Dave had kep' on gittin' wusser en wusser in his mine, 'tel he des got ter b'lievin' he wuz all done turnt ter a ham; en den he had gone en built a fier, en tied a rope roun' his neck, des lack de hams wuz tied, en had hung hisse'f up in de smoke-'ouse fer ter kyo.

"Dave wuz buried down by the swamp, in de plantation buryin'-groun'. Wiley did n' died fum de woun' he got in Mars McIntyre's hen-'ouse; he got well atter a w'ile, but Dilsey would n' hab nuffin mo' ter do wid 'im, en 't wa'n't long 'fo' Mars Dugal' sol' 'im ter a spekilater on his way souf,—he say he did n' want no sich a nigger on de plantation, ner in de county, ef he could he'p it. En w'en de een' er de year come, Mars Dugal' turnt Mars Walker off, en run de plantation hisse'f atter dat.

"Eber sence den," said Julius in conclusion, "w'eneber I eats ham, it min's me er Dave. I lacks ham, but I nebber kin eat mo' d'n two er th'ee poun's befo' I gits ter studyin' 'bout Dave, en den I has ter stop en leab de res' fer ernudder time."

There was a short silence after the old man had finished his story, and then my wife began to talk to him about the weather, on which subject he was an authority. I went into the house. When I came out, half an hour later, I saw Julius disappearing down the lane, with a basket on his arm.

At breakfast, next morning, it occurred to me that I should like a slice of ham. I said as much to my wife.

"Oh, no, John," she responded, "you shouldn't eat anything so heavy for breakfast."

I insisted.

"The fact is," she said, pensively, "I couldn't have eaten any more of that ham, and so I gave it to Julius."

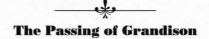

The Passing of Grandison

I

When it is said that it was done to please a woman, there ought perhaps to be enough said to explain anything; for what a man will not do to please a woman is yet to be discovered. Nevertheless, it might be well to state a few preliminary facts to make it clear why young Dick Owens tried to run one of his father's negro men off to Canada.

In the early fifties, when the growth of anti-slavery sentiment and the constant drain of fugitive slaves into the North had so alarmed the slaveholders of the border states as to lead to the passage of the Fugitive Slave Law,[30] a young white man from Ohio, moved by compassion for the sufferings of a certain bondman who happened to have a "hard master," essayed to help the slave to freedom. The attempt was discovered and frus-

---

30. A controversial part of the Compromise of 1850, the Fugitive Slave Law provided that slaves who had escaped to free states had to be returned to their owners.

trated; the abductor was tried and convicted for slave-stealing, and sentenced to a term of imprisonment in the penitentiary. His death, after the expiration of only a small part of the sentence, from cholera contracted while nursing stricken fellow prisoners, lent to the case a melancholy interest that made it famous in anti-slavery annals.

Dick Owens had attended the trial. He was a youth of about twenty-two, intelligent, handsome, and amiable, but extremely indolent, in a graceful and gentlemanly way; or, as old Judge Fenderson put it more than once, he was lazy as the Devil,—a mere figure of speech, of course, and not one that did justice to the Enemy of Mankind. When asked why he never did anything serious, Dick would good-naturedly reply, with a well-modulated drawl, that he didn't have to. His father was rich; there was but one other child, an unmarried daughter, who because of poor health would probably never marry, and Dick was therefore heir presumptive to a large estate. Wealth or social position he did not need to seek, for he was born to both. Charity Lomax had shamed him into studying law, but notwithstanding an hour or so a day spent at old Judge Fenderson's office, he did not make remarkable headway in his legal studies.

"What Dick needs," said the judge, who was fond of tropes, as became a scholar, and of horses, as was befitting a Kentuckian, "is the whip of necessity, or the spur of ambition. If he had either, he would soon need the snaffle[31] to hold him back."

But all Dick required, in fact, to prompt him to the most remarkable thing he accomplished before he was twenty-five, was a mere suggestion from Charity Lomax. The story was never really known to but two persons until after the war, when it came out because it was a good story and there was no particular reason for its concealment.

Young Owens had attended the trial of this slave-stealer, or martyr,—either or both,—and, when it was over, had gone to call on Charity Lomax, and, while they sat on the veranda after sundown, had told her all about the trial. He was a good talker, as his career in later years disclosed, and described the proceedings very graphically.

"I confess," he admitted, "that while my principles were against the prisoner, my sympathies were on his side. It appeared that he was of good family, and that he had an old father and mother, respectable people, dependent upon him for support and comfort in their declining years. He had been led into the matter by pity for a negro whose master ought to

31. Bit or restraint for a horse.

have been run out of the county long ago for abusing his slaves. If it had been merely a question of old Sam Briggs's negro, nobody would have cared anything about it. But father and the rest of them stood on the principle of the thing, and told the judge so, and the fellow was sentenced to three years in the penitentiary."

Miss Lomax had listened with lively interest.

"I've always hated old Sam Briggs," she said emphatically, "ever since the time he broke a negro's leg with a piece of cordwood. When I hear of a cruel deed it makes the Quaker blood that came from my grandmother assert itself. Personally I wish that all Sam Briggs's negroes would run away. As for the young man, I regard him as a hero. He dared something for humanity. I could love a man who would take such chances for the sake of others."

"Could you love me, Charity, if I did something heroic?"

"You never will, Dick. You're too lazy for any use. You'll never do anything harder than playing cards or fox-hunting."

"Oh, come now, sweetheart! I've been courting you for a year, and it's the hardest work imaginable. Are you never going to love me?" he pleaded.

His hand sought hers, but she drew it back beyond his reach.

"I'll never love you, Dick Owens, until you have done something. When that time comes, I'll think about it."

"But it takes so long to do anything worth mentioning, and I don't want to wait. One must read two years to become a lawyer, and work five more to make a reputation. We shall both be gray by then."

"Oh, I don't know," she rejoined. "it doesn't require a lifetime for a man to prove that he is a man. This one did something, or at least tried to."

"Well, I'm willing to attempt as much as any other man. What do you want me to do, sweetheart? Give me a test."

"Oh, dear me!" said Charity, "I don't care what you *do,* so you do *something*. Really, come to think of it, why should I care whether you do anything or not?

"I'm sure I don't know why you should, Charity," rejoined Dick humbly, "for I'm aware that I'm not worthy of it."

"Except that I do hate," she added, relenting slightly, "to see a really clever man so utterly lazy and good for nothing."

"Thank you, my dear; a word of praise from you has sharpened my wits already. I have an idea! Will you love me if *I* run a negro off to Canada?"

"What nonsense!" said Charity scornfully. "You must be losing your wits. Steal another man's slave, indeed, while your father owns a hundred!"

"Oh, there'll be no trouble about that," responded Dick lightly; "I'll run off one of the old man's; we've got too many anyway. It may not be quite as difficult as the other man found it, but it will be just as unlawful, and will demonstrate what I am capable of."

"Seeing's believing," replied Charity. "Of course, what you are talking about now is merely absurd. I'm going away for three weeks, to visit my aunt in Tennessee. If you are able to tell me, when I return, that you've done something to prove your quality, I'll—well, you may come and tell me about it."

II

Young Owens got up about nine o'clock next morning, and while making his toilet put some questions to his personal attendant, a rather bright looking young mulatto of about his own age.

"Tom," said Dick.

"Yas, Mars Dick," responded the servant.

"I'm going on a trip North. Would you like to go with me?"

Now, if there was anything that Tom would have liked to make, it was a trip North. It was something he had long contemplated in the abstract, but had never been able to muster up sufficient courage to attempt in the concrete. He was prudent enough, however, to dissemble his feelings.

"I wouldn't min' it, Mars Dick, ez long ez you'd take keer er me an' fetch me home all right."

Tom's eyes belied his words, however, and his young master felt well assured that Tom needed only a good opportunity to make him run away. Having a comfortable home, and a dismal prospect in case of failure, Tom was not likely to take any desperate chances; but young Owens was satisfied that in a free state but little persuasion would be required to lead Tom astray. With a very logical and characteristic desire to gain his end with the least necessary expenditure of effort, he decided to take Tom with him, if his father did not object.

Colonel Owens had left the house when Dick went to breakfast, so Dick did not see his father till luncheon.

"Father," he remarked casually to the colonel over the fried chicken, "I'm feeling a trifle run down. I imagine my health would be improved somewhat by a little travel and change of scene."

"Why don't you take a trip North?" suggested his father. The colonel added to paternal affection a considerable respect for his son as the heir of a large estate. He himself had been "raised" in comparative poverty, and had laid the foundations of his fortune by hard work; and while he despised the ladder by which he had climbed, he could not entirely forget it, and unconsciously manifested, in his intercourse with his son, some of the poor man's deference toward the wealthy and well-born.

"I think I'll adopt your suggestion, sir," replied the son, "and run up to New York; and after I've been there awhile I may go on to Boston for a week or so. I've never been there, you know."

"There are some matters you can talk over with my factor in New York," rejoined the colonel, "and while you are up there among the Yankees, I hope you'll keep your eyes and ears open to find out what the rascally abolitionists[32] are saying and doing. They're becoming altogether too active for our comfort, and entirely too many ungrateful niggers are running away. I hope the conviction of that fellow yesterday may discourage the rest of the breed. I'd just like to catch any one trying to run off one of my darkeys. He'd get short shrift; I don't think any Court would have a chance to try him."

"They are a pestiferous lot," assented Dick, "and dangerous to our institutions. But say, father, if I go North I shall want to take Tom with me."

Now, the colonel, while a very indulgent father, had pronounced views on the subject of negroes, having studied them, as he often said, for a great many years, and, as he asserted oftener still, understanding them perfectly. It is scarcely worth while to say, either, that he valued more highly than if he had inherited them the slaves he had toiled and schemed for.

"I don't think it safe to take Tom up North," he declared, with promptness and decision. "He's a good enough boy, but too smart to trust among those low-down abolitionists. I strongly suspect him of having learned to read, though I can't imagine how. I saw him with a newspaper the other day, and while he pretended to be looking at a woodcut, I'm almost sure he was reading the paper. I think it by no means safe to take him."

Dick did not insist, because he knew it was useless. The colonel would have obliged his son in any other matter, but his negroes were the outward and visible sign of his wealth and station, and therefore sacred to him.

"Whom do you think it safe to take?" asked Dick. "I suppose I'll have to have a body-servant."[33]

32. Abolitionism began in the northeastern United States in the 1840s and sought to "abolish" slavery.

33. Personal servant or valet.

"What's the matter with Grandison?" suggested the colonel. "He's handy enough, and I reckon we can trust him. He's too fond of good eating to risk losing his regular meals; besides, he's sweet on your mother's maid, Betty, and I've promised to let 'em get married before long. I'll have Grandison up, and we'll talk to him. Here, you boy Jack," called the colonel to a yellow [34] youth in the next room who was catching flies and pulling their wings off to pass the time, "go down to the barn and tell Grandison to come here."

"Grandison," said the colonel, when the negro stood before him, hat in hand.

"Yas, marster."

"Haven't I always treated you right?"

"Yas, marster."

"Haven't you always got all you wanted to eat?"

"Yas, marster."

"And as much whiskey and tobacco as was good for you, Grandison?"

"Y-a-s, marster."

"I should just like to know, Grandison, whether you don't think yourself a great deal better off than those poor free negroes down by the plank road, with no kind master to look after them and no mistress to give them medicine when they're sick and—and—"

"Well, I sh'd jes' reckon I is better off, suh, dan dem low-down free niggers, suh! Ef anybody ax 'em who dey b'long ter, dey has ter say nobody, er e'se lie erbout it. Anybody ax me who I b'longs ter, I ain' got no 'casion ter be shame' ter tell 'em, no, suh, 'deed I ain', suh!"

The colonel was beaming. This was true gratitude, and his feudal heart thrilled at such appreciative homage. What cold-blooded, heartless monsters they were who would break up this blissful relationship of kindly protection on the one hand, of wise subordination and loyal dependence on the other! The colonel always became indignant at the mere thought of such wickedness.

"Grandison," the colonel continued, "your young master Dick is going North for a few weeks, and I am thinking of letting him take you along. I shall send you on this trip, Grandison, in order that you may take care of your young master. He will need some one to wait on him, and no one can ever do it so well as one of the boys brought up with him on the old plantation. I am going to trust him in your hands, and I'm sure you'll

34. Light-complexioned person of mixed race who can sometimes "pass" as white.

do your duty faithfully, and bring him back home safe and sound—to old Kentucky."

Grandison grinned. "Oh yas, marster, I'll take keer er young Mars Dick."

"I want to warn you, though, Grandison," continued the colonel impressively, "against these cussed abolitionists, who try to entice servants from their comfortable homes and their indulgent masters, from the blue skies, the green fields, and the warm sunlight of their southern home, and send them away off yonder to Canada, a dreary country, where the woods are full of wildcats and wolves and bears, where the snow lies up to the eaves of the houses for six months of the year, and the cold is so severe that it freezes your breath and curdles your blood; and where, when runaway niggers get sick and can't work, they are turned out to starve and die, unloved and uncared for. I reckon, Grandison, that you have too much sense to permit yourself to be led astray by any such foolish and wicked people."

"'Deed, suh, I would n' low none er dem cussed, low-down abolitioners ter come nigh me, suh. I'd—I'd—would I be 'lowed ter hit 'em, suh?"

"Certainly, Grandison," replied the colonel, chuckling, "hit 'em, as hard as you can. I reckon they'd rather like it. Begad,[35] I believe they would! It would serve 'em right to be hit by a nigger!"

"Er ef I did n't hit 'em, suh," continued Grandison reflectively, "I'd tell Mars Dick, en *he'd* fix 'em. He'd smash de face off'n 'em, suh, I jes' knows he would."

"Oh yes, Grandison, your young master will protect you. You need fear no harm while he is near."

"Dey won't try ter steal me, will dey, marster?" asked the negro, with sudden alarm.

"I don't know, Grandison," replied the colonel, lighting a fresh cigar. "They're a desperate set of lunatics, and there's no telling what they may resort to. But if you stick close to your young master, and remember always that he is your best friend, and understands your real needs, and has your true interests at heart, and if you will be careful to avoid strangers who try to talk to you, you'll stand a fair chance of getting back to your home and your friends. And if you please your master Dick, he'll buy you a present, and a string of beads for Betty to wear when you and she get married in the fall."

"Thanky, marster, thanky, suh," replied Grandison, oozing gratitude at

35. "By God," mild oath.

every pore; "you is a good marster, to be sho', suh; yas, 'deed you is. You kin jes' bet me and Mars Dick gwine git 'long jes' lack I wuz own boy ter Mars Dick. En it won't be my fault ef he don' want me fer his boy all de time, w'en we come back home ag'in."

"All right, Grandison, you may go now. You needn't work any more to-day, and here's a piece of tobacco for you off my own plug."

"Thanky, marster, thanky, marster! You is de bes' marster any nigger ever had in dis worl'." And Grandison bowed and scraped and disappeared round the corner, his jaws closing around a large section of the colonel's best tobacco.

"You may take Grandison," said the colonel to his son. "I allow he's abolitionist-proof."

III

Richard Owens, Esq., and servant, from Kentucky, registered at the fashionable New York hostelry for Southerners in those days, a hotel where an atmosphere congenial to Southern institutions was sedulously maintained. But there were negro waiters in the dining-room, and mulatto bell-boys, and Dick had no doubt that Grandison, with the native gregariousness and garrulousness of his race, would foregather and palaver with them, sooner or later, and Dick hoped that they would speedily inoculate him with the virus of freedom. For it was not Dick's intention to say anything to his servant about his plan to free him, for obvious reasons. To mention one of them, if Grandison should go away, and by legal process be recaptured, his young master's part in the matter would doubtless become known, which would be embarrassing to Dick, to say the least. If, on the other hand, he should merely give Grandison sufficient latitude, he had no doubt he would eventually lose him. For while not exactly skeptical about Grandison's perfervid loyalty, Dick had been a somewhat keen observer of human nature, in his own indolent way, and based his expectations upon the force of the example and argument that his servant could scarcely fail to encounter. Grandison should have a fair chance to become free by his own initiative; if it should become necessary to adopt other measures to get rid of him, it would be time enough to act when the necessity arose; and Dick Owens was not the youth to take needless trouble.

The young master renewed some acquaintances and made others, and spent a week or two very pleasantly in the best society of the metropolis, easily accessible to a wealthy, well-bred young Southerner, with proper introductions. Young women smiled on him and young men of convivial habits pressed their hospitalities; but the memory of Charity's sweet, strong face and clear blue eyes made him proof against the blandishments of the one sex and the persuasions of the other. Meanwhile he kept Grandison supplied with pocket-money, and left him mainly to his own devices. Every night when Dick came in he hoped he might have to wait upon himself, and every morning he looked forward with pleasure to the prospect of making his toilet unaided. His hopes, however, were doomed to disappointment, for every night when he came in Grandison was on hand with a bootjack,[36] and a nightcap mixed for his young master as the colonel had taught him to mix it, and every morning Grandison appeared with his master's boots blacked and his clothes brushed, and laid his linen out for the day.

"Grandison," said Dick one morning, after finishing his toilet, "this is the chance of your life to go around among your own people and see how they live. Have you met any of them?"

"Yas, suh, I's seen some of 'em. But I don' keer nuffin fer 'em, suh. Dey're diffe'nt f'm de niggers down ou' way. Dey 'lows dey're free, but dey ain' got sense 'nuff ter know dey ain' half as well off as dey would be down Souf, whar dey'd be 'preciated."

When two weeks had passed without any apparent effect of evil example upon Grandison, Dick resolved to go on to Boston, where he thought the atmosphere might prove more favorable to his ends. After he had been at the Revere House for a day or two without losing Grandison, he decided upon slightly different tactics.

Having ascertained from a city directory the addresses of several well-known abolitionists, he wrote them each a letter something like this: —

DEAR FRIEND AND BROTHER: —

    A wicked slaveholder from Kentucky, stopping at the Revere House, has dared to insult the liberty-loving people of Boston by bringing his slave into their midst. Shall this be tolerated? Or shall steps be taken in the name of liberty to rescue a fellow-man from bondage? For obvious reasons I can only sign myself,

A FRIEND OF HUMANITY.

That his letter might have an opportunity to prove effective, Dick made it a point to send Grandison away from the hotel on various errands. On one of these occasions Dick watched him for quite a distance down the

36. Device for removing close-fitting leather boots.

street. Grandison had scarcely left the hotel when a long-haired, sharp-featured man came out behind him, followed him, soon overtook him, and kept along beside him until they turned the next corner. Dick's hopes were roused by this spectacle, but sank correspondingly when Grandison returned to the hotel. As Grandison said nothing about the encounter, Dick hoped there might be some self-consciousness behind this unexpected reticence, the results of which might develop later on.

But Grandison was on hand again when his master came back to the hotel at night, and was in attendance again in the morning, with hot water, to assist at his master's toilet. Dick sent him on further errands from day to day, and upon one occasion came squarely up to him—inadvertently of course—while Grandison was engaged in conversation with a young white man in clerical garb. When Grandison saw Dick approaching, he edged away from the preacher and hastened toward his master, with a very evident expression of relief upon his countenance.

"Mars Dick," he said, "dese yer abolitioners is jes' pesterin' de life out er me tryin' ter git me ter run away. I don' pay no 'tention ter 'em, but dey riles me so sometimes dat I'm feared I'll hit some of 'em some er dese days, an' dat mought git me inter trouble. I ain' said nuffin' ter you 'bout it, Mars Dick, fer I did n' wanter 'sturb yo' min'; but I don' like it, suh; no, suh, I don'! Is we gwine back home 'fo' long, Mars Dick?"

"We'll be going back soon enough," replied Dick somewhat shortly, while he inwardly cursed the stupidity of a slave who could be free and would not, and registered a secret vow that if he were unable to get rid of Grandison without assassinating him, and were therefore compelled to take him back to Kentucky, he would see that Grandison got a taste of an article of slavery that would make him regret his wasted opportunities. Meanwhile he determined to tempt his servant yet more strongly.

"Grandison," he said next morning, "I'm going away for a day or two, but I shall leave you here. I shall lock up a hundred dollars in this drawer and give you the key. If you need any of it, use it and enjoy yourself,—spend it all if you like,—for this is probably the last chance you'll have for some time to be in a free State, and you 'd better enjoy your liberty while you may."

When he came back a couple of days later and found the faithful Grandison at his post, and the hundred dollars intact, Dick felt seriously annoyed. His vexation was increased by the fact that he could not express his feelings adequately. He did not even scold Grandison; how could he, indeed, find fault with one who so sensibly recognized his true place in the economy of civilization, and kept it with such touching fidelity?

"I can't say a thing to him," groaned Dick. "He deserves a leather medal, made out of his own hide tanned. I reckon I'll write to father and let him know what a model servant he has given me."

He wrote his father a letter which made the colonel swell with pride and pleasure. "I really think," the colonel observed to one of his friends, "that Dick ought to have the nigger interviewed by the Boston papers, so that they may see how contented and happy our darkeys really are."

Dick also wrote a long letter to Charity Lomax, in which he said, among many other things, that if she knew how hard he was working, and under what difficulties, to accomplish something serious for her sake, she would no longer keep him in suspense, but overwhelm him with love and admiration.

Having thus exhausted without result the more obvious methods of getting rid of Grandison, and diplomacy having also proved a failure, Dick was forced to consider more radical measures. Of course he might run away himself, and abandon Grandison, but this would be merely to leave him in the United States, where he was still a slave, and where, with his notions of loyalty, he would speedily be reclaimed. It was necessary, in order to accomplish the purpose of his trip to the North, to leave Grandison permanently in Canada, where he would be legally free.

"I might extend my trip to Canada," he reflected, "but that would be too palpable. I have it! I'll visit Niagara Falls on the way home, and lose him on the Canadian side. When he once realizes that he is actually free, I'll warrant that he'll stay."

So the next day saw them westward bound, and in due course of time, by the somewhat slow conveyances of the period, they found themselves at Niagara. Dick walked and drove about the Falls for several days, taking Grandison along with him on most occasions. One morning they stood on the Canadian side, watching the wild whirl of the waters below them.

"Grandison," said Dick, raising his voice above the roar of the cataract, "do you know where you are now?"

"I's wid you, Mars Dick; dat's all I keers."

"You are now in Canada, Grandison, where your people go when they run away from their masters. If you wished, Grandison, you might walk away from me this very minute, and I could not lay my hand upon you to take you back."

Grandison looked around uneasily.

"Let's go back ober de ribber, Mars Dick. I's feared I'll lose you ovuh heah, an' den I won' hab no marster, an' won't nebber be able to git back home no mo'."

Discouraged, but not yet hopeless, Dick said, a few minutes later,—

"Grandison, I'm going up the road a bit, to the inn over yonder. You stay here until I return. I'll not be gone a great while."

Grandison's eyes opened wide and he looked somewhat fearful.

"Is dey any er dem dadblasted abolitioners roun' heah, Mars Dick?"

"I don't imagine that there are," replied his master, hoping there might be. "But I'm not afraid of *your* running away, Grandison. I only wish I were," he added to himself.

Dick walked leisurely down the road to where the whitewashed inn, built of stone, with true British solidity, loomed up through the trees by the roadside. Arrived there he ordered a glass of ale and a sandwich, and took a seat at a table by a window, from which he could see Grandison in the distance. For a while he hoped that the seed he had sown might have fallen on fertile ground, and that Grandison, relieved from the restraining power of a master's eye, and finding himself in a free country, might get up and walk away; but the hope was vain, for Grandison remained faithfully at his post, awaiting his master's return. He had seated himself on a broad flat stone, and, turning his eyes away from the grand and awe-inspiring spectacle that lay close at hand, was looking anxiously toward the inn where his master sat cursing his ill-timed fidelity.

By and by a girl came into the room to serve his order, and Dick very naturally glanced at her; and as she was young and pretty and remained in attendance, it was some minutes before he looked for Grandison. When he did so his faithful servant had disappeared.

To pay his reckoning and go away without the change was a matter quickly accomplished. Retracing his footsteps toward the Falls, he saw, to his great disgust, as he approached the spot where he had left Grandison, the familiar form of his servant stretched out on the ground, his face to the sun, his mouth open, sleeping the time away, oblivious alike to the grandeur of the scenery, the thunderous roar of the cataract, or the insidious voice of sentiment.

"Grandison," soliloquized his master, as he stood gazing down at his ebony encumbrance, "I do not deserve to be an American citizen; I ought not to have the advantages I possess over you; and I certainly am not worthy of Charity Lomax, if I am not smart enough to get rid of you. I have an idea! You shall yet be free, and I will be the instrument of your deliverance. Sleep on, faithful and affectionate servitor, and dream of the blue grass and the bright skies of old Kentucky, for it is only in your dreams that you will ever see them again!"

Dick retraced his footsteps toward the inn. The young woman chanced to look out of the window and saw the handsome young gentleman she had waited on a few minutes before, standing in the road a short distance away, apparently engaged in earnest conversation with a colored man employed as hostler [37] for the inn. She thought she saw something pass from the white man to the other, but at that moment her duties called her away from the window, and when she looked out again the young gentleman had disappeared, and the hostler, with two other young men of the neighborhood, one white and one colored, were walking rapidly towards the Falls.

IV

Dick made the journey homeward alone, and as rapidly as the conveyances of the day would permit. As he drew near home his conduct in going back without Grandison took on a more serious aspect than it had borne at any previous time, and although he had prepared the colonel by a letter sent several days ahead, there was still the prospect of a bad quarter of an hour with him; not, indeed, that his father would upbraid him, but he was likely to make searching inquiries. And notwithstanding the vein of quiet recklessness that had carried Dick through his preposterous scheme, he was a very poor liar, having rarely had occasion or inclination to tell anything but the truth. Any reluctance to meet his father was more than offset, however, by a stronger force drawing him homeward, for Charity Lomax must long since have returned from her visit to her aunt in Tennessee.

Dick got off easier than he had expected. He told a straight story, and a truthful one, so far as it went.

The colonel raged at first, but rage soon subsided into anger, and anger moderated into annoyance, and annoyance into a sort of garrulous sense of injury. The colonel thought he had been hardly used; he had trusted this negro, and he had broken faith. Yet, after all, he did not blame Grandison so much as he did the abolitionists, who were undoubtedly at the bottom of it.

As for Charity Lomax, Dick told her, privately of course, that be had run his father's man, Grandison, off to Canada, and left him there.

"Oh, Dick," she had said with shuddering alarm, "what have you done? If they knew it they'd send you to the penitentiary, like they did that Yankee."

37. Attendant for travelers' horses.

"But they don't know it," he had replied seriously; adding, with an injured tone, "you don't seem to appreciate my heroism like you did that of the Yankee; perhaps it's because I wasn't caught and sent to the penitentiary. I thought you wanted me to do it."

"Why, Dick Owens!" she exclaimed. "You know I never dreamed of any such outrageous proceeding."

"But I presume I'll have to marry you," she concluded, after some insistence on Dick's part, "if only to take care of you. You are too reckless for anything; and a man who goes chasing all over the North, being entertained by New York and Boston society and having negroes to throw away, needs some one to look after him."

"It's a most remarkable thing," replied Dick fervently, "that your views correspond exactly with my profoundest convictions. It proves beyond question that we were made for one another."

They were married three weeks later. As each of them had just returned from a journey, they spent their honeymoon at home.

A week after the wedding they were seated, one afternoon, on the piazza of the colonel's house, where Dick had taken his bride, when a negro from the yard ran down the lane and threw open the big gate for the colonel's buggy to enter. The colonel was not alone. Beside him, ragged and travel-stained, bowed with weariness, and upon his face a haggard look that told of hardship and privation, sat the lost Grandison.

The colonel alighted at the steps.

"Take the lines, Tom," he said to the man who had opened the gate, "and drive round to the barn. Help Grandison down,—poor devil, he's so stiff he can hardly move!—and get a tub of water and wash him and rub him down, and feed him, and give him a big drink of whiskey, and then let him come round and see his young master and his new mistress."

The colonel's face wore an expression compounded of joy and indignation,—joy at the restoration of a valuable piece of property; indignation for reasons he proceeded to state.

"It's astounding, the depths of depravity the human heart is capable of! I was coming along the road three miles away, when I heard some one call me from the roadside. I pulled up the mare, and who should come out of the woods but Grandison. The poor nigger could hardly crawl along, with the help of a broken limb. I was never more astonished in my life. You could have knocked me down with a feather. He seemed pretty far gone,—he could hardly talk above a whisper,—and I had to give him a mouthful of whiskey to brace him up so he could tell his story. It's just as I thought from the beginning, Dick; Grandison had no notion of running away; he knew when he was well off, and where his friends were. All the persuasions of abolition liars and runaway niggers did not move him. But the desperation of those fanatics knew no bounds; their guilty consciences gave them no rest. They got the notion somehow that Grandison belonged to a nigger-catcher, and had been brought North as a spy to help capture ungrateful runaway servants. They actually kidnapped him—just think of it!—and gagged him and bound him and threw him rudely into a wagon, and carried him into the gloomy depths of a Canadian forest, and locked him in a lonely hut, and fed him on bread and water for three weeks. One of the scoundrels wanted to kill him, and persuaded the others that it ought to be done; but they got to quarreling about how they should do it, and before they had their minds made up Grandison escaped, and, keeping his back steadily to the North Star, made his way, after suffering incredible hardships, back to the old plantation, back to his master, his friends, and his home. Why, it's as good as one of Scott's [38] novels! Mr. Simms [39] or some other one of our Southern authors ought to write it up."

"Don't you think, sir," suggested Dick, who had calmly smoked his cigar throughout the colonel's animated recital, "that that kidnapping yarn sounds a little improbable? Isn't there some more likely explanation?"

"Nonsense, Dick; it's the gospel truth! Those infernal abolitionists are capable of anything—everything! Just think of their locking the poor, faithful nigger up, beating him, kicking him, depriving him of his liberty, keeping him on bread and water for three long, lonesome weeks, and he all the time pining for the old plantation!"

There were almost tears in the colonel's eyes at the picture of Grandison's sufferings that he conjured up. Dick still professed to be slightly skeptical, and met Charity's severely questioning eye with bland unconsciousness.

The colonel killed the fatted calf [40] for Grandison, and for two or three weeks the returned wanderer's life was a slave's dream of pleasure. His fame spread through-out the county, and the colonel gave him a permanent place

---

38. Sir Walter Scott (1771–1832), British author whose historic novels of medieval feudalism were immensely popular, especially in the South.

39. William Gilmore Simms (1806–1870), perhaps the antebellum South's most admired writer.

40. When the prodigal son of Jesus' parable returned home from a life of dissipation, his joyful father butchered a calf that was being fattened up for a special feast (Luke 15:11–32).

among the house servants, where he could always have him conveniently at hand to relate his adventures to admiring visitors.

About three weeks after Grandison's return the colonel's faith in sable humanity was rudely shaken, and its foundations almost broken up. He came near losing his belief in the fidelity of the negro to his master,—the servile virtue most highly prized and most sedulously cultivated by the colonel and his kind. One Monday morning Grandison was missing. And not only Grandison, but his wife, Betty the maid; his mother, aunt Eunice; his father, uncle Ike; his brothers, Tom and John, and his little sister Elsie, were likewise absent from the plantation: and a hurried search and inquiry in the neighborhood resulted in no information as to their whereabouts. So much valuable property could not be lost without an effort to recover it, and the wholesale nature of the transaction carried consternation to the hearts of those whose ledgers were chiefly bound in black. Extremely energetic measures were taken by the colonel and his friends. The fugitives were traced, and followed from point to point, on their northward run through Ohio. Several times the hunters were close upon their heels, but the magnitude of the escaping party begot unusual vigilance on the part of those who sympathized with the fugitives, and strangely enough, the underground railroad [41] seemed to have had its tracks cleared and signals set for this particular train. Once, twice, the colonel thought he had them, but they slipped through his fingers.

One last glimpse he caught of his vanishing property, as he stood, accompanied by a United States marshal, on a wharf at a port on the south shore of Lake Erie. On the stern of a small steamboat which was receding rapidly from the wharf, with her nose pointing toward Canada, there stood a group of familiar dark faces, and the look they cast backward was not one of longing for the fleshpots of Egypt. [42] The colonel saw Grandison point him out to one of the crew of the vessel, who waved his hand derisively toward the colonel. The latter shook his fist impotently—and the incident was closed.

41. The system of safe havens, mostly in cramped hiding spaces, in the homes of abolitionists along the dangerous escape route from points in the South to Canada.

42. When the fleeing Israelites encountered starvation in the desert, they complained to Moses that they preferred the full pots of meat they had had as slaves in Egypt (Exodus 16:2–3).

Sarah Barnwell Elliott

(1848–1928)

CHRISTENED WITH the familial name of her distinguished maternal grandmother, Sarah Barnwell Bull Elliott (the fifth of six children) was born
November 29, 1848, in Montpelier, Georgia, where her father, the state's
first Episcopal bishop, had founded a school as he later would found the
University of the South in Sewanee, Tennessee. Sarah's ancestors included
colonial governors, prominent lawyers, physicians, a journal editor, an author of a sports' classic, and a host of wealthy rice and cotton planters. To
resolve his school's debts, Bishop Elliott sold his property and slaves (he
had always been troubled over owning human property) and moved his
family to Savannah in 1852.

At the family's comfortable summer residence near Beaufort, South
Carolina, and at her grandmother's nearby plantation, Sarah heard the
tales of slaves, whose humanity, loyalty, and struggles she would later
chronicle, and became familiar with the ways of their storytellers. This
idyllic life was shattered in November 1861 when federal troops seized the
Barnwells' Beaufort property. In Savannah Sarah and her family maintained some semblance of normalcy, despite the absence of her brothers
and her father, who were vigorous champions of the southern cause. Just
after her sixteenth birthday, the family was forced to flee Savannah, departing on the last train before the arrival of General Sherman's troops in
December 1864. The death of her father in 1866 left the family financially
destitute. Elliott, her mother, and sisters eventually settled in Sewanee,
where her brother held a university teaching position and where her
mother opened a student boarding house.

Throughout these hardships, Elliott had never ceased to refine herself
through study and voracious reading. Encouraged by her family to travel
with relatives in the Northeast, she became a welcome guest of U.S. Senator Samuel Greene Arnold, whose daughter Louisa had become a close
friend. Sarah based the manuscript of her first (unpublished) novel and

two subsequent novels on these visits; however, Sarah's frank pro-South sentiments estranged her from Louisa. Though her determination to write intensified, it was ten years before Elliott published *The Felmeres* (1879), which highlighted women's constraints in marriage. Encouraged by its moderately positive reviews, Elliott turned her four-month stay with her missionary brother in Texas into frontier fiction infused with dialect, picturesque settings, family feuds, and relocated southerners. In 1887, while traveling abroad with her brother, she translated her European experience into travel sketches and, later, into stories and a novel. Though her ailing brother returned home, Sarah spent additional months in Italy where she met the highly esteemed writer Constance Woolson. Woolson, whose own southern stories were quite popular, encouraged Elliott to write about what she knew best: her varied souths.

That welcome advice led Elliott to enter the flourishing and lucrative field of local color with "The Ex-brigadier" (*Harper's*, 1890). She then published *Jerry* (1891), a critically acclaimed and financially successful novel, which recounts the slow undoing of a transplanted mountaineer by the greed and materialism of the Gilded Age. Like Mary Noailles Murfree, Elliott published other works based on her many years in Tennessee, including a one-act tragedy and *The Durket Sperret* (1898), which recounts the lively "sperret" of a young mountain woman on her own.

Such spirit underlay Elliott's decision at forty-seven, following her mother's death, to relocate to New York and to birth her "real self," as she wrote on New Year's Day 1896. New York provided intellectual stimulation, a platform for social activism, and access to a wide circle of friends and literary acquaintances such as Thomas Nelson Page, Charles Dudley Warner, and William Dean Howells. Her passion for social justice found voice in her political activism (particularly the cause of woman's suffrage) and in her fiction. A lifelong friend of influential Cubans who had settled in South Carolina, she persuaded *McClure's* to send her to Cuba during the War of 1898 as a war correspondent. Although that assignment never materialized, she published "Hands All Round" (1898), in which a prosperous southern town's racial rivalries and divided loyalties arouse a debate over the war and its opportunities for nation-building.

Her 1899 collection, *An Incident and Other Happenings*, unmasked the violence of a white-supremacist South clinging to outworn prerogatives with its stories of lynching, white assaults, and unjustly acquitted murderers. Racial injustices, the deceptions and seductions of white privilege, and womanly courage provide the context for "The Heart of It," one of two stories about miscegenation that, along with seven other stories and two novels, remained unpublished in Elliott's lifetime. In the story, Elliott disrupts the tragic mulatta plot that often ends in death (or in the ambiguous convent of Alice Dunbar-Nelson's "Sister Josepha"); the story typifies Elliott's lifelong commitments to the ideal of women's self-determination, despite the severity of its costs.

The responsibility of raising her nephews drew Elliott back to Sewanee in 1904, where she continued her energetic support for women's rights as a lecturer, essayist, and suffrage leader. These efforts served as the catalyst for Tennessee's becoming the critical thirty-sixth state and the only southern state to ratify the Nineteenth Amendment (1921), which guaranteed women the vote. In 1913 she was awarded an honorary Doctor of Civil Law degree by the University of the South. She continued writing reviews, but she published no fiction after 1915 and led a quiet life, welcoming weekly visitors to her home, entertaining university guests, and enjoying her extended family. She died of cancer on August 30, 1928.

Works by Sarah Barnwell Elliott

The Felmeres, 1879

Jerry, 1891

The Durket Sperret, 1898

An Incident and Other Happenings, 1899

The Making of Jane, 1901

Some Data and Other Stories of Southern Life, ed. Clara Childs Mackenzie, 1981

Further Reading

Honey, Maureen. "Sarah Barnwell Elliott." In *American Women Prose Writers, 1820–1920*. Ed. Sharon Harris. Detroit: Gale, 2000.
Mackenzie, Clara Childs. *Sarah Barnwell Elliott*. Boston: Twayne, 1980.
Wright, Nathalia. "Sarah Barnwell Elliott." In *Notable American Women 1607–1950*. Vol. 1. 1971.

The Heart of It

It was a dark night and raining, and the level, sandy road could be distinguished only because of the greater dark of the wilderness on either side.

A broad, white road it was, that led by swamp, and river, and pine barren,[1] and now was greatly under water, not only because of rain, but because of a spring freshet that had swelled the great river that was an arm of the sea. Along this road a large blur was moving, with creakings and splashings; gradually emerging as a cart with a canvas cover and one horse, going at a leisurely gait. It was heavy traveling and slow, and reaching a little upward incline, the horse stopped.

"Mos' dead, is you Job?" said the man sitting just under the cover; "an' yo' travelin' ain't half done."

"Are we there?" a woman's voice asked from the recesses of the cart.

"In jest about five yards of it."

"You mean . . ."

"The railroad track; my horse is restin' a min'it; it ain't rainin' now, if you're sure goin' to git out."

"Yes, thank you, I must get this next train that passes."

"Well, if you git out here, you've got fo' miles to walk down the track; but I kin drive you three miles fu'ther on to Mr. Percy Lasston's place an' you might hire a horse there an' drive down to the nex' station."

"No, thank you, I'll get out here and walk."

"Fo' miles on the crossties."

"Yes."

"An' you ain't skeered?"

"No."

"Well, I'm right sorry, but I can't drive down the crossties."

"No, and I thank you for bringing me so far. You mentioned a name just now."

"Mr. Percy Lasston."

"Do you know the people about here?"

"No, I don't. I'm only a peddler sellin' to the niggers; but I knows the names of the planters. I've stopped tradin' round here though, its too po'. I never stops to sell nothin' this side o' Jonesborough, an' that's nigh to thirty miles fu'ther on; an' frum there I goes on to Greensborough. This is Friday night, an' I muss git to Jonesborough by Sat'day night, for then the man's gits paid off an' comes to town, an' that's my chance."

"Do you expect to travel all night?"

"I do; an' I hate to leave a white woman in the road 'leven o'clock of a rainy night; I certainly do."

---

1. Forest of pines in sandy soil.

"It doesn't matter. No, you need not bother to help me out. Good-bye."

"Good-bye, an' good luck to you, Lady; you're travelin' back to yo' own people, you say? They ought to be mightly proud you'd take sicher journey, an' I hopes you gits there safe; good-bye. You ain't skeered?"

"No, good-bye," and the woman stood still in the mist and the darkness, watching the wagon toil up the incline to the railway.

Not long, then the wagon became a blur, then the sounds faded. Still she stood there poised attentive as if one more "Git up" of the kindly voice; one more grind of wheel, or splash of hoof might reach her; waited in the silence where, gradually, there intruded a soft sound as of whispering rain, or sweeping wings; a sound that as she listened seemed to grow on her awakening senses into a tremulous terror! She caught the stem of a young tree; what was coming? People with panting dogs? A train with glaring lights that would reveal her?

The river! Only the old river; brimful, rushing, swirling, deep and strong; the river that went by home! The young tree swayed a little for she sobbed against it. Dogs, people, would they search for her? Would they bring the dogs? To the pond, to the swamp, to the river? The dogs could not tell, no, at the junction of the three ways the wagon had come. How kind the man had been, a stranger, and white, how fortunate.

Fortunate? The pond, the swamp, the river would have been better. Search for her? Never! As that morning—was it only that morning—? In the awful light that had searched her heart, her life; that had seemed to scorch her physical eyeballs as she had read the letter thrust under her door, so now, she went over slowly, but with the bitterness of death, all the things of her life that had hurt her. From her orphaned babyhood there had been a lack of love, a lack that Alan partly filled, and yet, she had never told him of the lack because he was her Aunt Alicia's only child. But Percy—the leaves of the young tree shivered as in a sudden gust of wind.

That was all past, and now—now it was only a few steps to the railway; here it was; now, four miles on the crossties to the station. The night train passed at two o'clock. The man had said it was eleven now; yes, she had time. Once at the station, she would look up a schedule and decide where she would go. Fifteen dollars she would spend on traveling; this would leave her ten dollars for expenses until she found work. Meanwhile, she would slip off her frock skirt and fold it under her coat where, for the sake of dryness, her thick veil now was. Just before she reached the station, she would put them on. The thick veil would hide her face. Besides, the man at the station would be too sleepy to observe much.

Tired—tired, too tired! The river was just beyond that bank? They'd find her body beaten up against one of the rice dams; or swept aside, entangled in brush and logs; and they would realize. But it did not matter what they realized. They had done what they thought was their duty by her. Better, less cruel, it seemed, to have drowned her as they did the worthless puppies, far better.

Yes, she had told Percy. Percy was her third cousin; lived on his own plantation, and was the head of the family. How he laughed at that; land-poor, tax-ridden, poverty-stricken. And talk of 'The Head of the Family'! But she had been so proud of it; it was fine, she declared, and it was. She—she was still a Lasston! She must go on; must think of something else.

Yes, Percy was older than Alan, and Alan older than she, and on the fateful day when she had been driven to the conclusion that her aunt did not love her—a day in February when the fires were still necessary—those great fires, how sweet they smelled—her despair had demanded outlet and she had told Percy; had poured out all the longings of her life, all the pain of loneliness that had been with her day and night, had told it all clinging to his arm. And he?

The rushing river was nearer now! The friendly river that would lodge her somewhere near the old place. And, yes, she had not hauled her boat up! She stopped a moment, they might think she'd gone out in the boat. Why had she not thought of that? Out on that wild, sweeping tide in her little boat; out with the wind and the rain beating in her face! And she could have fought for her life then; have had the battle that would have dulled her fear of death, and with all her fighting, not have saved her life.

Again she sobbed a little, a tearless sob with a catch in it, and plodded on in the darkness. She knew she would never have entered the boat. She had courage only to endure; endure life a little longer, a little longer until her vision cleared. Had she not endured—endured herself—her life, since—since when? How long was it? The morning before this night, the morning which she could only remember in fragments as she moved along the dark railway track.

She had been about to do something that morning. What was it? She was on her way out the door of the big old house which had always been home to her and Aunt Alicia—taking breakfast to old George. It was old George who had kept the place running after Aunt Alicia was left a widow, until Alan had become old enough to begin to look after things. All this had been her knowledge for all her life. Old George, good old George, the special care of the family—all who were left, her Aunt Alicia, Alan and—

not herself now—no. And old Mawm Sue, George's daughter, she was good too, was cook and general servant at the big house, and his great-granddaughter, little Juno, black little Juno, down at the cabin to wait on the old man. All her life they had been about her, and it was this morning she had gone down carrying George's breakfast in a basket, and with it a pitcher of hot coffee. This morning!

She must not hasten; she could not run away, not escape; this thing, no, it would be with her forever—forever. And it was too dark to run; she would fall, would injure herself, perhaps be unable to get even to the river! She must walk quietly, steadily.

The woolly little dog, dirty, but with a ribbon about its neck, had rushed out at her, had stopped her, not its small bark, but the surprise of such an anomaly. Instantly, old George had stood in the door, blocking the entrance. She could hear his—"Mawnin, Li'l Missy Hagar, mawnin' ma'm," and his call—"Juno, come teck dese t'ings! Come quick, gal!" And Juno had dodged under his arm that to steady him, was against the door frame, and had taken the basket and pitcher.

"But the dog," she had insisted. If she had not; if she had gone away, her curiosity unsatisfied, would it all have happened?

He said, "Lou's dawg, Li'l Missy Hagar; Lou come las' night." Then behind the old man, lolling in a rocking chair, she saw a figure in white. Old George had been careful to block the door, but she had moved forward. Her own fault. The old man had made way for her, but the figure in white had not moved from the rocking chair. Instead, she had said, "How do you do, Miss Lasston?"

Her face burned now, remembering. She had paused and had stood looking down on the girl who as a child had been a runner of messages up at the big house; a clever, light-footed little creature whom her Aunt Alicia had sent to a mission school in the city. The little thing had cried, had begged not to go, and all her own child sympathy had gone out to the black child. And that had been ten years ago; Lou must be twenty now.

Yes, even now her face burned as she remembered the interview; but then, she had said quietly, "How are you, Lou." How careful the girl's pronunciation had been, how emphasized the "Grandpar-par," how slowly and carelessly she had rocked, old George's great-granddaughter, Lou, yes all these things she must remember, and the old man leaning on his stick with his old wrinkled face so full of pain. But he was not well, he said, and Lou explained, "I told him all my plans, Miss Lasston, not wise at night; but I wished him to share my joy. I am engaged to be married, Miss Lasston, to a gentleman at the school, one of the teachers." Then old George's sharp interpolation; "A yaller nigger, Miss Hagar!"

"And Grandpar-par," Lou had gone on smoothly; "and Aunt Susan, and Juno must come to live with me. My family must not be servants any longer." But Old George would have none of it. His dim eyes flashed.

"No, ma'm, Miss Hagar!" he had cried quite loud, striking his stick on the floor; "no, ma'm en ef Missis 'll lemme stay, I ent gwine; no, ma'am; en Sue ent gwine, en Juno ent gwine nurrer, no, ma'm! En we is berry mad, Miss Hagar; en we ent to say been want you fuh see Lou, no, ma'm!" They had been wise, these old people; but she had pushed in.

Then Lou had talked of the unholy slavery to which her race had been subjected. And she had turned on the Negro girl. "Slavery raised your race," she had said sharply; "you came to this country, savages!" She seemed to hear her own voice now as she announced that; it was true; and once more she sobbed a little as she plodded on in the darkness. Then Lou's retort—"You mean that we are an inferior race," she cried; "made lower than the whites!" And old George's—"Cose, gal!" and he raised his stick as if to strike the girl. Quickly she had saved Lou from the stick, and pushing on, ever pushing on, she had asked, "What do you think, Lou?"

"That we are a little backward," had come glibly, then her voice sharpening; "it is a great tragedy; an awful tragedy! Yes, and you don't care! But there is an outlet, yes, an outlet to this terrible tragedy, yes, we cross over to you whites!" How the words seemed to echo about her out here in the darkness, and the cry, "We cross over and you don't know it, ah ha!"

It had been as a physical blow and she had caught her breath while all the teachings of her life as to the awfulness of amalgamation; the hopelessness of the hybrid; the horrors of the "Return to Race"[2] had swept over her. Her aunt had taught her all this—how carefully it had been done—it had sickened her at the time, and the assertion of the Negro girl was as a sword thrust!

"Impossible!" she had faltered, and at last had turned toward the open door, while through the horrid confusion old George had cried, "En who wants ter be er yaller-white nigger! Ole Mawsa always drown dem half-breed puppy." And she, weakly, "You could never be pure white, Lou, never!"

2. Late-nineteenth-century notion opposing racial mixing, which proposed that since racial characteristics were carried in the blood, descendants would inevitably "return" to the features of their racial forebears.

"But if nobody knows the black blood is in us?"

"Somebody always knows!" She had been taught that too.

"But I know better!" Lou had cried; "wait! Last night I found that my own family had crossed over! That I have white cousins; as white as you! Wait!" and she had run out of the room. Then old George had wailed, the tears running down his face. "Oh, Miss Hagar, Miss Hagar! Please ma'm scuze Lou? Please ma'm? Dee school is done meck she foolish, ma'm? She ent hab no manners, ma'm; en dat letter what she is gittin', Miss Hagar, she done git out she Mah trunk w'at is lef' yer w'en she Mah daid, yes, ma'm; en I ent know say she Mah is keep dat letter, no, ma'm, I ent know it. Dat letter hot my feelin's w'en I fust git it, Miss Hagar, en it hots my feelin's now, ma'm; hots my feelin's des dee same dis berry min'it. Oh, Lawd!"

It was almost a cry as Lou had rushed in. "Read that!" she ordered. Race instinct, race experience, all had then risen up within her, all were with her now as she remembered, even now! And would she ever forget the grime and dirt of the letter, the worn age of it! Written in the thirties, and to old George from his aunt, telling him that after she had gone North, her Negro husband had left her to return South, and that then she had married a 'very white man,' so she had expressed it; a German carpenter; that George's first cousin, her daughter by this German, had also married a white man and had gone west, where she was considered a white woman, and her name was 'Mrs. Henry Smithers.' That her advice to George was to run away from slavery and to do as she had done, so as to give his children a better place in life; and the letter was signed "Lualamba Siegers." And during the reading old George had sat with covered eyes, but Lou's eyes had watched her as she read. She had paused a second before looking up, then all that she could find to say was, "What a curious name."

"Her African name!" Lou cried.

Then at last she had stepped out of the open door which she had better never have entered, and in a maze of confusion had returned to the house, to her sewing with her aunt in the study. And for once she had felt that she must talk, must say all that was in her to say as to what she had been through, and her aunt had listened, quiet, unanswering, until she reached the letter, then, without one sign of interest she had said, "I have read the letter." And then had explained the story, how Lualamba and her brother, old George's father, had been bought by the Lasstons out of pity for their condition, as they seemed of a better tribe. "There was a great difference in the tribes," her aunt had added. How strange that seemed. Superior tribe. Lualamba had married a Negro! How foolish to shut her eyes. Of course a Negro, and on the Howard plantation. Then Lualamba had been

sold to the Howards, that was the custom, so that she would not be separated from her husband. Then old Mr. Howard dying, Mrs. Howard, having no children, and being a Northern woman, had sold to Mr. Howard's
nephew, everything except Lualamba and her husband; she had taken
them with her to the North. "When the letter came," her aunt had finished, "old George could not read it, and brought it to my mother. At her
death I found it, read it to see what I should do with it. I returned it to
George. He would not let me read it to him this second time; said it was a
wicked, sinful letter."

And she had cried—"It is, Aunt Alicia, it is!" "Yes," her aunt had answered in a toneless voice. "And what good does it do them to 'Cross
Over,'" she had pushed on. "It is forever in the blood; they are always
Negro, always, forever!" "Forever," her aunt had agreed. "I'd kill myself,"
she had cried! There had been a second's pause, and then, "Perhaps," was
all the answer, but in the voice there had been a strange tone and her aunt
had added, "But the Negroes would not feel it as you do; they have not
been trained—" and she had interrupted sharply—"They have not my
blood! My blood that goes back and back!"

"Nor your prejudices," came the quiet reply.

"Race instinct!" her aunt had cried. "Prejudices," was repeated.

"The world calls it prejudice; and the Negro does not mind," her aunt
had gone on; "and ambitious, they do not tell their secret, and many,
many people do not know the marks," then she had added slowly—"all
the marks."

"Do you know them?" and now she had leaned forward, and—"tell
me?" she had whispered, had slipped from off her low chair to her knees
close beside her aunt. Then like a physical blow came a low, fierce "No!"
and a quick movement away from her as if she were a repulsive thing—
"the subject is abhorrent to me! Hush!"

She felt the hot tears in her eyes, tears for the poor girl who was herself, kneeling there. She had got up slowly, had tried to go on with her
sewing. Her heart had seemed wrung, somehow; she longed that her aunt
should talk to her of this dreadful question; should say something, something pitiful for the poor Negroes. Never until that moment had she
thought of them as having any feeling on the subject of being black. That
they were black and were servants, had seemed to her a foregone conclusion. But that they had this hopeless desire—wicked, horrible desire, she
had called it—to be white, to mingle their blood with the blood of the
white race, was too appalling, it seemed almost to suffocate her! Poor
things, poor things! They could not escape their fate; they were blacks just

as birds were birds. "Cross Over!" Unendurable! Better raise themselves as a black race, as a black nation, so she had thought; had wondered why some leader did not rise to tell them this; to preach a hegira;[3] to take them quickly back to their own country, such a rich country, before the white nations took it all; rouse their self-respect, their ambition as blacks! "Poor things, poor things!" and in her absorption she had said this last aloud, and started, looking up, "I meant the Negroes, Aunt Alicia," she had explained; "the poor things who long to be white and cannot. I wonder if they know about the 'Return to Race.'" Then she had caught sight of the clock. "Already eleven," she said.

She stopped in her walk. Twelve hours ago! Twelve years—twelve centuries! All time had swept over her, had blighted her! What remained? She must not think, no, just walk. Her life lay all before her in which to think; now she must walk, step from crosstie to crosstie until she reached the station.

Twelve hours ago when her aunt had said, "You cannot go to walk, the dogs are out with Alan." Then she had got her hat and a small pistol that Percy had given her; she did not know it was an expensive one; "Just down the Avenue," she had explained.

"How could Percy afford it" was demanded; and—"Is he in the habit of giving you things?" And the look! One moment it held her, then, "You may go." And she had gone.

That look burned and seared her still! Down the avenue she had sped, under the live oaks, that draped in the long gray moss did what was possible to keep out the brilliant sunlight. On either side, beyond the avenue, had stretched the level pine woods, and wherever there was a hillock or any support for a vine, there grew the yellow jessamine,[4] filling the air with an ineffable sweetness. She could see it all, this dear home of all her life, could smell the jessamine; out here in the darkness as she walked, the picture seemed to shine about her, and yonder, at the end; there, by the big gate—Percy!

She had a right to dream—to remember? How fair and tall he was, how blue his eyes with ever a laugh in them. How strong the clasp of his hand, how rich his voice.

"And what are you running from?" he had demanded. But she had not told.

3. Flight of Muhammad from Mecca to Medina to escape persecution; here the flight of black slaves back to Africa.

4. Favorite southern vine with very fragrant flowers.

The haste had given her a color, it made her beautiful, he said, quite gave him "indigestion of the heart!" And she was so "Fizzy, always driving the cork out; not at all a Lasston; a changeling, with red-black eyes." His "Blossom" for whose love he was "hungry and thirsty."

And she—"I give you all! My life, my soul!"

"Hagar!" was all he said; her name that she hated, that she had not understood; why—why name her Hagar?[5]

Then, "We must tell Aunt Alicia," she had declared; "She murdered me with a look!"

"And so you ran—of course we'll tell; I've always wanted to tell, but you, little coward, would not. But now I've sold the pine lands, and we can be married at once."

For a little moment she had looked within the gates of Paradise, at least she had done that; then again fear had cowed her. "But that look!" she had whispered; "that look about the pistol; I felt burned up! Now that you love me perhaps she will love me." And to his assertions she had answered, "Never, and yet she adored my father; he was 'The Head of the Family' and if I had been a boy—"

She paused a moment. If she had been a boy? It was a new line of thought and she followed it as she tramped; if she had been a boy. She must think that out in the days to come.

Then Percy had untied his horse and had gone with her to the house. "It's unlucky touching perfect happiness," he said.

Then she—"I am not happy."

Once more he called her "little coward" as they walked together. From the garden gate where he tied his horse, she could see her aunt standing at the study window that was a door, and upstairs, in the sunshine by an open window, her cousin Sabina Lasston, sewing. How her fair hair glittered in the sunshine; and all the connection had wanted Percy to marry Sabina. A choking came in her throat. He would, in time.

He had laughed at her when they reached the gate. "I'll kiss you here where they can see," he said; "such an easy way to tell them. Why so terrified? You really are a coward." He had held her hand as they went around the big tea olive bush,[6] how sweet it smelled! Then her aunt had called

5. Egyptian slave who was the handmaid of Sarah, Abraham's wife, and mated with Abraham at the childless Sarah's suggestion. However, Sarah became jealous and cast out Hagar and her son, Ishmael, who became the father of the Arab nations and was associated by the Hebrews with the curse of slavery (Genesis 16−21).

6. Sweet olive, native of Asia, large evergreen shrub with fragrant flowers.

them in at the study window. How gay and debonair he had been about it all.

"Cousin Alicia wants us to go in there," he whispered; "trap us as it were; don't worry, I'll protect you. Here goes! Hullo, 'Bina!" and he waved his hand to the upstairs window. "Good morning, Cousin Alicia, how are you? Shall we come in there? I love this dear old study. Too cool? Let me close that window; the wind has still a little nip in it, only we've been walking."

Then——"You went to meet him, Hagar?"

"We are engaged, Cousin Alicia," he had struck in; "third cousins, no harm, and I've come to ask you to the wedding. Why——why, are you not well!"

"Yes, yes, I——I think so; I had, I have had, no suspicion of this; Hagar——"

Then for once she had been brave. "My fault," she had cried; "my fault, I would not let him tell you."

Then the order——"Leave the room." And she had gone despite Percy's order to stay, despite his clasp of her arm.

That was the end. She was glad she had got to the end; had it all clear of confusion in her mind even though she could not remember how she had got up the stairs.

Lying face downwards on her bed was the next clear thing she could remember, then to the window; and he had not turned his head, had gone slowly away from the house, as if suddenly crippled. In silence she had endured this, endured, yes.

She had eaten the food put down outside her door for the sake of the strength to endure. She had not died, no, she had endured the horrors of the letter thrust under her door, the hideous anticlimax of its ending: "I have said that you have a nervous headache and must not be disturbed"! All this she had endured; but not yet had she dared. She had not dared even to think; not dared to realize, not dared to feel——to die! Not yet. Recalling and arranging memories, scenes, that was all. "Afraid?" the man had asked. Yesterday, this walk would have been a terrifying impossibility. Now? Well, now, if anything further happened to her, perhaps, perhaps she would have the courage for the river; no, she was not afraid of this.

The day was still as death; a fine rain was falling noiselessly; the bright jessamine of the day before now were hanging heavy with moisture, the long moss showed a pale, dim green because of the wetness. Near one of the windows stood Mrs. Jarnigan, still and gray as the day. She seemed to be watching, listening. She walked from window to window, then out to the front door, standing for a moment to look down the avenue. Something sent a shiver through her, perhaps the rain, or the wind that now and then came in little gusts, and she went in again.

She was cold, colder than the rain or the wind could have made her. For twenty-four hours she had not rested, had not slept; had again and again gone over the scenes of the day before. How radiant Percy had looked; had come to ask her to his wedding—wedding with Hagar!

Great God! Blind! How blind she had been, how foolish; had she not eyes to see that the girl was beautiful? How his fair, level brows had drawn together when Hagar at her order had left the room, closing the door, how his blue eyes had flashed! What avail that she had pleaded to him, "Before God, I had no thought of this! I have kept the girl so secluded." How he had stared.

"What!" he had whispered it. Then her own voice answering, low, intense, that seemed to still the universe.

"It killed my brother," she had said; "it crucified me!" Then dimly, through the closed windows she had heard a mockingbird singing.

"Think," she had gone on, and she had come closer, peering into his face; "think had there ever before been a brunette Lasston?" A white line had settled about Percy's lips.

"Sit down, sit down," she had ordered; "it is a long story"; but he would not. Then with her hand on his shoulder, she had told him the story.

"My brother, so young, that when he finished his part in the war went to college, and there met his wife, older than he, but very beautiful. We opposed this stranger; he was infatuated. He brought her here a bride. Just before the child was born, an old German came on a visit, a scientific man. He stayed here for two days. The German said to me, 'You do not mind the Negro blood, then?'"

In telling the terrible story to Percy she had given the German's very words that for years had been burned into her heart, her memory.

"She has one mark of Negro blood," the German had said; "that may fade in her child; but she lacks, she has not the mark of the pure white. The hair, the modeling of the nose—one drop of Negro blood eliminated that delicate modelling."

The words seemed even now actually to sound in her ears; she shivered and went to the fire. How cold she was. She put on a fresh log, made it blaze cheerfully, then stood there warming herself. Why could she not forget; would she be always seeing Percy's face gone so gray, so drawn? And beyond that seeing again, as she had seemed to see the day before, the face of her young brother, dead all these years? He had overheard the German telling her! He had come in at the door—the door there behind Percy— and his fair young face had gone gray and drawn just as Percy's had; and yesterday he had come and stood behind Percy—she had had a vision of him and of his dead wife standing there!

And the wife had known that she had black blood; after the German left them, the whole story had been told. She had known that the Lasstons had owned her ancestors, but not that in old George and old Sue she had black cousins left there. That had been a terrible shock to her; unknowing, they had bowed down before her as their master's wife—before Hagar as their master's daughter! They had been as an awful nightmare to the young wife and she had died when her child was born. Hagar, the father had named the child; Hagar, " 'An alien,' he said, 'an outcast.' "

The story told, Percy had turned his dead eyes, his ashen face to her; "Thank you," he had said. "Thank you—may I go this way?" and had put his hand on the window latch. How loud the mockingbird had sounded as the window opened, singing its heart out! Still singing as when he and Hagar had come inside. The sun was still shining. Then he had crossed the broad piazza to the steps, down to the garden path, round the olive bushes to where his horse stood at the gate. He did not once turn, not once look back.

She drew a sobbing breath; how still the house was. Not a footstep, not a voice, no sound anywhere, just the wind outside, the drip of the rain from the roof. She started away from the cheerful fire so suddenly that she overturned a small screen; the sound seemed to echo, to come, to go. Hastily she went from the window to the door and back again; up and down; out to the piazza. And old George had hobbled up to the kitchen this morning, hearing the awful news that his young mistress was missing, and he was waiting there in the kitchen now for some word. His kinswoman. He had a right to know it all? Never!

She wrung her hands together; she must stop thinking. Would this terrible waiting never end—would no one ever come! Once more she went from window to door and back again; up and down the piazza. At last she bent her head, stopped, went quickly to the door. Yes, there, she could see her son now, and coming alone!

A horseman dismounted at the gate and tied his horse, slowly he came as if neither rain nor shelter meant anything to him. She met him at the step.

"No sign," he said, going into the study; "We've dragged the pond, have searched the swamp out to the river; the freshet makes the river impossible; but the dogs did not go to the river——"

"Where?" It was a whisper.

"They lost scent in the middle of the public road, and I found this." In his extended palm there lay a gray button.

Her whole being seemed to relax. "Her gray frock," she said; "that tells nothing; she had that on yesterday, too."

"You say that so quietly, mother," laying his hands on her two shoulders. "Mother," swaying her slightly; "why did you let her live here as our equal?"

"A girl, I could not cast her off; poverty-stricken, I had no money to place her elsewhere; I could not bring myself to explain, the disgrace would have killed me! The disgrace, the horror of it, killed my brother. But, where's Sabina?"

"She and the Doctor have ridden again to the river; she will not give up the search."

"She does not know our secret; and Percy?"

"Percy? Good God!"

"What?"

"Says, God has been merciful!"

"He has; and Hagar has been well trained."

"Mother!" Staring into Mrs. Jarnigan's eyes; "your niece, your——"

"Hush!"

"Your only brother's only child; trained by you; beautiful, gentle! Mother, did you not love her?"

"Love her? God! My life has been torture! When she touched me my blood turned backward in my veins! Eating at my table; sitting near you; treating you as a brother! The unspeakable misery! Her black hair, coarse, curly! Could you not see, boy? And I, I cut myself off from my people; I could not take her into their homes any more than I would take a disease there. Lonely, wretched, I've lived here with that calamity, turning over and over in my mind what to do for her—with her. A boy, I would have sent away, but a girl? A little black-eyed, black-haired baby, she killed her father. He died within the year. 'My blood!' he cried; 'My race!' "

"And now, mother, she has vanished; that is noble, mother."

"She has Lasston blood in her; she has been well trained."

"She might not have lived up to it."

"She may not yet."

"She may not be alive, mother."

"In all my training of her I looked forward to this day, and now, in the first trial, she has done the right thing."

"I say, she may not be alive."

"She is afraid; she would not kill herself. She loves the soft things; she was not direct; was hard to train. I taught her daily the 'Noblesse Oblige'[7] of the Lasstons; it became her creed; it is guiding her now; pray God it will continue. Her father named her 'Hagar Black'; if I should go out into the world to hunt for her, I should hunt for Hagar Black. Thank God, Percy needed no arguments! Your attitude, Alan, shames me."

"Suppose Sabina find trace of her?"

"I should send Percy to lose it."

"Oh, mother!"

"What would you have? Bring her back as our equal? Place her in old George's cabin? You have no answer. There is no answer. To lose herself to us; to make her own place in life, that is the only thing. Pray God she may remain true to her training and not marry a white man—"

"How dare you, mother!"

"Not marry at all; her children might—"

"Here is Sabina."

"We have ridden miles and miles, cousin, down the river. It is over the banks; the current is terrific!"

"Thank you, dear Sabina, you must be wet."

"No, the clouds are breaking."

"And Doctor Bruce?"

"He left me at the gate, cousin," she paused, "cousin, he has no hope."

"Yes, Sabina."

"She must have gone out early this morning in her boat; old George said she often did—she did not mind weather."

"Perhaps."

"And, cousin, if you do not mind, will you let Alan ride home with me now? And bring the buggy back for you? Won't you come too? A little change, cousin?"

"Oh, Sabina, yes! Thank you, dear."

"And Alan, too?"

"Thank you, dear," her voice faltering a little; "thank you."

---

7. "Nobility obligates" (Fr.), the moral obligation of the highborn or wealthy to act honorably and charitably to the less fortunate.

"Poor cousin," putting her arm about the elder woman; "Mama will be so glad to see you; the first time in all my life that you have come to us; you'd never bring Hagar, too many, you said; but now?"

"Yes, now I can come; I shall be ready when Alan returns."

"You've led such a hermit life; you seemed to need no one but dear Hagar; but now you must come out to us."

"I shall be glad; but none of you must be pitiful, sorrowful; it would kill me! Good-bye, dear Sabina; I shall be ready; yes, close the door."

She stood quite still until the door was fast, then she went to the window. "In her boat on the river; that story will do; and old George suggested it." She raised her arms above her head. "Free!" she said, looking up, while a great light broke over her face; "once more, once more myself—free among my own kind, once more!" Her voice broke and the sobs came, deep, heart-rending, almost cries, that shook her from head to foot. Down on her knees she prayed, "God have mercy! If I have failed, have mercy!"

And out in the olive bushes a bird was singing—singing.

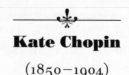

Kate Chopin

(1850–1904)

THOUGH KATE CHOPIN is today best known for her novel *The Awakening,* during her lifetime her reputation was based on her achievement as a writer of stories about the Acadians of southwest Louisiana. Born Katherine O'Flaherty in St. Louis on February 8, 1850, Chopin was the oldest surviving daughter of an Irish immigrant, Thomas O'Flaherty, and his second wife, Eliza Faris, sixteen years his junior and the daughter of a respectable family of French descent. After her father's death in a train accident when she was five, Chopin (known as "Katie" to her family) was raised in a female-centered household that included her grandmother and great-grandmother, whose love of French, stories, and music made lasting impressions. Chopin received her formal education from the Catholic sisters at the Academy of the Sacred Heart; her teenage diary reflects her lively reading interests and observational talents as well as an adolescent impatience with conventional young men. In 1869 she met Oscar Chopin, the son of a French émigré, who had settled in Louisiana and who sent his eldest son north to learn the banking business. They were married in June of 1870 and set out on a European wedding journey (whose highlights Chopin recorded), returning to New Orleans in September, where Oscar took up business as a cotton factor (trader).

The Chopins' life in Reconstruction New Orleans was reasonably comfortable. Kate was occupied with their children, five sons and a daughter between 1870 and 1879, but she clearly appreciated the city with its agreeable and lively French atmosphere. Oscar's business failed in 1879, however, and the family moved to Cloutierville, near Natchitoches, a small town in central Louisiana where Oscar's family owned plantations. There Kate became intimately acquainted with the singular culture and lilting speech of the rural Acadians, who were later to become central to her fiction. In December 1882 Oscar died of malaria. Kate remained in Louisiana another year while she settled her husband's estate (and probably had an affair with a neighboring, married planter).

Only a year after Chopin's return to St. Louis, her mother died, leaving Kate with six children under fourteen and her elderly grandmother. At that time her friend and former obstetrician, Austrian émigré Frederick Kolbenheyer, suggested that she write stories. After a false start or two (carefully recorded in her account book), she published her first short story, "A Point at Issue!" in the *St. Louis Post-Dispatch* in 1889. A steady stream of stories in a variety of settings followed, including her first Louisiana story, the children's tale "For Marse Chouchoute" in 1891. Chopin quickly recognized that her Louisiana material sold best, and, for several years, she used no other setting.

Published in 1890, her first novel, *At Fault*, uses the reconstruction plot of a North-South relationship to develop such contemporary topics as divorce, alcoholism, Darwinist philosophy, and religious scruples. In 1894 she published her first short-story collection, *Bayou Folk*, which established her, together with Ruth Stuart, Grace King, and George W. Cable, as a major figure of Louisiana local color. In this volume and in her 1897 collection, *A Night in Acadie*, Chopin creates the nineteenth-century's richest portrait of the Acadian people of central and south Louisiana.

Chopin often drew on the multicultural richness of New Orleans for her complex and deft sketches, as in "La Belle Zoraïde" (*Vogue*, 1894). Chopin's tragic story of the fair-skinned Zoraïde, whose cruel mistress thwarts her love for the black Mézor, offers a sophisticated view of the way dialect and language sustain difference. Though Chopin's work is hardly free of racial stereotyping, her representations of black life are often complex. Her most famous story, "Désirée's Baby," originally published in *Vogue* (1893), filters southern racial prejudices through exquisite narrative ambiguities: a foundling without a clear racial identity finds that the birth of her dark child threatens her marriage to a rich and proud white Creole. The famous twist at the story's conclusion (a narrative trick Chopin probably adapted from French realist author Guy de Maupassant, whose work she greatly admired) leaves little resolved about anyone's identity.

Both of these stories are somewhat unusual for Chopin in their antebellum settings. The majority of her fiction focuses on the plight of contemporary young women and men, whose dilemmas are made interesting by the details of their exotic Acadian contexts and by Chopin's interest in the conflicts that social conventions create for individuals. "In Sabine," which first appeared in *Bayou Folk*, is a remarkable instance of her ability to treat such serious issues as wife abuse, divorce, and racial relations with a lightness that almost obscures their dark implications. In fact, the modest success of Chopin's local-color fiction encouraged her to move away from what she described in her journal as the limits of the genre. After 1894 her fiction explores with even greater freedom the themes that most interested her: female sexuality and selfhood, the role of the senses in human understanding, and the complexities of male and female relationships.

In 1898 she completed her third novel (a second had been destroyed), a powerful account of a woman's "awakening" to the limits imposed on her life by gender. Like many of the stories that preceded it, *The Awakening* reflects issues surrounding the lively "woman question" of the late nineteenth century: the role of motherhood, female sexuality, marriage, adultery, and divorce. Though Chopin was evidently not prepared for the novel's negative reception, she certainly appreciated the dangers of treating female sexuality openly in nineteenth-century fiction. Before the April 1899 appearance of her daring novel, she had written "The Storm," a story that she never even tried to publish. A sequel to "At the 'Cadian Ball" (1892), an earlier and more conventional story, "The Storm" recounts a spontaneous act of adultery between former lovers during a violent storm. With its richly suggestive imagery, the tale presents adulterous sexuality as redemptive, a point of view that retains its startling flavor over a century later. It also demonstrates Chopin's mastery of short fiction: her economical uses of dialect, setting, and dialogue to create evocative and multidimensional stories. In Chopin's hands, local color produces art of a very high kind.

The critical rejection of *The Awakening*, together with failing health, served to diminish Chopin's literary production after 1899. While she wrote several more stories, they reflect a certain reticence and a return to more conventional themes. Afflicted with a stroke after a strenuous day at the St. Louis Louisiana Purchase Exposition in 1904, Chopin died at her home on August 22. Most of her fiction went out of print, though she was sometimes recalled as a talented writer of southern local color. With the rediscovery of *The Awakening* in the 1970s, however, she has been reclaimed as a major literary figure.

Works by Kate Chopin

At Fault, 1890, ed. Suzanne Disheroon Green and David J. Caudle, 2001

Bayou Folk, 1894, ed. Bernard Koloski, 1999

A Night in Acadie, 1897, ed. Bernard Koloski, 1999

The Awakening, 1899, ed. Kenneth Eble, 1964, ed. Lewis Leary, 1970,
ed. Sandra M. Gilbert, 1984, ed. Margo Culley, 1994, ed. Nancy A. Walker, 2000

The Complete Works of Kate Chopin, 2 vols., ed. Per Seyersted, 1969

A Kate Chopin Miscellany, ed. Per Seyersted and Emily Toth, 1979

A Vocation and a Voice: Stories, ed. Emily Toth, 1991

Kate Chopin's Private Papers, ed. Emily Toth and Per Seyersted, 1998

Further Reading

Beer, Janet. *Kate Chopin, Edith Wharton and Charlotte Perkins Gilman: Studies in Short Fiction*. New York: St. Martin's, 1997.

Benfey, Christopher E. G. *Degas in New Orleans: Encounters in the Creole World of Kate Chopin and George Washington Cable*. New York: Knopf, 1997.

Bonner, Thomas, ed. *The Kate Chopin Companion*. New York: Greenwood Press, 1988.

Dyer, Joyce. *The Awakening: A Novel of Beginnings*. New York: Twayne, 1993.

Ewell, Barbara C. *Kate Chopin*. New York: Frederick Ungar, 1986.

———. "Making Places: Kate Chopin and the Art of Fiction." *Louisiana Literature* 2.1 (1994): 157–71.

Green, Suzanne Disheroon, and David J. Caudle. *An Annotated Bibliography of Critical Works*. Westport, Conn.: Greenwood Press, 1999.

Koloski, Bernard. *Kate Chopin: A Study of the Short Fiction*. New York: Twayne, 1996.

Papke, Mary E. *Verging on the Abyss: The Social Fiction of Kate Chopin and Edith Wharton*. New York: Greenwood Press, 1990.

Petry, Alice Hall, ed. *Critical Essays on Kate Chopin*. New York: G. K. Hall, 1996.

Seyersted, *Kate Chopin: A Critical Biography*. Baton Rouge: Louisiana State University Press, 1969.

Toth, Emily. *Kate Chopin*. New York: Morrow, 1990.

———. *Unveiling Kate Chopin*. Jackson: University Press of Mississippi, 1999.

Désirée's Baby

As the day was pleasant, Madame Valmondé drove over to L'Abri[1] to see Désirée and the baby.

It made her laugh to think of Désirée with a baby. Why, it seemed but

1. "The Shelter" (Fr.).

yesterday that Désirée was little more than a baby herself; when Monsieur in riding through the gateway of Valmondé had found her lying asleep in the shadow of the big stone pillar.

The little one awoke in his arms and began to cry for "Dada." That was as much as she could do or say. Some people thought she might have strayed there of her own accord, for she was of the toddling age. The prevailing belief was that she had been purposely left by a party of Texans, whose canvas-covered wagon, late in the day, had crossed the ferry that Coton-Maïs kept, just below the plantation. In time Madame Valmondé abandoned every speculation but the one that Désirée had been sent to her by a beneficent Providence to be the child of her affection, seeing that she was without child of the flesh. For the girl grew to be beautiful and gentle, affectionate and sincere,—the idol of Valmondé.

It was no wonder, when she stood one day against the stone pillar in whose shadow she had lain asleep, eighteen years before, that Armand Aubigny riding by and seeing her there, had fallen in love with her. That was the way all the Aubignys fell in love, as if struck by a pistol shot. The wonder was that he had not loved her before; for he had known her since his father brought him home from Paris, a boy of eight, after his mother died there. The passion that awoke in him that day, when he saw her at the gate, swept along like an avalanche, or like a prairie fire, or like anything that drives headlong over all obstacles.

Monsieur Valmondé grew practical and wanted things well considered: that is, the girl's obscure origin. Armand looked into her eyes and did not care. He was reminded that she was nameless. What did it matter about a name when he could give her one of the oldest and proudest in Louisiana? He ordered the *corbeille*[2] from Paris, and contained himself with what patience he could until it arrived; then they were married.

Madame Valmondé had not seen Désirée and the baby for four weeks. When she reached L'Abri she shuddered at the first sight of it, as she always did. It was a sad looking place, which for many years had not known the gentle presence of a mistress, old Monsieur Aubigny having married and buried his wife in France, and she having loved her own land too well ever to leave it. The roof came down steep and black like a cowl, reaching out beyond the wide galleries that encircled the yellow stuccoed house. Big, solemn oaks grew close to it, and their thick-leaved, far-reaching branches shadowed it like a pall. Young Aubigny's rule was a strict one,

2. "Wedding presents" (Fr.), from the groom to the bride.

too, and under it his negroes had forgotten how to be gay, as they had been during the old master's easy-going and indulgent lifetime.

The young mother was recovering slowly, and lay full length, in her soft white muslins and laces, upon a couch. The baby was beside her, upon her arm, where he had fallen asleep, at her breast. The yellow nurse woman sat beside a window fanning herself.

Madame Valmondé bent her portly figure over Désirée and kissed her, holding her an instant tenderly in her arms. Then she turned to the child.

"This is not the baby!" she exclaimed, in startled tones. French was the language spoken at Valmondé in those days.

"I knew you would be astonished," laughed Désirée, "at the way he has grown. The little *cochon de lait!*[3] Look at his legs, mamma, and his hands and fingernails,—real finger-nails. Zandrine had to cut them this morning. Is n't it true, Zandrine?"

The woman bowed her turbaned head majestically, "Mais si,[4] Madame."

"And the way he cries," went on Désirée, "is deafening. Armand heard him the other day as far away as La Blanche's[5] cabin."

Madame Valmondé had never removed her eyes from the child. She lifted it and walked with it over to the window that was lightest. She scanned the baby narrowly, then looked as searchingly at Zandrine, whose face was turned to gaze across the fields.

"Yes, the child has grown, has changed," said Madame Valmondé, slowly, as she replaced it beside its mother. "What does Armand say?"

Désirée's face became suffused with a glow that was happiness itself.

"Oh, Armand is the proudest father in the parish, I believe, chiefly because it is a boy, to bear his name; though he says not,—that he would have loved a girl as well. But I know it is n't true. I know he says that to please me. And mamma," she added, drawing Madame Valmondé's head down to her, and speaking in a whisper, "he has n't punished one of them—not one of them—since baby is born. Even Négrillon, who pretended to have burnt his leg that he might rest from work—he only laughed, and said Négrillon was a great scamp. Oh, mamma, I'm so happy; it frightens me."

What Désirée said was true. Marriage, and later the birth of his son had softened Armand Aubigny's imperious and exacting nature greatly. This

3. "Suckling pig" (Fr.), a favorite food at country feasts in south Louisiana; also sounds like "milk chocolate."

4. "But yes" (Fr.), of course.

5. "The white one" (Fr.).

was what made the gentle Désirée so happy, for she loved him desperately. When he frowned she trembled, but loved him. When he smiled, she asked no greater blessing of God. But Armand's dark, handsome face had not often been disfigured by frowns since the day he fell in love with her.

When the baby was about three months old, Désirée awoke one day to the conviction that there was something in the air menacing her peace. It was at first too subtle to grasp. It had only been a disquieting suggestion; an air of mystery among the blacks; unexpected visits from far-off neighbors who could hardly account for their coming. Then a strange, an awful change in her husband's manner, which she dared not ask him to explain. When he spoke to her, it was with averted eyes, from which the old love-light seemed to have gone out. He absented himself from home; and when there, avoided her presence and that of her child, without excuse. And the very spirit of Satan seemed suddenly to take hold of him in his dealings with the slaves. Désirée was miserable enough to die.

She sat in her room, one hot afternoon, in her *peignoir*,[6] listlessly drawing through her fingers the strands of her long, silky brown hair that hung about her shoulders. The baby, half naked, lay asleep upon her own great mahogany bed, that was like a sumptuous throne, with its satin-lined half-canopy. One of La Blanche's little quadroon[7] boys—half naked too—stood fanning the child slowly with a fan of peacock feathers. Désirée's eyes had been fixed absently and sadly upon the baby, while she was striving to penetrate the threatening mist that she felt closing about her. She looked from her child to the boy who stood beside him, and back again; over and over. "Ah!" It was a cry that she could not help; which she was not conscious of having uttered. The blood turned like ice in her veins, and a clammy moisture gathered upon her face.

She tried to speak to the little quadroon boy; but no sound would come, at first. When he heard his name uttered, he looked up, and his mistress was pointing to the door. He laid aside the great, soft fan, and obediently stole away, over the polished floor, on his bare tiptoes.

She stayed motionless, with gaze riveted upon her child, and her face the picture of fright.

Presently her husband entered the room, and without noticing her, went to a table and began to search among some papers which covered it.

"Armand," she called to him, in a voice which must have stabbed him,

6. Woman's dressing gown (Fr.).

7. Offspring of a white parent and a mulatto (half black and half white).

if he was human. But he did not notice. "Armand," she said again. Then she rose and tottered towards him. "Armand," she panted once more, clutching his arm, "look at our child. What does it mean? tell me."

He coldly but gently loosened her fingers from about his arm and thrust the hand away from him. "Tell me what it means!" she cried despairingly.

"It means," he answered lightly, "that the child is not white; it means that you are not white."

A quick conception of all that this accusation meant for her nerved her with unwonted courage to deny it. "It is a lie; it is not true, I am white! Look at my hair, it is brown; and my eyes are gray, Armand, you know they are gray. And my skin is fair," seizing his wrist. "Look at my hand; whiter than yours, Armand," she laughed hysterically.

"As white as La Blanche's," he returned cruelly; and went away leaving her alone with their child.

When she could hold a pen in her hand, she sent a despairing letter to Madame Valmondé.

"My mother, they tell me I am not white. Armand has told me I am not white. For God's sake tell them it is not true. You must know it is not true. I shall die. I must die. I cannot be so unhappy, and live."

The answer that came was as brief:

"My own Désirée: Come home to Valmondé; back to your mother who loves you. Come with your child."

When the letter reached Désirée she went with it to her husband's study, and laid it open upon the desk before which he sat. She was like a stone image: silent, white, motionless after she placed it there.

In silence he ran his cold eyes over the written words. He said nothing. "Shall I go, Armand?" she asked in tones sharp with agonized suspense.

"Yes, go."

"Do you want me to go?"

"Yes, I want you to go."

He thought Almighty God had dealt cruelly and unjustly with him; and felt, somehow, that he was paying Him back in kind when he stabbed thus into his wife's soul. Moreover he no longer loved her, because of the unconscious injury she had brought upon his home and his name.

She turned away like one stunned by a blow, and walked slowly towards the door, hoping he would call her back.

"Good-by, Armand," she moaned.

He did not answer her. That was his last blow at fate.

Désirée went in search of her child. Zandrine was pacing the sombre gallery with it. She took the little one from the nurse's arms with no word of explanation, and descending the steps, walked away, under the live-oak branches.

It was an October afternoon; the sun was just sinking. Out in the still fields the negroes were picking cotton.

Désirée had not changed the thin white garment nor the slippers which she wore. Her hair was uncovered and the sun's rays brought a golden gleam from its brown meshes. She did not take the broad, beaten road which led to the far-off plantation of Valmondé. She walked across a deserted field, where the stubble bruised her tender feet, so delicately shod, and tore her thin gown to shreds.

She disappeared among the reeds and willows that grew thick along the banks of the deep, sluggish bayou;[8] and she did not come back again.

Some weeks later there was a curious scene enacted at L'Abri. In the centre of the smoothly swept back yard was a great bonfire. Armand Aubigny sat in the wide hallway that commanded a view of the spectacle; and it was he who dealt out to a half dozen negroes the material which kept this fire ablaze.

A graceful cradle of willow, with all its dainty furbishings, was laid upon the pyre, which had already been fed with the richness of a priceless *layette*.[9] Then there were silk gowns, and velvet and satin ones added to these; laces, too, and embroideries; bonnets and gloves; for the *corbeille* had been of rare quality.

The last thing to go was a tiny bundle of letters; innocent little scribblings that Désirée had sent to him during the days of their espousal. There was the remnant of one back in the drawer from which he took them. But it was not Désirée's; it was part of an old letter from his mother to his father. He read it. She was thanking God for the blessing of her husband's love:——

"But, above all," she wrote, "night and day, I thank the good God for having so arranged our lives that our dear Armand will never know that his mother, who adores him, belongs to the race that is cursed with the brand of slavery."

8. From the Choctaw word *bayuk*, slow-moving, marshy outflow of a lake or river.

9. Clothes and toilet articles for a newborn child (Fr.).

La Belle Zoraïde

The summer night was hot and still; not a ripple of air swept over the *marais*.[10] Yonder, across Bayou St. John,[11] lights twinkled here and there in the darkness, and in the dark sky above a few stars were blinking. A lugger[12] that had come out of the lake was moving with slow, lazy motion down the bayou. A man in the boat was singing a song.

The notes of the song came faintly to the ears of old Manna-Loulou, herself as black as the night, who had gone out upon the gallery[13] to open the shutters wide.

Something in the refrain reminded the woman of an old, half-forgotten Creole[14] romance, and she began to sing it low to herself while she threw the shutters open:—

> "Lisett' to kité la plaine,
> Mo perdi bonhair à moué;
> Ziés à moué semblé fontaine,
> Dépi mo pa miré toué."[15]

And then this old song, a lover's lament for the loss of his mistress, floating into her memory, brought with it the story she would tell to Madame, who lay in her sumptuous mahogany bed, waiting to be fanned and put to sleep to the sound of one of Manna-Loulou's stories. The old negress had

---

10. "Swamp" (Fr.).

11. From the Choctaw word *bayuk*, slow-moving, marshy outlet of a lake or river. Bayou St. John was the major route from Lake Pontchartrain into New Orleans; by 1800 it was lined with West Indies—style plantation houses.

12. Small vessel with square sails hung, or lug-rigged, on two or three masts, suited for low-wind, inland sailing.

13. Veranda or porch along one side of a house.

14. Technically, individuals born outside their parents' country of origin, especially of mixed racial heritage; in the nineteenth century, increasingly limited to upper-class landowners of French and/or Spanish descent.

15. Variation of a popular Creole French song first transcribed by Haitian collector Moreau de St. Mery in 1759:

> "Lisette has left these fields,
> And I have lost my happiness;
> My eyes seem like fountains,
> Since I last saw you."

already bathed her mistress's pretty white feet and kissed them lovingly, one, then the other. She had brushed her mistress's beautiful hair, that was as soft and shining as satin, and was the color of Madame's wedding-ring. Now, when she re-entered the room, she moved softly toward the bed, and seating herself there began gently to fan Madame Delisle.

Manna-Loulou was not always ready with her story, for Madame would hear none but those which were true. But to-night the story was all there in Manna-Loulou's head—the story of la belle Zoraïde[16]—and she told it to her mistress in the soft Creole patois,[17] whose music and charm no English words can convey.

"La belle Zoraïde had eyes that were so dusky, so beautiful, that any man who gazed too long into their depths was sure to lose his head, and even his heart sometimes. Her soft, smooth skin was the color of *café-au-lait.*[18] As for her elegant manners, her *svelte*[19] and graceful figure, they were the envy of half the ladies who visited her mistress, Madame Delarivière.[20]

"No wonder Zoraïde was as charming and as dainty as the finest lady of la rue Royale:[21] from a toddling thing she had been brought up at her mistress's side; her fingers had never done rougher work than sewing a fine muslin seam; and she even had her own little black servant to wait upon her. Madame, who was her godmother as well as her mistress, would often say to her:—

" 'Remember, Zoraïde, when you are ready to marry, it must be in a way to do honor to your bringing up. It will be at the Cathedral. Your wedding gown, your *corbeille,*[22] all will be of the best; I shall see to that myself. You know, M'sieur Ambroise is ready whenever you say the word; and his master is willing to do as much for him as I shall do for you. It is a union that will please me in every way.'

16. "The beautiful Zoraïde" (Fr.).

17. Dialect which is spoken (not written) among more rural or less educated people; here it applies to the local blend of French, English, Spanish, and African languages spoken across class lines in nineteenth-century Louisiana.

18. Coffee lightened with boiled milk (Fr.).

19. "Stretched out" (It.), that is, "slender."

20. Literally, "of the river" (Fr.).

21. "Royal Street" (Fr.), the main commercial and residential street of New Orleans's French Quarter.

22. "Wedding presents" (Fr.), from the groom to the bride.

"M'sieur Ambroise was then the body servant[23] of Doctor Langlé. La belle Zoraïde detested the little mulatto,[24] with his shining whiskers like a white man's, and his small eyes, that were cruel and false as a snake's. She would cast down her own mischievous eyes, and say:—

"'Ah, nénaine,[25] I am so happy, so contented here at your side just as I am. I don't want to marry now; next year, perhaps, or the next.' And Madame would smile indulgently and remind Zoraïde that a woman's charms are not everlasting.

"But the truth of the matter was, Zoraïde had seen le beau Mézor[26] dance the Bamboula[27] in Congo Square.[28] That was a sight to hold one rooted to the ground. Mézor was as straight as a cypress-tree and as proud looking as a king. His body, bare to the waist, was like a column of ebony and it glistened like oil.

"Poor Zoraïde's heart grew sick in her bosom with love for le beau Mézor from the moment she saw the fierce gleam of his eye, lighted by the inspiring strains of the Bamboula, and beheld the stately movements of his splendid body swaying and quivering through the figures of the dance.

"But when she knew him later, and he came near her to speak with her, all the fierceness was gone out of his eyes, and she saw only kindness in them and heard only gentleness in his voice; for love had taken possession of him also, and Zoraïde was more distracted than ever. When Mézor was not dancing Bamboula in Congo Square, he was hoeing sugar-cane, barefooted and half naked, in his master's field outside of the city. Doctor Langlé was his master as well as M'sieur Ambroise's.

"One day, when Zoraïde kneeled before her mistress, drawing on Madame's silken stockings, that were of the finest, she said:

"'Nénaine, you have spoken to me often of marrying. Now, at last, I have chosen a husband, but it is not M'sieur Ambroise; it is le beau Mézor

23. Valet, or personal servant.

24. Individual born to one black parent and one white parent.

25. Diminutive of "Nana" or woman (Fr.); also familiar address of child to godmother.

26. "The handsome Mézor" (Fr.).

27. African dance, accompanied by the "bamboula," a small drum or tambourine made from a large bamboo joint. Popular among blacks in the nineteenth century, the dance begins slowly and builds to a sexualized frenzy.

28. Unique area at the edge of the French Quarter, where slaves were permitted to gather on Sundays and other holidays.

that I want and no other.' And Zoraïde hid her face in her hands when she had said that, for she guessed, rightly enough, that her mistress would be very angry. And, indeed, Madame Delarivière was at first speechless with rage. When she finally spoke it was only to gasp out, exasperated:—

" 'That negro! that negro! Bon Dieu Seigneur,[29] but this is too much!'

" 'Am I white, nénaine?' pleaded Zoraïde.

" 'You white! *Malheureuse!*[30] You deserve to have the lash laid upon you like any other slave; you have proven yourself no better than the worst.'

" 'I am not white,' persisted Zoraïde, respectfully and gently. 'Doctor Langlé gives me his slave to marry, but he would not give me his son. Then, since I am not white, let me have from out of my own race the one whom my heart has chosen.'

"However, you may well believe that Madame would not hear to that. Zoraïde was forbidden to speak to Mézor, and Mézor was cautioned against seeing Zoraïde again. But you know how the negroes are, Ma'zélle Titite,"[31] added Manna-Loulou, smiling a little sadly. "There is no mistress, no master, no king nor priest who can hinder them from loving when they will. And these two found ways and means.

"When months had passed by, Zoraïde, who had grown unlike herself,—sober and preoccupied,—said again to her mistress:—

" 'Nénaine, you would not let me have Mézor for my husband; but I have disobeyed you, I have sinned. Kill me if you wish, nénaine: forgive me if you will; but when I heard le beau Mézor say to me, "Zoraïde, mo l'aime toi,"[32] I could have died, but I could not have helped loving him.'

"This time Madame Delarivière was so actually pained, so wounded at hearing Zoraïde's confession, that there was no place left in her heart for anger. She could utter only confused reproaches. But she was a woman of action rather than of words, and she acted promptly. Her first step was to induce Doctor Langlé to sell Mézor. Doctor Langlé, who was a widower, had long wanted to marry Madame Delarivière, and he would willingly have walked on all fours at noon through the Place d'Armes[33] if she wanted him to. Naturally he lost no time in disposing of le beau Mézor, who was

29. "Good Lord God" (Fr.), a mild epithet.

30. "Woman of bad fortune" (Fr.), "wicked wretch."

31. "Mademoiselle" (Creole Fr.). "Titite" is a diminutive, an affectionate childhood name.

32. "I love you" (Creole Fr.).

33. "Place for military assembly" (Fr.); now Jackson Square, the public center of the French Quarter in front of St. Louis Cathedral.

sold away into Georgia, or the Carolinas, or one of those distant countries far away, where he would no longer hear his Creole tongue spoken, nor dance Calinda,[34] nor hold la belle Zoraïde in his arms.

"The poor thing was heartbroken when Mézor was sent away from her, but she took comfort and hope in the thought of her baby that she would soon be able to clasp to her breast.

"La belle Zoraïde's sorrows had now begun in earnest. Not only sorrows but sufferings, and with the anguish of maternity came the shadow of death. But there is no agony that a mother will not forget when she holds her first-born to her heart, and presses her lips upon the baby flesh that is her own, yet far more precious than her own.

"So, instinctively, when Zoraïde came out of the awful shadow she gazed questioningly about her and felt with her trembling hands upon either side of her. 'Où li, mo piti a moin? (Where is my little one?)' she asked imploringly. Madame who was there and the nurse who was there both told her in turn, 'To piti à toi, li mouri' ('Your little one is dead'), which was a wicked falsehood that must have caused the angels in heaven to weep. For the baby was living and well and strong. It had at once been removed from its mother's side, to be sent away to Madame's plantation, far up the coast.[35] Zoraïde could only moan in reply, 'Li mouri, li mouri,' and she turned her face to the wall.

"Madame had hoped, in thus depriving Zoraïde of her child, to have her young waiting-maid again at her side free, happy, and beautiful as of old. But there was a more powerful will than Madame's at work—the will of the good God, who had already designed that Zoraïde should grieve with a sorrow that was never more to be lifted in this world. La belle Zoraïde was no more. In her stead was a sad-eyed woman who mourned night and day for her baby. 'Li mouri, li mouri,' she would sigh over and over again to those about her, and to herself when others grew weary of her complaint.

"Yet, in spite of all. M'sieur Ambroise was still in the notion to marry her. A sad wife or a merry one was all the same to him so long as that wife was Zoraïde. And she seemed to consent, or rather submit, to the approaching marriage as though nothing mattered any longer in this world.

"One day, a black servant entered a little noisily the room in which Zo-

34. A popular dance of syncopated rhythms from coastal Africa and the West Indies.

35. Many plantations fronted the "coast" or banks of the Mississippi River, both up- and down-river from New Orleans.

raïde sat sewing. With a look of strange and vacuous happiness upon her face, Zoraïde arose hastily. 'Hush, hush,' she whispered, lifting a warning finger, 'my little one is asleep; you must not awaken her.'

"Upon the bed was a senseless bundle of rags shaped like an infant in swaddling clothes. Over this dummy the woman had drawn the mosquito bar,[36] and she was sitting contentedly beside it. In short, from that day Zoraïde was demented. Night nor day did she lose sight of the doll that lay in her bed or in her arms.

"And now was Madame stung with sorrow and remorse at seeing this terrible affliction that had befallen her dear Zoraïde. Consulting with Doctor Langlé, they decided to bring back to the mother the real baby of flesh and blood that was now toddling about, and kicking its heels in the dust yonder upon the plantation.

"It was Madame herself who led the pretty, tiny little 'griffe'[37] girl to her mother. Zoraïde was sitting upon a stone bench in the courtyard, listening to the soft splashing of the fountain, and watching the fitful shadows of the palm leaves upon the broad, white flagging.

" 'Here,' said Madame, approaching, 'here, my poor dear Zoraïde, is your own little child. Keep her; she is yours. No one will ever take her from you again.'

"Zoraïde looked with sullen suspicion upon her mistress and the child before her. Reaching out a hand she thrust the little one mistrustfully away from her. With the other hand she clasped the rag bundle fiercely to her breast; for she suspected a plot to deprive her of it.

"Nor could she ever be induced to let her own child approach her; and finally the little one was sent back to the plantation, where she was never to know the love of mother or father.

"And now this is the end of Zoraïde's story. She was never known again as la belle Zoraïde, but ever after as Zoraïde la folle,[38] whom no one ever wanted to marry—not even M'sieur Ambroise. She lived to be an old woman, whom some people pitied and others laughed at—always clasping her bundle of rags—her 'piti.'[39]

"Are you asleep, Ma'zélle Titite?"

36. Light gauze draped over beds to keep out biting insects.

37. Individual born of one black parent and one half-black and half-white (mulatto) parent.

38. "Zoraïde the fool" (Fr.), madwoman.

39. "Petite," "little one" (Fr.).

"No, I am not asleep; I was thinking. Ah, the poor little one, Man Lou-lou, the poor little one! better had she died!"

But this is the way Madame Delisle and Manna-Loulou really talked to each other:—

"Vou pré droumi, Ma'zélle Titite?"

"Non, pa pré droumi; mo yapré zongler. Ah, la pauv' piti, Man Loulou. La pauv' piti! Mieux li mouri!"

In Sabine

The sight of a human habitation, even if it was a rude log cabin with a mud chimney at one end, was a very gratifying one to Grégoire.

He had come out of Natchitoches parish,[40] and had been riding a great part of the day through the big lonesome parish of Sabine.[41] He was not following the regular Texas road, but, led by his erratic fancy, was push-ing toward the Sabine River by circuitous paths through the rolling pine forests.

As he approached the cabin in the clearing, he discerned behind a pali-sade of pine saplings an old negro man chopping wood.

"Howdy, Uncle," called out the young fellow, reining his horse. The ne-gro looked up in blank amazement at so unexpected an apparition, but he only answered: "How you do, suh," accompanying his speech by a series of polite nods.

"Who lives yere?"

"Hit 's Mas' Bud Aiken w'at live' heah, suh."

"Well, if Mr. Bud Aiken c'n affo'd to hire a man to chop his wood, I reckon he won't grudge me a bite o' suppa an' a couple hours' res' on his gall'ry. W'at you say, ole man?"

"I say dit Mas' Bud Aiken don't hires me to chop 'ood. Ef I don't chop dis heah, his wife got it to do. Dat w'y I chops 'ood, suh. Go right 'long in, suh; you g'ine fine Mas' Bud some'eres roun', ef he ain't drunk an' gone to bed."

40. A "parish" or county in central Louisiana, which includes Cloutierville, Chopin's home from 1879 to 1884.

41. Parish or county west of Natchitoches, whose far border is the Sabine River, across which lies Texas.

Grégoire, glad to stretch his legs, dismounted, and led his horse into the small inclosure which surrounded the cabin. An unkempt, vicious-looking little Texas pony stopped nibbling the stubble there to look maliciously at him and his fine sleek horse, as they passed by. Back of the hut, and running plumb up against the pine wood, was a small, ragged specimen of a cotton-field.

Grégoire was rather undersized, with a square, well-knit figure, upon which his clothes sat well and easily. His corduroy trousers were thrust into the legs of his boots; he wore a blue flannel shirt; his coat was thrown across the saddle. In his keen black eyes had come a puzzled expression, and he tugged thoughtfully at the brown moustache that lightly shaded his upper lip.

He was trying to recall when and under what circumstances he had before heard the name of Bud Aiken. But Bud Aiken himself saved Grégoire the trouble of further speculation on the subject. He appeared suddenly in the small doorway, which his big body quite filled; and then Grégoire remembered. This was the disreputable so-called "Texan" who a year ago had run away with and married Baptiste Choupic's pretty daughter, 'Tite Reine, yonder on Bayou Pierre,[42] in Natchitoches parish. A vivid picture of the girl as he remembered her appeared to him: her trim rounded figure; her piquant face with its saucy black coquettish eyes; her little exacting, imperious ways that had obtained for her the nickname of 'Tite Reine, little queen. Grégoire had known her at the 'Cadian balls that he sometimes had the hardihood to attend.

These pleasing recollections of 'Tite Reine lent a warmth that might otherwise have been lacking to Grégoire's manner, when he greeted her husband.

"I hope I fine you well, Mr. Aiken," he exclaimed cordially, as he approached and extended his hand.

"You find me damn' porely, suh; but you 've got the better o' me, ef I may so say." He was a big good-looking brute, with a straw-colored "horse-shoe" moustache quite concealing his mouth, and a several days' growth of stubble on his rugged face. He was fond of reiterating that women's admiration had wrecked his life, quite forgetting to mention the early and sustained influence of "Pike's Magnolia" and other brands,[43] and wholly ignoring certain inborn propensities capable of wrecking unaided any

42. From the Choctaw word *bayuk*, a slow-moving, marshy tributary; here, of the Red River.
43. Of cheap whiskey.

ordinary existence. He had been lying down, and looked frouzy and half asleep.

"Ef I may so say, you 've got the better o' me, Mr.—er"—

"Santien, Grégoire Santien. I have the pleasure o' knowin' the lady you married, suh; an' I think I met you befo',—somew'ere o' 'nother," Grégoire added vaguely.

"Oh," drawled Aiken, waking up, "one o' them Red River[44] Sanchuns!" and his face brightened at the prospect before him of enjoying the society of one of the Santien boys. "Mortimer!" he called in ringing chest tones worthy a commander at the head of his troop. The negro had rested his axe and appeared to be listening to their talk, though he was too far to hear what they said.

"Mortimer, come along here an' take my frien' Mr. Sanchun's hoss. Git a move thar, git a move!" Then turning toward the entrance of the cabin he called back through the open door: "Rain!" it was his way of pronouncing 'Tite Reine's name. "Rain!" he cried again peremptorily; and turning to Grégoire: "she 's 'tendin' to some or other housekeepin' truck." 'Tite Reine was back in the yard feeding the solitary pig which they owned, and which Aiken had mysteriously driven up a few days before, saying he had bought it at Many.[45]

Grégoire could hear her calling out as she approached: "I 'm comin', Bud. Yere I come. W'at you want, Bud?" breathlessly, as she appeared in the door frame and looked out upon the narrow sloping gallery[46] where stood the two men. She seemed to Grégoire to have changed a good deal. She was thinner, and her eyes were larger, with an alert, uneasy look in them; he fancied the startled expression came from seeing him there unexpectedly. She wore cleanly homespun garments, the same she had brought with her from Bayou Pierre; but her shoes were in shreds. She uttered only a low, smothered exclamation when she saw Grégoire.

"Well, is that all you got to say to my frien' Mr. Sanchun? That 's the way with them Cajuns,"[47] Aiken offered apologetically to his guest; "ain't

44. The Red River, a major tributary of the Mississippi through central Louisiana, was lined with many prosperous plantations in the nineteenth century.

45. Small town in Sabine Parish.

46. Open porch extending the length of a house.

47. "'Cadians" or Acadians were French peasants who settled Nova Scotia in 1603 and were expelled by the British in 1755. Many resettled upriver from New Orleans in the rural areas

got sense enough to know a white man when they see one." Grégoire took her hand.

"I'm mighty glad to see you, 'Tite Reine," he said from his heart. She had for some reason been unable to speak; now she panted somewhat hysterically:—

"You mus' escuse me, Mista Grégoire. It's the truth I did n' know you firs', stan'in' up there." A deep flush had supplanted the former pallor of her face, and her eyes shone with tears and ill-concealed excitement.

"I thought you all lived yonda in Grant,"[48] remarked Grégoire carelessly, making talk for the purpose of diverting Aiken's attention away from his wife's evident embarrassment, which he himself was at a loss to understand.

"Why, we did live a right smart while in Grant; but Grant ain't no parish to make a livin' in. Then I tried Winn and Caddo[49] a spell; they was n't no better. But I tell you, suh, Sabine's a damn' sight worse than any of 'em. Why, a man can't git a drink o' whiskey here without going out of the parish fer it, or across into Texas. I'm fixin' to sell out an' try Vernon."[50]

Bud Aiken's household belongings surely would not count for much in the contemplated "selling out." The one room that constituted his home was extremely bare of furnishing,—a cheap bed, a pine table, and a few chairs, that was all. On a rough shelf were some paper parcels representing the larder. The mud daubing had fallen out here and there from between the logs of the cabin; and into the largest of these apertures had been thrust pieces of ragged bagging and wisps of cotton. A tin basin outside on the gallery offered the only bathing facilities to be seen. Notwithstanding these drawbacks, Grégoire announced his intention of passing the night with Aiken.

"I'm jus' goin' to ask the privilege o' layin' down yere on yo' gall'ry tonight, Mr. Aiken. My hoss ain't in firs'-class trim; an' a night's res' ain't goin' to hurt him o' me either." He had begun by declaring his intention of pushing on across the Sabine, but an imploring look from 'Tite Reine's eyes had stayed the words upon his lips. Never had he seen in a woman's

---

of Louisiana, where they maintained their distinctive language and customs until the late twentieth century.

48. Grant Parish is east of Natchitoches.

49. Winn and Caddo parishes are north and west of Natchitoches, suggesting Aiken's circling toward wilder territories.

50. An even less populated parish south of Sabine.

eyes a look of such heartbroken entreaty. He resolved on the instant to know the meaning of it before setting foot on Texas soil. Grégoire had never learned to steel his heart against a woman's eyes, no matter what language they spoke.

An old patchwork quilt folded double and a moss pillow which 'Tite Reine gave him out on the gallery made a bed that was, after all, not too uncomfortable for a young fellow of rugged habits.

Grégoire slept quite soundly after he laid down upon his improvised bed at nine o'clock. He was awakened toward the middle of the night by some one gently shaking him. It was 'Tite Reine stooping over him; he could see her plainly, for the moon was shining. She had not removed the clothing she had worn during the day; but her feet were bare and looked wonderfully small and white. He arose on his elbow, wide awake at once. "W'y, 'Tite Reine! w'at the devil you mean? w'ere 's yo' husban'?"

"The house kin fall on 'im, 't en goin' wake up Bud w'en he 's sleepin'; he drink' too much." Now that she had aroused Grégoire, she stood up, and sinking her face in her bended arm like a child, began to cry softly. In an instant he was on his feet.

"My God, 'Tite Reine! w'at 's the matta? you got to tell me w'at 's the matta." He could no longer recognize the imperious 'Tite Reine, whose will had been the law in her father's household. He led her to the edge of the low gallery and there they sat down.

Grégoire loved women. He liked their nearness, their atmosphere; the tones of their voices and the things they said; their ways of moving and turning about; the brushing of their garments when they passed him by pleased him. He was fleeing now from the pain that a woman had inflicted upon him. When any overpowering sorrow came to Grégoire he felt a singular longing to cross the Sabine River and lose himself in Texas. He had done this once before when his home, the old Santien place, had gone into the hands of creditors. The sight of 'Tite Reine's distress now moved him painfully.

"W'at is it, 'Tite Reine? tell me w'at it is," he kept asking her. She was attempting to dry her eyes on her coarse sleeve. He drew a handkerchief from his back pocket and dried them for her.

"They all well, yonda?" she asked, haltingly, "my popa? my moma? the chil'en?" Grégoire knew no more of the Baptiste Choupic family than the post beside him. Nevertheless he answered: "They all right well, 'Tite Reine, but they mighty lonesome of you."

"My popa, he got a putty good crop this yea'?"

"He made right smart o' cotton fo' Bayou Pierre."

"He done haul it to the relroad?"

"No, he ain't quite finish pickin'."

"I hope they all ent sole 'Putty Girl'?" she inquired solicitously.

"Well, I should say not! Yo' pa says they ain't anotha piece o' hossflesh in the pa'ish he 'd want to swap fo' 'Putty Girl.'" She turned to him with vague but fleeting amazement,—"Putty Girl" was a cow!

The autumn night was heavy about them. The black forest seemed to have drawn nearer; its shadowy depths were filled with the gruesome noises that inhabit a southern forest at night time.

"Ain't you 'fraid sometimes yere, 'Tite Reine?" Grégoire asked, as he felt a light shiver run through him at the weirdness of the scene.

"No," she answered promptly, "I ent 'fred o' nothin' 'cep' Bud."

"Then he treats you mean? I thought so!"

"Mista Grégoire," drawing close to him and whispering in his face, "Bud 's killin' me." He clasped her arm, holding her near him, while an expression of profound pity escaped him. "Nobody don' know, 'cep' Unc' Mort'mer," she went on. "I tell you, he beats me; my back an' arms—you ought to see—it 's all blue. He would 'a' choke' me to death one day w'en he was drunk, if Unc' Mort'mer had n' make 'im lef go—with his axe ov' his head." Grégoire glanced back over his shoulder toward the room where the man lay sleeping. He was wondering if it would really be a criminal act to go then and there and shoot the top of Bud Aiken's head off. He himself would hardly have considered it a crime, but he was not sure of how others might regard the act.

"That 's w'y I wake you up, to tell you," she continued. "Then sometime' he plague me mos' crazy; he tell me 't ent no preacher, it 's a Texas drummer[51] w'at marry him an' me; an' w'en I don' know w'at way to turn no mo', he say no, it 's a Meth'dis' archbishop, an' keep on laughin' 'bout me, an' I don' know w'at the truth!"

Then again, she told how Bud had induced her to mount the vicious little mustang[52] "Buckeye," knowing that the little brute would n't carry a woman; and how it had amused him to witness her distress and terror when she was thrown to the ground.

"If I would know how to read an' write, an' had some pencil an' paper, it 's long 'go I would wrote to my popa. But it 's no pos'office, it 's no rel-

51. "Drummer," traveling salesman.

52. Small, sturdy horse descended from Spanish stock and found on the North American plains.

road,—nothin' in Sabine. An' you know, Mista Grégoire, Bud say he 's goin' carry me yonda to Vernon, an' fu'ther off yet,—'way yonda, an' he 's goin' turn me loose. Oh, don' leave me yere, Mista Grégoire! don' leave me behine you!" she entreated, breaking once more into sobs.

"'Tite Reine," he answered, "do you think I 'm such a low-down scoundrel as to leave you yere with that"—He finished the sentence mentally, not wishing to offend the ears of 'Tite Reine.

They talked on a good while after that. She would not return to the room where her husband lay; the nearness of a friend had already emboldened her to inward revolt. Grégoire induced her to lie down and rest upon the quilt that she had given to him for a bed. She did so, and broken down by fatigue was soon fast asleep.

He stayed seated on the edge of the gallery and began to smoke cigarettes which he rolled himself of périque tobacco.[53] He might have gone in and shared Bud Aiken's bed, but preferred to stay there near 'Tite Reine. He watched the two horses, tramping slowly about the lot, cropping the dewy wet tufts of grass.

Grégoire smoked on. He only stopped when the moon sank down behind the pine-trees, and the long deep shadow reached out and enveloped him. Then he could no longer see and follow the filmy smoke from his cigarette, and he threw it away. Sleep was pressing heavily upon him. He stretched himself full length upon the rough bare boards of the gallery and slept until day-break.

Bud Aiken's satisfaction was very genuine when he learned that Grégoire proposed spending the day and another night with him. He had already recognized in the young creole[54] a spirit not altogether uncongenial to his own.

'Tite Reine cooked breakfast for them. She made coffee; of course there was no milk to add to it, but there was sugar. From a meal bag that stood in the corner of the room she took a measure of meal, and with it made a pone[55] of corn bread. She fried slices of salt pork. Then Bud sent her into the field to pick cotton with old Uncle Mortimer. The negro's cabin was the counterpart of their own, but stood quite a distance away hidden in the woods. He and Aiken worked the crop on shares.

53. Richly flavored tobacco unique to Louisiana and named after its developer, Pierre Chenet.

54. Technically, individuals born outside their parents' country of origin, especially of mixed racial heritage. In the nineteenth century, increasingly limited to persons of Spanish and/or French ancestry.

55. Oval loaf.

Early in the day Bud produced a grimy pack of cards from behind a parcel of sugar on the shelf. Grégoire threw the cards into the fire and replaced
them with a spic and span new "deck" that he took from his saddlebags.
He also brought forth from the same receptacle a bottle of whiskey, which
he presented to his host, saying that he himself had no further use for it,
as he had "sworn off" since day before yesterday, when he had made a fool
of himself in Cloutierville.[56]

They sat at the pine table smoking and playing cards all the morning, only desisting when 'Tite Reine came to serve them with the gumbo-
filé[57] that she had come out of the field to cook at noon. She could afford
to treat a guest to chicken gumbo, for she owned a half dozen chickens that
Uncle Mortimer had presented to her at various times. There were only
two spoons, and 'Tite Reine had to wait till the men had finished before
eating her soup. She waited for Grégoire's spoon, though her husband was
the first to get through. It was a very childish whim.

In the afternoon she picked cotton again; and the men played cards,
smoked, and Bud drank.

It was a very long time since Bud Aiken had enjoyed himself so well, and
since he had encountered so sympathetic and appreciative a listener to the
story of his eventful career. The story of 'Tite Reine's fall from the horse he
told with much spirit, mimicking quite skillfully the way in which she had
complained of never being permitted "to teck a li'le pleasure," whereupon
he had kindly suggested horseback riding. Grégoire enjoyed the story
amazingly, which encouraged Aiken to relate many more of a similar character. As the afternoon wore on, all formality of address between the two
had disappeared: they were "Bud" and "Grégoire" to each other, and Grégoire had delighted Aiken's soul by promising to spend a week with him.
'Tite Reine was also touched by the spirit of recklessness in the air; it moved
her to fry two chickens for supper. She fried them deliciously in bacon fat.
After supper she again arranged Grégoire's bed out on the gallery.

The night fell calm and beautiful, with the delicious odor of the pines
floating upon the air. But the three did not sit up to enjoy it. Before the
stroke of nine, Aiken had already fallen upon his bed unconscious of
everything about him in the heavy drunken sleep that would hold him
fast through the night. It even clutched him more relentlessly than usual,
thanks to Grégoire's free gift of whiskey.

56. In Chopin's novel *At Fault*, Grégoire killed a man in Cloutierville, which led to his rejection by a northern woman with whom he was in love.

57. Filé is powdered sassafras leaves added to thicken gumbo, a rich local soup.

The sun was high when he awoke. He lifted his voice and called imperiously for 'Tite Reine, wondering that the coffee-pot was not on the hearth, and marveling still more that he did not hear her voice in quick response with its, "I 'm comin', Bud. Yere I come." He called again and again. Then he arose and looked out through the back door to see if she were picking cotton in the field, but she was not there. He dragged himself to the front entrance. Grégoire's bed was still on the gallery, but the young fellow was nowhere to be seen.

Uncle Mortimer had come into the yard, not to cut wood this time, but to pick up the axe which was his own property, and lift it to his shoulder.

"Mortimer," called out Aiken, "whur 's my wife?" at the same time advancing toward the negro. Mortimer stood still, waiting for him. "Whur 's my wife an' that Frenchman? Speak out, I say, before I send you to h—l."

Uncle Mortimer never had feared Bud Aiken; and with the trusty axe upon his shoulder, he felt a double hardihood in the man's presence. The old fellow passed the back of his black, knotty hand unctuously over his lips, as though he relished in advance the words that were about to pass them. He spoke carefully and deliberately:

"Miss Reine," he said, "I reckon she mus' of done struck Natchitoches pa'ish sometime to'ard de middle o' de night, on dat 'ar swif' hoss o' Mr. Sanchun's."

Aiken uttered a terrific oath. "Saddle up Buckeye," he yelled, "before I count twenty, or I 'll rip the black hide off yer. Quick, thar! Thur ain't nothin' fourfooted top o' this earth that Buckeye can't run down." Uncle Mortimer scratched his head dubiously, as he answered:—

"Yes, Mas' Bud, but you see, Mr. Sanchun, he done cross de Sabine befo' sun-up on Buckeye."

The Storm

A SEQUEL TO "AT THE 'CADIAN BALL"[58]

I

The leaves were so still that even Bibi thought it was going to rain. Bobinôt, who was accustomed to converse on terms of perfect equality with his little son, called the child's attention to certain somber clouds that were

58. In "At the 'Cadian Ball," Bobinôt decides to attend the weekly community dance when he hears that Alcée Laballière, a wealthy planter, will be there courting Calixta. Alcée, despon-

rolling with sinister intention from the west, accompanied by a sullen, threatening roar. They were at Friedheimer's store and decided to remain there till the storm had passed. They sat within the door on two empty kegs. Bibi was four years old and looked very wise.

"Mama'll be 'fraid, yes," he suggested with blinking eyes.

"She'll shut the house. Maybe she got Sylvie helpin' her this evenin'," Bobinôt responded reassuringly.

"No; she ent got Sylvie. Sylvie was helpin' her yistiday," piped Bibi.

Bobinôt arose and going across to the counter purchased a can of shrimps, of which Calixta was very fond. Then he returned to his perch on the keg and sat stolidly holding the can of shrimps while the storm burst. It shook the wooden store and seemed to be ripping great furrows in the distant field. Bibi laid his little hand on his father's knee and was not afraid.

II

Calixta, at home, felt no uneasiness for their safety. She sat at a side window sewing furiously on a sewing machine. She was greatly occupied and did not notice the approaching storm. But she felt very warm and often stopped to mop her face on which the perspiration gathered in beads. She unfastened her white sacque [59] at the throat. It began to grow dark, and suddenly realizing the situation she got up hurriedly and went about closing windows and doors.

Out on the small front gallery [60] she had hung Bobinôt's Sunday clothes to air and she hastened out to gather them before the rain fell. As she stepped outside, Alcée Laballière rode in at the gate. She had not seen him very often since her marriage, and never alone. She stood there with Bobinôt's coat in her hands, and the big rain drops began to fall. Alcée rode his horse under the shelter of a side projection where the chickens had huddled and there were plows and a harrow piled up in the corner.

"May I come and wait on your gallery till the storm is over, Calixta?" he asked.

dent over losing his rice crop in a storm, urges Calixta to go with him again south to Assumption Parish, a few miles upriver from New Orleans, where rumors say they have already had an affair. But before Calixta can respond, Clarisse arrives to fetch Alcée home. Clarisse, the goddaughter of Alcée's mother, soon confesses her love for Alcée, who has left Calixta alone in the dark. Calixta then resignedly agrees to marry the overjoyed Bobinôt.

59. Loose-fitting dress.

60. Open porch extending the length of a house.

"Come 'long in, M'sieur Alcée."

His voice and her own startled her as if from a trance, and she seized Bobinôt's vest. Alcée, mounting to the porch, grabbed the trousers and snatched Bibi's braided jacket that was about to be carried away by a sudden gust of wind. He expressed an intention to remain outside, but it was soon apparent that he might as well have been out in the open: the water beat in upon the boards in driving sheets, and he went inside, closing the door after him. It was even necessary to put something beneath the door to keep the water out.

"My! what a rain! It's good two years sence it rain' like that," exclaimed Calixta as she rolled up a piece of bagging and Alcée helped her to thrust it beneath the crack.

She was a little fuller of figure than five years before when she married; but she had lost nothing of her vivacity. Her blue eyes still retained their melting quality; and her yellow hair, disheveled by the wind and rain, kinked more stubbornly than ever about her ears and temples.

The rain beat upon the low, shingled roof with a force and clatter that threatened to break an entrance and deluge them there. They were in the dining room — the sitting room — the general utility room. Adjoining was her bedroom, with Bibi's couch along side her own. The door stood open, and the room with its white, monumental bed, its closed shutters, looked dim and mysterious.

Alcée flung himself into a rocker and Calixta nervously began to gather up from the floor the lengths of a cotton sheet which she had been sewing.

"If this keeps up, *Dieu sait*[61] if the levees[62] goin' to stan' it!" she exclaimed.

"What have you got to do with the levees?"

"I got enough to do! An' there's Bobinôt with Bibi out in that storm — if he only didn' left Friedheimer's!"

"Let us hope, Calixta, that Bobinôt's got sense enough to come in out of a cyclone."

She went and stood at the window with a greatly disturbed look on her face. She wiped the frame that was clouded with moisture. It was stiflingly hot. Alcée got up and joined her at the window, looking over her shoulder. The rain was coming down in sheets obscuring the view of far-

61. "God (only) knows!" (Fr.).

62. Embankments built to prevent flooding, these are major features in the landscape along the lower Mississippi River.

off cabins and enveloping the distant wood in a gray mist. The playing of the lightning was incessant. A bolt struck a tall chinaberry tree at the edge of the field. It filled all visible space with a blinding glare and the crash seemed to invade the very boards they stood upon.

Calixta put her hands to her eyes, and with a cry, staggered backward. Alcée's arm encircled her, and for an instant he drew her close and spasmodically to him.

"*Bonté!*" [63] she cried, releasing herself from his encircling arm and retreating from the window, "the house'll go next! If I only knew w'ere Bibi was!" She would not compose herself; she would not be seated. Alcée clasped her shoulders and looked into her face. The contact of her warm, palpitating body when he had unthinkingly drawn her into his arms, had aroused all the old-time infatuation and desire for her flesh.

"Calixta," he said, "don't be frightened. Nothing can happen. The house is too low to be struck, with so many tall trees standing about. There! aren't you going to be quiet? say, aren't you?" He pushed her hair back from her face that was warm and steaming. Her lips were as red and moist as pomegranate seed. Her white neck and a glimpse of her full, firm bosom disturbed him powerfully. As she glanced up at him the fear in her liquid blue eyes had given place to a drowsy gleam that unconsciously betrayed a sensuous desire. He looked down into her eyes and there was nothing for him to do but to gather her lips in a kiss. It reminded him of Assumption.

"Do you remember—in Assumption, Calixta?" he asked in a low voice broken by passion. Oh! she remembered; for in Assumption he had kissed her and kissed and kissed her; until his senses would well nigh fail, and to save her he would resort to a desperate flight. If she was not an immaculate dove in those days, she was still inviolate; a passionate creature whose very defenselessness had made her defense, against which his honor forbade him to prevail. Now—well, now—her lips seemed in a manner free to be tasted, as well as her round, white throat and her whiter breasts.

They did not heed the crashing torrents, and the roar of the elements made her laugh as she lay in his arms. She was a revelation in that dim, mysterious chamber; as white as the couch she lay upon. Her firm, elastic flesh that was knowing for the first time its birthright, was like a creamy lily that the sun invites to contribute its breath and perfume to the undying life of the world.

63. "Gracious!" (Fr.).

The generous abundance of her passion, without guile or trickery, was like a white flame which penetrated and found response in depths of his own sensuous nature that had never yet been reached.

When he touched her breasts they gave themselves up in quivering ecstasy, inviting his lips. Her mouth was a fountain of delight. And when he possessed her, they seemed to swoon together at the very borderland of life's mystery.

He stayed cushioned upon her, breathless, dazed, enervated, with his heart beating like a hammer upon her. With one hand she clasped his head, her lips lightly touching his forehead. The other hand stroked with a soothing rhythm his muscular shoulders.

The growl of the thunder was distant and passing away. The rain beat softly upon the shingles, inviting them to drowsiness and sleep. But they dared not yield.

The rain was over; and the sun was turning the glistening green world into a palace of gems. Calixta, on the gallery, watched Alcée ride away. He turned and smiled at her with a beaming face; and she lifted her pretty chin in the air and laughed aloud.

III

Bobinôt and Bibi, trudging home, stopped without at the cistern to make themselves presentable.

"My! Bibi, w'at will yo' mama say! You ought to be ashame'. You oughtn' put on those good pants. Look at 'em! An' that mud on yo' collar! How you got that mud on yo' collar, Bibi? I never saw such a boy!" Bibi was the picture of pathetic resignation. Bobinôt was the embodiment of serious solicitude as he strove to remove from his own person and his son's the signs of their tramp over heavy roads and through wet fields. He scraped the mud off Bibi's bare legs and feet with a stick and carefully removed all traces from his heavy brogans.[64] Then, prepared for the worst— the meeting with an over-scrupulous housewife, they entered cautiously at the back door.

Calixta was preparing supper. She had set the table and was dripping coffee at the hearth. She sprang up as they came in.

"Oh, Bobinôt! You back! My! but I was uneasy. W'ere you been during the rain? An' Bibi? he ain't wet? he ain't hurt?" She had clasped Bibi and

64. Tied shoes of thick leather.

was kissing him effusively. Bobinôt's explanations and apologies which he had been composing all along the way, died on his lips as Calixta felt him to see if he were dry, and seemed to express nothing but satisfaction at their safe return.

"I brought you some shrimps, Calixta," offered Bobinôt, hauling the can from his ample side picket and laying it on the table.

"Shrimps! Oh, Bobinôt! you too good fo' anything!" and she gave him a smacking kiss on the cheek that resounded. "*J'vous réponds,*[65] we'll have a feas' to night! umph-umph!"

Bobinôt and Bibi began to relax and enjoy themselves, and when the three seated themselves at table they laughed much and so loud that any-one might have heard them as far away as Laballière's.

IV

Alcée Laballière wrote to his wife, Clarisse, that night. It was a loving let-ter, full of tender solicitude. He told her not to hurry back, but if she and the babies liked it at Biloxi,[66] to stay a month longer. He was getting on nicely; and though he missed them, he was willing to bear the separation a while longer—realizing that their health and pleasure were the first things to be considered.

V

As for Clarisse, she was charmed upon receiving her husband's letter. She and the babies were doing well. The society was agreeable; many of her old friends and acquaintances were at the bay. And the first free breath since her marriage seemed to restore the pleasant liberty of her maiden days. Devoted as she was to her husband, their intimate conjugal life was something which she was more than willing to forego for a while.

So the storm passed and every one was happy.

65. "I tell you" (Fr.).

66. Popular summer resort on the Mississippi Gulf Coast.

Paul Laurence Dunbar

(1872–1906)

THE SON OF FORMER Kentucky plantation slaves, Paul Laurence Dunbar was born in Dayton, Ohio, on June 17, 1872. Dunbar's literate and strong-willed father, Joshua, had escaped to Canada, but returned to fight for the Union, eventually settled in Dayton, and married Matilda Glass Burton Murphy. Matilda, a widow almost thirty years younger, had relocated to Dayton after the Civil War with her two sons. When Paul was four, the couple divorced. Matilda worked as a laundress to support Paul and his much older half-brothers, who soon moved to Chicago. The only African American in his high school, the bright and popular Paul was school newspaper editor and literary society president. At sixteen, he published his first poem in a Dayton paper and, with a school friend, founded a black newspaper that lasted six issues. These early literary successes were soon cut short. The recently graduated Dunbar, who had hoped to attend Harvard and study law, was denied employment because of his race. His eventual position as an elevator operator provided a modest income that at least permitted him to write.

Among his favorite authors (Shakespeare, Tennyson, Keats, Poe, Longfellow) was the Indiana poet James Whitcomb Riley, whose dialect poems Dunbar emulated. Determined to publish, Dunbar submitted short pieces and stories to local newspapers and, thanks to a former teacher, was invited to address the Western Association of Writers at its 1892 Dayton meeting. There he met Riley and other authors who were favorably impressed with Dunbar's poetry. Heartened, he gathered sufficient funds to publish his first collection of fifty-six poems, *Oak and Ivy* (1893). Carrying the volume with him to sell, Paul attended the World's Columbian Exposition in Chicago where he met the aging Frederick Douglass, who arranged for Dunbar to read. His performance gained the attention of two white benefactors (lawyer Charles A. Thatcher and psychiatrist Henry A. Tobey), who supported Dunbar throughout his life and who funded Dunbar's next volume of verse, *Majors and Minors* (1896). This volume attracted the interest of William Dean Howells, himself an Ohioan, who praised it in *Harper's Weekly* (1896) and found a publisher for Dunbar's third and best-selling poetry collection, *Lyrics of Lowly Life* (1896). Although other black writers preceded Dunbar and other black contemporaries (notably James Edwin Campbell and Daniel Webster Davis) wrote similar kinds of verse, none achieved the national celebrity that Dunbar would attain in the next decade. The appearance of his poems in leading magazines and a reading tour in England gained him international fame.

Dunbar's literary success was mirrored in his personal life. In 1895 he had begun corresponding with the highly educated and gifted New Orleanian writer Alice Ruth Moore. They married secretly in 1898, evading their families' disapproval: her mother's displeasure with his lack of education and dark complexion and his mother's uneasiness toward his beautiful fiancée's "uppity" family. By his early twenties, newlywed Dunbar had become the most popular poet in America, black or white. His dialect poetry endeared him to readers who had also delighted in the antics of black folk in plantation poetry by white apologists like Irwin Russell, whose poetic portraits of black folk influenced both Thomas Nelson Page and Joel Chandler Harris.

Dunbar wrote easily and rapidly, publishing novels, short fiction, dialect and nondialect poetry, essays, songs, and New York musicals. Even though Dunbar later eschewed his dialect poetry as "a jingle in a broken tongue," his poems secured his fame and have shaped his literary reputation, sometimes to the detriment of his other achievements. Dunbar walked, at times ungracefully, the line between commercial necessity and artistic integrity as an outspoken and well-read black man, committed to preserving the tenor, voice, and substance of African American heritage while, at the same time, identifying racial injustice.

Drawing on the popularity of local-color fiction and its capacity for realistic portraits of black life, Dunbar published his first volume of short stories, *Folks from Dixie* (1898), which included "Nelse Hatton's Vengeance." With Dunbar's adaptation of the popular plot of an ex-slave who meets and saves his former master, "Nelse Hatton" suggests the balance Dunbar sought between engaging and critiquing the antebellum stereotypes. Unlike Page and others, Dunbar fully recognizes the freedman's power and highlights the dignity, compassion, and self-sufficiency of blacks who prosper spiritually and economically in the north. That same year, Dunbar published a less favorably reviewed novel, *The Uncalled*, which presents the odyssey of a white, Midwestern protagonist who is likely Dunbar's surrogate. While Dunbar's fiction, like his poetry, often incorporates elements of nostalgia, it also takes thematic risks, including lynching, mob violence, political corruption, and white fanaticism.

With his literary fame relatively secure in the late 1890s, Dunbar used his national celebrity to address the increasing constraints on black life, as in "The Lynching of Jube Benson" from Dunbar's last collection, *The Heart of Happy Hollow* (1904). The story recounts the horror of "blood guilt" in a reluctant retrospective account by a white physician whose belief in the individual goodness of a gentle black man is swept away by the deep-seated stereotypes that draw the doctor into an act of racist violence. As the collection's ironic title and this grim story suggest, at the heart of these final Dunbar stories is a bitter recognition that the happiness of freed blacks is inevitably compromised and "hollow." Such pessimism likewise characterizes Dunbar's final novels—those with white protagonists, like *The Fanatics* (1901), and black, as in *The Sport of the Gods* (1902), whose account of the disintegration of a black family is a pioneering work of naturalism.

Dunbar's health began failing in 1898. Seeking a more temperate climate, he and his wife moved to Colorado, but financial problems soon forced them back to Washington, D.C. Dunbar's return was celebrated by the black community, and he was awarded an honorary doctorate in 1899 by Atlanta University. Recuperating with his longtime friend, admirer, and fellow poet James Weldon Johnson in Florida, Dunbar continued to be plagued with ill health and began drinking to lessen the pain. He and Alice separated in 1902, and he returned to live with his mother in Dayton. Suffering from alcoholism and tuberculosis, Dunbar, only thirty-four, died at his home on February 9, 1906.

Works by Paul Laurence Dunbar

POETRY

Oak and Ivy, 1893
Majors and Minors: Poems, 1895
Lyrics of Lowly Life, 1896
Lyrics of the Hearthside, 1899
Poems of Cabin and Field, 1899

Candle-lightin' Time, 1901

Lyrics of Love and Laughter, 1903

When Malindy Sings, 1903

Lil' Gal, 1904

Howdy, Honey, Howdy, 1905

Lyrics of Sunshine and Shadow, 1905

Joggin' Erlong, 1906

The Collected Poetry of Paul Laurence Dunbar, ed. Joanne M. Braxton, 1993

FICTION

Folks from Dixie, 1898

The Uncalled, a Novel, 1898

The Love of Landry, 1900

The Strength of Gideon and Other Stories, 1900

The Fanatics, 1901

The Sport of the Gods, 1902

In Old Plantation Days, 1903

The Heart of Happy Hollow 1904

The Best Stories of Paul Laurence Dunbar, ed. Benjamin Brawley, 1938

The Paul Laurence Dunbar Reader, ed. Jay Martin and Gossie H. Hudson, 1975

Further Reading

Baker, Houston A., Jr., *Blues, Ideology, and Afro-American Literature: A Vernacular Theory.* Chicago: University of Chicago Press, 1984.
———. *Singers of Daybreak: Studies in Black American Literature.* Washington: Howard University Press, 1974.
Brawley, Benjamin Griffith. *Paul Laurence Dunbar, Poet of His People.* Chapel Hill: University of North Carolina Press, 1936.
Bruce, Dickson D., Jr. *Black American Writing from the Nadir.* Baton Rouge: Louisiana State University Press, 1989.
Cunningham, Virginia. *Paul Laurence Dunbar and His Song.* New York: Dodd, Mead, 1947.
Dunbar, Alice Ruth Moore. *The Poet and His Song.* Philadelphia: AME Publishing House, 1914.
Harris, Trudier. *Exorcising Blackness: Historical and Literary Lynching and Burning Rituals.* Bloomington: Indiana University Press, 1984.

Martin, Jay, ed. *A Singer in the Dawn: Reinterpretations of Paul Laurence Dunbar.* New York: Dodd, Mead, 1975.

Metcalf, E. W. *Paul Laurence Dunbar: A Bibliography.* Metuchen, N.J.: Scarecrow Press, 1975.

Redding, J. Saunders. *To Make a Poet Black.* Chapel Hill: University of North Carolina Press, 1939.

Revell, Peter. *Paul Laurence Dunbar.* Boston: Twayne, 1979.

Wiggins, Lida Keck, and William Dean Howells. *The Life and Works of Paul Laurence Dunbar.* 1907; New York: Kraus Reprint, 1971.

Nelse Hatton's Vengeance

It was at the close of a summer day, and the sun was sinking dimly red over the hills of the little Ohio town which, for convenience, let us call Dexter.

The people had eaten their suppers, and the male portion of the families had come out in front of their houses to smoke and rest or read the evening paper. Those who had porches drew their rockers out on them, and sat with their feet on the railing. Others took their more humble positions on the front steps, while still others, whose houses were flush with the street, went even so far as to bring their chairs out upon the sidewalk, and over all there was an air of calmness and repose save when a glance through the open doors revealed the housewives busy at their evening dishes, or the blithe voices of the children playing in the street told that little Sally Waters was a-sitting in a saucer or asserted with doubtful veracity that London Bridge was falling down. Here and there a belated fisherman came straggling up the street that led from the river, every now and then holding up his string of slimy, wiggling catfish in answer to the query "Wha' 'd you ketch?"

To one who knew the generous and unprejudiced spirit of the Dexterites, it was no matter of wonder that one of their soundest and most highly respected citizens was a coloured man, and that his home should nestle unrebuked among the homes of his white neighbors.

Nelse Hatton had won the love and respect of his fellow-citizens by the straightforward honesty of his conduct and the warmth of his heart. Everybody knew him. He had been doing chores about Dexter,—cutting grass in summer, cleaning and laying carpets in the spring and fall, and tending furnaces in the winter,—since the time when, a newly emancipated man, he had passed over from Kentucky into Ohio. Since then through thrift he had attained quite a competence, and, as he himself expressed it, "owned some little propity." He was one among the number who had arisen to the dignity of a porch; and on this evening he was sitting thereon, laboriously spelling out the sentences in the *Evening News*— his reading was a *post-bellum*[1] accomplishment—when the oldest of his three children, Theodore, a boy of twelve, interrupted him with the intelligence that there was an "old straggler at the back door."

After admonishing the hope of his years as to the impropriety of applying such a term to an unfortunate, the father rose and sought the place where the "straggler" awaited him.

Nelse's sympathetic heart throbbed with pity at the sight that met his eye. The "straggler," a "thing of shreds and patches," was a man about his own age, nearing fifty; but what a contrast he was to the well-preserved, well-clothed black man! His gray hair straggled carelessly about his sunken temples, and the face beneath it was thin and emaciated. The hands that pulled at the fringe of the ragged coat were small and bony. But both the face and the hands were clean, and there was an open look in the bold, dark eye.

In strong contrast, too, with his appearance was the firm, well-modulated voice, somewhat roughened by exposure, in which he said, "I am very hungry; will you give me something to eat?" It was a voice that might have spoken with authority. There was none of the beggar's whine in it. It was clear and straightforward; and the man spoke the simple sentence almost as if it had been a protest against his sad condition.

"Jes' set down on the step an' git cool," answered Nelse, "an' I'll have something put on the table."

The stranger silently did as he was bidden, and his host turned into the house.

Eliza Hatton had been quietly watching proceedings, and as her husband entered the kitchen she said, "Look a-here, Nelse, you shorely ain't a-goin' to have that tramp in the kitchen a-settin' up to the table?"

"Why, course," said Nelse; "he's human, ain't he?"

"That don't make no difference. I bet none of these white folks round here would do it."

"That ain't none of my business," answered her husband. "I believe in every person doin' their own duty. Put somethin' down on the table; the man's hungry. An' don't never git stuck up, 'Lizy; you don't know what our children have got to come to."

---

1. "After the war" (*post* + *bellum*) (Gr.).

Nelse Hatton was a man of few words; but there was a positive manner about him at times that admitted of neither argument nor resistance.

His wife did as she was bidden, and then swept out in the majesty of wounded dignity, as the tramp was ushered in and seated before the table whose immaculate white cloth she had been prudent enough to change for a red one.

The man ate as if he were hungry, but always as if he were a hungry gentleman. There was something in his manner that impressed Nelse that he was not feeding a common tramp as he sat and looked at his visitor in polite curiosity. After a somewhat continued silence he addressed the man: "Why don't you go to your own people when you're hungry instead of coming to us coloured folks?"

There was no reproof in his tone, only inquiry.

The stranger's eyes flashed suddenly.

"Go to them up here?" he said; "never. They would give me my supper with their hypocritical patronage and put it down to charity. You give me something to eat as a favor. Your gift proceeds from disinterested kindness; they would throw me a bone because they thought it would weigh something in the balance against their sins. To you I am an unfortunate man; to them I am a tramp."

The stranger had spoken with much heat and no hesitation; but his ardour did not take the form of offense at Nelse's question. He seemed perfectly to comprehend the motive which actuated it.

Nelse had listened to him with close attention, and at the end of his harangue he said, "You had n't ought to be so hard on your own people; they mean well enough."

"My own people!" the stranger flashed back. "My people are the people of the South,—the people who have in their veins the warm, generous blood of Dixie!"

"I don't see what you stay in the North fur ef you don't like the people."

"I am not staying; I 'm getting away from it as fast as I can. I only came because I thought, like a lot of other poor fools, that the North had destroyed my fortunes and it might restore them; but five years of fruitless struggle in different places out of Dixie have shown me that it is n't the place for a man with blood in his veins. I thought that I was reconstructed; but I 'm not. My State did n't need it, but I did."

"Where 're you from?"

"Kentucky; and there's where I 'm bound for now. I want to get back where people have hearts and sympathies."

The coloured man was silent. After a while he said, and his voice was tremulous as he thought of the past, "I 'm from Kintucky, myself."

"I knew that you were from some place in the South. There's no mistaking our people, black or white, wherever you meet them. Kentucky's a great State, sir. She did n't secede; but there were lots of her sons on the other side. I was; and I did my duty as clear as I could see it."

"That's all any man kin do," said Nelse; "an' I ain't a-blamin' you. I lived with as good people as ever was. I know they would n't 'a' done nothin' wrong ef they'd 'a' knowed it; an' they was on the other side."

"You 've been a slave, then?"

"Oh, yes, I was born a slave; but the War freed me."

"I reckon you would n't think that my folks ever owned slaves; but they did. Everybody was good to them except me, and I was young and liked to show my authority. I had a little black boy that I used to cuff around a good deal, altho' he was near to me as a brother. But sometimes he would turn on me and give me the trouncing that I deserved. He would have been skinned for it if my father had found it out; but I was always too much ashamed of being thrashed to tell."

The speaker laughed, and Nelse joined him. "Bless my soul!" he said, "ef that ain't jes' the way it was with me an' my Mas' Tom——"

"Mas' Tom!" cried the stranger; "man, what's your name?"

"Nelse Hatton," replied the Negro.

"Heavens, Nelse! I'm your young Mas' Tom. I'm Tom Hatton; don't you know me, boy?"

"You can't be——you can't be!" exclaimed the Negro.

"I am, I tell you. Don't you remember the scar I got on my head from falling off old Baldy's back? Here it is. Can't you see?" cried the stranger, lifting the long hair away from one side of his brow. "Does n't this convince you?"

"It's you——it's you; 't ain't nobody else but Mas' Tom!" and the ex-slave and his former master rushed joyously into each other's arms.

There was no distinction of colour or condition there. There was no thought of superiority on the one hand, or feeling of inferiority on the other. They were simply two loving friends who had been long parted and had met again.

After a while the Negro said, "I'm sure the Lord must 'a' sent you right here to this house, so's you wouldn't be eatin' off o' none o' these poor white people 'round here."

"I reckon you 're religious now, Nelse; but I see it ain't changed your feeling toward poor white people."

"I don't know about that. I used to be purty bad about 'em."

"Indeed you did. Do you remember the time we stoned the house of old Nat, the white wood-sawyer?"[2]

"Well, I reckon I do! Was n't we awful, them days?" said Nelse, with forced contrition, but with something almost like a chuckle in his voice.

And yet there was a great struggle going on in the mind of this black man. Thirty years of freedom and the advantages of a Northern State made his whole soul revolt at the word "master." But that fine feeling, that tender sympathy, which is natural to the real Negro, made him hesitate to make the poor wreck of former glory conscious of his changed estate by using a different appellation. His warm sympathies conquered.

"I want you to see my wife and boys, Mas' Tom," he said, as he passed out of the room.

Eliza Hatton sat in her neatly appointed little front room, swelling with impotent rage.

If this story were chronicling the doings of some fanciful Negro, or some really rude plantation hand, it might be said that the "front room was filled with a conglomeration of cheap but pretentious furniture, and the walls covered with gaudy prints"—this seems to be the usual phrase. But in it the chronicler too often forgets how many Negroes were house-servants, and from close contact with their master's families imbibed aristocratic notions and quiet but elegant tastes.

This front room was very quiet in its appointments. Everything in it was subdued except—Mrs. Hatton. She was rocking back and forth in a light little rocker that screeched the indignation she could not express. She did not deign to look at Nelse as he came into the room; but an acceleration of speed on the part of the rocker showed that his presence was known.

Her husband's enthusiasm suddenly died out as he looked at her; but he put on a brave face as he said,—

"'Lizy, I bet a cent you can't guess who that pore man in there is."

The rocker suddenly stopped its violent motion with an equally violent jerk, as the angry woman turned upon her husband.

"No, I can't guess," she cried; "an' I don't want to. It's enough to be settin' an on'ry ol' tramp down to my clean table, without havin' me spend my time guessin' who he is."

"But look a-here, 'Lizy, this is all different; an' you don't understand."

"Don't care how different it is, I do' want to understand."

2. One who saws rather than chops wood to produce shingles, planks, and boards.

"You 'll be mighty su'prised, I tell you."

"I 'low I will; I'm su'prised already at you puttin' yourself on a level with tramps." This with fine scorn.

"Be careful, 'Lizy, be careful; you don't know who a tramp may turn out to be."

"That ol' humbug in there has been tellin' you some big tale, an' you ain't got no more sense 'an to believe it; I 'spect he's crammin' his pockets full of my things now. Ef you don't care, I do."

The woman rose and started toward the door, but her husband stopped her. "You must n't go out there that way," he said. "I want you to go out, you an' the childern; but I want you to go right—that man is the son of my ol' master, my young Mas' Tom, as I used to call him."

She fell back suddenly and stared at him with wide-open eyes.

"Your master!"

"Yes, it 's young Mas' Tom Hatton."

"An' you want me an' the childern to see him, do you?"

"Why, yes, I thought—"

"Humph! that 's the slave in you yet," she interrupted. "I thought thirty years had made you free! Ain't that the man you told me used to knock you 'round so?"

"Yes, 'Lizy; but—"

"Ain't he the one that made you haul him in the wheelbar', an' whipped you because you could n't go fast enough?"

"Yes, yes; but that—"

"Ain't he the one that lef' that scar there?" she cried, with a sudden motion of her hand toward his neck.

"Yes," said Nelse, very quietly; but he put his hand up and felt the long, cruel scar that the lash of a whip had left, and a hard light came into his eyes.

His wife went on: "An' you want to take me an' the childern in to see that man? No!" The word came with almost a snarl. "Me an' my childern are free born, an', ef I kin help it, they sha'n't never look at the man that laid the lash to their father's back! Shame on you, Nelse, shame on you, to want your childern, that you 're tryin' to raise independent,—to want 'em to see the man that you had to call 'master'!"

The man's lips quivered, and his hand opened and shut with a convulsive motion; but he said nothing.

"What did you tell me?" she asked. "Didn't you say that if you ever met him again in this world you 'd—"

"Kill him!" burst forth the man; and all the old, gentle look had gone out of his face, and there was nothing but fierceness and bitterness there, as his mind went back to his many wrongs.

"Go on away from the house, 'Lizy," he said hoarsely; "if anything happens, I do' want you an' the childern around."

"I do' want you to kill him, Nelse, so you'll git into trouble; but jes' give him one good whippin' for those he used to give you."

"Go on away from the house"; and the man's lips were tightly closed. She threw a thin shawl over her head and went out.

As soon as she had gone Nelse's intense feeling got the better of him, and, falling down with his face in a chair, he cried, in the language which the Sunday sermons had taught him, "Lord, Lord, thou hast delivered mine enemy into my hands!"

But it was not a prayer; it was rather a cry of anger and anguish from an overburdened heart. He rose, with the same hard gleam in his eyes, and went back toward the kitchen. One hand was tightly clinched till the muscles and veins stood out like cords, and with the other he unconsciously fingered the lash's scar.

"Could n't find your folks, eh, Nelse?" said the white Hatton.

"No," growled Nelse; and continued hurriedly, "Do you remember that scar?"

"Well enough — well enough," answered the other, sadly; "and it must have hurt you, Nelse."

"Hurt me! yes," cried the Negro.

"Ay," said Tom Hatton, as he rose and put his hand softly on the black scar; "and it has hurt me many a day since, though time and time again I have suffered pains that were as cruel as this must have been to you. Think of it, Nelse; there have been times when I, a Hatton, have asked bread of the very people whom a few years ago I scorned. Since the War everything has gone against me. You do not know how I have suffered. For thirty years life has been a curse to me; but I am going back to Kentucky now, and when I get there I'll lay it down without a regret."

All the anger had melted from the Negro's face, and there were tears in his eyes as he cried, "You sha'n't do it, Mas' Tom, — you sha'n't do it."

His destructive instinct had turned to one of preservation.

"But, Nelse, I have no further hopes," said the dejected man.

"You have, and you shall have. You 're goin' back to Kintucky, an' you 're goin' back a gentleman. I kin he'p you, an' I will; you 're welcome to the last I have."

"God bless you, Nelse——"

"Mas' Tom, you used to be jes' about my size, but you 're slimmer now; but——but I hope you won't be mad ef I ask you to put on a suit o' mine. It's put' nigh brand-new, an'——"

"Nelse, I can't do it! Is this the way you pay me for the blows——"

"Heish your mouth; ef you don't I 'll slap you down!" Nelse said it with mock solemnity, but there was an ominous quiver about his lips.

"Come in this room, suh"; and the master obeyed. He came out arrayed in Nelse's best and newest suit. The coloured man went to a drawer, over which he bent laboriously. Then he turned and said: "This 'll pay your passage to Kintucky, an' leave somethin' in your pocket besides. Go home, Mas' Tom,——go home!"

"Nelse, I can't do it; this is too much!"

"Doggone my cats, ef you don't go on——"

The white man stood bowed for a moment; then, straightening up, he threw his head back. "I 'll take it, Nelse; but you shall have every cent back, even if I have to sell my body to a medical college and use a gun to deliver the goods! Good-bye, Nelse, God bless you! goodbye."

"Good-bye, Mas' Tom, but don't talk that way; go home. The South is changed, an' you 'll find somethin' to suit you. Go home——go home; an' ef there 's any of the folks a-livin', give 'em my love, Mas' Tom——give 'em my love——good-bye——good-bye!"

The Negro leaned over the proffered hand, and his tears dropped upon it. His master passed out, and he sat with his head bowed in his hands.

After a long while Eliza came creeping in.

"Wha' 'd you do to him, Nelse——wha' 'd you do to him?" There was no answer. "Lawd, I hope you ain't killed him," she said, looking fearfully around. "I don't see no blood."

"I ain't killed him," said Nelse. "I sent him home——back to the ol' place."

"You sent him home! how 'd you send him, huh?"

"I give him my Sunday suit and that money——don't git mad, 'Lizy, don't git mad——that money I was savin' for your cloak. I could n't help it, to save my life. He 's goin' back home among my people, an' I sent 'em my love. Don't git mad an' I 'll git you a cloak anyhow."

"Pleggone³ the cloak!" said Mrs. Hatton, suddenly, all the woman in her rising in her eyes. "I was so 'fraid you 'd take my advice an' do some-

---

3. "A plague on" (Old English).

thin' wrong. Ef you're happy, Nelse, I am too. I don't grudge your master nothin'—the ol' devil! But you 're jes' a good-natured, big-hearted, weak-headed ol' fool!" And she took his head in her arms.

Great tears rolled down the man's cheeks, and he said: "Bless God, 'Lizy, I feel as good as a young convert."

The Lynching of Jube Benson

Gordon Fairfax's library held but three men, but the air was dense with clouds of smoke. The talk had drifted from one topic to another much as the smoke wreaths had puffed, floated, and thinned away. Then Handon Gay, who was an ambitious young reporter, spoke of a lynching story in a recent magazine, and the matter of punishment without trial put new life into the conversation.

"I should like to see a real lynching," said Gay rather callously.

"Well, I should hardly express it that way," said Fairfax, "but if a real, live lynching were to come my way, I should not avoid it."

"I should," spoke the other from the depths of his chair, where he had been puffing in moody silence. Judged by his hair, which was freely sprinkled with gray, the speaker might have been a man of forty-five or fifty, but his face, though lined and serious, was youthful, the face of a man hardly past thirty.

"What, you, Dr. Melville? Why, I thought that you physicians wouldn't weaken at anything."

"I have seen one such affair," said the doctor gravely, "in fact, I took a prominent part in it."

"Tell us about it," said the reporter, feeling for his pencil and note-book, which he was, nevertheless, careful to hide from the speaker.

The men drew their chairs eagerly up to the doctor's, but for a minute he did not seem to see them, but sat gazing abstractedly into the fire, then he took a long draw upon his cigar and began:

"I can see it all very vividly now. It was in the summer time and about seven years ago. I was practising at the time down in the little town of Bradford. It was a small and primitive place, just the location for an impecunious medical man, recently out of college.

"In lieu of a regular office, I attended to business in the first of two rooms which I rented from Hiram Daly, one of the more prosperous of the townsmen. Here I boarded and here also came my patients—white and black—whites from every section, and blacks from 'nigger town,' as the west portion of the place was called.

"The people about me were most of them coarse and rough, but they were simple and generous, and as time passed on I had about abandoned my intention of seeking distinction in wider fields and determined to settle into the place of a modest country doctor. This was rather a strange conclusion for a young man to arrive at, and I will not deny that the presence in the house of my host's beautiful young daughter, Annie, had something to do with my decision. She was a beautiful young girl of seventeen or eighteen, and very far superior to her surroundings. She had a native grace and a pleasing way about her that made everybody that came under her spell her abject slave. White and black who knew her loved her, and none, I thought, more deeply and respectfully than Jube Benson, the black man of all work about the place.

"He was a fellow whom everybody trusted; an apparently steady-going, grinning sort, as we used to call him. Well, he was completely under Miss Annie's thumb, and would fetch and carry for her like a faithful dog. As soon as he saw that I began to care for Annie, and anybody could see that, he transferred some of his allegiance to me and became my faithful servitor also. Never did a man have a more devoted adherent in his wooing than did I, and many a one of Annie's tasks which he volunteered to do gave her an extra hour with me. You can imagine that I liked the boy and you need not wonder any more that as both wooing and my practice waxed apace, I was content to give up my great ambitions and stay just where I was.

"It wasn't a very pleasant thing, then, to have an epidemic of typhoid[4] break out in the town that kept me going so that I hardly had time for the courting that a fellow wants to carry on with his sweetheart while he is still young enough to call her his girl. I fumed, but duty was duty, and I kept to my work night and day. It was now that Jube proved how invaluable he was as a coadjutor. He not only took messages to Annie, but brought sometimes little ones from her to me, and he would tell me little secret things that he had overheard her say that made me throb with joy and swear at him for repeating his mistress' conversation. But best of all, Jube was a perfect Cerberus,[5] and no one on earth could have been more effective in keeping away or deluding the other young fellows who visited

4. An infectious, often fatal disease spread under unsanitary conditions in food, drink, bathing water, and through personal contact.

5. In Greek myth, a fierce three-headed hound who guards the gates of Hades, permitting only the dead to enter and none to leave.

the Dalys. He would tell me of it afterward, chuckling softly to himself. 'An,' Doctah, I say to Mistah Hemp Stevens, "'Scuse us, Mistah Stevens, but Miss Annie, she des gone out," an' den he go outer de gate lookin' moughty lonesome. When Sam Elkins come, I say, "Sh, Mistah Elkins, Miss Annie, she done tuk down," an' he say, "What, Jube, you don' reckon hit de—" Den he stop an' look skeert, an' I say, "I feared hit is, Mistah Elkins," an' sheks my haid ez solemn. He goes outer de gate lookin' lak his bes' frien' done daid, an' all de time Miss Annie behine de cu'tain ovah de po'ch des' a laffin' fit to kill.'

"Jube was a most admirable liar, but what could I do? He knew that I was a young fool of a hypocrite, and when I would rebuke him for these deceptions, he would give way and roll on the floor in an excess of delighted laughter until from very contagion I had to join him—and, well, there was no need of my preaching when there had been no beginning to his repentance and when there must ensue a continuance of his wrong-doing.

"This thing went on for over three months, and then, pouf! I was down like a shot. My patients were nearly all up, but the reaction from overwork made me an easy victim of the lurking germs. Then Jube loomed up as a nurse. He put everyone else aside, and with the doctor, a friend of mine from a neighbouring town, took entire charge of me. Even Annie herself was put aside, and I was cared for as tenderly as a baby. Tom, that was my physician and friend, told me all about it afterward with tears in his eyes. Only he was a big, blunt man and his expressions did not convey all that he meant. He told me how my nigger had nursed me as if I were a sick kitten and he my mother. Of how fiercely he guarded his right to be the sole one to 'do' for me, as he called it, and how, when the crisis came, he hovered, weeping, but hopeful, at my bedside, until it was safely passed, when they drove him, weak and exhausted, from the room. As for me, I knew little about it at the time, and cared less. I was too busy in my fight with death. To my chimerical vision there was only a black but gentle demon that came and went, alternating with a white fairy, who would insist on coming in on her head, growing larger and larger and then dissolving. But the pathos and devotion in the story lost nothing in my blunt friend's telling.

"It was during the period of a long convalescence, however, that I came to know my humble ally as he really was, devoted to the point of abjectness. There were times when for very shame at his goodness to me, I would beg him to go away, to do something else. He would go, but before I had time to realise that I was not being ministered to, he would be back at my side, grinning and pottering just the same. He manufactured duties for the joy of performing them. He pretended to see desires in me that I never had, because he liked to pander to them, and when I became entirely exasperated, and ripped out a good round oath, he chuckled with the remark, 'Dah, now, you sholy is gittin' well. Nevah did hyeah a man anywhaih nigh Jo'dan's sho'[6] cuss lak dat.'

"Why, I grew to love him, love him, oh, yes, I loved him as well—oh, what am I saying? All human love and gratitude are damned poor things; excuse me, gentlemen, this isn't a pleasant story. The truth is usually a nasty thing to stand.

"It was not six months after that that my friendship to Jube, which he had been at such great pains to win, was put to too severe a test.

"It was in the summer again, and as business was slack, I had ridden over to see my friend, Dr. Tom. I had spent a good part of the day there, and it was past four o'clock when I rode leisurely into Bradford. I was in a particularly joyous mood and no premonition of the impending catastrophe oppressed me. No sense of sorrow, present or to come, forced itself upon me, even when I saw men hurrying through the almost deserted streets. When I got within sight of my home and saw a crowd surrounding it, I was only interested sufficiently to spur my horse into a jog trot, which brought me up to the throng, when something in the sullen, settled horror in the men's faces gave me a sudden, sick thrill. They whispered a word to me, and without a thought, save for Annie, the girl who had been so surely growing into my heart, I leaped from the saddle and tore my way through the people to the house.

"It was Annie, poor girl, bruised and bleeding, her face and dress torn from struggling. They were gathered round her with white faces, and, oh, with what terrible patience they were trying to gain from her fluttering lips the name of her murderer. They made way for me and I knelt at her side. She was beyond my skill, and my will merged with theirs. One thought was in our minds.

" 'Who?' I asked.

"Her eyes half opened, 'That black ———' She fell back into my arms dead.

"We turned and looked at each other. The mother had broken down and was weeping, but the face of the father was like iron.

6. "Near Jordan's shore," that is, the Jordan River, the site of Jesus' baptism, also prefigures the Christian's "crossing over" into death.

" 'It is enough,' he said; 'Jube has disappeared.' He went to the door and said to the expectant crowd, 'She is dead.'

"I heard the angry roar without swelling up like the noise of a flood, and then I heard the sudden movement of many feet as the men separated into searching parties, and laying the dead girl back upon her couch, I took my rifle and went out to join them.

"As if by intuition the knowledge had passed among the men that Jube Benson had disappeared, and he, by common consent, was to be the object of our search. Fully a dozen of the citizens had seen him hastening toward the woods and noted his skulking air, but as he had grinned in his old good-natured way, they had, at the time, thought nothing of it. Now, however, the diabolical reason of his slyness was apparent. He had been shrewd enough to disarm suspicion, and by now was far away. Even Mrs. Daly, who was visiting with a neighbour, had seen him stepping out by a back way, and had said with a laugh, 'I reckon that black rascal's a-running off somewhere.' Oh, if she had only known.

" 'To the woods! To the woods!' that was the cry, and away we went, each with the determination not to shoot, but to bring the culprit alive into town, and then to deal with him as his crime deserved.

"I cannot describe the feelings I experienced as I went out that night to beat the woods for this human tiger. My heart smouldered within me like a coal, and I went forward under the impulse of a will that was half my own, half some more malignant power's. My throat throbbed drily, but water nor whiskey would not have quenched my thirst. The thought has come to me since that now I could interpret the panther's desire for blood and sympathise with it, but then I thought nothing. I simply went forward, and watched, watched with burning eyes for a familiar form that I had looked for as often before with such different emotions.

"Luck or ill-luck, which you will, was with our party, and just as dawn was graying the sky, we came upon our quarry crouched in the corner of a fence. It was only half light, and we might have passed, but my eyes had caught sight of him, and I raised the cry. We leveled our guns and he rose and came toward us.

" 'I t'ought you wa'n't gwine see me,' he said sullenly, 'I didn't mean no harm.'

" 'Harm!'

"Some of the men took the word up with oaths, others were ominously silent.

"We gathered around him like hungry beasts, and I began to see terror

294 · PAUL LAURENCE DUNBAR

dawning in his eyes. He turned to me, 'I's moughty glad you's hyeah, doc,' he said, 'you ain't gwine let 'em whup me.'

" 'Whip you, you hound!' I said, 'I'm going to see you hanged,' and in the excess of my passion I struck him full on the mouth. He made a motion as if to resent the blow against even such odds, but controlled himself.

" 'W'y, doctah,' he exclaimed in the saddest voice I have ever heard, 'w'y, doctah! I ain't stole nuffin' o' yo'n, an' I was comin' back. I only run off to see my gal, Lucy, ovah to de Centah.'

" 'You lie!' I said, and my hands were busy helping the others bind him upon a horse. Why did I do it? I don't know. A false education, I reckon, one false from the beginning. I saw his black face glooming there in the half light, and I could only think of him as a monster. It's tradition. At first I was told that the black man would catch me, and when I got over that, they taught me that the devil was black, and when I had recovered from the sickness of that belief, here were Jube and his fellows with faces of menacing blackness. There was only one conclusion: This black man stood for all the powers of evil, the result of whose machinations had been gathering in my mind from childhood up. But this has nothing to do with what happened.

"After firing a few shots to announce our capture, we rode back into town with Jube. The ingathering parties from all directions met us as we made our way up to the house. All was very quiet and orderly. There was no doubt that it was as the papers would have said, a gathering of the best citizens. It was a gathering of stern, determined men, bent on a terrible vengeance.

"We took Jube into the house, into the room where the corpse lay. At sight of it, he gave a scream like an animal's and his face went the colour of storm-brown water. This was enough to condemn him. We divined, rather than heard, his cry of 'Miss Ann, Miss Ann, oh, my God, doc, you don't t'ink I done it?'

"Hungry hands were ready. We hurried him out into the yard. A rope was ready. A tree was at hand. Well, that part was the least of it, save that Hiram Daly stepped aside to let me be the first to pull upon the rope. It was lax at first. Then it tightened, and I felt the quivering soft weight resist my muscles. Other hands joined, and Jube swung off his feet.

"No one was masked. We knew each other. Not even the culprit's face was covered, and the last I remember of him as he went into the air was a look of sad reproach that will remain with me until I meet him face to face again.

"We were tying the end of the rope to a tree, where the dead man might hang as a warning to his fellows, when a terrible cry chilled us to the marrow.

" 'Cut 'im down, cut 'im down, he ain't guilty. We got de one. Cut him down, fu' Gawd's sake. Here's de man, we foun' him hidin' in de barn!'

"Jube's brother, Ben, and another Negro, came rushing toward us, half dragging, half carrying a miserable-looking wretch between them. Someone cut the rope and Jube dropped lifeless to the ground.

" 'Oh, my Gawd, he's daid, he's daid!' wailed the brother, but with blazing eyes he brought his captive into the centre of the group, and we saw in the full light the scratched face of Tom Skinner—the worst white ruffian in the town—but the face we saw was not as we were accustomed to see it, merely smeared with dirt. It was blackened to imitate a Negro's.

" 'God forgive me; I could not wait to try to resuscitate Jube. I knew he was already past help, so I rushed into the house and to the dead girl's side. In the excitement they had not yet washed or laid her out. Carefully, carefully, I searched underneath her broken finger nails. There was skin there. I took it out, the little curled pieces, and went with it to my office.

"There, determinedly, I examined it under a powerful glass, and read my own doom. It was the skin of a white man, and in it were embedded strands of short, brown hair or beard.

"How I went out to tell the waiting crowd I do not know, for something kept crying in my ears, 'Blood guilty! Blood guilty!'

"The men went away stricken into silence and awe. The new prisoner attempted neither denial nor plea. When they were gone I would have helped Ben carry his brother in, but he waved me away fiercely, 'You he'ped murder my brothah, you dat was *his* frien', go 'way, go 'way! I'll tek him home myse'f.' I could only respect his wish, and he and his comrade took up the dead man and between them bore him up the street on which the sun was now shining full.

"I saw the few men who had not skulked indoors uncover as they passed, and I—I—stood there between the two murdered ones, while all the while something in my ears kept crying, 'Blood guilty! Blood guilty!' "

The doctor's head dropped into his hands and he sat for some time in silence, which was broken by neither of the men, then he rose, saying, "Gentlemen, that was my last lynching."

Alice Ruth Moore Dunbar-Nelson

(1875–1935)

BORN IN NEW ORLEANS on July 19, 1875, Alice Ruth Moore was the daughter of Patricia Wright, a former slave from southwest Louisiana, and Joseph Moore, a (probably white and mostly absent) seaman. Though her mother worked as a seamstress to support her two daughters, Alice had a relatively privileged childhood. She attended public schools and graduated from the two-year teacher's program of Straight College (now Dillard University) in 1892. At Straight, she came into contact with many of the city's elite activists, including Louis A. Martinet, an attorney involved in the *Plessy v. Ferguson* court case. She later studied at Cornell, Columbia, and the University of Pennsylvania. For four years after graduation she taught elementary school and was active in Creole literary and social circles. Regal, well-versed in opera and fine arts, she was also an accomplished violinist and cellist. She began publishing poetry and in 1895 published her first book, *Violets and Other Tales,* an eclectic collection of poems and sketches, the first such compilation by an African American woman.

One of her poems caught the attention of Paul Dunbar, who, though only two years her senior, already had a national reputation as a writer of black dialect poetry. He initiated a two-year correspondence that culminated in their marriage on March 6, 1898. Neither mother particularly approved of the relationship, in part because of color differences: the Creole Alice was very fair while Paul was very dark. Nonetheless, the two settled first in New York and later in Washington, D.C. The marriage, however, proved volatile, and in 1902 Alice moved with her mother and her sister's family to Wilmington, Delaware. Dunbar died in 1906, still estranged from his wife, though she retained his name even after a brief, ill-fated union to a high-school teacher in 1910 and her much happier marriage in 1916 to journalist Robert Nelson.

With Dunbar's support, Dunbar-Nelson published her second book, *The Goodness of St. Rocque and Other Stories* (1899), as a companion volume to Dunbar's *Poems of Cabin and Field.* Dunbar-Nelson stated in an early letter that she felt challenged by the popularity of George W. Cable and Grace King to tell her version of New Orleans culture. While most of the stories do reflect the complexities of that famous city, Dunbar-Nelson carefully codes their racial implications and even more discreetly couples issues of race with gender. She might well have been wary of a national audience that was not sympathetic to black perspectives; however, her self-described "pretty creole" stories often reflect shocking domestic violence, working-class conflict, male deceit, women's economic oppression, and racial strife. Dunbar-Nelson also explores interethnic tensions between Germans and Italians in "Tony's Wife," a bitter portrait of an immigrant woman's life in a culture that barely sees her as human. Similarly, "The Praline Woman" evokes in its miniature monologue the suppressed anger and despair of Tante Marie, who tells about her life as she sells her sweet wares for strangers' consumption. One of the collection's most highly re-garded stories, "Sister Josepha," takes up the plight of the "tragic mu-latta," a woman of uncertain heritage caught on the color line, who re-treats to the white safety of a convent when she recognizes the liability of her "namelessness." Unlike similar stories by white writers, Josepha's di-lemma is not settled by death, but by a chilling erasure of all identity.

While "Sister Josepha" suppresses the dilemma of being a racially mixed woman at the end of the nineteenth century, "The Stones of the Village," a later unpublished story that Dunbar-Nelson had hoped to expand into a novel, straightforwardly portrays the cruelties of racism and racial self-loathing. The anguish and bitterness of this story, echoed in au-tobiographical essays like "Brass Ankles Speaks," betray Dunbar-Nelson's own experience of prejudice, both from within and without the black community, on account of color. Dunbar-Nelson's frustration at the *Atlan-tic* editor's rejection of "Stones" because of the public's "dislike" for ma-terial on "the color-line" may have led her to redirect her artistic energies to journalism. Her stories and poetry were appearing in leading maga-zines with a general (white) readership, and she published two plays. How-ever, she increasingly channeled her creative efforts into editorials, essays, and social commentary for periodicals specializing in black materials. In-sistent on bringing black voices and issues to national attention, she ed-ited a collection of "Negro" oratory in 1914 and a Paul Laurence Dunbar anthology in 1920.

Throughout her many years in Wilmington, including eighteen as a popular and influential English teacher at Howard High School (the only black secondary school in the area), she was prominently engaged in a myriad of social-justice organizations and racial causes (often as an officer or president). She even campaigned for women's suffrage in 1915, although her public views on women's issues often seem more conventional than her views on race. Fired in 1920 from her teaching position because of her ardent support for the Republican party, she intensified her work in journalism, founding and editing with her husband *The Wilmington Advocate* (1920–22). She also became a popular columnist for the *Pittsburgh Courier* (1926, 1930) and the *Washington Eagle* (1926–30).

Until recently, Dunbar was considered a minor poet; however, her short fiction has gained increasing critical attention. Of note is her voluminous diary written during times of personal and professional crisis (1921, 1926, 1931). It includes evidence of at least two intense, intimate relationships with other women and, in the opinion of its twentieth-century editor, may well be Dunbar-Nelson's most important literary contribution with its "staggering" revelations about "the meaning of being a Black woman in twentieth-century America."

On September 18, 1935, Dunbar-Nelson died at sixty of heart disease in Philadelphia. She, who had so long battled the cruelties of the color line, died its victim. She was cremated in Wilmington because no Philadelphia funeral home would handle arrangements for a person of color, and her husband scattered her ashes on the Delaware River. At her death, she left unpublished manuscripts (novels, a screenplay, and several remarkable short stories) that substantiate her continuing interest in fiction as well as her ability to deal more directly with racial issues than her earlier stories might intimate.

Works by Alice Ruth Moore Dunbar-Nelson

Violets and Other Tales, 1895

The Goodness of St. Rocque and Other Stories, 1899; rpt., 1969

The Letters of Paul and Alice Dunbar: A Private History, ed. E. W. Metcalf, 1973

Give Us Each Day: The Diary of Alice Dunbar-Nelson, ed. Gloria T. Hull, 1984

The Works of Alice Dunbar-Nelson, ed. Gloria T. Hull, 1988

Further Reading

Ammons, Elizabeth. "The Limits of Freedom: The Fiction of Alice Dunbar-Nelson, Kate Chopin, and Pauline Hopkins." In *Conflicting Stories: American Women Writers at the Turn into the Twentieth Century*. New York: Oxford University Press, 1991.

Bryan, Violet Harrington. "Race and Gender in the Early Works of Alice Dunbar-Nelson." In *Louisiana Women Writers: New Essays and a Comprehensive Bibliography*. Ed. Dorothy H. Brown and Barbara C. Ewell. Baton Rouge: Louisiana State University Press, 1992.

Hull, Gloria T. *Color, Sex, and Poetry: Three Women Writers of the Harlem Renaissance*. Bloomington: Indiana University Press, 1987.

———. "Shaping Contradictions: Alice Dunbar-Nelson and the Black Creole Experience." *New Orleans Review* 15 (1988).

Whitlow, Roger. "Alice Dunbar-Nelson: New Orleans Writer." In *Regionalism and the Female Imagination: A Collection of Essays*. Ed. Emily Toth. New York: Human Sciences, 1985.

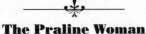

The Praline Woman

The praline[1] woman sits by the side of the Archbishop's quaint little old chapel on Royal Street,[2] and slowly waves her latanier fan[3] over the pink and brown wares.

"Pralines, pralines. Ah, ma'amzelle, you buy? S'il vous plaît,[4] ma'amzelle, ces pralines,[5] dey be fine, ver' fresh.

"Mais non, maman,[6] you are not sure?

"Sho', chile, ma bébé, ma petite, she put dese up hissef.[7] He's han's so small, ma'amzelle, lak you's, mais brune.[8] She put dese up dis morn'. You tak' none? No husban' fo' you den!

"Ah, ma petite, you tak'? Cinq sous, bébé, may le bon Dieu[9] keep you good!

"Mais oui, madame, I know you étrangér.[10] You don' look lak dese New Orleans peop'. You lak' dose Yankee dat come down 'fo' de war."

Ding-dong, ding-dong, ding-dong, chimes the Cathedral bell across Jackson Square, and the praline woman crosses herself.

1. Confection made of pecans and brown sugar.

2. Main commercial street of the Vieux Carré or French Quarter of New Orleans.

3. Fan made from palmetto branches.

4. "Please" (Fr.).

5. "These pralines" (Fr.).

6. "But no, mama" (Creole Fr.).

7. "Herself" (Creole English often interchanges the gender of pronouns).

8. "But brown" (Creole Fr.).

9. "Five pennies (French copper coins), child, may the good God . . ." (Creole Fr.).

10. "Stranger" (Creole Fr.).

"Hail, Mary, full of grace——[11]

"Pralines, madame? You buy lak' dat? Dix sous,[12] madame, an' one lil' piece fo' lagniappe[13] fo' madame's lil' bébé. Ah, c'est bon!

"Pralines, pralines, so fresh, so fine! M'sieu would lak' some fo' he's lil' gal' at home? Mais non, what's dat you say? She's daid! Ah, m'sieu, 't is my lil' gal what died long year ago. Misère, misère![14]

"Here come dat lazy Indien squaw. What she good fo', anyhow? She jes' sit lak dat in de French Market an' sell her filé,[15] an' sleep, sleep, sleep, lak' so in he's blanket. Hey, dere, you, Tonita, how goes you' beezness?

"Pralines, pralines! Holy Father, you give me dat blessin' sho'? Tak' one, I know you lak dat w'ite one. It tas' good, I know, bien.

"Pralines, madame? I lak' you' face. What fo' you wear black? You' lil' boy daid? You tak' one, jes' see how it tas'. I had one lil' boy once, he jes' grow 'twell he's big lak' dis, den one day he tak' sick an' die. Oh, madame, it mos' brek my po' heart. I burn candle in St. Rocque,[16] I say my beads, I sprinkle holy water roun' he's bed; he jes' lay so, he's eyes turn up, he say 'Maman, maman,' den he die! Madame, you tak' one. Non, non, no l'argent,[17] you tak' one fo' my lil' boy's sake.

"Pralines, pralines, m'sieu? Who mak' dese? My lil' gal, Didele, of co'se. Non, non, I don't mak' no mo'. Po' Tante Marie get too ol'. Didele? She's one lil' gal I 'dopt. I see her one day in de strit. He walk so; hit col' she shiver, an' I say, 'Where you gone, lil' gal?' and he can' tell. He jes' crip close to me, an' cry so! Den I tak' her home wid me, and she say he's name Didele. You see dey wa'nt nobody dere. My lil' gal, she's daid of de yellow fever; my lil' boy, he's daid, po' Tante Marie all alone. Didele, she grow fine, she keep house an' mek' pralines. Den, when night come, she sit wid he's guitar an' sing,

> " 'Tu l'aime ces trois jours,
> Tu l'aime ces trois jours,

11. The first line of a Roman Catholic prayer recited while touching each bead in a rosary.

12. "Ten (French copper) pennies."

13. South Louisiana practice of adding a small gift to a customer's purchase.

14. "Sad, sad" (Creole Fr.).

15. Powder of sassafras leaves used to thicken soup, especially gumbo.

16. St. Roche, the patron saint of invalids, whose popular church in New Orleans is in a Creole neighborhood.

17. "Money" (Creole Fr.).

Ma coeur à toi,
Ma coeur à toi,
Tu l'aime ces trois jours!'[18]

"Ah, he's fine gal, is Didele!

"Pralines, pralines! Dat lil' cloud, h'it look lak' rain, I hope no.

"Here come dat lazy I'ishman down de strit. I don't lak' I'ishman me, non, dey so funny. One day one I'ishman, he say to me, 'Auntie, what fo' you talk so?' and I jes' say back, 'What fo' you say "Faith an' be jabers"?'[19] Non, I don' lak' I'ishman, me!

"Here come de rain! Now I got fo' to go. Didele, she be wait fo' me. Down h'it come! H'it fall in de Meesseesip, an' fill up—up—so, clean to de levee, den we have big crivasse,[20] an' po' Tante Marie float away. Bon jour, madame, you come again? Pralines! Pralines!"

Tony's Wife

"Gimme fi' cents worth o' candy, please." It was the little Jew girl who spoke, and Tony's wife roused herself from her knitting to rise and count out the multi-hued candy which should go in exchange for the dingy nickel grasped in warm, damp fingers. Three long sticks, carefully wrapped in crispest brown paper, and a half dozen or more of pink candy fish for lagniappe,[21] and the little Jew girl sped away in blissful contentment. Tony's wife resumed her knitting with a stifled sigh until the next customer should come.

A low growl caused her to look up apprehensively. Tony himself stood beetle-browed and huge in the small doorway.

"Get up from there," he muttered, "and open two dozen oysters right away; the Eliots want 'em." His English was unaccented. It was long since he had seen Italy.

She moved meekly behind the counter, and began work on the thick shells. Tony stretched his long neck up the street.

---

18. "You love him these three days / my heart is yours" (Creole Fr.). Probably the chorus of a popular song.

19. Saying commonly attributed to nineteenth-century Irish immigrants.

20. Crack in the levee or embankment built to prevent the river from overflowing.

21. South Louisiana custom of adding a small gift to a customer's purchase.

302 · ALICE RUTH MOORE DUNBAR-NELSON

"Mr. Tony, mama wants some charcoal." The very small voice at his feet must have pleased him, for his black brows relaxed into a smile, and he poked the little one's chin with a hard, dirty finger, as he emptied the ridiculously small bucket of charcoal into the child's bucket, and gave a banana for lagniappe.

The crackling of shells went on behind, and a stifled sob arose as a bit of sharp edge cut into the thin, worn fingers that clasped the knife.

"Hurry up there, will you?" growled the black brows; "the Eliots are sending for the oysters."

She deftly strained and counted them, and, after wiping her fingers, resumed her seat, and took up the endless crochet work, with her usual stifled sigh.

Tony and his wife had always been in this same little queer old shop on Prytania Street,[22] at least to the memory of the oldest inhabitant in the neighbourhood. When or how they came, or how they stayed, no one knew; it was enough that they were there, like a sort of ancestral fixture to the street. The neighbourhood was fine enough to look down upon these two tumble-down shops at the corner, kept by Tony and Mrs. Murphy, the grocer. It was a semi-fashionable locality, far up-town, away from the old-time French quarter. It was the sort of neighbourhood where millionaires live before their fortunes are made and fashionable, high-priced private schools flourish, where the small cottages are occupied by aspiring school-teachers and choir-singers. Such was this locality, and you must admit that it was indeed a condescension to tolerate Tony and Mrs. Murphy.

He was a great, black-bearded, hoarse-voiced, six-foot specimen of Italian humanity, who looked in his little shop and on the prosaic pavement of Prytania Street somewhat as Hercules[23] might seem in a modern drawing-room. You instinctively thought of wild mountain-passes, and the gleaming dirks[24] of bandit contadini[25] in looking at him. What his last name was, no one knew. Someone had maintained once that he had been christened Antonio Malatesta,[26] but that was unauthentic, and as little to be believed as that other wild theory that her name was Mary.

22. Prytania Street runs through New Orleans's "uptown" or "American" sector, parts of which were also home to many European immigrants.

23. Roman god of supreme strength, but not supreme intelligence.

24. A small dagger.

25. Tenant farmers or peasants (It.).

26. *Mala* is Italian for "sick," *testa* for "head." *Mal di testa* means "headache," *mal a testa* means "sick in the head."

She was meek, pale, little, ugly, and German. Altogether part of his arms and legs would have very decently made another larger than she. Her hair was pale and drawn in sleek, thin tightness away from a pinched, pitiful face, whose dull cold eyes hurt you, because you knew they were trying to mirror sorrow, and could not because of their expressionless quality. No matter what the weather or what her other toilet, she always wore a thin little shawl of dingy brick-dust hue about her shoulders. No matter what the occasion or what the day, she always carried her knitting with her, and seldom ceased the incessant twist, twist of the shining steel among the white cotton meshes. She might put down the needles and lace into the spool-box long enough to open oysters, or wrap up fruit and candy, or count out wood and coal into infinitesimal portions, or do her housework; but the knitting was snatched with avidity at the first spare moment, and the worn, white, blue-marked fingers, half enclosed in kid-glove stalls for protection, would writhe and twist in and out again. Little girls just learning to crochet borrowed their patterns from Tony's wife, and it was considered quite a mark of advancement to have her inspect a bit of lace done by eager, chubby fingers. The ladies in larger houses, whose husbands would be millionaires some day, bought her lace, and gave it to their servants for Christmas presents.

As for Tony, when she was slow in opening his oysters or in cooking his red beans and spaghetti, he roared at her, and prefixed picturesque adjectives to her lace, which made her hide it under her apron with a fearsome look in her dull eyes.

He hated her in a lusty, roaring fashion, as a healthy beefy boy hates a sick cat and torments it to madness. When she displeased him, he beat her, and knocked her frail form on the floor. The children could tell when this had happened. Her eyes would be red, and there would be blue marks on her face and neck. "Poor Mrs. Tony," they would say, and nestle close to her. Tony did not roar at her for petting them, perhaps, because they spent money on the multi-hued candy in glass jars on the shelves.

Her mother appeared upon the scene once, and stayed a short time; but Tony got drunk one day and beat her because she ate too much, and she disappeared soon after. Whence she came and where she departed, no one could tell, not even Mrs. Murphy, the Pauline Pry and Gazette[27] of the block.

Tony had gout,[28] and suffered for many days in roaring helplessness,

27. Idiomatic for someone who extracts and then broadcasts secrets.

28. Painful inflammation of joints, often caused by rich food and drink.

the while his foot, bound and swathed in many folds of red flannel, lay on the chair before him. In proportion as his gout increased and he bawled from pure physical discomfort, she became light-hearted, and moved about the shop with real, brisk cheeriness. He could not hit her then without such pain that after one or two trials he gave up in disgust.

So the dull years had passed, and life had gone on pretty much the same for Tony and the German wife and the shop. The children came on Sunday evenings to buy the stick candy, and on week-days for coal and wood. The servants came to buy oysters for the larger houses, and to gossip over the counter about their employers. The little dry woman knitted, and the big man moved lazily in and out in his red flannel shirt, exchanged politics with the tailor next door through the window, or lounged into Mrs. Murphy's bar and drank fiercely. Some of the children grew up and moved away, and other little girls came to buy candy and eat pink lagniappe fishes, and the shop still thrived.

One day Tony was ill, more than the mummied foot of gout, or the wheeze of asthma; he must keep his bed and send for the doctor.

She clutched his arm when he came, and pulled him into the tiny room.

"Is it—is it anything much, doctor?" she gasped.

Æsculapius[29] shook his head as wisely as the occasion would permit. She followed him out of the room into the shop.

"Do you—will he get well, doctor?"

Æsculapius buttoned up his frock coat, smoothed his shining hat, cleared his throat, then replied oracularly,

"Madam, he is completely burned out inside. Empty as a shell, madam, empty as a shell. He cannot live, for he has nothing to live on."

As the cobblestones rattled under the doctor's equipage rolling leisurely up Prytania Street, Tony's wife sat in her chair and laughed,—laughed with a hearty joyousness that lifted the film from the dull eyes and disclosed a sparkle beneath.

The drear days went by, and Tony lay like a veritable Samson[30] shorn of his strength, for his voice was sunken to a hoarse, sibilant whisper, and his black eyes gazed fiercely from the shock of hair and beard about a white face. Life went on pretty much as before in the shop; the children paused to ask how Mr. Tony was, and even hushed the jingles on their bell

---

29. Roman god of medicine and healing.

30. Samson, an Israelite hero, was betrayed to the Philistines when his long hair was cut, the sign of his religious commitment and source of his prodigious strength (Judges 13–16).

hoops[31] as they passed the door. Red-headed Jimmie, Mrs. Murphy's nephew, did the hard jobs, such as splitting wood and lifting coal from the bin; and in the intervals between tending the fallen giant and waiting on the customers, Tony's wife sat in her accustomed chair, knitting fiercely, with an inscrutable smile about her purple compressed mouth.

Then John came, introducing himself, serpent-wise, into the Eden of her bosom.

John was Tony's brother, huge and bluff too, but fair and blond, with the beauty of Northern Italy. With the same lack of race pride which Tony had displayed in selecting his German spouse, John had taken unto himself Betty, a daughter of Erin,[32] aggressive, powerful, and cross-eyed. He turned up now, having heard of this illness, and assumed an air of remarkable authority at once.

A hunted look stole into the dull eyes, and after John had departed with blustering directions as to Tony's welfare, she crept to his bedside timidly.

"Tony," she said,—"Tony, you are very sick."

An inarticulate growl was the only response.

"Tony, you ought to see the priest; you must n't go any longer without taking the sacrament."

The growl deepened into words.

"Don't want any priest; you 're always after some snivelling old woman's fuss. You and Mrs. Murphy go on with your church; it won't make *you* any better."

She shivered under this parting shot, and crept back into the shop. Still the priest came next day.

She followed him in to the bedside and knelt timidly.

"Tony," she whispered, "here's Father Leblanc."

Tony was too languid to curse out loud; he only expressed his hate in a toss of the black beard and shaggy mane.

"Tony," she said nervously, "won't you do it now? It won't take long and it will be better for you when you go—Oh, Tony, don't—don't laugh. Please, Tony, here's the priest."

But the Titan[33] roared aloud: "No; get out. Think I'm a-going to give you a chance to grab my money now? Let me die and go to hell in peace."

31. Nineteenth-century toy.

32. Ancient name for Ireland.

33. Primordial Greek god, associated with great size and power.

Father Leblanc knelt meekly and prayed, and the woman's weak pleadings continued,—

"Tony, I've been true and good and faithful to you. Don't die and leave me no better than before. Tony, I do want to be a good woman once, a real-for-true married woman. Tony, here's the priest; say yes." And she wrung her ringless hands.

"You want my money," said Tony, slowly, "and you sha'n't have it, not a cent; John shall have it."

Father Leblanc shrank away like a fading spectre. He came next day and next day, only to see re-enacted the same piteous scene,—the woman pleading to be made a wife ere death hushed Tony's blasphemies, the man chuckling in pain-racked glee at the prospect of her bereaved misery. Not all the prayers of Father Leblanc nor the wailings of Mrs. Murphy could alter the determination of the will beneath the shock of hair; he gloated in his physical weakness at the tenacious grasp on his mentality.

"Tony," she wailed on the last day, her voice rising to a shriek in its eagerness, "tell them I'm your wife; it'll be the same. Only say it, Tony, before you die!"

He raised his head, and turned stiff eyes and gibbering mouth on her; then, with one chill finger pointing at John, fell back dully and heavily.

They buried him with many honors by the Society of Italia's Sons. John took possession of the shop when they returned home, and found the money hidden in the chimney corner.

As for Tony's wife, since she was not his wife after all, they sent her forth in the world penniless, her worn fingers clutching her bundle of clothes in nervous agitation, as though they regretted the time lost from knitting.

Sister Josepha

Sister Josepha told her beads [34] mechanically, her fingers numb with the accustomed exercise. The little organ creaked a dismal "O Salutaris," [35] and she still knelt on the floor, her white-bonneted head nodding suspiciously. The Mother Superior gave a sharp glance at the tired figure; then,

34. Said one prayer for each bead on her rosary.

35. "O Salutaris Hostia" ("Oh Saving Victim," Lat.). Roman Catholic hymn associated with the service of benediction.

as a sudden lurch forward brought the little sister back to consciousness, Mother's eyes relaxed into a genuine smile.

The bell tolled the end of vespers,[36] and the sombre-robed nuns filed out of the chapel to go about their evening duties. Little Sister Josepha's work was to attend to the household lamps, but there must have been as much oil spilled upon the table to-night as was put in the vessels. The small brown hands trembled so that most of the wicks were trimmed with points at one corner which caused them to smoke that night.

"Oh, cher Seigneur,"[37] she sighed, giving an impatient polish to a refractory chimney,[38] "it is wicked and sinful, I know, but I am so tired. I can't be happy and sing any more. It doesn't seem right for le bon Dieu[39] to have me all cooped up here with nothing to see but stray visitors, and always the same old work, teaching those mean little girls to sew, and washing and filling the same old lamps. Pah!" And she polished the chimney with a sudden vigorous jerk which threatened destruction.

They were rebellious prayers that the red mouth murmured that night, and a restless figure that tossed on the hard dormitory bed. Sister Dominica called from her couch to know if Sister Josepha were ill.

"No," was the somewhat short response; then a muttered, "Why can't they let me alone for a minute? That pale-eyed Sister Dominica never sleeps; that's why she is so ugly."

About fifteen years before this night some one had brought to the orphan asylum connected with this convent, du Sacré Coeur,[40] a round, dimpled bit of three-year-old humanity, who regarded the world from a pair of gravely twinkling black eyes, and only took a chubby thumb out of a rosy mouth long enough to answer in monosyllabic French. It was a child without an identity; there was but one name that any one seemed to know, and that, too, was vague,—Camille.

She grew up with the rest of the waifs; scraps of French and American

---

36. Evening prayers or worship services.

37. "Dear Lord" (Fr.).

38. Clear glass globe that protects an oil flame from drafts.

39. "The good God" (Fr.).

40. "Of the Sacred Heart" (Fr.). The Society of the Sacred Heart was a French religious community dedicated to education and founded just after the French revolution by Madeleine-Sophie Barat. In 1818 Sr. Philipine du Chesne established convents and schools in the Louisiana Territory. The sisters in the Vieux Carré behind St. Louis Cathedral moved in 1900 to their present location on St. Charles Avenue.

civilization thrown together to develop a seemingly inconsistent miniature world. Mademoiselle Camille was a queen among them, a pretty little tyrant who ruled the children and dominated the more timid sisters in charge.

One day an awakening came. When she was fifteen, and almost fully ripened into a glorious tropical beauty of the type that matures early, some visitors to the convent were fascinated by her and asked the Mother Superior to give the girl into their keeping.

Camille fled like a frightened fawn into the yard, and was only unearthed with some difficulty from behind a group of palms. Sulky and pouting, she was led into the parlour, picking at her blue pinafore[41] like a spoiled infant.

"The lady and gentleman wish you to go home with them, Camille," said the Mother Superior, in the language of the convent. Her voice was kind and gentle apparently; but the child, accustomed to its various inflections, detected a steely ring behind its softness, like the proverbial iron hand in the velvet glove.

"You must understand, madame," continued Mother, in stilted English, "that we never force children from us. We are ever glad to place them in comfortable—how you say that?—quarters—maisons—homes—bien! But we will not make them go if they do not wish."

Camille stole a glance at her would-be guardians, and decided instantly, impulsively, finally. The woman suited her; but the man! It was doubtless intuition of the quick, vivacious sort which belonged to her blood that served her. Untutored in worldly knowledge, she could not divine the meaning of the pronounced leers and admiration of her physical charms which gleamed in the man's face, but she knew it made her feel creepy, and stoutly refused to go.

Next day Camille was summoned from a task to the Mother Superior's parlour. The other girls gazed with envy upon her as she dashed down the courtyard with impetuous movement. Camille, they decided crossly, received too much notice. It was Camille this, Camille that; she was pretty, it was to be expected. Even Father Ray lingered longer in his blessing when his hands pressed her silky black hair.

As she entered the parlour, a strange chill swept over the girl. The room was not an unaccustomed one, for she had swept it many times, but to-day

41. Large work apron, originally pinned to the front of a woman's dress ("pinned a'fore"), later tied on.

the stiff black chairs, the dismal crucifixes, the gleaming whiteness of the walls, even the cheap lithograph of the Madonna which Camille had always regarded as a perfect specimen of art, seemed cold and mean.

"Camille, ma chère,"[42] said Mother, "I am extremely displeased with you. Why did you not wish to go with Monsieur and Madame Lafayé yesterday?"

The girl uncrossed her hands from her bosom, and spread them out in a deprecating gesture.

"Mais, ma mère,[43] I was afraid."

Mother's face grew stern. "No foolishness now," she exclaimed.

"It is not foolishness, ma mère; I could not help it, but that man looked at me so funny, I felt all cold chills down my back. Oh, dear Mother, I love the convent and the sisters so, I just want to stay and be a sister too, may I?"

And thus it was that Camille took the white veil[44] at sixteen years. Now that the period of novitiate was over, it was just beginning to dawn upon her that she had made a mistake.

"Maybe it would have been better had I gone with the funny-looking lady and gentleman," she mused bitterly one night. "Oh, Seigneur,[45] I'm so tired and impatient; it's so dull here, and, dear God, I'm so young.

There was no help for it. One must arise in the morning, and help in the refectory[46] with the stupid Sister Francesca, and go about one's duties with a prayerful mien, and not even let a sigh escape when one's head ached with the eternal telling of beads.

A great fête[47] day was coming, and an atmosphere of preparation and mild excitement pervaded the brown walls of the convent like a delicate aroma. The old Cathedral[48] around the corner had stood a hundred years, and all the city was rising to do honour to its age and time-softened beauty. There would be a service, oh, but such a one! with two Cardinals,

42. "My dear" (Fr.).

43. "But, my Mother . . ." (Fr.); ordinary term of address to sisters in this community.

44. A novice or person training to join a Roman Catholic religious order of women is typically distinguished from the professed members by her white veil; a novitiate typically lasts a year and a day.

45. "Lord" (Fr.).

46. Dining hall, especially in a religious institution.

47. "Feast day" (Fr.).

48. St. Louis Cathedral was built in 1794 on the Place d'Armes (now Jackson Square) in New Orleans.

and Archbishops and Bishops, and all the accompanying glitter of soldiers and orchestras. The little sisters of the Convent du Sacré Coeur clasped their hands in anticipation of the holy joy. Sister Josepha curled her lip, she was so tired of churchly pleasures.

The day came, a gold and blue spring day, when the air hung heavy with the scent of roses and magnolias, and the sunbeams fairly laughed as they kissed the houses. The old Cathedral stood gray and solemn, and the flowers in Jackson Square smiled cheery birthday greetings across the way. The crowd around the door surged and pressed and pushed in its eagerness to get within. Ribbons stretched across the banquette [49] were of no avail to repress it, and important ushers with cardinal colours could do little more.

The Sacred Heart sisters filed slowly in at the side door, creating a momentary flutter as they paced reverently to their seats, guarding the blue-bonneted orphans. Sister Josepha, determined to see as much of the world as she could, kept her big black eyes opened wide, as the church rapidly filled with the fashionably dressed, perfumed, rustling, and self-conscious throng.

Her heart beat quickly. The rebellious thoughts that will arise in the most philosophical of us surged in her small heavily gowned bosom. For her were the gray things, the neutral tinted skies, the ugly garb, the coarse meats; for them the rainbow, the ethereal airiness of earthly joys, the bonbons [50] and glacés [51] of the world. Sister Josepha did not know that the rainbow is elusive, and its colours but the illumination of tears; she had never been told that earthly ethereality is necessarily ephemeral, nor that bonbons and glacés, whether of the palate or of the soul, nauseate and pall upon the taste. Dear God, forgive her, for she bent with contrite tears over her worn rosary, and glanced no more at the worldly glitter of femininity.

The sunbeams streamed through the high windows in purple and crimson lights upon a veritable fugue of color. Within the seats, crush upon crush of spring millinery; within the aisles erect lines of gold-braided, gold-buttoned military. Upon the altar, broad sweeps of golden robes, great dashes of crimson skirts, miters and gleaming crosses, the soft neutral hue of rich lace vestments; [52] the tender heads of childhood in pic-

49. "Sidewalk" (Fr.), originally raised a few feet above muddy or dusty streets.

50. "Goodies" (Fr.), especially filled chocolate candies.

51. "Candied fruit" (Fr.).

52. Richly embroidered satin ritual robes for clergy. Miters: tall, double-peaked hats worn by bishops.

turesque attire; the proud, golden magnificence of the domed altar with its weighting mass of lilies and wide-eyed roses, and the long candles that sparkled their yellow star points above the reverent throng within the altar rails.

The soft baritone of the Cardinal intoned a single phrase in the suspended silence. The censer[53] took up the note in its delicate clink clink, as it swung to and fro in the hands of a fair-haired child. Then the organ, pausing an instant in a deep, mellow, long-drawn note, burst suddenly into a magnificent strain, and the choir sang forth, "Kyrie Eleïson, Christe Eleïson."[54] One voice, flute-like, piercing, sweet, rang high over the rest. Sister Josepha heard and trembled, as she buried her face in her hands, and let her tears fall, like other beads, through her rosary.

It was when the final word of the service had been intoned, the last peal of the exit march had died away, that she looked up meekly, to encounter a pair of youthful brown eyes gazing pityingly upon her. That was all she remembered for a moment, that the eyes were youthful and handsome and tender. Later, she saw that they were placed in a rather beautiful boyish face, surmounted by waves of brown hair, curling and soft, and that the head was set on a pair of shoulders decked in military uniform. Then the brown eyes marched away with the rest of the rear guard, and the white-bonneted sisters filed out the side door, through the narrow court, back into the brown convent.

That night Sister Josepha tossed more than usual on her hard bed, and clasped her fingers often in prayer to quell the wickedness in her heart. Turn where she would, pray as she might, there was ever a pair of tender, pitying brown eyes, haunting her persistently. The squeaky organ at vespers intoned the clank of military accoutrements to her ears, the white bonnets of the sisters about her faded into mists of curling brown hair. Briefly, Sister Josepha was in love.

The days went on pretty much as before, save for the one little heart that beat rebelliously now and then, though it tried so hard to be submissive. There was the morning work in the refectory, the stupid little girls to teach sewing, and the insatiable lamps that were so greedy for oil. And always the tender, boyish brown eyes, that looked so sorrowfully at the fragile, beautiful little sister, haunting, following, pleading.

Perchance, had Sister Josepha been in the world, the eyes would have

53. An incense burner of perforated metal suspended from a chain.

54. "Lord have mercy, Christ have mercy" (Lat.), an opening prayer from the Catholic Mass.

been an incident. But in this home of self-repression and retrospection, it was a life-story. The eyes had gone their way, doubtless forgetting the little sister they pitied; but the little sister?

The days glided into weeks, the weeks into months. Thoughts of escape had come to Sister Josepha, to flee into the world, to merge in the great city where recognition was impossible, and, working her way like the rest of humanity, perchance encounter the eyes again.

It was all planned and ready. She would wait until some morning when the little band of black-robed sisters wended their way to mass at the Cathedral. When it was time to file out the side-door into the courtway, she would linger at prayers, then slip out another door, and unseen glide up Chartres Street to Canal,[55] and once there, mingle in the throng that filled the wide thoroughfare. Beyond this first plan she could think no further. Penniless, garbed, and shaven[56] though she would be, other difficulties never presented themselves to her. She would rely on the mercies of the world to help her escape from this torturing life of inertia. It seemed easy now that the first step of decision had been taken.

The Saturday night before the final day had come, and she lay feverishly nervous in her narrow little bed, wondering with wide-eyed fear at the morrow. Pale-eyed Sister Dominica and Sister Francesca were whispering together in the dark silence, and Sister Josepha's ears pricked up as she heard her name.

"She is not well, poor child," said Francesca. "I fear the life is too confining."

"It is best for her," was the reply. "You know, sister, how hard it would be for her in the world, with no name but Camille, no friends, and her beauty; and then—"

Sister Josepha heard no more, for her heart beating tumultuously in her bosom drowned the rest. Like the rush of the bitter salt tide over a drowning man clinging to a spar, came the complete submerging of her hopes of another life. No name but Camille, that was true; no nationality, for she could never tell from whom or whence she came; no friends, and a beauty that not even an ungainly bonnet and shaven head could hide. In a flash she realised the deception of the life she would lead, and the cruel self-torture of wonder at her own identity. Already, as if in anticipation of the world's questionings, she was asking herself, "Who am I? What am I?"

55. Chartres Street crosses in front of the cathedral continuing several blocks upriver to Canal Street, which divides the French Quarter from the "American" sectors of New Orleans.
56. Veiled religious women typically wore their hair very close-cropped.

The next morning the sisters du Sacré Coeur filed into the Cathedral at High Mass, and bent devout knees at the general confession. "Confiteor Deo omnipotenti," [57] murmured the priest; and tremblingly one little sister followed the words, "Je confesse à Dieu, tout puissant—que j'ai beaucoup péché par pensées—c'est ma faute—c'est ma faute—c'est ma très grande faute." [58]

The organ pealed forth as mass ended, the throng slowly filed out, and the sisters paced through the courtway back into the brown convent walls. One paused at the entrance, and gazed with swift longing eyes in the direction of narrow, squalid Chartres Street, then, with a gulping sob, followed the rest, and vanished behind the heavy door.

57. "I confess to God the almighty" (Lat.); part of the Catholic Mass.

58. "I confess to almighty God—that I have sinned much in my thoughts—it is my fault—it is my fault—it is my great fault" (Fr.). A French translation of the prayer being recited by the priest in Latin.

Appendix

FURTHER READINGS IN SOUTHERN LOCAL COLOR

The following list identifies notable stories and collections by authors of southern local color. For those included in this anthology, we have indicated specific volumes or stories that further illustrate their achievements. We have also included works by other significant writers, identifying the states with which they are associated and the collections and/or stories that best exemplify their art and contributions to the genre.

James Lane Allen (Kentucky, 1849–1925), "King Solomon of Kentucky," "Two Gentlemen of Kentucky," in *Flute and Violin and Other Kentucky Tales and Romances* (1891); *A Kentucky Cardinal* (1894).

Katharine (Sherwood Bonner) McDowell (1849–1883), "Gran'mammy's Last Gifts," in *Suwanee River Tales* (1884).

Virginia Frazer Boyle (Tennessee, African American folk tales, 1863–1938), "The Triumph of Shed," *Century* (1886); *Devil Tales* (1900).

George Washington Cable (1844–1925), "Jean-ah Poquelin," "Belles Demoiselles Plantation," "'Tite Poulette," in *Old Creole Days* (1879).

Charles Chesnutt (1855–1932), "A Matter of Principle," "The Wife of His Youth," "The Sheriff's Children," in *The Wife of His Youth and Other Stories of the Color Line* (1899); "Po' Sandy," in *The Conjure Woman* (1899); "The Doll," *The Crisis* (1912).

Kate Chopin (1851–1904), "A No-Account Creole," "At the 'Cadian Ball," "A Gentleman of Bayou Têche," in *Bayou Folk* (1894); "Nég Créol," in *A Night in Acadie* (1897).

Mollie E. Moore Davis (1844?–1909), "Mr. Benjamin Franklin Gish's Ball," in *An Elephant's Track and Other Stories* (1897).

Paul Laurence Dunbar (1872–1906), "At Shaft 11," in *Folks from Dixie* (1898); "The Strength of Gideon," "A Council of State," in *The Strength of Gideon* (1900).

Alice Ruth Moore Dunbar-Nelson (1875–1935), "Carnival Jangle," "When the Bayou Overflows," "Mr. Baptiste," in *The Goodness of St. Rocque and Other Stories* (1899); "The Stones of the Village," in *The Works of Alice Dunbar-Nelson*, ed. Gloria Hull (1988).

Harry Stillwell Edwards (Georgia, 1855–1938), "Sister Todhunter's Heart," in *Two Runaways and Other Stories* (1889); "His Defense," in *His Defense and Other Stories* (1899).

Sarah Barnwell Elliott (1848–1928), "An Incident," "Squire Kayley's Conclusions," "An Ex-Brigadier," in *An Incident and Other Happenings* (1899).

John Fox Jr. (Kentucky and Appalachia, 1863?–1919), *A Cumberland Vendetta and Other Stories* (1896); *The Little Shepherd of Kingdom Come* (1903).

Alice French (Octave Thanet) (Arkansas and Mississippi, 1850–1934), *Knitters in the Sun* (1887); "The Court of Last Resort," in *A Book of True Lovers* (1897); "The Mortgage on Jeffy," in *Otto the Knight and Other Trans-Mississippi Stories* (1891).

Ambrose Elliott Gonzales (coastal South Carolina, 1857–1926), "The Gator Hunter," "Conductor Smith's Dilemma," in *The Black Border: Gullah Stories of the Carolina Coast* (1922); "A Riever of the Black Border," "The Trencherman and the Shark," "The Green Calabash," in *The Captain: Stories of the Black Border* (1924).

Joel Chandler Harris (1848–1908), "Why the Negro is Black," in *Uncle Remus: His Songs and Sayings* (1880); "Free Joe," "Trouble on Lost Mountain," "Aunt Fountain's Prisoner," in *Free Joe and Other Sketches* (1887); *The Chronicles of Aunt Minervy Ann* (1899); "Rosalie," *Century* (1901).

Richard Malcolm Johnston (Middle Georgia, 1822–1898), *Georgia Sketches* (1864); *Dukesborough Tales* (1871); "A Critical Account of Mr. Absalom Billingslea," in *Mr. Absalom Billingslea and Other Georgia Folk* (1888); "King William and His Armies," in *The Chronicles of Mr. Bill Williams* (1892).

Grace King (1852–1932), "Bonne Maman," in *Tales of a Time and Place* (1892); "One of Us," "A Delicate Affair," "A Crippled Hope," in *Balcony Stories* (1893).

Mary Noailles Murfree (1850–1922), "The Dancin' Party at Harrison's Cove," "The 'Harn't' That Walks Chilhowee," "Over on the T'other Mounting," in *In the Tennessee Mountains* (1884).

Thomas Nelson Page (1853–1922), "Run to Seed," in *Elsket and Other Stories* (1891); "Marse Chan," "Meh Lady: A Story of the War," in *In Ole Virginia* (1887); "The Prosecution of Mrs. Dullet," "How Jinny Eased Her Mind," in *Pastime Stories* (1898).

Julia Peterkin (South Carolina, 1880–1961), "Green Thursday," in *Green Thursday* (1924); "A Baby's Mouth" (1922), "Over the River" (1924), in *Collected Short Stories of Julia Peterkin,* ed. Frank Durham (1970).

William Gilmore Simms (Georgia, 1806–1870), "The Lazy Crow," "Caloya, or, the Love of the Driver," in *Wigwam and the Cabin* (1845; 1882).

F. Hopkinson Smith (Virginia and Kentucky, 1838–1915), *Colonel Carter of Cartersville* (1891); "Six Hours in Squantico," in *A Day at Laguerre's* (1892); "A Kentucky Cinderella," in *The Other Fellow* (1899).

Ruth McEnery Stuart (Louisiana and Arkansas, 1856–1917), "Christmas Gifts," in *A Golden Wedding and Other Tales* (1893); "Queen o' Sheba's Triumph," in *Holly and Pizen and Other Stories* (1899); *The Woman's Exchange of Simpkins-ville* (1899); "Egypt," in *The Second Wooing of Salina Sue and Other Stories* (1905).

Fannie Barrier Williams (Virginia, 1855–1944), "After Many Days: A Christmas Story " (1902), in *Centers of the Self*, ed. Judith Hamer and Martin Hamer.

Constance Fenimore Woolson (1840–1894), "Miss Elisabetha," "Rodman the Keeper," "Old Gardiston," "King David," in *Rodman the Keeper: Southern Sketches* (1880).

Bibliography

Ammons, Elizabeth. *Conflicting Stories: American Women Writers at the Turn into the Twentieth Century.* New York: Oxford University Press, 1991.

Ammons, Elizabeth, and Valerie Rohy, eds. Introduction to *American Local Color Writing, 1880–1920.* New York: Penguin, 1998. vii–xxx.

Ayers, Edward L. *The Promise of the New South: Life after Reconstruction.* New York: Oxford University Press, 1992.

Baskervill, William Malone. *Southern Writers: Biographical and Critical Studies.* 2 vols. Nashville, Tenn.: M. E. Church, 1897.

Berthoff, Warner. *The Ferment of Realism: American Literature, 1884–1919.* New York: Macmillan, 1965.

Bone, Robert. *Down Home: Origins of the Afro-American Short Story.* New York: Columbia University Press, 1975.

Brodhead, Richard H. *Cultures of Letters: Scenes of Reading and Writing in Nineteenth-Century America.* Chicago: University of Chicago Press, 1993.

Brown, Dorothy H., and Barbara C. Ewell, eds. *Louisiana Women Writers: New Essays and a Comprehensive Bibliography.* Baton Rouge: Louisiana State University Press, 1992.

Bryan, Violet Harrington. *The Myth of New Orleans in Literature: Dialogues of Race and Gender.* Knoxville: University of Tennessee Press, 1993.

Buck, Paul H. *The Road to Reunion, 1866–1900.* 1937. Reprint, New York: Vintage, 1959.

Campbell, Donna M. *Resisting Regionalism: Gender and Naturalism in American Fiction, 1885–1915.* Athens: Ohio University Press, 1997.

Cash, W. J. *The Mind of the South.* New York: Random House, 1941.

Chopin, Kate. "'Crumbling Idols' by Hamlin Garland." In *The Complete Works of Kate Chopin.* Ed. Per Seyersted. Baton Rouge: Louisiana State University Press, 1969. 693–94.

Cohen, Hennig, and William B. Dillingham. *Humor of the Old Southwest.* Boston: Houghton Mifflin, 1964.

Current-García, Eugene, and Bert Hitchcock, eds. *American Short Stories.* Glenview, Ill.: Scott, Foresman, 1990.

Deleuze, Gilles, and Félix Guattari. *Kafka: Toward a Minor Literature.* Trans. Dana Polan. Minneapolis: University of Minnesota Press, 1986.

Donaldson, Susan V. "Gender and the Profession of Letters in the South." In

Rewriting the South: History and Fiction. Ed. Lothar Honnighausen and Valeria Gennaro Lerda. Tübingen: Franke Verlag, 1993. 35–46.

Donovan, Josephine. "Breaking the Sentence: Local-Color Literature and Subjugated Knowledges." In *The (Other) American Traditions: Nineteenth-Century Women Writers.* Ed. Joyce W. Warren. New Brunswick, N.J.: Rutgers University Press, 1993. 226–43.

Douglas [Wood], Ann. "The Literature of Impoverishment: The Women Local Colorists in America, 1865–1914." *Women's Studies* 1 (1972): 3–45.

Edwards, Laura F. *Gendered Strife and Confusion: The Political Culture of Reconstruction.* Urbana: University of Illinois Press, 1997.

Elfenbein, Anna Shannon. *Women on the Color Line: Evolving Stereotypes and the Writings of George Washington Cable, Grace King, Kate Chopin.* Charlottesville: University Press of Virginia, 1989.

Ewell, Barbara C. "Changing Places: Women, the Old South; or, What Happens When Local Color Becomes Regionalism." *American Studies: A Quarterly, German Association of American Studies* (Heidelberg) 42.2 (1997): 159–79.

Fetterley, Judith, ed. *Provisions: A Reader from Nineteenth-Century American Women.* Bloomington: Indiana University Press, 1985.

Fetterley, Judith, and Marjorie Pryse, eds. *American Women Regionalists: 1850–1910.* New York: W. W. Norton, 1992.

Fiske, John. "The Theory of a Common Origin for All Languages." *Atlantic* 48 (November 1881): 655–64.

Foner, Eric. *Reconstruction: America's Unfinished Revolution, 1863–1877.* New York: Harper & Row, 1988.

Foster, Gaines M. *Ghosts of the Confederacy: Defeat, the Lost Cause, and the Emergence of the New South.* New York: Oxford University Press, 1987.

Fusco, Richard. *Maupassant and the American Short Story: The Influence of Form at the Turn of the Century.* University Park: Pennsylvania State University Press, 1994.

Gebhard, Caroline. "Reconstructing Southern Manhood: Race, Sentimentality, and Camp in the Plantation Myth." In *Haunted Bodies: Gender and Southern Texts.* Ed. Anne Goodwyn Jones and Susan V. Donaldson. Charlottesville: University Press of Virginia, 1997. 132–55.

————. "The Spinster in the House of American Criticism." *Tulsa Studies in Women's Literature* 10.1 (1991): 79–91.

Glasgow, Ellen. *A Certain Measure: An Interpretation of Prose Fiction.* New York: Harcourt Brace, 1943.

Gottesman, Ronald, et al., eds. *William Dean Howells: Selected Literary Criticism.* Vol. 3. Bloomington: Indiana University Press, 1993.

Grady, Henry. *The New South and Other Addresses.* New York: Maynard, Merrill, 1904.

Green, Elna C. *Southern Strategies: Southern Women and the Woman Suffrage Question.* Chapel Hill: University of North Carolina Press, 1997.

Hibbard, Addison. *Stories of the South, Old and New.* Chapel Hill: University of North Carolina Press, 1931.

Hoganson, Kristin L. *Fighting for American Manhood: How Gender Politics Provoked the Spanish American and Philippine American Wars.* New Haven: Yale University Press, 1998.

Holman, David Marion. *A Certain Slant of Light: Regionalism and the Form of Southern and Midwestern Fiction.* Baton Rouge: Louisiana State University Press, 1995.

Howells, William Dean. *Selected Literary Criticism.* Vol. 3: 1898–1920. Edited by Ronald Gottesman et al. Bloomington: Indiana University Press, 1993.

Hubbell, Jay B. *The South in American Literature, 1607–1900.* Durham: Duke University Press, 1954.

Irons, Susan. "Southern Literary (Re)Construction: Formulating the Early Southern Literary Canon." Paper read at the Society for the Study of Southern Literature, Richmond, Virginia, April 1996.

Jones, Anne Goodwyn. *Tomorrow Is Another Day: The Woman Writer in the South, 1859–1936.* Baton Rouge: Louisiana State University Press, 1981.

Jones, Gavin. *Strange Talk: The Politics of Dialect Literature in Gilded Age America.* Berkeley: University of California Press, 1999.

Jones, Jacqueline. *Labor of Love, Labor of Sorrow: Black Women, Work and the Family, from Slavery to the Present.* New York: Vintage, 1985.

Jordan, David. *Regionalism Reconsidered: New Approaches to the Field.* New York: Garland, 1994.

Kaplan, Amy. "Nation, Region, and Empire." In *The Columbia History of the American Novel.* Ed. Emory Elliott et al. New York: Columbia University Press, 1991. 240–66.

King, Edward. *Southern States of North America: A Record of Journeys.* 3 vols. London: Blackie & Son, 1875.

Kolodny, Annette. "Letting Go Our Grand Obsessions: Notes Toward a New Literary History of the American Frontiers." *American Literature* 64 (1992): 1–18.

Ladd, Barbara. *Nationalism and the Color Line in George W. Cable, Mark Twain, and William Faulkner.* Baton Rouge: Louisiana State University Press, 1996.

MacKethan, Lucinda Hardwick. *The Dream of Arcady: Place and Time in Southern Literature.* Baton Rouge: Louisiana State University Press, 1980.

Martin, Jay. *Harvests of Change: American Literature, 1865–1914.* Englewood Cliffs, N.J.: Prentice-Hall, 1967.

McCullough, Kate. *Regions of Identity: The Construction of America in Women's Fiction, 1885–1914.* Stanford, Calif.: Stanford University Press, 1999.

Michaels, Walter Benn. "Local Colors." *Modern Language Notes* 113.4 (1998): 734–56.

Morrison, Toni. *Playing in the Dark: Whiteness and the Literary Imagination.* New York: Random House, 1993.

Moss, Elizabeth. *Domestic Novelists in the Old South: Defenders of Southern Culture.* Baton Rouge: Louisiana State University Press, 1992.

Nagel, James, and Tom Quirk, eds. *The Portable American Realism Reader.* New York: Penguin, 1997.

North, Michael. *The Dialect of Modernism: Race, Language, and Twentieth-Century Literature.* New York: Oxford University Press, 1994.

Parrington, Vernon L. *Main Currents in American Thought: The Beginnings of Critical Realism in America, 1860–1920.* Vol. 3. New York: Harcourt Brace, 1930.

Pattee, Fred Lewis. *The Development of the American Short Story: An Historical Survey.* New York: Harper, 1923.

Pizer, Donald, ed. *The Cambridge Companion to American Realism and Naturalism, Howells to London.* New York: Cambridge University Press, 1995.

Price, Kenneth M., and Susan Belasco Smith, eds. *Periodical Literature in Nineteenth-Century America.* Charlottesville: University Press of Virginia, 1995.

Rhode, Robert D. *Setting in the American Short Story of Local Color, 1865–1900.* The Hague: Mouton, 1975.

Ridgely, J. V. *Nineteenth-Century Southern Literature.* Lexington: University Press of Kentucky, 1980.

Rowe, Anne. *The Enchanted Country: Northern Writers in the South, 1865–1910.* Baton Rouge: Louisiana State University Press, 1978.

Rubin, Louis D., Jr., ed. *The History of Southern Literature.* Baton Rouge: Louisiana State University Press, 1985.

Sedgwick, Ellery. "Magazines and the Profession of Authorship in the United States: 1840–1900." Paper read at the American Literature Association Conference, Baltimore, Md., May 30, 1999.

Silber, Nina. *The Romance of Reunion: Northerners and the South, 1865–1900.* Chapel Hill: University of North Carolina Press, 1993.

Simms, William Gilmore. *Views and Reviews in American Literature, History, and Fiction.* 1845. Reprint, Cambridge: Harvard University Press, 1962.

Simpson, Claude M. *The Local Colorists: American Short Stories, 1857–1900.* New York: Harper, 1960.

Skaggs, Merrill Maguire. *The Folk of Southern Fiction.* Athens: University of Georgia Press, 1972.

Sundquist, Eric. *To Wake the Nations: Race in the Making of Literature.* Cambridge: Belknap Press of Harvard University Press, 1993.

Taylor, Helen. *Gender, Race, and Region in the Writings of Grace King, Ruth McEnery Stuart, and Kate Chopin.* Baton Rouge: Louisiana State University Press, 1989.

Tolnay, Stewart E., and E. M. Beck. *A Festival of Violence: An Analysis of Southern Lynchings, 1882–1930.* Urbana: University of Illinois Press, 1995.

Toth, Emily, ed. *Regionalism and the Female Imagination: A Collection of Essays.* New York: Human Sciences, 1985.

Tourgée, Albion W. "The South as a Field for Fiction." *The* ber 1888): 7–34.

Turner, Arlin. Introduction to *Chita: A Memory of Last Island,* Hearn. Chapel Hill: University of North Carolina Press, 1969.

Wald, Priscilla. *Constituting Americans: Cultural Anxiety and Narrati.* Durham: Duke University Press, 1995.

Warfel, Harry R., and G. Harrison Orians, eds. *American Local Color Sto.* New York: Cooper Square, 1970.

Wells, Ida B. *Southern Horrors and Other Writings: The Anti-Lynching Campaign of Ida B. Wells, 1892–1900.* Ed. Jacqueline Jones Royster. Boston: Bedford Books, 1997.

Wheeler, Marjorie Spruill. *New Women of the New South: The Leaders of the Woman Suffrage Movement in the Southern States.* New York: Oxford University Press, 1993.

———. "The Woman Suffrage Movement in the Inhospitable South." In *Votes for Women! The Woman Suffrage Movement in Tennessee, the South, and the Nation.* Ed. Marjorie Spruill Wheeler. Knoxville: University of Tennessee Press, 1995. 25–52.

Whites, LeeAnn. *The Civil War as a Crisis in Gender: Augusta, Georgia, 1860–1890.* Athens: University of Georgia Press, 1995.

Wilson, Charles Reagan, and William Ferris, eds. *Encyclopedia of Southern Culture.* Chapel Hill: University of North Carolina Press, 1989.

Woodward, C. Vann. *Origins of the New South: 1877–1913.* Baton Rouge: Louisiana State University Press, 1951.

Ziff, Larzer. *The American 1890s: Life and Times of a Lost Generation.* New York: Viking, 1966.

Zinn, Howard. *The Twentieth Century: A People's History.* Rev. ed. New York: Harper Collins, 1998.